# HIGHLAND
# FOLK WAYS

# HIGHLAND
# FOLK
# WAYS

by

I. F. GRANT

M.B.E., LL.D.

Routledge & Kegan Paul
LONDON AND BOSTON

*First published in 1961*
*by Routledge & Kegan Paul Ltd*
*Broadway House, 68-74 Carter Lane,*
*London EC4V 5EL and*
*9 Park Street,*
*Boston, Mass. 02108, USA*
*Reprinted and first published as a paperback 1975*
*Printed in Great Britain by*
*Redwood Burn Limited*
*Trowbridge & Esher*

*ISBN 0 7100 1466 X (c)*
*ISBN 0 7100 8064 6 (p)*

TO
THE FRIENDS OF
AM FASGADH

# CONTENTS

# FIGURES

## MAPS

# ACKNOWLEDGEMENTS

It is pleasant to begin this book by thanking the many people to whose help it owes so much and I should like to express my special indebtedness to Mrs. M. de Glehn, Mrs. Mary Grant, Mr. D. J. Macdonald, Mr. and Mrs. Eric Cregeen, Mr. J. W. M. Gunn, Mr. J. S. Gibson, Professor I. Whitaker and Mr. R. W. Plenderleith. I have met with unfailing kindness and helpfulness in the Libraries where I have worked and I owe a special debt for the assistance given to me by Miss Dickson and Mr. J. H. Stewart of the Reference Department of the Edinburgh Public Library. But besides all these my thoughts go back in gratitude to the older members of my family who made me heir to a background of their memories and to the many Highland folk whom it was my pleasure to meet when I was collecting or who were welcome visitors to *Am Fasgadh* and who taught me so much about the land and the people that I belong to.

Miss Mollie MacEwen, in seeking for the originals of her sensitive drawings, visited *Am Fasgadh* and other Museums and would like to express her thanks to their curators and especially for the help given her by Miss MacDougall of the Inverness Museum.

I should like to thank Major C. I. Fraser of Reelig for his constructive help when he kindly read the proofs.

The maps of rainfall and of population are reproduced by courtesy of *Chambers's Encyclopaedia* and the map of St. Kilda village by permission of the National Trust for Scotland.

I.F.G.

# INTRODUCTION

## THE CONFESSION OF
## A PERSONAL ATTITUDE OF MIND

In this age of urbanization and mechanization, the evocation of a picture of ancient folk ways—of life in a well-knit, self-supporting community bound closely to the land—has the same spell-binding charm as that of *Tir nan Og* to the Gael and of Arcady to the sophisticates of the eighteenth century. The notes of Illyrian pipes seem to linger in the music of the gapped scale of some ancient melody. The homely setting of some folk-tale of princes, swineherds and milkmaids calls up dreams of a Utopia where Adam delved and Eve spun. More potent still is the actual feel of homely, bygone implements, of stone, metal and wood smoothed and worn by the handling of a sequence of long-dead hands and fashioned by ancient and simple techniques that reveal the individualities of the craftsman who made them and of the actual pieces of material upon which he worked.

What we look for in these 'by-gones' varies with the infinite variety that lies within our own minds. They may furnish us with a link with a past remoter than written history, a past that has engulfed the thoughts, beliefs and ideals of the folk whose artefacts survive. Or with the handiwork of peoples of widely diverse races and traditions where the connection may merely be the limitations in supplying the materials that they use.

To a dwindling number of people the homely relics of a Highland past can re-create memories of their own young days. When I had charge of *Am Fasgadh*, the little Highland Folk Museum that I founded, it was my great privilege to show the collection to old men and women who were revisiting the Highlands from Overseas. Often they would stand in silence for so long that the poor curator began to long for overdue meals and the relief of shutting up the Museum for the night. But some would speak of their young days when my carefully labelled exhibits were part of the everyday setting of people's lives. One old man, as he gazed at the wooden churns and milk-bowls, murmured, 'Och, the dear hands I've seen about them.' There are stories that other people can sometimes share the vision of those who have second sight if they put their foot upon that of the seer and make bodily contact with him. Once, almost as vividly, a visitor to the Museum shared with me her memories. A little grey, old, Highland lady had been brought to the Museum by some younger relations. They wandered about, exclaiming over the strangeness of this and that, but the little old lady, shy and withdrawn, hardly spoke and scarcely raised her voice above a whisper. At last the party came to a wall where a variety of cruisie lamps was hanging, and I explained to the younger ones what I had been told about a cruisie. Then the old lady suddenly said 'but I can *remember*'. Her face flushed, her voice grew full and round as she went on to tell how, as a girl, she had gone with her companions to the threshing barn and how there, in every one of the four corners, a cruisie lamp was flaring, and as the young men who were threshing swung up and down their flails they were sometimes dark against the light and sometimes the sweat glistened as it ran down their bare arms. It was warm in the threshing barn and there was laughter and singing. Then the greyness came back to her face and her voice dropped as she went on to say that you could now hardly find the place where the threshing barn had stood and, except for herself, every one of the people who had been there was dead or gone away. 'And yet,' she ended, 'the sight of the cruisie lamps has brought it all back to my mind.'

Although I am of Highland blood myself and the home of my people is still in the Highlands, so greatly have the old ways changed, that it is only vicariously that I can share such experiences. Collecting for the Museum I have seen old implements actually in use; the wraith-like survivors from the past. Some I have used myself, but any completer picture of life in the Highlands in the old days has been derived from the recollections of other people, from the reading of family papers and from the delving that was the pleasantest part of writing some books on Highland Social and Economic History. It is as a narrative of continuity through changes, and of adjustment to outside influences, that I have built up my mental image of Highland folk ways and it is simply to a picture of this life, within the period for which we have records and traditions, that I have confined myself. Perhaps this narrows the field of study but it also accentuates its individuality. It seems to me that the everyday life of Highland people has been something different from the general idea one is apt to form of 'folk life', because as far back as even the sketchiest records go, and in spite of the direst poverty, it was not a peasant community but a closely integrated and complete social organism. In this it is very exceptional. To make clear this concept of the past life of my people I ask the reader to bear with a certain amount of historical narrative.

Edinburgh,                                                          I. F. GRANT
    September, 1960.

# I

## THE FASHIONING OF THE HUMAN FABRIC

IT may seem strange to describe the people before their geographical setting. I do so because the study of Highland Folk Life is not merely an account of how the people managed to live in an inhospitable northern land but how they adapted this environment to their particular social ideas. In Highland history the story of the rise and vicissitudes of the clans is of cardinal importance. This is the distinctive feature of Highland social life. It forms a marked contrast to the social patterns of other countries of Western Europe which show either a wide gulf between the landowners and the tillers of the soil or mainly peasant communities. Within the clans, on the other hand, one finds the microcosm of a wider type of society closely bound together as an integrated whole.[1]

It is, however, important to remember that the clans in no case were the survival of an ancient tribal system, and to recall a little of what went before them. The equation 'tribe or clan'[2] is apt to call up the idea of a patriarch wandering into the virgin wilderness, and of his descendants, huntsmen, herdsmen and, lastly, agriculturalists, peopling it, and of various customs of the allocation of their common tribal land growing up.

[1]As the 1884 Commission appointed to inquire into the Conditions of the Crofters and Cotters in the Highlands and Islands of Scotland points out, on page 6, one of the great advantages of life in the Highlands in the old days was that 'The various orders of Society were more fully represented in a resident community; the natural leaders of the people lived among them'. (Henceforth noted as 1884 Crofters Commission.)

[2]Older writers, notably W. F. Skene, to whose work readers are so deeply indebted, tended to confuse the issue by the use of the word 'tribe'.

1

Highland history is not as simple as that. There are abundant traces of the survival of very ancient ideas and customs but they did so through many changes and disruptions. Our physical appearance shows that we are a people of many different origins.[1] Although one can tell Highland people by their manner and intonation there is no physical 'Highland type'. The difference in our appearance is not merely the result of very modern changes. 'A descriptive Roll' of the recruits enlisted by MacLean of Lochbuie in 1794 shows that of the twenty men who came from Argyllshire, twelve were described as 'dark', three had dark hair and ruddy colouring, two had reddish hair and seven were fair. The men from other districts also varied although there was a rather higher number of fair men from the eastern districts. (This document was in the possession of the late Sheriff MacPhail who kindly allowed me to read it.)

The patient work of the archaeologists has shown us how ancient are the different types of humanity in Scotland and something of the identity of the many waves of immigration into northern Britain. Of the coming of hunters and fishermen, of herdsmen and of those who lived, partly at least, by agriculture. Of folk who wore skins and of those who had learnt to weave and to wear textiles. Of the users of stone and of bronze and then of iron. The long sequence of immigrations have left behind them the squalid debris of the early kitchen middens; the great collective tombs— the chambered cairns—made by a people who seem to have been preoccupied with death; the Standing Stones of various types;

[1]Various fallacious explanations of the physical variations are given. People describe tall fair men as 'of the Viking type' although these physical characteristics are constantly ascribed to the heroes of the Gaelic epics and the presence of a dark type in the Hebrides is sometimes said to be due to the survivors of the Spanish Armada although the archaeologists have proved the existence of a Mediterranean race in days before history. Red hair, generally supposed to show a mixed race, is described as a characteristic of the ancient Caledonians. Among books on Scots anthropology are—J. Beddoes: *Races of Britain*, pp. 26, 42, 54, 368. D. A. MacKenzie: *Earliest Man in Britain*, Ch. X. T. H. Bryce: 'Certain Points in Scottish Ethnology', *Scottish History Review*, Vol. I, p. 295. J. Brownlees: *Origin and Details of Racial Types in Scotland* (Pub. by the Henderson Trust). J. F. Tocher: *Records of Measurements, Weights and other Factors Relative to Man* (Pub. by the Henderson Trust). It must be remembered that the Gael of Ireland, whose language and culture became predominant in the Highlands, were themselves of very mixed origin. This is the main theme of F. T. Rahilly's: *Early Irish History and Mythology*. See also E. MacNeill: *Phases of Irish History*, pp. 74–75 and his *Celtic Ireland*, pp. 4, 146–7, 152–4, 344, 349.

the vestiges of human dwellings on artificial islands in lakes and in forts upon hill-top—these last the hill-forts of iron-using warlords.[1] After this sequence there followed four or five hundred years about which little has been discovered. Professor Gordon Childe has traced the continuity that underlay the well-marked social changes that are revealed in the surviving relics and he postulates the domination of a succession of incomers mingling with the survivors of earlier inhabitants and considerably affected by their ways of life.[2] So much for prehistory.

In the first glimmerings of the dawn of recorded Scots history, about the sixth century, we find several distinct peoples struggling for the possession of what is now Scotland. The Picts, the Britons and the Gael in occupation. The Angles encroaching from the south, while the influence that the Romans had exerted can also be traced because tribes retreating before them were pushed into what is now Scotland and because their social ideas of government had a considerable effect. The introduction of the rotary quern is attributed to them. Copies of their coins became recognized currency among tribes in Britain. A fascinating relic is a little model of a bale of hides in terra-cotta, that was found in a Dun in Skye and is thought to have been the charm or the votive offering of a trader. We know that furs and pelts were exported from Scotland to the Roman world. The Britons, who were still occupying the Kingdom of Strathclyde with their capital at Dumbarton, may have been the channel through which the earlier Celtic ornaments—the divergent spirals and the interlaced patterns that were adopted both by the Picts and the Gael—have made their way north. The Picts occupied the greater part of Scotland north of the Forth and extraordinarily little is known about them. The *Problem of the Picts*, a book containing studies by different authorities, Professor Jackson, Professor Stuart Piggott, R. B. K. Stevenson, Doctor Feacham and T. F. Wainwright, reaches by quite different methods of approach an extraordinary unanimity of opinion (see p. 12). It was agreed that the Picts

[1]The records of these excavations are recorded in the *Proceedings of the Society of Antiquaries* (*Scots*) and there are excellent summaries in Prof. V. Gordon Childe: *Prehistory of Scotland*. See also article by M. Kilbride Jones and M. E. Crichton Mitchell in *Proc. Soc. Antiq.* (*Scotl.*), 6th Series, Vol. I, p. 227 and by A. O. Curle, ibid, 17th Series, Vol. III, p. 35; also Prof. Stuart Piggott: *Scotland before History*.
[2]V. Gordon Childe: *Prehistory of Scotland*, pp. 264–5.

were the imperfectly fused elements of the previous inhabitants of the different regions of north-eastern Scotland. The remarkable thing from our point of view is how recessive was their influence. Their language has vanished. The meaning of their symbols has been lost.

The earliest settlement of the Gael recorded in history took place on the Argyllshire coast about 498, but there are many traditions of earlier settlements. They brought the culture—the epic stories, the whole concept of living that was to have the deepest influence on the later people of the Highlands. Their comparatively small kingdom, after a troublous history, was almost overrun by the Picts yet, in 844, their king succeeded to the throne of the Picts and the Gaelic culture entirely dominated the whole kingdom of Alba (as Scotland was then called). The Gaels, however, in the very century that they were able to make this great advance, were exposed to the raids of the Norsemen from 793 and eventually the Western Isles as well as a good part of the mainland came into Norse permanent occupation. The Norsemen, however, although they came as conquerors arrived as a people in a more backward stage of civilization. They were still pagan and illiterate and were only advancing towards the social concept of a king. And although abundant traces of their influence have been found, yet that which became predominant, even in the districts held by Norway for centuries, was eventually that of the Gaels.

Nevertheless, in spite of racial movements and conquests, a great deal that pertains to our Highland folk life has its roots in the remote past. One has only to think of how many of our folk traditions are obviously pre-christian, such as the widespread veneration for wells.[1] Sometimes the pagan tradition is stronger than a later christian one. On Iona, the hillock where the angels are said to have visited St. Columba while he was praying[2] is still

[1] J. Anderson: *Scotland in Early Christian Times*, p. 193, has a list. M. Martin, writing at the end of the seventeenth century, notes the strange attributes of many Hebridean wells (M. Martin: *A Description of the Western Islands of Scotland* (1934 ed.), p. 197, henceforth noted as Martin, *Western Isles*. See also Lachlan Shaw: *History of the Province of Moray* (Second Edition), pp. 87, 329, henceforth noted as L. Shaw, *Province of Moray*.

[2] Saint Adamnan: *Life of Saint Columba* (tr. W. Reeves, Historians of Scotland Series), p. 89.

4

pointed out but it is now called the Sithean—the Fairy Mound.[1] In this island, so famous as the cradle of Highland Christianity, people living in 1840 could still remember that an offering of porridge used to be poured into the sea to the God of the Ocean to induce him to provide plenty of sea-wrack.[2] Instances of the burying of bones under a house probably show the survival of traditions of human sacrifices. I know of two cases, a horse's skull under the farm of Cradlehall, near Inverness, and the vertebrae of a sheep under that of Dalraddie, near Aviemore. There is a tradition that a live man was buried under Redcastle in Ross-shire, one of the earliest castles built by a feudal baron in the north, and Hugh Miller writes that he was told that Craighouse Castle (near Cromarty) was haunted by a man who had been killed on the foundation stone and built into the walls to *keep* the castle and that there were similar traditions about all the other old castles in the district.[3] A stranger tale is that St. Columba buried St. Oran alive to prevent his new church from being destroyed by evil spirits.

Another persistent custom was that of veneration for rounded pebbles. Their association with burials goes back to the bronze age.[4] The custom persisted during the clan period. Visitors to the Cathedral, Iona, may notice small pebbles embedded in the cement of the floor. A man who was employed during the restoration told me that they were taken from the crypt which was full of bodies in the remains of wickerwork coffins and beside each a little pile of such pebbles. Four larger pebbles still rest on the corners of the tombstone said to be that of Shaw, the leader of Clan Chattan at the Combat on the Inches of Perth (1396), buried in the churchyard at Rothiemurchis.[5] There are stories in the clan traditions that show the Highlanders' veneration for rounded stones. When I visited Kilchoman in Islay, some years ago, there was still a rounded stone in a hollow in the base of the carved

---

[1] It is probably an ancient burial mound.

[2] A. Carmichael: *Carnima Gadelica*, Vol. 1, p. 163. W. C. Mackenzie: *The Book of Lewis*, pp. 148, 208. See also Martin, *Western Isles*, p. 28.

[3] Hugh Miller: *My Schools and Schoolmasters* (1909 ed.), p. 232.

[4] *Proc. Soc. Antiq.* (*Scots*), 1870–2, Vol. IX (5th Series), Vol. XIII, p. 90. See also Vol. LXXXI, p. xxi, also Vol. XVIII, pp. 433, 286–93.

[5] The inscription of the stone was unfortunately re-cut and is erroneous.

cross there and women who desired a son were still said to turn it.[1]

The Scots veneration for the sites of standing stones also lasted far into the Middle Ages.[2] Among many examples is the well-documented account of how Alexander, son of Robert II and known as the Wolf of Badenoch, held his feudal court at 'the Standard Stanys of Kyngucy' in 1380. There a scandalous quarrel with the Bishop of Moray took place which eventually led to the burning down of Elgin Cathedral.[3] One also remembers the account of the inauguration of Alexander III upon the Stone of Destiny, still incorporated in the Coronation Chair at Westminster Abbey.

Limitation of materials and similarity of circumstances were no doubt partly responsible for more survivals. The habit of living in 'lake dwellings' or crannogs was very widespread among ancient peoples. In many parts of the Highlands the remains of fortified and often artificial islands abound and it is evident that some of these were in use down to comparatively late times. In a fairly accurate manuscript history of the Mackintoshes there is the account of how a chief who lived about 1580 constructed an island in Loch Lochy. It 'was called Eilan-darroch, that is, oaken island, for it was built upon oaken beams'.[4] And in a series of measures designed to bring the chiefs of the Western Isles under control that were passed by the Scots Privy Council in 1608, one of the requirements was the destruction of 'all houses of defence, strongholds and crannaks'.[5] In collecting flails for my museum I found a difference between those found in districts where Norse place-names predominate and those from districts mainly Gaelic which seems to show the survival of folk custom, but as the

[1] Associated with such beliefs is probably the veneration for the charm stones that belonged to certain Highland families and to which curative properties or the gift of victory in fight was ascribed. One of the most famous pebbles of all was that which enabled the seer Coinneach Odhar (Dun Kenneth) to make the prophecies, so many of which have been fulfilled.

[2] For examples see I. F. Grant: *Social and Economic Development of Scotland before 1603*, p. 57, henceforth noted as Grant, *Social and Economic Development*.

[3] *Reg. Epis, Moraviense*, p. 159.

[4] *Macfarlane's Genealogical Collections* (Ed. T. Clark, Scottish History Society), Vol. II, p. 242 (henceforth noted as Macfarlane's *Genealogical Collections*).

[5] D. Gregory: *History of the Western Highlands and Islands*, p. 313 (henceforth noted as Gregory, *Western Highlands*).

'Gaelic Type' is carefully made of ash and hazel and the other is a more simply constructed kind of flail of any suitable bit of wood and sometimes partly of rope, the local timber supplies also probably had something to do with the survival of the differentiation.[1]

I have often wondered whether the aversion to the keeping of pigs and the eating of swine's flesh that used to characterize the people of the Eastern and Central Highlands, and which has not entirely died out, has a connexion with the fact that these districts were once part of Pictland. The Gael of Erin, to judge by their stories, were particularly fond of the meat of boars[2] and the Irishman's pig has become proverbial. The Scandinavians, as their sagas show, also ate pork and in the eighteenth century pigs were very largely kept in those districts where Norse influence was once paramount, in Lewis and Kintyre as well as in Caithness and the Shetland and Orkney Islands.[3]

There are two widely held beliefs in the Highlands that lack foundations within the historical period and may throw back to more primitive times. In spite of laws preserving game dating at least from feudal times and the possession of deer forests by many of the Highland chiefs, the old idea that a Highlander has a right to take a stag from the hill or a salmon from the pool is far from being dead in the Highlands.[4] The other belief is of far greater importance. There was a widespread belief that the prolonged occupation of land gave a right to a 'kindness', a right of permanent occupation (not possession) of it. There was no general principle as to the length of time required to acquire this right and the definiteness of the claim varied in different districts.[5]

[1]See also Chapter V.
[2]See for instance Mac Datho's Feast in the Ultonian Cycle, D. Hyde: *Literary History of Ireland*, p. 355.
[3]T. Pennant: *Tour in Scotland and Voyage to the Hebrides*, Vol. I, pp. 115, 167 (henceforth noted as Pennant, *Tour*). A. McKerral: *Kintyre in the Sixteenth Century*, p. 142 (henceforth noted as McKerral, *Kintyre*).
[4]The proverb is:
> Breac a Linne, slat a coille
> Is fiadh a fireach
> Meirle anns nach do ghabh
> Gaidheal riamh nàire.
[5]The Kindly Tenants of Lochmaben acquired legal status. In Kintyre the right was said to be acquired by occupation for eighty-two years by three generations. For examples see Grant, *Social and Economic Development*, pp. 91, 239, 247–92, 283–4. MacKerrall, *Kintyre*, pp. 13, 135.

In most of the Highlands the term 'kindness' was particularly vague and yet the right was strongly felt. It appears in many claims for land. Occasionally such a right was recognized. For instance, a certain Mackintosh, who was tenant for half a davoch of land in Farr (in Strath Nairn) 'having exhausted his means, sold his birthright of the place (commonly called a duchas) for five hundred merks' and in addition twenty pounds Scots from the superior (the Earl of Moray) for the right of occupation.[1] When the MacGregors were being dispossessed of their lands during the sixteenth century they again and again vainly claimed a right of 'kindness' to them, often on very flimsy pretexts.[2] This old feeling has persisted and it exacerbated the bitterness caused by the Clearances. The first famous Commission appointed in 1884 to inquire into the grievances of the crofters noted the strength of this feeling. 'The opinion was often expressed before us that the small tenantry of the Highlands have an inherited inalienable title to security of tenure in their possessions while rent and service are duly rendered, is an impression indigenous to the country though it has never been sanctioned by legal recognition, and has long been repudiated by the action of the proprietors.' Among the reasons for innovations in the land tenure of the crofters proposed by the Commission was 'the argument of public expediency', because not only had the feelings of dissatisfaction 'of native origin' caused many acts of opposition and even violence to legal proceedings but they had received wide support from Highland people who had left the Highlands, and land agitation 'is not likely to pass away without some adjustment of the claims of occupiers acceptable to the greater number. . . .'[3]

The legal concept of the right to land in Scotland was, however, definitely established during the eleventh and twelfth centuries. This had its effect on the rural organization of the Highlands and requires some explanation.

[1] *Macfarlane's Genealogical Collections*, Vol. II, p. 353.
[2] A. Cunningham: *The Loyal Clans*, p. 133, and though sympathetic to the MacGregors, acknowledges this.
[3] The Report of the 1884 Crofter Commission, pp. 8, 110, also p. 4. The Commission which met at a date prior to much research on the Clans, announced that the claim to this right to permanent occupation was due to the Clan system—see p. 8. I would suggest that it arose from earlier ideas.

After Kenneth MacAlpine had united the Scots and Pictish kingdoms in the ninth century, the whole of Scotland north of the Forth, exclusive of the districts colonized by the Norsemen, became Gaelic in culture although there were surviving Pictish features such as the division of the Kingdom into seven provinces ruled over by the Mormaers.[1] This Gaelic kingdom was distracted by warfare with the Angles and the Norsemen, by internal struggles with insubordinate provinces and by dynastic quarrels. From the eleventh century the policy of its kings became more and more directed to pushing their power southwards, and southern influences were increasingly felt. This was notably so in the case of Malcolm IV (known as Canmore).[2]

Under the rule of Malcolm Canmore and his eight successors (from 1057–1289) Scotland underwent drastic changes and its social structure was transformed. Saxon and then Norman influences became preponderant and a feudal system of landholding was introduced all over the country.[3] The Saxon Lothians became increasingly important as they were integrated into the kingdom which was becoming steadily consolidated. One after another, the old provinces lost their individuality, some like Moray, which had twice rebelled, had been 'planted' with more amenable subjects. Other districts, for instance Argyll, were peacefully feudalized and charters granted to some of the older inhabitants. Buchan, Angus and Menteith passed with the marriages of heiresses to Scoto-Normans. Mar was greatly reduced in area to make room

[1]The Provinces were: Circinn, later Enegus cum Moerne; Fotla, later Adtheodle cum Gouerin; Fortrenn, later Straderne cum Menetess; Fib, later Fif et Fortrenn; Fidach, later Muref et Ros; Cait, later Cathania.

[2]He reigned from 1057–93. He married the sister of the Atheling, the heir of Harold, last Saxon King of England.

[3]A feature special to Scotland in the reorganization of the country was the grant of privileges to certain newly founded towns known as Royal Burghs. They were made the collecting points for trading dues and customs and were given monopoly rights over districts that covered the whole country. To this is probably due the lack of older villages in the Highlands and Lowlands alike, also the relative backwardness of the rural industries that played so important a part in English development. References: Grant: *Social and Economic Development*, pp. 130–3. A. Ballard: *British Burgh Charters*, Vol. I, p. 109. See also Scottish History Review, Vol. XIII, p. 18. Th. Keith: 'Trading Privileges of the Royal Burghs of Scotland', *English History Review*, Vol. XXVIII, p. 298. J. Anderson, *Present State of the Hebrides and Western Coasts of Scotland* (1785) said that north of the Mull of Kintyre there was scarcely a settlement with more than a dozen houses in the Western Highlands and stressed the bad effects, p. xxi.

for a large grant to an incoming favourite. By degrees all the provinces were brought within the feudal system.[1] The kings were lavish in their grants of land in the Lowlands to the incomers from the south who, although not all Norman by blood, were so closely identified with that race that it is convenient to call them Scoto-Normans. They also penetrated to the far north and deeply within the hill country.[2] Meanwhile the Norwegians were gradually expelled from the mainland and finally, in 1266, the Hebrides were ceded to the King of Scots.

The laws of the land became feudal in character, deeply affecting the tenure of the land. The social changes, however, were more strongly felt in some parts than in others and, by the end of the period, the differentiation between the Highlands and the Lowlands had appeared. The Highland Line was mainly determined by conditions of physical geography. It followed the line of the hills bounding the belt of lower country that extends between the Firths of the Tay and the Clyde then, turning northwards, it clung to the edge of the central hill massif which rises from the shelf of lower coastwise country. At Nairn the Line reached the shores of the Moray Firth but in the extreme north it excluded the wedge-shaped County of Caithness.[3] In 1363–5, Fordoun, one of our earliest chroniclers, who evidently knew the Highlands, wrote: 'The manners and customs of the Scots vary with the diversity of their speech. For two languages are spoken among them, the Scottish and the Teuton, the last of which is

[1] The old title of Mormaer had become equated with that of Earl. Feudal charters were granted for Menteith in 1213, for Mar in 1171, for Atholl before the end of the twelfth century, for Fife earlier and in 1228 the earl granted a feudal charter to a vassal. See *Scots Peerage*, also *Scottish Historical Records*, Vol. III, p. 222.

[2] No complete list of Norman incomers to the Highlands has been compiled but among them were Olifards and Maynes in Glen Lyon and Fortingal (Perthshire), Comyns in Strathspey, Badenoch and Lochaber (Inverness-shire), Stewarts in Bute and Cowal, Bissets at the head of the Beauly Firth and in Strathherrick (Inverness-shire), de Boschos in the Black Isle (Ross-shire), de Raitts near Nairn, de Lundins in Glen Urquhart, de Chiens in Strath Naver. Two collections of documents illustrate how the land was feudalized and administered, (*a*) *Highland Papers I* (Scottish History Society). Ed. J. R. N. MacPhail contains a collection of early legal documents relating to Glassary in Argyllshire (henceforth noted as *Highland Papers*), (*b*) E. Chisholm Batten: *History of Beauly Priory* gives a well documented account of the establishment of the Bissets in the Aird. See also A. Stewart: *A Highland Parish*, pp. 11, 75.

[3] It thus cut through the old provinces of Lennox, Menteith, Gowry, Strathearn and Angus.

the language of those who occupy the seaboard and the plains, while the race of Scottish speech inhabit the Highlands and out-lying islands. The people of the coast are of domestic and civilized habits, patient and urbane'—and much more to the same effect. 'The Highlanders and people of the islands, on the other hand, are a savage and untamed nation, rude and independent, given to rapine, ease-loving, of a docile and warm disposition, comely in persons but unsightly in dress, hostile to the English people and language and, owing to diversity of speech, even to their own nation, and exceedingly cruel. They are, however, faithful and obedient to their king and country and easily made to submit if properly governed.' The tragedy of the Highlands was to be that they were so very seldom so governed![1]

At the end of the twelfth century, the most formative period in Scots history, Scotland had to fight for her existence against her more powerful neighbour, England, in the Wars of Independence. These were followed by sweeping forfeitures of the lands of the powerful pro-English party and the reallocation of such land materially assisted the rise of a new and distinctive social system, that of the clans, that was growing up in the High-lands.

It would be idle to speculate how far the innate attitude of mind of the Scots is responsible for the clan organization and how far the clan system has produced the Highland character. Although the changes and reorganizations in her past, and especially the feudalization of the laws of land-holding and the paramount in-fluence of the incoming Normans, precluded the survival of actual tribes or tribal customs, the influence of older styles of society continued to shape the social pattern of the Lowlands as well as the Highlands. Pride of kinship and descent knit wide sections of the people together. As Sir Thomas Innes of Learney, the present Lyon King at Arms, has pointed out: '. . . Between the Peerage, the Houses of Chiefs and Chieftains, the Baronage, the Gentlemen or lesser Lairds and Tacksmen it has been cal-culated that at the time of the Union there were (in a population of about a million) over ten thousand houses, each as proud and as nobly descended as any of the great Continental *noblesses*. Allowing for the expansion of even the near circle of these houses

[1]cf. *Fordoun's Chronicle* (Historians of Scotland Series). Ed. W. F. Skene, p. 58.

and lines of chieftains, it follows that about one in each twenty-four people were actually members of a titled or chiefly house, and that about one-half of the Scottish nation consciously regarded themselves as members of the aristocracy. Such a proportion is unknown in any other nation, and the moral and social effect upon the Scottish nation has been incalculable.'[1]

In the Highlands this unique state of social organization was far more marked. Once more to quote Sir Thomas Innes, 'the younger members of the family of the chief were expected by degrees to subside in an ever extending pyramid into the *duine uasail* and body of the clan, carrying with them through all ranks of the nation the pride and glory of lineage and achievement, and the sense of acknowledged blood-brotherhood upon either side stretching throughout the whole gamut of the Caledonian Social System.'[2]

The continuity through change that one finds in Highland institutions is well illustrated by the terms used for denoting the extent of land. I should explain that they were not linear measurements but were applied to an area from which it was estimated a certain due could be exacted. On poor land they were therefore more extensive than on good land. The term *davoch* is associated with the heart of what was once the kingdom of the Picts and it is probably derived from a Pictish word very closely analogous to a British one although there are other possible derivations. It appears in some notes upon grants of land to the monastery of Deer in Aberdeenshire, written upon the margins of a ninth-century copy of the Gospels that belonged to that Monastery. The notes which were continued down to the twelfth century also mention the old Pictish official, the Mormaer, and many of the personal names are Pictish. After that the word davoch vanished from written documents for a time, but then, in the post-medieval period, it reappeared.

Meanwhile the Gael had made their settlements in the south-west and had brought the land organization of Erin with them

---

[1]Sir Thomas Innes: *Tartans of the Clans and Families of Scotland*, p. 13 (henceforth noted as Sir T. Innes, *Tartans*). As a corollary it may be noted that Sir John Clapham notices the absence in early Scotland of a specialized artisan class because everyone occupied some fraction of land and other work was supplemental. Sir John Clapham: *A Concise Economic History of Britain*, pp. 215–18.

[2]Sir T. Innes, *Tartans*, p. 13.

12

and although the terms for many of the denominations disappeared and the lay-out was much altered, the old division of the larger holdings into eighths and quarters persisted in Islay down to the agricultural reforms, and the division of farms into four horsegangs, each contributing a horse to the characteristic Gaelic plough-team of four horses, was general in Perthshire down to the end of the eighteenth century.[1]

The Norse conquest of the Hebrides and of much of the mainland that overlaid the old Gaelic settlements, brought new developments. Such place-names as Ormidale—Orm's dale and Colonsay—Kolbein's Island, indicate Norse occupation and assessments for new taxes were introduced. The terms 'Ounceland', that is, land assessed as an ounce of silver with its components of twenty 'Pennylands', subdivided into 'Farthinglands' came into use in Skye, the Long Island, Mull and Kintyre, although not in the more predominantly Gaelic Islay.[2] The word Ounceland became Gaelicized into *Tirunga*, that is *tir*—land and *unga*—ounce and the lesser denominations survive in many place-names such as Pennygheal in Mull or Feorlinn in Skye. Within living memory the 'soumings' (proportions of animals allowed upon the common grazings) of a township in Bernera were based upon the number of farthinglands within it held by a crofter.[3]

When the Kings of Scotland adopted the feudal system during the twelfth century a totally new conception of the legal rights to land was introduced. It was held to belong to the King who granted it by charters to chosen subjects in return for feudal dues, including military service or money payments. The military service of a knight's fee was a convenient contribution to the military forces of the king and land was often allocated into 'Baronies', the extent that could be expected to provide the services of an armed and mounted man. In early feudal charters the

---

[1] For traces of the Gaelic land divisions in Islay see W. N. Lamont: *Old Land Divisions and Old Extent in Islay*, Scottish Studies, No. 1, part 2, p. 182; No. 2, part 1, p. 86 (henceforth noted as Lamont, *Old Land Divisions*). For examples of persistence of horse gangs see M. McArthur: *Survey of Lochtayside* (Scottish History Society), pp. vii, xxx (henceforth noted as McArthur, *Lochtayside*).

[2] A. MacKerral: 'Ancient Denominations of Land in Scotland'. *Proc. Soc. Antiq.* (*Scotl.*), Vol. LXXVIII (1943), p. 39.

[3] Information supplied by Mr Alick Morrison. For late eighteenth century survival of the terms in Harris and South Uist, see *Old Statistical Account*, Vol. X, p. 366, Vol. XIII, p. 309 (henceforth noted as *O.S.A.*).

terms for lesser denominations were *Carucate* and *Bovate*, these were the equivalent of the English terms Ploughgate and Oxgate which became general in the Lowlands and also in the Eastern Highlands till the eighteenth century.

During the feudalizing period another term came into use when land was assessed for taxation—the *Merkland*, the extent of land that was expected to pay a merk in taxation.[1] While this term continued to be used in official documents and sometimes in rentals, unofficially the older terms survived.[2]

Because these old land denominations were founded upon the subsistence that a given piece of land was expected to supply they were often equated. The davoch was often co-terminous with the Barony upon which feudal services were calculated, which generally contained four ploughgates, each divided into eight oxgates, but it might be calculated to contain twenty pennylands like the tirunga. The subject however is full of exceptions and pitfalls.[3] But that all these divisions went on being used gives some idea of the survivals, changes and adjustments that existed in the Highlands down to the eighteenth century.

[1] A merk was equal to 13s 4d Scots or 1s 8d sterling.
[2] This comes out in M. McArthur's *Lochtayside*, pp. vii, xxx. See also Lamont, *Old Land Divisions*, Scottish Studies, No. 2, part 1, p. 86.
[3] W. N. Lamont, *Old Land Divisions*, Scottish Studies, No. 2, part 1, p. 186.

# II

## THE CLANS

ALTHOUGH the following historical survey may seem outside the scope of a book about folk ways, in order to understand the position of the clansmen it is essential to have some
idea of how the Highland clans came into being. Furthermore, as
the clans varied very much in their origins, it seems best to outline the story of the rise of a few individual ones. Pride of place
belongs to the clans descended from Somerled (who flourished in
the twelfth century, the period when the feudalizing activities of
the Scots kings were in full vigour). His name is Norse but the
clan pedigree traces his descent back to Conn of the Hundred
Battles, High King of Ireland. Some of the later names in this
pedigree have been equated with those of historical personages
living in the Hebrides during the period of mixed Norse and
Gaelic occupation there. About the earlier origin modern research is doubtful but it is highly important to remember that
Somerled's descendants, the members of Clan Donald, strongly
believed in this kingly descent. For instance, when MacMhuirich,
their *filé* incited their battle ardour before Red Harlaw in a rousing *Brosnachadh* (Incitement to Battle), he began it with: 'Sons
of Con remember hardihood in time of Battle'. In Somerled's
days the Hebrides were under the rule of the King of Man as a
vassal of the King of Norway and Somerled, who had married a
daughter of this king, laid claim to them on behalf of his and her
eldest son and conquered them. He appears in Scots historical
records. In 1159 he made a treaty with Malcolm IV, King of
Scots, and in 1164, having raised a large fleet to attack him, he
was assassinated and his forces dispersed. After his death his
possessions were broken up but two sons founded clans; Dougal,

who received the mainland districts of Lorne, the islands of Coll, Tiree and Jura and a share at least of Mull, is the ancestor of the MacDougalls, who in spite of many vicissitudes, have clung to a small fraction of these territories. Reginald received Islay, Kintyre, a share of Arran and some claim to Mull. His son Donald is the eponymus of Clan Donald. Another of Reginald's sons, Ruari, founded a line that eventually held North and South Uist and the district of Garmoran—now Moidart and Knoydart. By the fourteenth century a descendant of Donald, by marriage with the heiress, had secured these lands and his possessions had already been augmented by grants of lands forfeited during the Wars of Independence. In 1354 he assumed the title of Lord of the Isles. Clan Donald formed a number of large and small branches, all vassals of the Lord of the Isles, and after the forfeiture of the Lordship, in 1493, these branches became independent of each other.[1]

Nearly all the clans claimed for their founder a long and generally mythical pedigree—in many cases more than one such line of descent. For instance the Campbells have pedigrees tracing their descent from King Arthur, from Diarmaid who was a character in the Fenian Cycle (one of the old Gaelic groups of stories), and from a French family named de Campo Bello. Firmer ground is reached with Duncan O'Duine, who is said to have been granted

---

[1]The following is a list of the more important branches:

| Descended from— | | |
|---|---|---|
| Alasdair, s. of Donald Lord of Islay | MacAlisters of Loup | |
| Iain Sprangach, s. of Angus Mor, Lord of Islay | MacIains of Ardnamurchan | Obtained a Crown Charter |
| Iain, illeg. s. of Angus Og, Lord of Islay | MacDonalds (MacIains) of Glencoe | |
| Ranald, s. of John 1st Lord of the Isles | MacDonalds of Clanranald, Cadets, Glengarry, Knoydart, Morar | Obtained a Crown Charter |
| Iain Mor, s. of John, 1st Lord of the Isles | MacDonalds of Kintyre and Islay (Clan Donald South) Cadet, Largy | Obtained a Crown Charter |
| Alasdair Carrach, s. of John, 1st Lord of the Isles | Macdonells of Keppoch | |
| Celestine, s. of Alasdair 3rd Lord of the Isles | MacDonalds of Loch Alsh | Obtained a Crown Charter |
| Hugh, s. of Alasdair 3rd Lord of the Isles | MacDonalds of Sleat (Clan Donald North) | Obtained a Crown Charter |

16

a charter for lands on Loch Awe about the time that Alexander II
is known to have been feudalizing Argyll. His grandson, Big
Colin, about whom there is a wealth of tradition, gave the
patronymic *MacCaillean Mor* to the head of Clan Campbell. His
son was the famous Sir Niel Campbell, the devoted adherent of
Robert the Bruce in the days of his adversity, and who was
munificently rewarded by the King.[1]

The origin of the comparatively small clan, the Macfarlanes, is
unusually clear. They descend from a younger brother of the Earl
of Lennox who gave him a charter for the lands of Arrochar on
Loch Lomondside in 1230 but they derive their name from the
fourth chief Parlan (Bartholomew). Similar probable origins are
those of the MacNabs, who claim to be the descendants of the
Lay Abbots of Glendochart, and the Robertsons, who it is now
thought are descended from a collateral male heir to the old
Earldom of Atholl which went to an heiress, although their first
recorded chief Donnachadh (who gives the clan its Gaelic name
of Clan Donachie) was contemporary with Robert the Bruce and
they take their English name from his descendant Robert, who
received a Crown Charter for his lands in 1451 as a reward for
hunting down the murderers of James I. There is strong probability that the MacLeods are descended from Leod, a younger
brother of the last King of Man. They are the most important of
the small group of clans claiming Norse origin.

There are several theories about the origin of the MacLeans,
but the most probable one is from 'Old Dougald of Scone', who
is known to have lived about 1100.[2] The family fortunes were,
however, founded by two brothers, Hector and Lachlan, who
enjoyed the patronage of John, First Lord of the Isles (fl. first
half of the fourteenth century). They received grants in Mull and
later of Coll, in Morven and Lochaber and elsewhere. Other

[1] The early records of Scotland are scanty because Edward I carried off most of
them, but the following are a few clans of which there is early record. Duncan
Lamont, son of Fearchar, granted a charter to the monks of Paisley in 1230.
Gillespie MacLachlan received a charter in 1292. Nachtan Mor, eponymus of the
MacNaughtons, in 1267 got a charter from Alexander II for the keeping of the
Castle of Fraoch Eilean on Loch Awe. Monro of Fowlis was occupying land that the
family still holds, for he got a charter of confirmation from the Earl of Ross in 1350.

[2] Another clan probably derived from him is that of the Colquhouns, whose
founder got a charter for the lands of Colquhoun from the Earl of Lennox about the
time of Alexander II and adopted this name.

clans, of varying origin, who flourished under the Lordship were the MacDuffies, the MacMillans and the MacNeills.[1]

The MacKenzies emerge into history rather later. Like the MacLeans they have a fanciful claim to a Hiberno-Norman origin but are now thought to be descended from a younger son of one of the O'Beolan line of Earls of Ross[2] and to have been established in Kintail as vassals of these Earls. But they became important when they helped the royal forces to subdue the Lords of the Isles (who had also succeeded to the Earldom of Ross) and the head of the family, after the Forfeiture, received a Crown Charter in 1476 for the lands of Strathconnan and Strathgarve in Central Ross-shire. From this time the chiefs increased their powers till their clan became the second most powerful in the Highlands. The Camerons also emerge into recorded history as a well established clan in the fifteenth century.

The MacKays are among the clans that became established upon land that had already been occupied by the incoming Scoto-Normans. They are now usually thought to be descended from a member of the family of the ancient Mormaers of Moray, who fled northwards to Caithness. The first chief of whom we have information was Iye (fl. 1330–70). His lands in Farr (Sutherland) belonged to a member of the de Chien family and MacKay was a tenant till 1499 when he was able to obtain a Crown Charter. The fertile district at the head of the Beauly Firth had been granted on feudal tenure to the Bissets and other adherents of the king in the thirteenth century. But in the fourteenth century, by marriage and by royal favour (which was often much the same thing) it passed to a member of the Scoto-Norman family of Fraser. (Their first charter is dated 1367.) His successors extended their lands but until 1512 no head of the family married a Highland girl. It would be difficult to say when they became a clan. They were certainly one by the end of the sixteenth century. The story of the Chisholms, whose ancestor is said to have come to England with William the Conqueror and who became the close neighbours of the Frasers, is rather similar. It is significant that so early

[1]The MacNeills claim to be descended from an Irish High King, Niel of the Nine Hostages.

[2]This Earldom was created by William the Lyon in the thirteenth century and granted to a Gaelic supporter.

as 1362 they are mentioned in a charter as 'Shishlach', evidently an attempt at Siosalich, the Gaelic rendering of their name.[1]

There are several traditional tales of the origin of the Grants but they were probably of Anglo-Norman stock and the name occurs in records of the north-east several times, but a permanent line was not established till the fifteenth century when a Grant married the heiress of the Lord of Glencharnie, who was a cadet of the Earls of Strathearn owning land in Strathspey. Her son, who inherited, first appears as a landholder in 1453. In 1537, in a formal agreement, the words 'lye Clan Grantes' occurs. The transactions by which Duncan's descendants gradually built up their estates are well documented. Strathspey had been divided piecemeal among a large number of landholders. By about seven major purchases of land and many lesser transactions within the next two hundred years, the whole of Strathspey was acquired.[2]

This may seem a rather prosaic story; that of the establishment of a branch of Stewarts in Appin is one of the most dramatic episodes in Highland history. Of all the incomers during the feudalizing period, the House of Stewart was one of the most successful. Its head eventually succeeded to the throne of Scotland[3] and many important cadet branches had been founded in the Lowlands and also Bute. A younger son of one of these succeeded by marriage to the district of Lorne, which had once been among the possessions of Dougal, the son of Somerled. There the family remained for three generations. The last Stewart Lord of Lorne was anxious that his illegitimate son should succeed him instead of his male heir who was his brother, or his legitimate heiresses, two daughters, one of them married to a Campbell. He tried to gain the support of the male representative of the old line of the MacDougalls, a collateral of the forfeited family, by giving him the district round Dunolly (which his descendants by direct descent still hold). The Lord of Lorne was murdered under peculiarly dramatic circumstances as he was actually marrying the mother of his son, in order to legitimize him. The son, supported by some of the people of Lorne, after a struggle, took

[1]William MacKay, *Glen Urquhart and Glen Moriston*, p. 41.
[2]For a good summary see opening chapters of Sir William Fraser: *The Chiefs of Grant*, Vol. I.
[3]He succeeded through his mother, the daughter of Robert the Bruce, who was the next in succession after her childless brother, David II.

revenge upon the murderer and was able to establish himself in Appin and to found the small but vigorous clan of the Stewarts of Appin there. Lorne, itself, passed to the heiress who had married a Campbell.

These summaries of the rise of a good many of the clans bring out two points. Whatever their theories of remote origin, there is generally much later an individual who founds the family fortunes by obtaining the occupation of land and whose name appears about the time that the clan enters the region of history and who is often its eponymus. The land is held by the founder and his successors. There is no vestige of clan territories held as such.

Moreover, the possessions of most chiefs were built up gradually and many of them held different parts of their lands on different tenures and they were not infrequently scattered. The lands held by Mackintosh are an example. Among many theories about the origin of his family, that claimed for it in the clan's own MSS. history of 1679 is probably the true one and the founder was Shaw, son of Duncan, 3rd Earl of Fife, who had come north with Malcolm IV in 1163 to suppress a revolt by the men of Moray, and Shaw, in reward for his services, is said to have been made keeper of Inverness Castle with lands in Petty and Brauchlie on the Moray Firth and the Forest of Strathdearn (the upper valley of the Findhorn).[1] The superiority of these lands passed to the Earl of Moray and a rental, made in 1487 when the earldom was temporarily in the hands of the Crown, shows that Mackintosh was then tenant of Petty and Brauchlie and we know, from written evidence, that he was acting as seneschal of the lands of the Bishop of Moray in Badenoch in 1434. (He also got a feu of Rothiemurchus from the Bishop in 1464 but lost this when Huntly succeeded the Bishop as superior.) In 1442 he got a heritable right to Geddes and Raitts (near Nairn) from the Earl of Huntly and, later, he obtained Dunachton and other land in Badenoch within Huntly's superiorities. He also claimed the lands of Glenlui and Locharkaig in Lochaber (traditionally by a marriage with the heiress of the chief of Clan Chattan) which were occupied by the Camerons. The Lord of the Isles, as superior, gave him heritable possession of these and other lands

[1]For a good summary see A. M. Mackintosh: *The Mackintoshes and Clan Chattan* (henceforth noted as Mackintosh, *The Mackintoshes*), opening chapters.

and the office of hereditary bailliary and, when the Lordship was forfeited, he received a Crown Charter of confirmation. These were the only lands he held of the King and, in spite of a bitter feud that went on intermittently till the middle of the seventeenth century, he was never able to dislodge the Camerons and Mac-Donells who were established there and he eventually had to accept a composition. On the other hand he was able successfully to resist ejectment by Moray from Petty and Brauchlie, the most valuable lands that he held.[1]

The summary of the acquisition of Mackintosh's lands brings out a cardinal point about the development of the clans and the distribution of land-holding. No title to possession was worth anything without the backing of an armed force to hold it. Chiefs able to protect their dependants were able to pay rent and so were successful in obtaining leases and feus, and for years together others occupied land against the wishes of its rightful possessor and sometimes of the king. Upon the vital need for mutual defence depended the adherence of chief and clansmen and the urge upon all chiefs to build up a numerous following. This had a deep effect upon their allocation of their lands.

A few more generalizations about the clans may be noted. Lesser clans often lived upon the lands of more powerful chiefs. For instance, the MacColls lived upon the lands of Stewart of Appin and there is the touching tradition that the chief of the larger clan was always buried between two MacColls. The list of the losses of the Stewarts in the '45 show how devotedly the MacColls had suffered with them. Upon the lands of the Mac-Kenzies, in amity lived the MacRaes, Mathesons and Mac-Lennans. The MacRaes, in particular, were devoted adherents of MacKenzie of Kintail and held the office of hereditary keeper of his castle of Eilean Donan. We have the actual agreements made

---

[1] Among many other examples of chiefs holding land of different superiors and by different tenures, MacLeod of MacLeod got a Crown Charter in the fourteenth century for Glenelg. The rest of his land he occupied under the Lord of the Isles but if he had a formal charter the record has not survived. After the forfeiture of the Lordship he gradually acquired Crown Charters but he lost the superiority of Glenelg to Argyll. The superiority of Cameron of Lochiel's lands became a bone of contention between Huntly and Argyll. Gunn's lands were held of the bitterly quarrelling Earls of Caithness and Sutherland and of MacKay of Strathnaver. Robertson had a Crown Charter for some of his land but his clan largely lived upon the estate of the Earl of Atholl.

between the Campbells of Craignish and of Glenurchy, powerful cadets of the house of Argyll, with several septs of dependant 'nativemen'.[1] Moreover within lands occupied by a clan there were nearly always men bearing other names. This is shown in surviving rentals, as for instance of MacLean lands in Mull.[2] On the lands of MacLeod of MacLeod are a family of Shaws who came from Strathspey to Skye in the fifteenth century and of Campbells who came from Kintyre to Harris in the sixteenth century and are there still. Moreover, the whole of the Highlands were never completely parcelled out among the chiefs. In Perthshire, under the superiority of the Earl of Atholl, there were several wide straths with no dominant clan and in Glen Urquhart, which was granted to the Laird of Grant in 1509, at a time when the clan-making impulse seems largely to have died out, many of the inhabitants continued to follow their own chiefs. No name was predominant in Kintyre.[3] There were also districts, generally the most fertile ones, where the claims of different chiefs conflicted. Lochaber is a notable example. The Earls of Huntly and Argyll had contesting claims to its superiority and Cameron of Lochiel, Mackintosh, MacDonnell of Keppoch and two branches of the MacLeans were at feud for occupation of parts of it. The districts of Trotternish, in Skye, and of the Rinns in Islay are other examples. The authorities were largely to blame for these troubles because, either from careless indifference or with the desire to provoke trouble, they several times granted conflicting or ill-defined charters. The clans varied so much in size and composition that it is difficult to define them exactly. Sometimes the great families, such as the Gordons in Eastern Scotland and the Border Lairds are included.[4]

[1] Other examples are the MacAskills and MacCrimmons on the lands of MacLeod of Skye. The Maceacherns, who were skilled armourers, lived upon the lands of Campbell of Craignish and of various MacDonald chiefs. For examples see *Collectanea Rebus Albanicis* (Iona Club), pp. 197–200 (henceforth noted as *Collectanea*). *Black Book of Taymouth* (Ed. Cosmo Innes, Bannatyne Club), p. 405 onwards (henceforth noted as *Black Book of Taymouth*).

[2] *Highland Papers*, Vol. I, p. 206.

[3] D. Campbell, *Reminiscences and Reflections of an Octogenarian Highlander*, pp. 57, 247 (henceforth noted as Campbell, *Octogenarian Highlander*). W. Mackay, *Glenurquhart*, App. L. A. MacKerral: *Kintyre*, p. 12.

[4] When James VI made special regulations for what was known as 'the peccant parts of the Kingdom' at the end of the sixteenth century, such names were all lumped together.

The Highland clans were important organizations for about 400 years. As we have seen, their founders appear during the period from the twelfth to the fifteenth centuries.[1] The collapse of the Rising of the '45 is the culminating point in a decline in the powers of the chiefs that had already begun and did not immediately end. The word *Clann*, i.e. children, used in the Irish sense as the close personal descendants of the eponymus, was true at first and only gradually took on the wider meaning it has come to bear in the Highlands.[2] The comparative insignificance of the early clans is shown by the fact that in contemporary accounts of the Battle of Bannockburn (fought in 1314), the lists of the Scots forces engaged do not mention any clan and the only name of a chief is that of the Lord of Islay, who appears among those of the feudal magnates who brought contingents to the battle. No doubt, as their own traditions tell, members of many clans were there but they fought as the retainers of the great feudatories.

During the fourteenth and fifteenth centuries several incidents concerning clans were of sufficient importance to be recorded in public records and contemporary chronicles. Best known is the Combat on the Inches of Perth in 1396, in which thirty clansmen from each of two opposing clans fought a sort of mass duel before the king. We have the sober records of the cost of erecting the lists in which the combat took place, but such were the vagaries

[1]That twenty-six recognizable clans were in existence before the fifteenth century is shown by a group of Highland pedigrees given in the Irish *Book of Ballimote* (1383) and *Book of Lecan* (1407). The actual pedigrees, however, are mostly in flat contradiction to the clans' own traditions and the inferences of probability. For instance eighteen clans are traced from the Dalriadic tribe of Loarne annihilated by the Picts in 736. The Gael, both in Ireland and Scotland were very skilful in manufacturing pedigrees that would support policies and alliances or family pride. See W. F. Skene: *Celtic Scotland*, Vol. III, p. 338.

[2]The earliest recorded use of the word in twelfth-century *Book of Deer* (published by the Spalding Club) tells us little. In Sir John Skene's *De Verborum Significatorum* occurs the Law of Clan MacDuff. MacDuff was the family name of the Earls of Fife. Among this earl's special privileges within this law, was that any man-slayer who was 'within the ninth degree of the kin and blood to MacDuff sometime Earl of Fife', if he comes to the Cross of MacDuff and gives a fine of cattle should be free of the guilt of manslaughter. As late as 1421 a Hugh de Arbuthnot claimed protection under this law, and when the Earldom passed to a Ramsay in the reign of David II the privilege passed to him with the title. See W. F. Skene: *Celtic Scotland*, Vol. III, p. 304. Two charters of David II (fourteenth century) to individuals in the southwest described them as 'capitanus de tota parentela sua' which is translated in a Scots index of 1622 as 'captain of his clan'. See *Register of the Great Seal*, Vol. I, App. 11, Nos. 912, 913, 914, 982, 1953; see also p. 508.

of Lowland spelling that histories still debate which clans were meant although they are most often thought to be Clan Cameron and Clan Chattan.[1] In 1427, James I, in his efforts to bring law and order into his kingdom, summoned the leading men of the north to meet him at Inverness and executed summary jurisdiction upon them. Some of the men mentioned in contemporary accounts have been identified; they are the Lord of the Isles (Chief of Clan Donald), Alexander, the head of a branch of the MacDonalds now extinct, John MacArthur, leader of an Argyllshire clan by some thought to be a branch of the Campbells and, more doubtfully, the chief of the MacKays.[2] An agreement made in 1364 between the Lord of the Isles and John, Lord of Lorne about the surrender of Mull by the latter, stipulates that Kerneburgh Castle shall not be given to any of the race of Clan Finnon.[3]

It is not possible to state the growth of individual clans in exact terms. There are, however, many indications. For instance, there were five branches of the Frasers in 1650, by 1745 there were thirty. The increase is also well documented for the Grants, Campbells and MacKenzies.[4] There is less definite information about how far lesser clansmen were not actually descended from the chief. The use of patronymics complicates matters. But there is a tradition that one Fraser of Lovat gave a boll of meal to any of his tenants who would take his name and that the term 'meal Frasers' became a byword. Old people have told me that in their youth it was still not unknown for tenants to take the surname of their landlord. A document of 1569 gives the names of fifty-nine parishioners in Duthil (in Strathspey) none with the name

[1] For an analysis of this episode see A. M. Mackintosh, *The Mackintoshes*, Chapter IV.

[2] See W. Bower's *Scotichronicon*, Vol. II, p. 489. J. Major: *History of Greater Britain* (Scottish History Society), p. 357. The meeting is often described as a Parliament. This however is doubtful. See E. Balfour Melville, *James I, King of Scots*, pp. 165, 284.

[3] D. MacKinnon, *History of Clan MacKinnon*, p. 7. A list of people put to the horn (declared outlaw) for a raid into Angus in 1391 that was led by a son of Alexander, Earl of Buchan and Lord of Badenoch, the disreputable 'Wolf of Badenoch', shows that they were nearly all his vassals but included members of two clans (the Robertsons and Clan Chattan). This analysis was made by W. F. Skene, *Celtic Scotland*, Vol. III, p. 309.

[4] The pedigrees of the chiefs of many more clans show that offset branches were constantly thrown off.

of Grant but in a document of 1569 there are the names of forty-three Grants coming from that parish.[1] The custom, however, varied very much from clan to clan. Rentals of MacLeod of MacLeod show that on his estate tenants tended to keep their own surnames.

These centuries that saw the emerging importance of the clans also saw the rise of the Lordship of the Isles, which has had a deep influence upon the development of Highland life. As we have seen the line descended from Reginald son of Somerled prospered greatly, and his successor, John, in 1345 took the proud title of *Dominus Insularum*. His grandson, through his mother, succeeded to the Earldom of Ross, with lands more considerable than the extent of the present county. His combined possessions stretched across the north of Scotland and also included all the Hebrides except Bute and Arran, and also Kintyre, Lochaber and Morven. The Lordship of the Isles lasted for about 150 years (the Earldom of Ross was forfeited in 1476 and the Lordship of the Isles in 1493). When they were strong enough, the four successive Lords of the Isles claimed to be more than subjects, a claim in which the Kings of England encouraged them. Seven times they swept across the country and occupied Inverness for years at a time. The Kings of Scots, however, during their brief periods of power, were able to force the Lords of the Isles to submit. The interest in the Lordship lies in the fact that as the last powerful Gaelic principality it formed a focus for Gaelic culture. To intrude a personal note—the late A. O. Curle, the distinguished Scots archaeologist, once asked me if there had been an important political and cultural force within the Western Highlands and Islands to account for the distinctive style of the stone carvings found there, mostly apparently dating from round about the fifteenth century. It was in replying to him that I began to appreciate the connexion between this school of carving and the old Lordship.[2] These beautiful standing crosses and tombstones clearly showed influences derived from eighth and ninth century work of Erin and Alba and, in their turn, from

[1]Grant: *Social and Economic Development*, p. 501.

[2]Contemporary Scots history was written by Lowlanders who say as little as they can about the Gaelic Lordship. The scraps I gathered about it are embodied in my *Lordship of the Isles*.

them are derived the interlaced designs of the later Highland circular brooches, dirk handles, targes and powder horns, popularly called 'Celtic Patterns'. With a few outliers, the carvings are found within the bounds of the old Lordship and, with some exceptions, within a few years after its fall there was a marked deterioration in their workmanship and designs (see ch. XIV).

The period was also a flowering time for Gaelic literature and poetry.[1] Professional poets highly trained in the complex metres of old Ireland flourished in the Highlands.[2] The composition of the Council of the Isles, with representatives of the greater and lesser magnates and also of free-holders, men 'of competent estate', the ceremonial of the Lords of the Isles Court, has been handed down in tradition and traces of it appear in the customs of other clans.[3] The Lords of the Isles maintained their hereditary poets, the MacMhuirich family, descended from Muireach O'Daly (fl. in 1213) from Sligo. After the fall of the Lordship the Mac-Mhuirichs were attached to the Macdonalds of Clanranald who gave them two farms in South Uist till the eighteenth century.[4] The Lords of the Isles' hereditary physicians were members of the Beaton family. Members of the family afterwards became hereditary doctors to MacLeod of MacLeod, MacDonald of Sleat, MacLean of Duart, the Earl of Sutherland and to Lovat.[5] Some of their extremely learned treatises, written in Gaelic but quoting

[1]Literature and Poetry. Among the surviving manuscripts are versions of the finest epics of Gaeldom and also of some of the current romantic tales of Western Europe, such as that of Roland, lives of the saints and much old and contemporary poetry. There were even versions of the *Togail Troy*, the Destruction of Troy and other classical themes told with modifications. There was a strange survival of this story for in the eighteenth century a visitor heard a tale of a fight between Nestor and Achilles, fought with Highland weapons and ending with a feast of herring at the head of Loch Fyne. J. Leyden, *Journal of a Tour in the Highlands and Islands* (1800), p. 115.

[2]For the wealth that has survived see Professor D. MacKinnon's *Catalogue of Gaelic MSS.*, also *Book of the Dean of Lismore* compiled by James MacGregor about 1512 translated by MacLaughlan in 1862 and by N. Ross and J. D. Watson (Scottish Gaelic Text Society), two vols. (1936).

[3]See Hugh MacDonald's *History of Clan Donald*, translated in *Collectanea* and *Highland Papers*, Vol. I.

[4]Evidence of Lachlan MacMhuirich, eighteenth descendant, in 1808, before the Committee appointed by the Highland Society of Edinburgh to inquire into the Authenticity of Ossian, p. 275.

[5]Besides the wandering bands of poets hospitably received wherever they went, many chiefs as well as the great Lords of the Isles had their hereditary poets.

from Greek and Arabic sources, have survived.[1] The Earl of Argyll also had his hereditary physician. From allusions we know that there were Brieves, Gaelic judges, in the various districts of the Lordship with a court of appeal in Islay, but the only family of Brieves of which the name has come down to us is that of the Morrisons in Lewis. MacKinnon kept the records (which have unfortunately disappeared). Besides the officers of the Lord of the Isles Court, such as the marshal and the chancellor, there were hereditary families of harpers, armour-bearers, sword-makers, etc.[2]

The surviving charters of the Lords of the Isles are nearly all conventional Latin documents. They show the sovereign state he held and his great dominions, but one Gaelic charter (from 1408) has come down to us, granting lands in Islay. It is framed in quite different terms, the date is calculated from the Gaelic festival of Beltane and it is signed simply 'MacDhomnal'=Mac-Donald, the chief of the great clan Donald.[3]

After the forfeiture of the Lordship the vassals and cadets of the family rose five times to try to restore it, and the memory of its glories were a source of rightful pride to the clans descended from Donald. So late as the eighteenth century, a bitterly Whig visitor to the Highlands wrote: 'The poorest and most despicable Creature of the name of MacDonald looks upon himself as a Gentleman of far Superior Quality than a man in England of £1,000 a year.'[4]

The fall of the Lordship was followed by a century of anarchy in the Highlands, during which the houses of Argyll and of MacKenzie of Kintail rose into power. Argyll and his Campbell clansmen in particular, secured much of the land formerly held by the MacDonalds. But neither Argyll nor MacKenzie replaced the Lords of the Isles as great patrons of the arts of the Gael. By the seventeenth century the learned classes of Gaeldom were disappearing and Highlanders were getting their education at Lowland universities. The degradation of the old Gaelic civilization to a folk culture was beginning. For instance, the old Gaelic

[1]See MacKinnon, *Catalogue of Gaelic MSS.* for many examples.
[2]A. MacKerral, *Kintyre*, pp. 10, 119.
[3]G. Gregory Smith, *The Book of Islay* has a reproduction of this charter, p. 16.
[4]*The Highlands of Scotland in 1700.* Anonymous tract edited by Andrew Lang, p. 49.

physicians who had been learned in the best contemporary medical science were being superseded by Lowland doctors and only the use of charms and simples by country people lingered on.

The fall of the great Lordship and the rise of the Campbells and MacKenzies are only outstanding examples of the vicissitudes of fortune many clans underwent. The seventeenth century saw the virtual elimination of several powerful clans[1] and the growing ability of the authorities to exercise control in the Highlands.[2] The worst of the long drawn out feuds were brought to an end, largely because the lands in dispute were properly demarcated. It says much for the usefulness of the clan organization and the enduring ties that bound the clansmen together that both were very slow in weakening. In spite of the growing economic difficulties of the chiefs, who found their revenues inadequate to support the Lowland standards of living that they were now adopting and so plunged into debt and in many cases had to sell their lands. The aftermath of the last Jacobite Rising, although not more than a small proportion of the Highlanders rose for the Stuarts,[3] marks a definite milestone in the ending of the old clan organization. An official estimate of the manpower that the different chiefs could put into the field, made about 1724 and generally attributed to Duncan Forbes of Culloden, shows how very powerful the chiefs were. Twenty-six chiefs of clans could call out 18,890 men, their followings varying from the 5,000 and 2,500 men that followed Argyll and Seaforth (MacKenzie) respectively to the followings of twelve medium-sized clans and as many much smaller ones.[4]

[1] As, for instance, the MacLeods of Lewis, the MacIains of Ardnamurchan and the MacDonalds of Islay.
[2] Yet, paradoxically, because the feudal organization of the Lowlands was dying away more quickly, the political influences of the chiefs became greatly increased. One has only to compare contemporary accounts of the campaigns of Montrose and Dundee in the seventeenth century and the Jacobite Risings of the '15, '19 and '45 in the eighteenth with those of the Scots Wars of Independence to realize this.
[3] In the '15 about 10,000, in the '45 never more than 8,000 at one time. E. M. Barron, *Scottish Wars of Independence*, p. lxv.
[4] ESTIMATE ATTRIBUTED TO DUNCAN FORBES OF CULLODEN OF THE FIGHTING MANPOWER OF THE HIGHLANDS (ABOUT 1724).
Out of a total of 31,830, those of the great feudatories and families were 12,900.

The influence of the clan organization deeply influenced the life of the Highland people. The welfare of a clan largely depended upon the ability of the chief who led it. In the lawless state of the country the function of being their leader in fighting was an essential one, but he fulfilled many other duties till far down the eighteenth century and even later. In fact the destruction of the family of the chief generally led to the break-up of the clan as an entity. Bishop Leslie, writing in the seventeenth century of the Mackintoshes, said that 'their custom as that of many others in the Irish country (Highlands), has been at all times to acknowledge one principal for their chief captain to whom they are obedient in time of war and peace, for he is mediator between them and the Prince. He defends them against the invasions of their enemies, their neighbours, and he causes justice to be

| Campbells | .. | .. | .. | .. | .. | .. | 5,000 men |
|---|---|---|---|---|---|---|---|
| MacKenzies | .. | .. | .. | .. | .. | .. | 2,500 men |
| Grants .. | .. | .. | .. | .. | .. | .. | 850 men |
| Camerons | .. | .. | .. | .. | .. | .. | 800 men |
| Mackintoshes | .. | .. | .. | .. | .. | .. | 800 men |
| MacDonalds of Sleat | .. | .. | .. | .. | .. | 700 men |
| MacDonalds of Clanranald | .. | .. | .. | .. | 700 men |
| MacLeods | .. | .. | .. | .. | .. | .. | 700 men |
| Frasers .. | .. | .. | .. | .. | .. | .. | 900 men |
| MacLeans | .. | .. | .. | .. | .. | .. | 500 men |
| MacDonalds of Glengarry | .. | .. | .. | .. | 500 men |
| MacGregors | .. | .. | .. | .. | .. | .. | 700 men |
| Farquharsons | .. | .. | .. | .. | .. | .. | 500 men |
| MacKays .. | .. | .. | .. | .. | .. | .. | 800 men |
| Stewarts of Appin.. | .. | .. | .. | .. | .. | 300 men |
| Macphersons | .. | .. | .. | .. | .. | .. | 400 men |
| Munros .. | .. | .. | .. | .. | .. | .. | 350 men |
| Rosses .. | .. | .. | .. | .. | .. | .. | 500 men |
| MacLachlans | .. | .. | .. | .. | .. | .. | 200 men |
| McDougalls | .. | .. | .. | .. | .. | .. | 200 men |
| McKinnons | .. | .. | .. | .. | .. | .. | 200 men |
| Robertsons | .. | .. | .. | .. | .. | .. | 200 men |
| Chisholms | .. | .. | .. | .. | .. | .. | 200 men |
| MacDonald of Keppoch | .. | .. | .. | .. | 150 men |
| MacDonald of Glencoe | .. | .. | .. | .. | .. | 130 men |
| Grants of Glenmoriston .. | .. | .. | .. | .. | 150 men* |

*Major-General D. Stewart of Garth, *Sketch of the Character, Manners and Present State of the Highlanders of Scotland* (1825). Printed as an appendix (henceforth noted as Gen. D. Stewart, *Manners of the Highlanders*).

ministered to them all in the manner of the country.'[1] The history of individual clans, especially those so lucky as to have preserved their muniments, well illustrates how much the chief did as the administrator of justice, especially in the many districts in which 'the king's writ did not run'—in adjusting by negotiation numberless disputes with other chiefs and the authorities and as being the social centre of his people.

Many clans illustrate the bonds uniting Highland society from the chiefs to the humblest of their followers. Without exception, the chiefs were addressed by their patronymic, the Earl of Argyll as Mac Cailein Mor, the Lord of the Isles and Earl of Ross as Macdhomnal, etc. With this familiarity went an intense devotion. In the fifteenth century Major wrote that the people of Argyll swore by 'the hand of Macallum' (Mac Cailein Mor) as the Egyptians had sworn by Pharaoh's head[2] and the eighteenth century Burt that their chief was the Highlander's idol.[3] A report to the Government of 1724 stated that, in spite of all measures that had been taken, the chiefs of eleven clans 'have an inherent attractive virtue which makes their people follow as iron claps to the loadstone'.[4] Successive Lords Lovat were known to their people as MacSimi (Son of Simon) and it was said of one of them that he prided himself upon knowing the pedigree of even his least tenant.[5] It was a special obligation on the chief to provide for the dependants of those who had rendered him service, especially of those who had lost their lives. A letter from Campbell of Glenurchy, dated 1570, ordered the keeper of his Castle of

[1]Bishop J. Leslie, (16th Century) History of Scotland (English Historical Text Society), p. 210. A summary of the duties of a chief written in the 1720s is extremely similar, see E. Burt, Letters from a Gentleman in the North of Scotland, Vol II, pp. 108, 109 (henceforth noted as Burt, Letters). See also Gen. D. Stewart, Manners of the Highlanders.
[2]Highland Papers, Vol. II, p. 84.
[3]Burt, Letters, Vol. II, p. 106.
[4]Historical Papers relating to the Jacobite Period (New Spalding Club), Vol. I, p. 173. The clans were the MacLeans, Camerons, MacLeods, MacDonalds of Sleat, Clanranald, Keppoch and Glengarry, MacLachlans, MacKinnons and Stewarts of Appin. For other examples see 'Ewill Troubles of the Lewis', Highland Papers, Vol. II, p. 27 and Culloden Papers, Vol. IV, p. 97.
[5]Jas. Fraser, Wardlaw Manuscript (Scottish History Society), p. 309 (henceforth noted as Wardlaw MSS.). This book gives detailed accounts of the duties fulfilled by good chiefs. According to MacMartin, MacNeil of Barra did even more. See Western Isles, p. 97.

Kilchurn not to spare using his gear in supplying people who had suffered in a recent raid. He added that God willing he would get gear 'eneuch' by means not stated,[1] and after the Frasers' heavy losses at the Battle of Auldearn (1645) 'in our country there were 87 widdowes about the Lord Lovates ears'.[2] It was said to be 'the use and wont' of a Highland laird to give his tenants 'rests' (from paying their rent) in bad years. His hereditary smith did essential work for the community. The snobbish Boswell wondered to find that the country people of Coll shook the hand of the son of their Laird.[3] The equally snobbish Captain Burt expressed similar surprise.[4] All the clansmen were entertained in the hall of their chief, although strictly according to their degree.[5] The chief's piper and fiddler made music for them. MacLeod of MacLeod regularly employed three pipers, one in each section of his lands. This chief even supplied 'ferriers' from one island to another.[6] Mackintosh enjoyed attending the weddings of his tenants.[7] The weddings and above all the funerals of members of the chief's family were tremendous events for the whole clan in which everyone joined in the conviviality. When the chiefs ceased to live among their people the loss of their presence was greatly felt and the people became 'soured'.

It was, however, as the holder of the land occupied by the clansmen which, as already stated, depended not only upon legal title but upon his ability to defend it, that the chief was specially important. Originally, the clansmen seem to have occupied their land as tenants at will, and there are abundant illustrations to show that a chief moved his people about as circumstances required. For instance, when Sir James MacDonald was vainly trying to make his peace with the authorities in the early seventeenth century he first offered to remove all his clansmen from

[1] *Black Book of Taymouth*, p. 387.
[2] *Wardlaw MSS.*, p. 296.
[3] J. Boswell, *Journal of a Tour in the Hebrides* (1936 ed.), pp. 258, 287.
[4] E. Burt, *Letters*, Vol. II, p. 109.
[5] Cf. *Memoirs of Sergeant Donald MacLeod*, ed. by J. G. Fyfe, p. 45.
[6] The relations between MacLeod and his clansmen are well documented. See I. F. Grant, *The MacLeods, the Making of a Clan*, pp. 349, 351, 357–9, 362, 376, 387, 387–8, 490–3, 508, 541–2, 555, 558 (henceforth noted as *The MacLeods*).
[7] Sir Eneas Mackintosh of Mackintosh, *Notes, Descriptive and Historical, principally relating to the Parish of Moy in Strathdearn* (1774–83), privately printed, p. 33 (henceforth noted as Sir E. Mackintosh, *Notes*).

Kintyre to Islay and later to anywhere that the King should direct. Records are unusually full for MacLeod of MacLeod. His lands were diminished by the encroachments of the MacDonalds, and successive MacLeod chiefs, to provide for their own families, had to reshuffle the lands of retainers and the relations of earlier chiefs. Of course, when new land was acquired, as in the case of Lewis by MacKenzie or Islay by Campbell of Cawdor, it is not surprising that rentals show that members of his clan were soon in possession of the larger farms. This infiltration from the top downwards is of great social importance. On the other hand there was no social ladder upwards and it is most exceptional to hear of a clansman bettering himself permanently.

By the seventeenth century a chief with expanding lands occasionally provided for a specially favoured son with the permanent holding of a feu[1] or more often of a wadset.[2] When a chief gave a son a wadset he usually gave him occupation of the land and the succeeding chief had to buy him out. But, more generally, a chief gave them a long lease, perhaps for a life or more than one life and a specified number of years afterwards. The tacksmen, as they were called, became very common in most parts of the Highlands. They let off most of their land to sub-tenants and their presence was an integral part of the agrarian system on which present conditions in the Highlands grew up.

Whatever the chiefs did for their own family, the state of lawlessness of the country was such that their prosperity or even existence depended upon maintaining as many followers as possible upon their lands. And it was an understood thing that a chief must provide land for his clansmen, if necessary dividing existing holdings for the purpose.[3] One can see from rentals and also from traditions that families of even the smallest landholders, although they might be moved about, continued to farm land in the same district for generations. For instance, a family named Fergusson claims to have occupied land on Bernera from the thirteenth century when they came there during the Wars of

[1] A Scots form of land tenure giving permanent tenure in return for the payment of a yearly feu duty.
[2] An old Scots form of mortgage under which the creditor has the occupation and produce of the land until the loan is repaid. This generally gave a very long tenure.
[3] E. Burt, *Letters*, Vol. I, p. 109.

Independence till almost the present day.[1] It was a constant complaint by the Privy Council that, in addition to their own clansmen, chiefs would welcome 'broken men' upon their land to increase their followings.[2] A following was a necessity for a chief and was his main distinction. For instance, the story is told of MacDonnell of Keppoch, who occupied land nominally owned by Mackintosh and on more than one occasion successfully resisted ejectment, that when he was asked the amount of his income retorted: 'I can call out and command 500 men.'[3] So late as 1726 a Highland chief told Captain Burt that he preferred his estate, which was worth £500 a year, to an English one worth £30,000 because of his following.[4] In the case of some of the poorer clans, notably the MacDonalds of Glencoe, the Chief's land was inadequate to support his following without systematic cattle rieving from the Lowlands.

As a result the utmost population that the land could support was encouraged. In the words of William Marshall, who in 1793 made one of the fullest agricultural reports on the Highlands: 'A good soldier or a foolhardy desperado was of more value than a good husbandman' and therefore the farms had been 'frittered down' and the country 'burdened with a load of tenantry'.[5] As I shall hope to show, the crowding of people strongly attached to the land upon even smaller portions of it became intensified and led to the most painful readjustments.

This summary of the history of the development of the clans, brief as it is, may seem to be outside the scope of a book on present-day folklife. But although the conditions that favoured the functioning of the clan organization have disappeared and clan sentiments have largely died away among the country people, especially during the past seventy years,[6] yet the old

[1]Local tradition.
[2]Cf. Register Privy Council, Vol. III, p. 37 (henceforth noted as Reg.P.C.S.).
[3]Gen. D. Stewart, *Manners of the Highlanders*, p. 31.
[4]E. Burt, *Letters*, Vol. II, p. 164.
[5]W. Marshall, *General View of the Agriculture of the Central Highlands of Scotland*, p. 25 (henceforth noted as W. Marshall, *Agriculture of the Central Highlands*). To quote a more terrible statement, the minister of Harris wrote that: 'the lowest class of People were a burden on the hands of the landholders, an annoyance to one another and in many instances rather a nuisance than useful members of Society'. *O.S.A.*, Vol. X, p. 387.
[6]Contemporary descriptions down to the second half of the nineteenth century

ideas have largely moulded the outlook and bearing of the present day people of the Highlands. The old feeling of clannish pugnacity shows itself in their devotion to their own strath or island as opposed to all neighbouring ones. The survival of standards of behaviour of a society where everyone carried arms and where a feeling of kinship, real or fictitious, ran through the whole social fabric has given the people of the Highlands their self-respecting pride of descent, their breeding and fine manners and their pioneering and soldierly qualities.

suggest that such feelings were then stronger. For instance, A. Carmichael, in 1884, described how the people of Barra 'still fondly cling to the memory' of their chiefs: Evidence before the 1884 Crofters Commission, p. 457, and Miss Goodrich Freer wrote of the strong attachment of the people of Tiree to the MacLeans, who had lost the island in the seventeenth century: *The Outer Isles* (1902), p. 14. Nevertheless, as recent developments among the MacLeods show, under favourable circumstances, where the chief has retained some of his land and continues to be in touch with his people, the old feeling persists, notably among the Highlanders who have settled outside their native land.

# III

## THE LIE OF THE LAND AND THE SHAPE OF HUMAN SETTLEMENTS

THE word Highland is extremely expressive. A physical map of the area is almost covered with the shades of brown that denote altitudes of 800 ft. and over. It will be remembered that the boundary, the Highland Line, on the south and east runs along the outskirts of the central mass of the hill country, only coming down to the sea-level far up the Moray Firth (at Nairn) and then, in the extreme north-east, cutting off the wedge-shaped County of Caithness. On the west, as a rule, the hills plunge straight down to the many sea-lochs. The general level of the hill country—with a few exceptions such as the spired Cuillin in Skye and the fantastically carved sandstone hills of the north-west —is very uniform. In the words of *Chambers's Encyclopaedia*: 'The Highlands consist of a plateau dissected by glens and straths.' The plateaux are divided by the great cleft that runs diagonally across the country between Inverness and Fort William and by the wide straths of the Spey, the Tay and some other rivers, with lesser glens running into them. The Highland area also covers the Western Isles, the Hebrides—'the Long Island' (now often called the Outer Isles), consisting of the kite-shaped string of the islands of Lewis, Harris, North and South Uist with Benbecula in between them, Barra with lesser islands and what is now termed the Inner Isles—the host of very diverse islands, large, small, lesser and least, nearer to the mainland—Skye, Mull, Islay, Jura, etc.

Geological descriptions of the Highlands are complex but, to venture on a generalization, the Long Island and the extreme north-west are mainly formed of extremely ancient archaean rocks, planed to flat rock faces by the eons of erosion. The greater part of the mainland is formed of schists, forming massive hills such as the Cairngorm and the Grampians. Three entirely diverse regions are the volcanic intrusions, so noticeable in Skye and Mull, the sandstone peaks of a part of the north-west and, in the south-west, an area of slates and mica schists forming shapely conical peaks and providing the kindliest material for dry-stone walling.[1]

Whatever the geological formations underneath, the vegetation of the area is that common to many sterile, northern regions —heather, juniper, birch, coarse moor grass and fine, sweet turf, freckled with elegant little flowers, predominate. The distribution of the vegetation is less affected by what lies beneath it than by the geographic position—the actual lie of the land. Exceptional is the wonderful grass of the Machair lands that fringe the western shores of many of the islands, which is due to the accumulation of myriads of particles of shells forming a strand of dazzling whiteness and not to special rocks beneath. The Eastern and Central Highlands are exposed to cold winds from the northern Continent of Europe and especially to the destructive 'late and early frosts'. The winters are long and can be severe; more serious, the coming of spring is fickle and late. On the other hand, the western coasts and islands enjoy the milder air, the constant gales and the heavy rainfall brought them by the Atlantic, the high winds being a greater disadvantage than the rain.[2] The hill ramparts of the Central Highlands cause the precipitation of the moisture-laden air, so that the Eastern Highlands are generally drier if much colder. (See map.) When one crosses the Highlands from east to west, almost everywhere at a certain point, there is a sudden change in the vegetation. The moss and lichen on the tree-trunks and the ferns in the clefts of the rocks grow more luxuriantly and, in many places, a little farther on, there is a point where grass tends to replace heather.

Altitude and shelter are the determining factors in the growth of the trees. On lower ground, in the Eastern and Central Highlands, hardwood forest trees, such as the ash, beech and oak will

[1] *British Regional Geography, Scotland: The Western Highlands*, J. Phemiston, pp. 1, 17. *The Grampians*, H. N. Read and A. G. MacGregor, pp. 1, 3, 4, Plate II.
[2] Cf. M. F. Fraser Darling, *Crofting Agriculture*, p. 8.

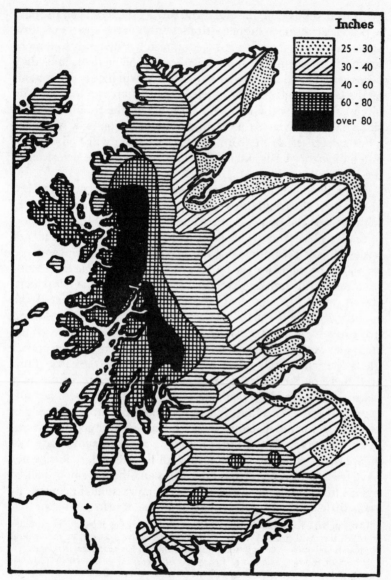

Rainfall map of Scotland.

grow well. The birch, the alder, the rowan, the hazel and the pine will flourish at much higher altitudes.[1] But in the west, even low down, the trees are often reduced in size by the gales to a mere scrub and on the more exposed peninsulas and on the islands they become more and more wind-battered and will hardly grow at all on the Long Island. Shelter is indeed the all-important factor. The birch and alder will climb very high where the fold in the hill-sides made by even a tiny burn gives protection and, when the gales sweep across the bare moors, there one will find congregated the hardy birds and beasts who can endure the severities of the high hills.

If one flies over the Highlands one sees, for miles upon miles, nothing but the rough brown hide of the heather, spangled over with lochans and pools. If one wanders among the hills it is easy to reach a place from which no human habitation can be seen. Yet traces of man's handiwork of the present or the not so long ago can easily be found for the looking. When sheep came to the hill-pastures much drainage was undertaken. Older travellers constantly allude to the dangerous quagmires that infested the country.[2] Captain Burt's account about 1723 of an expedition from Inverness to Strathspey has a dramatic description of the struggles of the hill-ponies to get through the bog.[3] In the upland glens one can see the grassy patches enriched by the cattle gathered there on the long abandoned sheilings, or, sign of the next phase of Highland agriculture, the drystone walls of a half-ruined sheep-fank. A line of turf-built shooting butts, probably in bad repair, for the spacious days of grouse shooting are over, tell of a yet later attempt to turn the hills to some account.[4] Latest of all are the great sheets of water into which hydro-electric schemes have transformed many natural valleys and the marching lines of pylons that carry away the power. The impression of grim sterility is little affected by such puny evidence of man's efforts.

[1]Although the north and the south also affects the growing of trees. The altitudes at which they will grow is about 1,700–1,900 ft. above sea-level in the Central Highlands and only 1,200 or 1,400 ft. in Sutherland. (*Encyclopaedia Britannica*.)

[2]Bishop R. Forbes, *Journals of Episcopal Visitations*, Ed. J. Craven (1762), had to engage a guide between Langwell and Thurso because of the dangerous bogs, even so, two of the party's horses became bogged and had to be hauled out, p. 196 (henceforth noted as Bp. R. Forbes, *Journals*).

[3]*Letters*, Vol. II, p. 48.

[4]For value of shootings see I. F. Grant, *Economic Journal*, January 1928, p. 405.

Where a burn has torn its peat banks in a recent spate or where the peat itself has decayed into dark hags, one can see the traces of primeval forests, that in times of a kindlier climate, formed a green fleece over the greater part of the country. Even in later times there was a great deal more forest. Traditions of it still live among the people. In the Long Island the passing of the forests is so remote that their destruction is attributed to a witch sent by a pagan Norse princess to take revenge on her faithless Island lover.[1] But in many districts the people say that the forests were destroyed because of the robbers or the wolves that harboured in them. In Strathdearn I have been told that once upon a time the strath was all forest with only three 'smokes' (human habitations) in it and Slochd Muich (the pass to the south) was said to have been covered with oak wood down to the time of Mary, Queen of Scots.[2] Old accounts and traditions show that even two hundred years ago there was a great deal more woodland even on the barest regions,[3] and in historic times the Caledonian Forest provided exports of timber for the chiefs fortunate enough to own part of it. Even yet, the remains of its great spreading pines survive in such places as Rothiemurchus and Glen Nevis.[4] So abundant was wood that in the times of acute timber shortage, before the use of coal for smelting iron was developed, English iron-masters used to send their ore up to favoured spots in the Highlands to be smelted—for instance, to Furnace on Loch Fyne, Bunawe on Loch Etive and Kinlochewe in Wester Ross. The native wood, however, was mainly destroyed piecemeal by the nibbling of sheep and goats, cutting for firewood, etc.

Timber is now extensively planted in the Highlands and the dense, symmetrical plantings and the introduction of larch, spruce and many other varieties of soft woods show man's influence. Afforestation began in the eighteenth century as part of the great agrarian reforms. The massive plantings of Central Perthshire and of Strathspey are early examples on the grand scale. The timber from the old woods had supplied the local

[1]Alexander Carmichael, *Carmina Gadelica*, Vol. I, p. xx.
[2]See Sir Eneas Mackintosh, *Notes*, pp. 2, 12.
[3]Cf. Macfarlane's *Geographical Collections*, Ed. R. Mitchell (Scottish History Society), Abertarf, 1720, p. 220. F. Fraser Darling, *Crofting Agriculture*, p. 105.
[4]James Ritchie, *Influences of Man on Animal Life in Scotland*, p. 314, gives a fuller list.

people with timber for building and the making of home-made furniture and plenishings. Late eighteenth century lumbering operations in the Caledonian Forest were for export for such archaic purposes as wooden ships and drain pipes, and the produce of the modern artificial plantings is still sent south, now largely for pit-props. (One sees the same trend from production for subsistence to production for sale in Highland farming.) The social history of the country is shown in the recent change from planting by private landowners to increased activities by the State. Since 1919 the Forestry Commission has been entrusted with the work. By 1957 it owned over a million acres in Scotland.[1] It is now replacing the terrible sacrifice of Highland timber during the wars and the work of planting, maintenance and felling in its forests is a valuable source of employment in the Highlands.[2]

The plantings lead down the hill slopes into the straths and glens where the changes wrought by man are increasingly obvious. Two of such changes that are quickly noticed are that, with the introduction of tile drainage, the alluvial land along the rivers has come increasingly into use and that, with roads and railways, means of communication also tend to follow the lower ground instead of ranging by means of foot-tracks over the hills. A less desirable change is the spread of unproductive bracken, muffling the pastures and encouraged by the spread of sheep-farming.

The most casual survey brings out the fact that the Highlands always have been, and still are, more fit for pastoral than arable farming. In the present century the percentages of the use of land in Scotland as a whole and in the Highlands are:

|  | Scotland | Highlands |
|---|---|---|
| Percentage under crops and[3] sown grass | 24.11 | 7.4 |
| Percentage under rough grazing | 54.45 | 65.37 |

[1]*Conditions of the Highlands and Islands of Scotland* (published by the Scottish Economic Committee), p. 111 (henceforth noted as *Condition of the Highlands*). State aid in 1958 was granted to 272,800 acres of private forests. Forestry Commission, 38th Report, p. 6.

[2]See 38th Ann. Rept. Forestry Commission, p. 26. In 1956–7 15,200 acres were planted by private owners and 26,700 by the Forestry Commission, pp. 35, 45.

[3]*Conditions of the Highlands*, p. 16.

Under such conditions the human population is very thin on the ground. The density of the population of the whole of Scotland averages 171.4 per square mile whereas that of the counties of Inverness-shire, Ross and Cromarty, Sutherland and Argyllshire only averages 14 per square mile. (See map, p. 42.)

Within the Highlands, the areas of fertile land are very limited. Among specially favoured districts are part of the Black Isle, the Aird at the head of the Beauly Firth, the coastal lands of Easter Ross, the Islands of Tiree and Lismore, much of Islay, the western side of Kintyre and both Sleat and Trotternish in Skye. Elsewhere there are many relatively fertile spots, on the slopes of glens and straths, the raised beaches along the sea-shores and the western side of the Long Island with its machair lands. In such places, from ancient times, human settlements have maintained themselves.[1] Often the land round these old settlements is marginal and the uncultivated hill-sides show traces of where cultivation has been extended to meet such times of special need as that of the desperate requirements of the early nineteenth century population that was increasing at the very time when much of the land was being taken for sheep-farming or in response to the food shortages, high returns and drives for production of the two world war periods.

The traces of the past are, however, generally much blurred because the layout of most of the land has been so constantly altered.[2] The traces of life under the clan system are sparse. Here and there one sees the ruins of a powerful chief's castle. It is significant that on the west coast they are almost always to be found close to the sea because travel by boats was so much more convenient than that by land. Dunvegan Castle, although it was in continuous occupation, could only be entered by scrambling up the rock to the 'sea gate' until the eighteenth century.

As we have seen, it was the duty and also to the interest of a

[1]See excellent map of distribution of Highland population in *Chambers's Encyclopaedia* and map of settlements in Wester Ross. See I. D. Duff, 'Human Geography in South West Ross-shire', *Scottish Geographical Magazine*, September 1929, p. 277.

[2]It may be worth while to remind English readers that in Scotland the tenure of copyholding did not exist and that a Scots Commonty is legally different to an English Common and that until the nineteenth century, except in very exceptional cases, no legal process was necessary for the re-allocation of holdings. For summary see Grant, *Social and Economic Development*, pp. 247, 727.

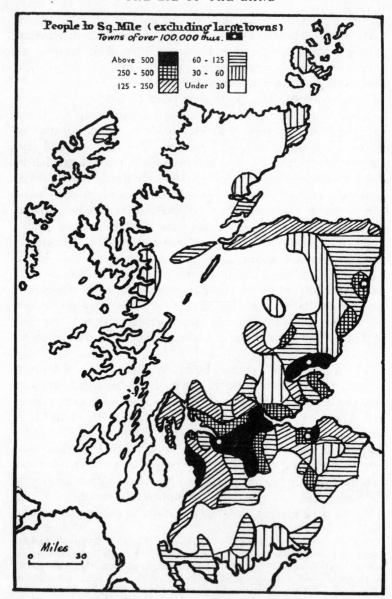

The distribution of population in Scotland.

Highland chief to support as many people upon his land as he could, and he was also obliged to provide for his relations. By the seventeenth century, in most parts of the Highlands it had become usual for the chief to provide for kinsmen and for connexions by leasing them large portions of his estate and for them to sublet their lands to groups of joint subtenants. Some of his land the chief let directly to groups of joint tenants. Although a very few small, severally held, pendicles of land existed on the east, joint tenancy by the smaller cultivators was universal on the west and usual everywhere. The great social importance of the tacksmen is better dealt with elsewhere. The proportion of the land held by tacksmen was generally considerable. For instance, on the MacLeod estates in the eighteenth century there were 73 tacksmen paying a total rent of £917 Scots while twenty-four farms were occupied by 105 joint tenants paying a total rent of £246 Scots.[1] In Kintyre the proportion was similar.[2] In Breadalbane, where there was no predominant clan although Campbell of Glenorchy had acquired the superiority, there were no tacksmen.[3] On the other hand, in Badenoch, where the Huntly family had wide superiorities, there were numbers, generally cadets of local chiefs.[4] The tacksmen have vanished even more completely than the chiefs. Their earlier houses of drystone walling and turf were as transient as those of the country people, but the slated masonry-built houses that some of them built in the late eighteenth or early nineteenth century can still be picked out, plain, unpretentious, four-square little buildings, often with a touch of Regency grace about the staircase or interior mouldings. Often they are surrounded by a tuft of ancient trees, the relics of an eighteenth-century gentleman's urge to plant. On the west, like the castles, they are generally accessible to the sea.[5] In districts well opened to the tourist trade, such as Skye or Strathspey, they often survive as farm-cum-boarding houses with the emphasis on one or the other.

[1]L. MacDonald, *The Past and Present Position of the Skye Crofters*, p. 4 (henceforth noted as L. MacDonald, *Skye Crofters*).
[2]A. MacKerral, *Kintyre*, p. 134.
[3]M. MacArthur, *Loch Tayside*, p. xxxiii.
[4]Gordon Estate Rent Roll, Spalding Club Miscellany, Vol. IV.
[5]Two fine examples, with pleasant panelling, survive near Laide in Wester Ross.

The actual cultivation of the land was done by groups, either of joint tenants holding directly of the chief or of sub-tenants holding of his tacksmen.[1] The custom of joint cultivation, of course, is not a peculiarly Gaelic feature and was common to most northern countries, but the system fitted in well with the social organization of the clans. The joint farms varied in size but would tend to consist of one, two or even three ploughgates, that age-old unit of the team of work-beasts—oxen or horses according to the district. Here and there, where land has long gone out of cultivation, one can pick out the huddle of heaps of loose stones that were once the foundations of the primitive little houses and, under the grass and heather, the irregular patches of high crooked ridges which were once the township's precious 'infield' land under constant cultivation. The old head-dyke that separated the lower and better land that was under permanent or intermittent cultivation from the more sterile hill-side above can sometimes be traced. Or one may be able to find old estate maps that show the joint farms in some detail.[2] The lay-out naturally depended upon the lie of the land. In inland districts in the wider straths, such as those of the Spey, Garry and Tay, the little settlements were generally strung along the slopes where there was land most suitable for cultivation but, where the ground was broken and the straths were narrower, the various holdings might be scattered in twos and threes.[3] On the west and the islands the settlements were generally by the sea-shore because of facilities for transport in those roadless days. Captain Dymes wrote of Lewis in 1630 that the groups of joint tenants occupied 'towns', 'which towns are some half a score of cottages built together neare some piece of arable land where they make theire abode in winter, for the most part of the common people in the somer they remaine in the hills to graze theire cattle'. Another account has it that 'a joint

[1]For details of actual agricultural methods see Chapter IV.
[2]The maps prepared for the Commissioners of the Forfeited Estates now in H.M. Register House, Edinburgh, have some good examples.
[3]Cf. descriptions by W. Marshall, *Agriculture of the Central Highlands*, p. 16. Jas. Robertson, *General View of the Agriculture of the County of Inverness*, p. 109 (henceforth noted as Jas. Robertson, *Agriculture of Inverness*). Sir J. Sinclair, *General View of the Agriculture of the Northern Counties and Islands of Scotland*, p. 76 (henceforth noted as Sir J. Sinclair, *Northern Counties*). The variations in lay-out were very great, there are many good descriptions in the accounts of individual parishes in the *O.S.A.*

FIG. 1. Reconstruction of old settlement with irregular cluster of houses; rigs of 'infield' and more distant 'outfield'.

45

tenant farm is like a commonwealth of villagers'.[1] (See Fig. 1.) It will be simplest to deal with the actual methods of cultivation separately and to outline the great changes in the life of Highland people as written on the face of the land.

Many of the old implements and work processes and social customs can be traced back to ways of folk life in these clustered settlements, but nevertheless many changes in the lay-out of the land and in the lives of the people upon it have taken place, probably more than most people realize until they study the general social history of the Highlands and the individual alterations that have taken place in practically every existing human settlement. Even as early as 1884, in the exhaustive *Report of the Crofters Commission*, evidence of these great changes is said not only to depend on tradition or even 'solid contemporary records' but 'is written in indelible characters on the surface of the soil'.[2] A map published by the National Trust for Scotland shows the superimposure of the regular strip cultivation over the irregular patches of cultivation in St. Kilda. (See map, p. 47.)

The sweeping changes in little Highland homes were the result of great industrial and social movements. As the chiefs and lairds no longer had to defend themselves and their people and were brought more and more into touch with the more affluent gentry of the south, a change took place in their social standards. A story is attributed to Sir Walter Scott that an old Argyllshire chief said: 'I have lived in woeful times; when I was young the only question asked concerning a man of rank was—How many men lived on his estate—then it was, How many black cattle it could keep, but now it is, How many sheep will it carry?'[3] In many parts of the Highlands one can see the visible sign of this change of attitude in the rather ambitious although pleasant Georgian and Regency mansions that were taking the place of the older and extremely uncomfortable castles of the landowners.

[1]Captain Dymes report is printed by W. C. MacKenzie, *History of the Outer Hebrides*, Appendix F. See also *O.S.A.*, Vol. X, p. 365. J. Leyden, *Journal of a Tour in the Highlands and Islands of Scotland*, p. 40. E. Burt, *Letters*, Vol. II, p. 130.

[2]Report, *1884 Crofters Commission*, p. 23. For Lewis, see *Tolsta bho Thuath* (published monthly in *Stornoway Gazette*, 1951). For Kintyre, see F. F. MacKay, *MacNeill of Carskey*, p. 22. For Bernera, A. Morrison, *Orain Chaluim*, pp. 5, 7, 10.

[3]G. Gray Graham, *Social Life in Scotland in the Eighteenth Century*, p. 210 (henceforth noted as G. Gray Graham, *Social Life*).

Although the emphasis upon monetary returns rather than the support of manpower took effect all over the Highlands, the changes followed quite different lines in the Southern, Central and Eastern Highlands as compared to the North-West, and this contrast is still very marked. In the Southern, Central and

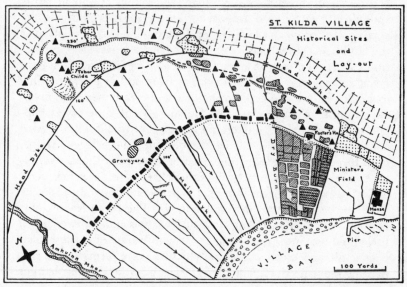

ST. KILDA VILLAGE

Historical Sites
and
Lay-out

▲ Vestige of early building    ▨ Early cultivation plot    ⌒ Vestige of early track
▮● 19th. century building    ⊕ 19th. century enclosure    ⁖ Edge of village street

Eastern Highlands the new methods of husbandry that were coming into Scotland during the eighteenth century—the introduction of a regular rotation of crops including the cultivation of turnips and of sown hay—led to the erection of stone dykes to enclose rectangular fields, replacing the inter-mixed strips of the joint farms, and at the same time the old tacksmen and the groups of joint tenants were replaced by working farmers, who received long leases. Sometimes these farmers were incomers and specially skilled men but, with better methods of working the land, the farms became more productive and some of the old joint tenants tended to remain on as farm workers. For others there were rural handicrafts, which at that time were very flourishing, and abundant openings in the south where the Industrial Revolution was beginning. Far less isolated than were the inhabitants of the north-west, the local people do not seem to have been unwilling to accept such openings. The whole social pattern of the countryside thus became changed; the process, however, was gradual. During the second half of the eighteenth century many individual Highland lairds sporadically introduced 'improving leases' (leases enforcing the sowing of turnips and hay, the enclosing of fields, etc.) all over the Highlands but with little effect. The main work of reorganization started in the most favoured districts, especially in the Aird (near Inverness), in Breadalbane, in Islay and in Kintyre.[1] One example, well documented by rentals and estate maps and probably typical of what went on elsewhere, will show what happened. The estate of Newton in the parish of Kirkhill in the Aird consisted in 1754 of a davoch divided into three larger farms, with three, two and four joint tenants respectively, and twenty-six smaller holdings, nearly all of them held jointly and in several cases tenants had shares in more[2] than one holding. By 1786 the land had been laid out in regular fields. The three larger joint holdings had been made into two single farms and the twenty-six little holdings into three smaller farms. Groups of cottages had been built and there was employment on the farms which had become more productive and, very significantly, the new hamlet was called Drum-Chardny (the Ridge of the Weavers) and a considerable hand loom linen weaving industry developed there.[3] The population of the parish rose from 950 in 1760 to 1,571 in 1789.

The pattern of holdings that was laid down by these changes has in the main survived. The many farm names beginning Easter or Wester and the name Middleton generally give a clue to the re-allocations that took place with the main agricultural reforms

[1]M. MacArthur *Lochtayside*, p. lxv. M. Gray, *The Highland Economy, 1750–1850*, pp. 75–86 (henceforth noted as *The Highland Economy*). J. Robertson, *Agriculture of Inverness-shire*, p. 189.

[2]This was not exceptional. On Dunachton the same thing occurred and it shows up very strongly in some rentals relative to the upper alley of the Findhorn which I was able to examine.

[3]I. F. Grant, 'Development of an Estate in Eastern Inverness-shire', *Estate Magazine* (pub. E.S.A.), November 1924, p. 823.

and the sites of many of the sturdy, stone-built farm-houses, generally built at a central spot overlooking the holding, date from this time.

Nevertheless, there have been further developments. The introduction of field drainage has made the appearance of the fields far more uniform by removing many wet, unproductive patches and has made possible the reclamation of alluvial land in the valley bottoms, often the best land on the farm. The drains built of flat stones that were an exciting innovation in the late eighteenth century have long given place to tile drainage.[1] One can see examples of holdings that have literally 'gone down hill'. The upper slope is now marginal land with the remains of dry-stone buildings, below are the present fields and farm-house. Meanwhile, with the introduction of turnips and sown hay, it was no longer necessary to send the cattle up to the shielings in summer and the land is well enriched from the well-fed beasts at grass in the summer and housed during the winter. The drystone dykes that gave such emphasis to the contours of the land have almost entirely given place to wire fences and now the range of byres on three sides of the open manure heap, wasteful but what a sign of farming opulence! are giving place to covered cattle courts. The size of the holdings had been largely correlated to the work of the horses required for the two-horse iron plough that was one of the earliest agricultural improvements but, as horses are giving place to tractors and mechanization proceeds, a good deal of reorganization in the lay-out and size of the holdings must go on. A new development is the establishment of large dairy farms in more favoured places in the Highlands. The social implications of this can better be dealt with elsewhere.[2]

The formal lay-out of some villages, as for instance, Grant-town, Kenmore and Kingussie, are associated with the agricultural reforms of the Central and Eastern Highlands. Because of the ancient monopolies tenaciously held by the Scots burghs there had been few old villages in Scotland and the development of rural industries had been much hampered.[3] But by the eighteenth

[1]The older form of drain is however still the best on peaty land in the west.
[2]See Chapter IV.
[3]I. F. Grant, *Social and Economic Development*, p. 368. A. Ballard, *Scottish Historical Review*, Vol. XIII, pp. 22, 28. Jas. Anderson, *Present State of the Hebrides and Western Garth of Scotland*, pp. 18, 225.

century powers of the burghs to enforce their rights had declined and those lairds who were interested in agricultural reforms were generally also interested in encouraging craftsmen and several of them laid out villages to encourage handicraft workers, especially in the flourishing textile industries. Handicraft work is now, of course, about as obsolete as open-field farming and, where these villages have continued to flourish, it is because they are conveniently placed with regard to railways, the tourist industry and the shopping and marketing needs of the local people. The villages laid out for the fishery industry about the same time—Ullapool and Tobermory are good specimens—are contemporary examples of the same sort of movement in the west.

About the same time (the second half of the eighteenth century) as the revolution in the lay-out of arable holdings in the Eastern Highlands, another kind of farming was making its appearance on the less productive hilly land of the Central Highlands and of the western mainland; a change that was to have dire and lasting consequences for the people of the Highlands. The ancient breed of Highland sheep had been small, delicate animals with fine though scanty fleeces.[1] They were generally housed at night and were kept in relatively small numbers for their milk and for the people's own requirements in wool. But about the middle of the eighteenth century it was discovered that the hardy, coarse-woolled sheep of the Borders could be kept all the year round on the higher hills of the Highlands upon land which had only been partially grazed by cattle in high summer. The Border sheep-masters accordingly began to rent great stretches of the Highlands for sheep-walks. The movement started about 1762 and steadily spread over the north. By 1782 flocks of Border sheep were being introduced into Glengarry and in the next decade they had reached Cromarty and Sutherland.[2]

The market for wool and for mutton was expanding as the

[1] See Chapter IV.
[2] H. Hamilton, *The Industrial Revolution in Scotland*, pp. 66–68 (henceforth noted as *The Industrial Revolution*). Sir J. Sinclair, *Northern Counties*, pp. 162–79. T. Robertson, *General Report on the Size of Farms* (1795), p. 104. J. Stoddart, *Remarks on the Scenery and Manners of Scotland* (1799 and 1800), Vol. II, pp. 299, 364 (henceforth noted as Stoddart, *Scenery and Manners in Scotland*).

great industrial towns of the south grew and Sir John Sinclair, a practical agriculturist, confidently asserted that the value of a farm stocked with Highland cattle would be quadrupled if these were replaced by sheep.[1] This was a matter of sober fact, for instance, a shieling in Glengarry that had been let to local men for a rent of £15 per annum was rented by a sheep-farmer for £350. When the whole estate was mainly let to sheep-farmers between 1762 and 1802 the total rental was increased from £700 to £5,000.[2] But unfortunately the sheep occupied the hill-grazings that had been essential to the old economy of the Highlanders who had depended upon their cattle for the dairy products upon which they largely lived and, by the sale of the beasts, for what ready money they required. They had been mainly clothed from the wool of their sheep and saved much drudgery by their work ponies.[3] And, moreover, to winter the sheep-farmers' ewes and hoggs much of the precious land suitable for arable cultivation was required. To take a favourable illustration of what only too often happened. Lord Seaforth (the descendant of the long line of MacKenzies of Kintail, chiefs of that clan) had for long refused to let part of his lands as sheep walks but in 1802, being in dire financial difficulties, he did so. The displaced people tended to crowd into neighbouring townships. For instance, that of Duirinish (on Loch Alsh) originally had four tenants who had pastured eighty cattle. By 1852 there were ten tenants and the people had lost their hill grazings. The men had to take seasonal work in the south in order to support themselves.[4] In other cases people who had lost their holdings rented patches of barren land which it had not been thought worthwhile to till or were planted by the sea-shore to earn their living by

[1]Sir J. Sinclair, *Northern Counties*, p. 110.
[2]C. Fraser Mackintosh, *Antiquarian Notes*, Vol. II, pp. 299, 364.
[3]For good accounts see statements in *1884 Crofters Commission* by the Rev. J. S. Macphail, Appendix A, p. 10, and the Rev. M. McRitchie, p. 141.
[4]I. D. Duff, *Human Geography, West Ross-shire*, p. 277. For many other examples see evidence *Crofters Commission, 1884*. Doctor Garnett overtook groups of people, men, women and some children tramping from Sutherland to help with the harvest in the south 'a yearly custom with many of them'. They each carried a bundle with a few clothes and a bag of oatmeal on which 'They chiefly subsist during their journey'. T. Garnett, *Observations on a Tour through the Highlands and Part of the Western Isles of Scotland* (1800), Vol. II, p. 36 (henceforth noted as, T. Garnett, *Tour*).

fishing[1] although they lacked experience, boats or gear or money to buy these. Some of these miserable settlements were upon the rocky and stormy coasts of the extreme north. In other cases the people were faced with emigration or starvation. Clearing the tenantry off the land to make room for sheep farms bears a heavy responsibility for abandoned townships and the congestion within those that remained.[2] Clearing began in the late eighteenth century and was then intermittent: the worst period was after 1820; after the 1840s there was little clearing on a large scale. More than anything else the clearing for sheep broke the old ties of affection between the people who owned and those who lived on the land, and it has left an enduring feeling of bitterness that is part of the mental heritage of present-day people. It must, however, be remembered that the clearing was not the sole cause of misery and congestion in the Highlands. Conditions were very serious in the Long Island long before large-scale sheep-farming reached there about the middle of the nineteenth century, and in many other districts where the people's cattle stocks were not depleted, their condition showed improvement from about the end of the eighteenth century. Alternative sources of work were opening for them and the movement of the prices that they got for their cattle and had to pay for their meal was favourable to them.[3] Moreover the people showed great courage and spirit in acquiring stock of the new breeds of hardy black-faced and Cheviot sheep and in learning the different technique required in keeping them, so that these sheep are now the mainstay of many crofters

[1]For good account see *Statement on Tongue*, by the Rev. W. Hall Telford, *Crofters Commission, 1884*, Appendix A., pp. 334–9. He calculated that the pieces of land rented to the people evicted in 1807–20 from good holdings in Strath Strathey, Strath Naver and Strath Halladale could not supply more than four-sevenths of the needs of the people. For examples from Bernera and Harris see A. Morrison, *Orain Chaluim*, pp. 10, 80.

[2]For general accounts of clearing see *Conditions of the Highlands* (Scottish Economic Committee), pp. 14, 16. J. P. Day, *Public Administration in the Highlands and Islands of Scotland*, p. 26 (henceforth noted as *Public Administration*) H. Hamilton, *The Industrial Revolution*, p. 91. Gen. D. Stewart, *Manners of the Highlanders*, p. 148. For more localized accounts see C. Fraser Mackintosh, *Antiquarian Notes*, Vol. I, pp. 126–7, 130. D. Campbell, *Octogenarian Highlander*, pp. 56, 59, 117, 173, 188, 199. A. MacKerral, *Kintyre*, p. 143. T. Johnston, *History of the Working Classes in Scotland*, pp. 198–200. For some of the most notorious clearances, those in Sutherland, the subject of bitter controversy, see J. G. Fyfe, *Scottish Diaries and Memoirs, 1746–1843*, for a good summary.

[3]M. Gray, *Highland Economy*, p. 143. A. Morrison, *Orain Chaluim*, p. 11.

and from the black-faced sheep comes the special wool used in the Harris tweed industry.

The large-scale keeping of sheep did not continue to flourish. From the 1870s onwards the imports of wool and then of meat from overseas made it less and less profitable.[1] In the districts most suitable for such farming, especially in the north, one can see the large establishments of the great flock-masters, and in many other hilly districts older farms have largely gone in for sheep, as one can see from the massive fanks. But one can also trace the decline of the industry in great derelict steadings planted high on the moors.[2] Pleasanter results of sheep-farming are the trig shepherds' cottages with a patch of cultivation and grazing for a cow or two, that are a welcome sign of humanity in the loneliness of many an austere glen.

In spite of the clearances the population of the Highlands continued to rise. According to an estimate by a Doctor Webster, made in 1755, it was 257,153. From 1801 census returns are available and by 1811 the population was 362,000. By 1841, when the clearances were coming to an end, it was 396,000, the maximum figure it was to reach. The increase, however, was not uniform. It was comparatively slight in the districts where the improved agriculture was able to maintain the people in a reasonable degree of comfort and was mainly concentrated in the north-west. There the introduction of a new industry was to lead to permanent changes in the lay-out of the holdings and to the immediate gathering of a dense, local population.

In Wester Ross, Skye and the Long Island the joint farms had not been rearranged upon a more modern pattern. The old race of tacksmen were dying out there as elsewhere, but their holdings were generally let directly to the existing groups of sub-tenants or new tacksmen, generally strangers, had taken them over. About the middle of the eighteenth century, the discovery had been made that the calcined ash of the tangle, a tawny seaweed that fringes the rocky shores of much of the west, was rich in alkali. Alkali was a most valuable product because it was then

[1] *Report of Departmental Committee on Deer Forests, 1922*, p. 5. See *Historical Survey in Report of the Committee on Hill Sheep-farming in Scotland, 1944* (Cmd. 6494) p. 7.
[2] There is a very good example near Ruthven in Badenoch.

used for bleaching linen—and linen in the eighteenth century was Scotland's most valuable industry—as well as in the manufacture of glass and soap. Soon the manufacture of kelp (the calcined seaweed) became spectacularly profitable because, in the sequence of great wars of the period that culminated in the Napoleonic Wars, barilla, the alternative source of alkali, had to be imported from Spain and supplies were reduced and then stopped. The price of kelp rose from £1 a ton to as much as £20 and there was a corresponding jump in the value of the land on the shores of which this 'golden fringe' grew.

In order to attract people to come and make the kelp inducements were offered. The work was seasonal. The sea-ware had to be gathered at low tide in the summer and brought to the shore to be calcined between layers of burning peat in trenches dug in the ground. The maintenance of the right temperature in burning the kelp required considerable skill. A number of farms were divided into small separate holdings in order to support the kelp makers. For instance, in Skye, one of the kelping districts, thirty-five of the seventy-three farms formerly leased to tacksmen on the MacLeod estate, were divided into these little holdings which were known as *crofts*, while of seventy-seven smaller farms formerly leased to joint tenants, thirty-six were divided up for the same purpose. On the estates of MacDonald of Sleat the same thing was done although not to such an extent.[1] This was a most significant change in the organization of the holdings. The existence of a few small separate holdings had been an old feature of the eastern districts and had already been introduced farther south when the Argyll estates were reorganized, but in the north-west it was an innovation from the joint farms. MacLeod of MacLeod himself, in a memorandum to the 1884 Crofters Commission, stated that in the eighteenth century there had been no tenants on the estates of his family 'who could be called *crofters*, as that appellation is understood today'. The same process occurred in the other kelping districts to provide for the influx of population attracted by the kelping industry. On the Long Island, where the industry especially flourished, the population increased by 137 per cent between 1755 and 1831. It was from

---

[1] L. MacDonald, *Skye Crofters*. Plates X, XI, XXII, XXIII. See also A. Morrison, *Orain Chaluim*, p. 7 for Bernera.

now on that the term *crofter* came into general use and the new pattern of separate holdings in communities with joint grazings very gradually spread to the joint farms. Reporting to the Crofters Commission of 1884, Alexander Carmichael summarized the position in the Long Island. All the crofters lived in townships with joint grazings, but the partial re-allocation of the arable land was going out and on only three farms was it all held in common and individually re-allocated.[1] More slowly the crofters have tended to introduce a regular rotation of oats, barley, turnips, potatoes and hay and even to fence their land although, even now, in some cases, the long strips are merely divided by ditches.[2] This distinctive arrangement of narrow strips of the vividly contrasting colours of the different crops— the intenser verdure of potatoes and turnips, the more vivid green of the cereal crops and the softer tones of the hay and grass —is familiar to anyone visiting the crofting counties.

Unfortunately the kelp industry itself soon practically collapsed. When peace came the price of barilla was only kept high by an import duty and when, as part of a general change in British fiscal policy, this was repealed in 1825 without any alternative concession to those who would suffer, the price quickly fell. By 1834 the price of a ton had fallen to £3 and the industry died out in most districts.[3] I have been told that in Bernera the latest consignment of kelp was left lying by the jetty because it was not worth the freight. The lairds were hard hit and the only profitable use that they could make of their land was to let it for sheep-farming, displacing many of the crofters. The kelp-makers themselves were in far more desperate straights.[4] They were faced with the alternatives of starvation or emigration.

The old joint tenants had been mainly dependent upon their cattle for a livelihood but, by the eighteenth century, families had

[1]*Crofters Commission, 1884.* Appendix A, pp. 213, 451, 463.

[2]F. Fraser Darling, *Crofting Agriculture*, p. 132. Jas. Robertson, *Agriculture of Inverness-shire*, p. 335. M. Gray, *Highland Economy*, pp. 66, 67. A map of St. Kilda, published by the National Trust in their *Newsletter No. 18*, p. 7, shows the more modern strips superimposed upon a wider area of the old irregular patches of cultivation.

[3]Only lingering on in a few places in North and South Uist and Barra where kelp wages had been commuted into rent. M. Gray, *Highland Economy*, pp. 156, 158.

[4]For instance, in the small island of Bernera, there were 700 more people than the crofts alone could sustain. A. Morrison, *Orain Chaluim*, p. 7.

often earned something by spinning and fishing. The new crofters were even more dependent upon outside sources of income. For a time fishing was an important source of revenue. Markets for herring and salt fish were good. The rise and decline of the Highland fishing industry requires fuller treatment.[1] Today, beyond a few deserted 'salting houses' and the traditions of where, on the open shores of the Western Isles, the hardy fishermen would beach their boats, there is little remaining evidence of a phase that greatly affected the Long Island. In the north, strung along the coast are the almost deserted fishing villages which lost their livelihood as the industry became concentrated on the east coast. As another subsidiary source of income numbers of the people went to join the bands of reapers on the Lowland farms before mechanical reaping machinery was introduced. By such attempts to eke out a living the people within the crofting areas clung desperately to their homes. Fathers provided for sons and sons-in-law by subdividing their already inadequate holdings and such 'squatters' were tolerated by the kindly people. It was calculated that in 1884, in the most crowded districts of South Uist, Uig, Farr and Duirinish, out of 3,226 families, 3,091 depended on the land for a livelihood. Of these 25 per cent were not on any rent roll and therefore were squatters, and of the remaining rent-paying families only 30 per cent had holdings large enough to support them adequately.[2]

In their increasing poverty, the people had subsisted more and more upon the potato, the food of direst poverty. It is said to have been introduced into the Islands about 1739 by Clanranald. The story goes that he made his people grow the tubers but that, when the crop was lifted, they brought it to him and declared that although he could force them to grow such things he could not make them eat them.[3] The people were, however, quick to appreciate the value of this enormously productive crop, which does

[1]See Chapter XII.
[2]*Crofters Commission, 1884*, pp. 13–14. For general figures and instances (Lewis) *Crofters Commission, 1884*, pp. 152, 155. In Skye to quote two among many instances there had been fourteen families in Waternish, by 1884 there were thirty-eight. The figures for Geary were twelve to thirty-three. *Crofters Commission, 1884*, pp. 17, 18.
[3]R. Salaman, *History and the Social Influence of the Potato*, p. 367. Correspondence Relative to the Relief of Distress in Scotland, 1844 (Blue Book), pp. 49, 51.

well in the north-west, and late eighteenth-century travellers noticed how widely it was being grown. By 1840 potatoes were said to form three-fourths to seven-eighths of the food consumed by Highland families. When the potato blight became severe in 1846 and the following years, and the crop completely failed, the people were faced with calamity. In Skye, at the worst of the potato famine, one-third of the population was receiving food in relief. Many of the local lairds impoverished themselves in meeting the first impact of the famine. MacLeod of MacLeod bankrupted himself in his efforts to provide for his people and relief funds were organized in the south. The Highland potato famine did not produce the lasting effects of that of Ireland and it seems to be little remembered, but a memento of that grim time is many long stretches of road in Mull, Skye and in Wester Ross constructed by the local lairds with Government loans to provide work for the hungry people.

At last, in the 1880s, as the result of strong public sympathy for the poverty-stricken crofters and with their struggles to resist evictions and to extend their inadequate holdings, the famous First Crofters Commission was appointed and reported in 1884. This report stated that the sufferings of the people were mainly due to the smallness of their holdings, the insecurity of their tenure with no compensation for improvements, to high rents and defective transport. As a result the Crofters' Holdings (Scotland) Act was passed in 1886 which 'marked a turning point in the history of the crofting districts'.[1] It was years in advance of other similar social legislation. It recognized the crofters' organization in townships, gave them security of tenure, enabled them to apply to a statutory body[2] for the fixing of fair rents, and when they gave up their tenancy enabled them to claim compensation for improvements that they had made. These rights have tended to make the structure of the crofting townships rigid,[3] but a series of Commissions and of Acts have tried to make provision for making more land available for small holdings and to provide machinery for improving the lay-out of the crofts. State

[1]*Report of the Commission of Enquiry into Crofting Conditions, 1954*, p. 10 (Cmd. 9091).
[2]To the Crofters Commission, later to the Land Court.
[3]*Report of the Commission of Enquiry into Crofting Conditions, 1954*, p. 13.

help in improving stock and in free advice has also been given and it is not surprising that the whole look of the settlements and the agricultural interests and domestic economy of the people has changed.

The most important of such measures were the 1892 Commission to try to find scope for further settlements, the Congested Districts Board (Scotland·) Act of 1897 which set up the Congested Districts Board to try to carry out this intention. The 1911 Small Holders (Scotland) Act which extended the 1886 legislation to the whole of Scotland and substituted the Scottish Board of Agriculture for the Congested Districts Board. An important effect was that it removed the obligation of residence and has produced a class of absentee crofters. The Land Settlement (Scotland) Act of 1919 and finally the Commission of Enquiry into Crofting Legislation of 1954, following which a further Crofter Commission was set up. The crofters have also received a large proportion of a number of public grants such as the Hill Cattle, the Hill Sheep and the Calf Subsidies. In 1952 for the counties of Argyll, Inverness, Ross and Cromarty and Sutherland these grants totalled £449,258. The crofters also received a proportion of other grants totalling £293,541.[1]

It may be worth while to quote a few figures to show the results of all this effort. In 1885 there were 28,825 crofts and the 1884 Report estimated that 40,000 families of 200,000 people lived on them. In 1886, in the twenty-six mainly crofting parishes there were 70,232 acres under tillage, 95,041 head of cattle and 947,955 sheep. By 1952 the crofts had increased to 29,858.[2] Meanwhile the tillage had shrunk to 38,000 acres, the cattle had decreased to 58,000 (in spite of the fact that the cattle-stocks in the Highlands had risen by 17 per cent between 1870 and 1950) and the sheep, the least exacting stock to keep but also the least beneficial to the land, had increased to 1,090,000. The population of these parishes in 1851 had been 395,540 and by 1951 it had decreased to 285,164. The decrease moreover in those actually engaged in crofting was more marked. In Lewis it was estimated

[1]*Report of the Commission of Enquiry into Crofting Conditions, 1954*, pp. 15, 24, 25, 26. As agriculturists crofters do not have to pay county rates.

[2]There had been a slight increase in the proportion of larger ones but there were cases where a crofter occupied more than one holding and some where he was virtually an absentee.

at 16 per cent in five typical crofting parishes and on the mainland at 20 per cent.[1] Meanwhile the fundamental character of the crofts—that they do not as a rule furnish a complete and adequate maintenance for the crofters—has materially changed. According to a classification by the Scottish Board of Agriculture there are 6,009 whole-time crofts and 20,909 part-time ones.[2]

It is the considered opinion of the latest Commission of Enquiry into Crofting Conditions (that of 1954) that crofting 'as now organized, is fighting a losing battle against the social and economic powers of the day', although, as the Report states and as is evident to anyone visiting different districts, some crofting areas are doing much better than others. The newly formed small holdings (not a township) in the fertile Black Isle (Easter Ross) are flourishing and in Lewis, in spite of a poor soil, there is a crowded, lively, vivid community. Skye and Tiree are keeping up their cattle stocks.[3] On South Uist and Benbecula there are good crofts.[4] On the other hand the decline in vitality is all too marked among many of the crofts on the north-western mainland.

The grinding penury of the crofters, so evident at the time of the *1884 Report*, is mercifully a thing of the past. Even fifty years ago one saw many ragged children, very primitive housing, and other signs of poverty. That has entirely disappeared. The surplus population of squatters, so pitifully clinging to the land, has disappeared and, except in a few places, there is no longer an unsatisfied hunger for land.[5] Although local fishing has declined, there are new sources of subsidiary employment, such as construction work by the Local Authorities and the Hydro-Electric Board, the new sea-weed industry and the tourist industry. The old stand-by of service in H.M. Forces, notably the R.N.V.R. and the Merchant Navy is still important, and from all over the world help comes from members of the family who have gone overseas—for many years the most valuable export from the Hebrides has been *men*.

[1]*Commission of Enquiry into Crofting Conditions, 1954*, pp. 13, 15, 19.
[2]Ibid., pp. 16, 17.
[3]*Report of Commission of Enquiry into Crofting Conditions, 1954*, pp. 8, 9, 19. App. 8.
[4]*Scottish Mothers and Children*, ed. W. Leslie Mackenzie (published by Carnegie Trust), p. 426.
[5]*Report of Commission of Enquiry into Crofting Conditions, 1954*, p. 8.

There is, however, one feature, and perhaps the most ominous of all, that one cannot help noticing if one travels much in the crofting areas, and that is the preponderance of elderly people and the low proportion of children, especially in some of the mainland districts of Wester Ross.[1] Figures bear out this impression. In 1861 the percentage of people over 45 was 19.61 for the whole of Scotland but nearly 24 per cent in the Highlands. By 1931 the percentages were 27.72 and 33.56, and the preponderance of the aged is more marked in the crofting communities. In 1931 in five crofting parishes there were 1,104 male crofters of whom 425 were aged between 55–70 and 251 over 70.

The crofting areas are of special interest because of the greater continuity of folk-life there, but this is only relative, for besides their special vicissitudes, these areas, with the rest of the Highlands, have undergone great changes that have left their marks upon the land and the people. Apart from the military roads begun by General Wade in 1725, the Highlands were almost destitute of roads before the nineteenth century.[2] Since then roads and the mainland railways have transformed the accessibility of many districts. Looking down from the hills one can watch the distant trains and the ribbons of road with their glittering strings of motors, lorries and buses winding along the straths or climbing over passes. In many places roads have been more than once remade to increase the ease of transport, but toilfully climbing or gingerly descending the old road over Glencoe with its hairpin bends certainly gave one a thrill that is lost to the speed merchants on the modern road![3] On the western seas steamer traffic has greatly facilitated communication between the islands and now we have the aeroplane.

With improved transport has come the Sassenach for sport or for enjoyment, and his coming has had considerable economic and social effects. Grouse shooting had begun to become fashionable in the 1820s. By 1850 the letting of grouse moors had become 'a common practice'. Rents for shooting then averaged about £50

[1] *Report of the Commission of Enquiry into Crofting Conditions, 1954*, p. 19, terms the proportion of old people and children as 'abnormal'.
[2] See also Chapter XIII.
[3] Where the high road passes from Strathspey to Strathdearn at Slochd-Muich one can trace four successive roads.

to £750.[1] These shooting rents went on rising in value and, after the decline in agriculture, and especially in sheep-farming, that set in with the 1880s, the letting of sporting rights became the main source of income on Highland properties. The demand for deer forests had begun to arise in the 1870s and there was a considerable change-over from sheep-walks to moors and forests.[2] The large shooting lodges with the keepers' cottages with their ranges of kennels that one sees all over the Highlands and Islands are the visible signs of the coming of a good deal of well-paid seasonable employment not only to the country people as gillies and beaters but to the local shops, besides regular and extremely congenial employment to a number of stalkers and keepers. The influx of the shooting tenants and their staffs introduced a note of gaiety into many a strath. Since the last war there has been far less demand for expensive shootings and the industry might be described as 'depressed'. Salmon and trout fishing, carried on from hotels frequented by anglers, is more flourishing. It also gives a good deal of local work.

The roads, railways and steamers have also brought an increase in the tourist traffic. This has been responsible for the rise of many Highland villages. A striking example is Oban, which only had one house before 1770 and was 'a small village' in 1800[3] and is now known as 'the Charing Cross of the north'. Nowadays holiday-makers, especially hikers, are going farther and farther afield and are bringing in revenue to a wider range of hosts. They can be a material source of income to crofters who reap a considerable benefit from the fact that as they are on agricultural holdings their houses are free from rates.

The importance of the roads is shown by the changes in the lay-out of a great many crofter townships.[4] Instead of being built in clusters, the houses are now dotted along the roads. It is better to devote a special chapter to the great alterations in the construction of the houses themselves although one may note that the tourist industry and the taking in of boarders has had

---

[1]Estimate by Snowie, the Inverness gun-maker, who did most of the letting. See Anderson's *Guide to the Highlands and Islands of Scotland* (1850 ed.), p. 18.
[2]*Report on Deer Forests, 1922*, p. 5. D. Campbell, *Octogenarian Highlander*, p. 544.
[3]T. Garnett, *Tour*, Vol. I, p. 140.
[4]The change in an individual township is well described in the articles, 'Tolsta bho Thuath', *Stornoway Gazette*, 13.7.51.

some influence on this. It is a charming sight to look across a sea-loch and to see the long line of four-square little houses, each surrounded by its patchwork of fields, and strung along the opposite coast where the road runs. As dusk falls, it is even pleasanter to see the lights in numbers of small windows gleaming between the darkly looming outline of the hill and the reaches of the untamed sea. (See Fig. 2.)

The changes brought about by easier means of transport are, moreover, deeply pervasive through many aspects of the people's own lives. Although from ancient times the sparsity of the resources of Highland farmers has prevented them from being entirely self-supporting,[1] the shift from at least partial subsistence production to production entirely for sale is very marked. Anyone with an eye for agriculture will notice that the crops (except potatoes) are all grown for feeding the livestock for sale and unfortunately, under modern market requirements, a good deal of material, fertilizers and concentrated feeding stuffs have to be purchased. From the people's appearance it is obvious that their clothes are almost entirely boughten and, should one enjoy their hospitality, one can see that the same is true of the furniture and plenishings of their houses. Even in the remotest districts one may notice shop catalogues lying about. The importance of their own dairy products in the people's dietary has declined, in some cases almost to vanishing point. Cheese is almost invariably bought, butter (or margarine) to a large extent. Even milk is increasingly supplied by the dairies. White wheaten bread, often made in Glasgow factories, penetrates to the Outer Islands. The use of many of these commodities represents world-wide links in transportation. The reduction in the price of wheat flour when overseas were able to undersell British production led to near tragedy in the south, but the north of Scotland, as an oatmeal-producing district, stood to gain. Tea has long been a constant drink.[2] This change from partial home production to dependence on more distant markets has left its traces in the ruins of the little, water-driven meal and wool mills that sprang up all over the

[1]M. Gray, *Highland Economy*, p. 10.
[2]In remoter districts, especially in Lewis, the influence of the First World War when so many men went overseas, has also been very marked. For more details of the people's food see Chapter XIV.

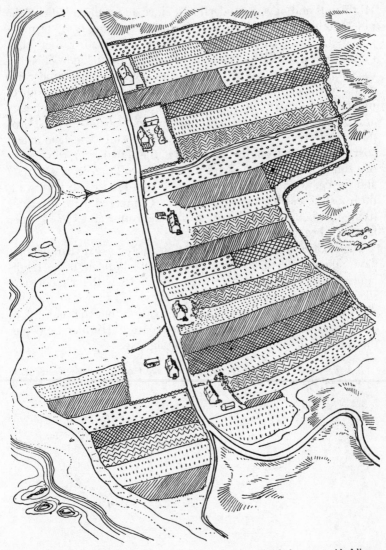

FIG. 2. Modern crofter settlement strung along road and with demarcated holdings.

Highlands and have been declining since about the middle of the nineteenth century. As ways of life and methods of farming changed, the transport difficulty has increased rather than diminished in the Highland and especially the Islands. The old exports of unfinished cattle on the hoof was a simple and comparatively cheap undertaking. To meet modern market requirements for younger and more finished animals the cost is heavy and becomes progressively so the more out-of-the-way the producer may live. To quote actual figures, besides the labour and cost of transport from the pier-head to the actual croft, the freight of a ton of fertilizer or hay from Glasgow to Portree is £5 0s 9d and the cost of a float to carry beasts from Portree to Dingwall, the most accessible market, is £18. Compared with a farmer living on the spot it will cost an Island crofter an extra £3 per head per beast to get it to a market.[1]

Such is a summary of the indications of the great changes that have taken place that even a casual rambler through the Highlands and Islands may notice. Here and there, with luck, one may see some ancient agricultural implement still in use or the survival of some obsolete method of cultivation, but the real link of continuity, the distinctive character of the Highland people, though it is fundamental, is more intangible.

[1] *Report of the Commission of Enquiry into Crofting Conditions, 1954*, quotes these and many other actual figures and stresses the heaviness of this burden, pp. 29, 70.

# IV

## THE BEASTS THAT SET THE
## PATTERN OF HUMAN LIFE

### CATTLE

THE nature of the physical conditions of the Highlands of
Scotland make them, and have always made them, more suitable for the raising of livestock than for the cultivation of crops,
or perhaps one should say, bearing in mind the natural unpro-
ductiveness of the land during the long winters and late springs,
the Highlands are less unsuitable for the raising of animals than
for the growing of grain. The Highlanders have mainly depended
on their livestock ever since our remote predecessors first became
herdsmen rather than hunters!

As we have seen, the change from a predominantly cattle-
raising economy to one of sheep-farming is responsible for great
social changes. Even although, for a hundred and fifty years, the
emphasis has been so largely upon sheep-farming, yet the raising
of cattle continued to be, and still is, very important in Highland
economy. In earlier times the keeping of stocks of cattle was even
more vital. Dairy products were the main source of food for a
considerable part of the year and the beasts were almost the only
way in which the Highlanders could earn money to supplement
the inadequate produce of their poor little holdings and for other
needs. Not only were they the most suitable product that could
be raised in 'Caledonia stern and wild' but, in the roadless days
of the past, they were an export that could transport itself to
market even from the remotest districts. They were the main
source of wealth. For instance, in 1609—when the Privy Council
were able to force some of the more powerful west coast chiefs

to sign a code of regulations for the Western Highlands, an important provision was that men of a certain position were required to send their eldest son to be educated in the 'in country' and to learn to speak and write English—the standard of wealth was the possession of sixty cows.

The influence of animal keeping is shown upon very ancient things. For instance, the main Highland festivals in the old days were *Beltane* and *Samhain* (the first day of May and the first of November), the dates when the livestock went out to pasturage on the higher ground and returned to be housed or fed on the herbage near the human settlements. Sir James Frazer[1] points out that this division of the year was also observed in the pastoral regions of Central Europe. Samhain festivals were held in the late eighteenth century by the herdsmen on the hills all over the Highlands. The custom similar to eighteenth century accounts lingered on till within living memory in the Long Island. Every fire in the country was extinguished and a bonfire was lit on the top of a hill and the cattle were driven round it to safeguard them from harm during the coming year. Then everyone carried home fire from the bonfire with which to rekindle their hearth.[2] A great feature was the making of a Beltane Bannock, a flat oatmeal cake covered with custard. Pennant describes how a herding lad threw pieces of the bannock over his shoulder as offerings to the foxes and eagles and all the enemies of the herds. The bannocks were also used for divination. Each member of the party rolled a cake marked with a cross down the hill: if it broke or did not roll far, or if the marked side came uppermost, misfortune was foretold. Accounts of similar festivals survive for the Hebrides and Badenoch. The making of the Beltane Bannock has lingered on after the rest of the festival. Father Allan MacDonald, priest of Eriskay, said he remembered his mother baking one, and the slope of the hill between Slochd and Findhorn Bridge was pointed out to me as the place where the local people rolled the Samhain bannocks.[3]

[1]Sir J. Frazer, *The Golden Bough* (Abridged Edition), pp. 617, 634.

[2]Father Allan MacDonald, *Gaelic Words from South Uist and Eriskay*, Ed. J. L. Campbell, p. 240 (henceforth noted as Father A. MacDonald, *Gaelic Words*).

[3]Sir J. Frazer, *The Golden Bough*, pp. 617, 620. T. Pennant, *Tour*, p. 110. Lachlan Shaw, *History of the Province of Moray*, Vol. II, p. 145. For later day Halloween celebrations see Chapter XVI.

One of the most important of ancient rites, with an element of magic in it, was the making of 'need fire' to stop a plague on the cattle. All the fires in the district were extinguished and a fresh fire was kindled by the friction of dry wood and from it every hearth was rekindled.[1] The pernicious habits of the Little Folk in shooting cattle with elf-bolts (prehistoric stone arrow heads) and of witches in drawing off the substance of the milk of the cows, figure in endless Highland yarns and various devices, such as the placing of rowan twigs at the doors of the byres, were used to counter them. The water bull, a creature far less sinister than the water horse, was to be found in many Highland lochs and the MacLeods of Gesto had a herd of white fairy cattle. Sometimes Brownies and especially *Gruagachs* were the devoted tutelary spirits who looked after the cattle, and it was usual for the milkmaids to pour an offering of milk into a hallowed stone to recompense them. Carmichael has preserved a Prayer of the Cattlefold.[2]

The Highlanders inherited, with the rest of the traditions of the Gael of Erin, a great treasury of heroic tales in which cattle raiding figured as part of the essential life of the people, the greatest of them all the *Tain bo Chuailagne*—the Cattle Raid of Cooley—tells of a war between Ulster and Connaught over the possession of two bulls and of the heroic deeds of Cuchullin in defence of Ulster.

During the period of the clans, the raiding of cattle was a constant and congenial occupation and had a considerable prestige value. There can hardly be a clan that has not its traditions or sober histories of the 'lifting' of cattle. Besides large-scale forays when a clan feud flared up as, for instance, in 1545 when the Laird of Grant claimed compensation on behalf of his tenants for the loss of over 2,000 cattle, besides horses and goats raided from Glen Urquhart by Clanranald, Glengarry and other Mac-Donalds,[3] the young men, especially the heir of a chief, would prove their manhood by taking a 'spreidh' of cattle from a neighbouring clan or from the Lowlands. Cattle lifting was the main source of livelihood of the Caterans and 'the broken men' (un-

[1] Well summarized in Sir J. Frazer, *The Golden Bough*, pp. 617, 634, 641.
[2] A. Carmichael, *Carmina Gadelica*, Vol. II, p. 131.
[3] See William MacKay, *Urquhart and Glenmoriston*, p. 97 and App. B.

fortunates who had lost their clan and land). It was also an economic necessity to some of the poorer clans as, for instance, the Macfarlanes, the MacDonalds of Glencoe and the poorer members of Clan Cameron. A letter survives from Cameron of Lochiel to the Laird of Grant in 1645 promising compensation for the action of some of his clansmen who had driven some cattle belonging to a Grant thinking that he was a 'Moray man', 'where all men taken their prey'.[1] Members of more settled clans were able to earn a subsidy from the Lowland farmers in return for keeping 'watches' in the glens through which the raiders passed. Strathdearn was such a passage-way and, in my youth, stories of the exploits of John Beg MacAndrew, a member of the watch, were still told and the site of his home at Dalnahaitnich, on the Dulnan, was pointed out. The young people nowadays do not know such stories. The levying of blackmail comes into the well-known story of Rob Roy Macgregor. In the years after the '45 there was a serious increase in cattle reiving.

Besides lifting his neighbour's cattle the ancient Highlander sent large numbers of his beasts to market. On a map made by Matthew Paris (ob. 1259) two entries are noted on the Highlands stating that the country was marshy and impassable and fit for cattle and inhabited by a people 'rude and pastoral'.[2] Scotland herself was miserably poor and from the fourteenth century, the earliest period for which we have such records, her main exports were hides and skins and wool.[3] The wool in these early times came almost entirely from the Borders but many of the hides and skins were of Highland origin. In 1503 the royal rents for the district of Trotternish in Skye were paid by cattle sent to Inverness; the ransom of MacKenzie of Kintail, who was captured at the Battle of Pinkie (1547) was paid with cows which were collected throughout his dominions for the purpose and two Acts of the Privy Council ordered that the Highlanders should not be molested when bringing their cattle to the Lowland markets. Nevertheless, from time to time, there were bitter complaints

[1]Sir William Fraser, *Chiefs of Grant*, Vol. II, p. 76. When members of one clan drove a spreidh through lands belonging to another chief the 'Raiders collop', a share of the booty was given. A dispute over the adequacy of the share led to a fierce battle between the Munros and Mackintoshes at Clachnaharry near Inverness.

[2]Reprinted as frontispiece in P. Hume Brown, *Early Travellers in Scotland*.

[3]I. F. Grant, *Social and Economic Development*, pp. 187, 311.

by the Highlanders of interception on their way to the markets.[1]

Before 1603 most of the animals that were sent to the Lowlands were no doubt eaten there, for hides were the most important of contemporary exports but, with the Union of the Crowns of Scotland and England, the cattle droving industry, which had previously been discouraged, came into its own and the beasts were sent on the hoof from the remotest Highlands to England and the whole social life of the North came to depend upon this industry. The numbers of cattle that were raised under the old, hard conditions was extraordinary. The autumn 'trysts' at Crieff (on the borders of the hill country of Perthshire) became important at the end of the seventeenth century and by 1723, no less than 20,000 cattle are said to have been sold there annually.[2] In that year a traveller visited one of these fairs. He said that 30,000 guineas were spent by the English drovers. He wrote more fully of the people at the fair than of the cattle: 'The Highland Gentlemen were mighty civil, dress'd in their slashed short Waistcoats, a Trousing (which is Breeches and Stockings of one piece of striped stuff) with a Plaid for a Cloak and a blue Bonnet. They had a Ponyard, Knife and Fork in one Sheath, hanging at one side of their Belt, their Pistol at the other, and their Snuff Mill (mull) before, with a great broad Sword by their side. Their Attendants were very numerous, all in belted Plaids, girt like a Woman's Petticoats down to the Knees, their Thighs and half of the Leg all bare.' They had also 'each their broad Sword and Ponyard, and spoke the Irish, an unintelligible Language to the English.'[3]

The principal trysts were shifted from Crieff to Falkirk later in the century to meet the convenience of the increasing number of English drovers who came north to attend them. By 1777 it was estimated that 30,000 head of cattle were sold at the three yearly sales held there in August, September and October, and the numbers went on increasing until 1850 when 150,000 cattle were sold.[4] After this the droving industry quickly declined. In

[1] I. F. Grant, *Social and Economic Development*, pp. 542–6.
[2] A. R. B. Haldane, *The Drove Roads of Scotland*, p. 135 (henceforth noted as *The Drove Roads*).
[3] John MacKay, *Journey through the Highlands*, pp. 194–6.
[4] A. R. B. Haldane, *The Drove Roads*, pp. 56, 135, 142.

the heyday of the trade the cattle were gathered into droves and sent to these trysts from the remotest parts of the Highlands and from the Hebrides. They were ferried across the Minch in small, open boats; they swam from Skye to the mainland at Kyle Rhea, they forded rivers in the bridgeless days and made their leisurely way by hill and glen, along the old drove tracks in great herds of perhaps as many as 1,000 beasts. The business started in the early summer when the tacksmen gathered in their own beasts and bought stock from the lesser tenants and either sold them at some local fair—there were well known ones at Broadford in Skye, at Muir of Ord at the head of the Beauly Firth and at Pitmain in the Upper Valley of the Spey—or else engaged men to drive them the whole way. The financial structure of Highland society became based on the sales of cattle during the eighteenth century. We have contemporary records which show how dependent on the trade were the lairds and tacksmen. Nearly all financial transactions were carried through after October by means of dealers' bills given at the trysts.[1] For instance, the accounts of MacLeod of MacLeod show that this income mainly depended on the trade in the first half of the eighteenth century.[2] When the trade was temporarily interrupted as, for instance by the disturbed state of the country and the very severe winters of 1745–6, or the disastrous cattle plague of 1781, the lairds and tacksmen were very severely hit and of course the lesser people must have suffered with them.[3] As the last of the old drovers die out the memories of the cattle droving days are being lost. These men slept among their cattle on the journey south and sometimes accompanied the beasts, after the English dealers had bought them, down to the pasturages of south-eastern England for the final stages of fattening. I have been told that the drovers in olden days often wore fine silver buttons so that, if they fell ill or died in the south, their expenses could be paid. And a few older people have pointed out to me the old tracks over the hills that the cattle

---

[1] For general account see A. R. B. Haldane, *The Drove Roads*, p. 204. For details of actual transactions see *Letter Book of Bailie John Steuart* (Scottish History Society), pp. 42, 200, 334, 337.

[2] I. F. Grant, *The MacLeods*, p. 487.

[3] I. F. Grant, *The MacLeods*, pp. 478, 497. Canon R. MacLeod, *Book of Dunvegan*, Vol. II, pp. 10, 498. 'A Letter from MacLeod of Talisker,' National Library of Scotland, Delvine Papers. *Manuscript Collections*, Book II, Fo. 117.

followed, the places where they rested and the site of the black-smith's forge in Glen Tromie that was one of those where the beasts were shod before they came to harder ground.

The keeping of numbers of cattle was absolutely essential to the ancient Highlanders to supply the dairy products upon which they largely subsisted, to buy meal in order to supplement their inadequate home-grown supplies, to pay their rent and to buy necessaries that they were unable to supply themselves with, such as iron and fishing hooks. For instance, Thomas Moser wrote in 1715 that the Highlanders had not enough grain and yearly came down with their cattle, of which they had great plenty, to traffic for oats and barley for their needs.[1] Grain was regularly brought by sea to the Western Highlands from the Eastern Lowlands and from England.[2] In the sixteenth century rent had largely been paid in cattle and in dairy products. For instance, fifty-eight score of cattle beside dairy produce, were given in rent in Harris and $339\frac{1}{2}$ stones of butter and cheese from Skye. It was only gradually that these rents in kind were commuted.[3] The inadequacy of High-land holdings to supply enough grain for the needs of the people who worked them varied, of course, with the pressure of the population upon the land available and the suitability of the local soil. The stocks of cattle and the amount of the arable were, as a rule, correlated: for instance, in districts where even before the re-allocations of land of the late eighteenth century, the average holdings were very small, perhaps with 2 acres of arable, as Kinlochmoidart and Barrisdale, the cattle stocks were twice as large as on the holdings of Strathspey which averaged about 13 acres of arable, or parts of Argyllshire and Perthshire with about 10 acres of arable.[4] In many parts of the Highlands cattle had to

[1] *A short account of Scotland*, p. 5.

[2] Donald MacLeod, who acted as Prince Charles Edward's guide and crossed with him to the Long Island in his wanderings had acquired his knowledge of the west coast in carrying on this trade. For actual figures of imports see M. Gray, *Highland Economy*, pp. 43, 44.

[3] Dean Munro's contemporary 'Report on the Islands' gives details for all the islands during the sixteenth century, printed in W. F Skene, *Celtic Scotland*, Vol. III, p. 429. For examples of changes in the eighteenth century see I. F. Grant, *The MacLeods*, pp. 352, 487. Canon R. MacLeod, *Book of Dunvegan*, Vol. I, pp. 155, 271. See also G. Gregory Smith, *Book of Islay*, App. III for a long sequence of Rentals.

[4] Malcolm Gray, *The Highland Economy*, pp. 7, 24 gives exact details.

be sold regularly to buy meal.[1] Even in other districts, during the frequent bad harvests, meal had to be imported, as for instance in the very fertile island of Islay[2], and the careful accounts show that an old forbear of my own, who farmed a considerable amount of good land in Lower Badenoch had to buy corn in bad years and that when he had a surplus it was mainly sold locally.[3]

These supplies of meal were always only a small part of the people's dietary and they lived very much upon the milk, butter and cheese of their cattle. In Assynt we are told that the people in the higher districts, in a good year, had enough grain to last them for six or seven months and in the more favourable parts for ten months.[4] So much did the people depend upon their cattle that when the harvest failed, if the spring were not unfavourable to the cattle the Lowlands were sometimes said to be worse off than the Highlands.[5] Supplies of dairy cattle must have been very large. For instance, in a seventeenth century raid on Glenelg, a tenant complained that 20 stone of butter and cheese had been stolen from him.[6] A less attractive food derived from the people's cattle was made from their blood. The beasts were bled, some authorities say, 'several times a year' but others imply that drawing the cattle's blood was resorted to in time of scarcity. The blood was boiled and 'eaten like bread'.[7] Black puddings, a sort of sausage made with blood (not of course drawn from living cattle) are still much eaten in Scotland.

All important as cattle were, the keeping of sufficient stocks

[1]See for instance *Old Statistical Accounts for Stornoway*, Vol. XIII, p. 330; *Kilfinichen*, Vol. XIV, p. 176; *Lairg*, Vol II p. 571; T. Pennant, *Tour*, Vol. II, pp. 363, 365–6.

[2]T. Pennant, *Tour*, Vol. II, p. 262.

[3]I. F. Grant, *Everyday Life on an Old Highland Farm*, p. 36 (henceforth noted as *Highland Farm*). Other examples are noted in *Old Statistical Account for South Uist*, Vol. XIII, p. 308; *Edderachilis*, Vol. VI, p. 278. See also T. Pennant, *Tour*, Vol. II, p. 251, for 'Skye', and T. Garnett, *Tour*, Vol. I, p. 116 for 'Lochtayside'. The *Old Statistical Account for South Uist* gives details of the yearly sale of a beast by the tenant of 'a half penny land' and of how largely the price went to supply meal in all but good years. Vol. XIII, p. 309.

[4]*Old Statistical Account*, Vol. XVI p. 192.

[5]*Wardlaw Manuscript*, pp. 236, 244. T. Pennant, *Tour*, Vol. II, pp. 311–2, for account of Canna.

[6]Canon R. MacLeod, *Book of Dunvegan*, Vol. I, p. 119.

[7]*Old Statistical Account*, Fortingall, Vol. II, p. 459. E. Burt, *Letters*, Vol. II, p. 131.

under the unkindly physical conditions of the Highlands has always been a matter of difficulty. The Highlands do not grow natural hay and good pasturage is not to be found everywhere, that of the nearer hill slopes in Badenoch and some other districts was poor and all over the country the natural grass dies completely away in the winter—the machairs on the western coasts of the Long Island are exceptional. In the summer, where the crops were growing on the unfenced strips of cultivation, the beasts had to be watched day and night to keep them out of the corn.[1] The night watching of the cattle figures in many tales of meetings with ghosts, fairies and other unchancy beings. For instance, a Lewis story tells how the mother of Coinneach Odhar (Dun Kenneth), a famous seer of the seventeenth century, obtained the stone in which he saw the future from the ghost of a Norse princess when she was herding cattle at midnight. One version of how the Dunvegan Cup came into the possession of the MacLeods describes how a lad herding cattle at night saw a fairy mound open and he went in and stole the cup.

In the crofter townships of the nineteenth century, the constable, the official elected by the people, was responsible for overseeing the common grazings and cattle folds and assessed damage to crops through careless watching.[2] A series of cattle folds were arranged so that in spring and early summer the cattle could be sent farther and farther up the moors.[3] There is no information about how the communal grazings were organized in earlier times, but then, as now, the joint cultivators were soumed, i.e. the number of animals they were allowed to keep on the common grazings was fixed according to the size of their holding in the joint farm. An employee of the tacksman or laird, known as the grass or grazing bailiff, is occasionally mentioned.

In the summer, continuing the ancient practice of transhumance, a considerable proportion of the community migrated, with most of their beasts, to the shielings in the sheltered glens among the hills. There the cattle fed on the sweet hill grass

---

[1]Even in the Eastern Highlands I have met old people who remember how, as children, they spent long days herding the cattle. Where the agriculture was more primitive the burden of herding was very heavy. For a late example see 'Tolsta bho Thuath', *Stornoway Gazette*, 20.7.51.

[2]Evidence by A. Carmichael, before *Crofters Commission, 1884*, pp. 453–4.

[3]'Tolsta bho Thuath', *Stornoway Gazette*, 13. 7. 58.

herded by the lads and the women and girls made the milk into the butter and cheese upon which the community would subsist. The saleable beasts were brought into condition on the plentiful hill grass for disposal in the autumn.[1]

In the Eastern and Central Highlands the practice died out when, under an improved system of agriculture, it became more profitable to keep the animals at home; in my young days the tradition of it still survived. In parts of the Long Island the practice lasted till within living memory.[2] One can trace the sites of some of the mainland shielings (*Airidh, Airidhean*) by the green patches caused by the enrichment of the ground where the cattle had gathered, although the simple huts of sods or branches have long since crumbled away. They are said generally to have been built in pairs. One contained the bed of heather on which the dairy maids slept together and a hearth, the other the dairying utensils and the butter and the cheeses.[3] On the Long Island the drystone shieling huts are, many of them, still in a fair state of preservation—some of them examples of the ancient bee-hive method of construction. One can see the niches in the walls where the dairying vessels were kept.[4]

Life at the shielings was a happy one for the beasts as well as for the people. But they came home to increasing times of starvation. As the herbage died down during the long Highland winters and springs, the cattle were forced to subsist on the stubbles. So reduced were the animals that they would not have been worth eating if killed during the winter and therefore the animals required for the winter food of the lairds and tacksmen were always killed and salted in the autumn. Marshall described how the land was 'gnawed to the quick' and even in normal years the mortality

[1]The Saeter of the Norwegians and the Swiss on their Alps are of course well known examples of similar customs by pastoral peoples in hilly country. The summer migration of the Highlanders was probably the uninterrupted survival of an age-old and widely diffused pastoral habit.

[2]For detailed account see 'Tolsta bho Thuath', *Stornoway Gazette*, 24.8.51.

[3]In T. Pennant's *Tour*, Vol. I, Plate XV, there is an illustration of conical shieling huts in Islay and Bishop Forbes, writing in 1762 has a good description of a group of shielings 'almost by the High-way side to the right' of the main road north of Dalwhinnie, R. Forbes, *Journals of Episcopal Visitations*, p. 142.

[4]A. Mitchell in *Past and in the Present*, p. 58, gives details of the bee-hive shielings. For a minute description of life at the shielings see 'Tolsta bho Thuath', *Stornoway Gazette*, 24.7.51. See also chapter VI for the life of the people.

was high—Sinclair put it at one in five of the outdoor stock.[1] The milch cows were housed during the winter but had no food beyond straw and the scanty gatherings of the inferior natural hay of the Highlands. How wretched was the feeding is shown by the fact that only 1s 6d was allowed for the wintering of a young beast and 2s for a heifer in calf at a time when hay cost 5d a stone, which would only allow 5 stone for the winter. Nowadays housed cattle get turnips and oil-cake; if they only got hay they would need about 281 lb a day and it would be poor feeding.[2] In the spring the cattle were so weakened by hunger that the people had to combine together to lift them from the byre to the pasture.[3]

The winter scarcity of food limited the number of cattle that could be pastured on the hills in the summer, and it retarded the growth of the cattle so that they were only fit to send south to the markets when they were four years old, and therefore large stocks had to be maintained until the beasts reached maturity. So underfed were the cows that they only calved every second year and only gave one Scots pint of milk a day,[4] and the period of lactation was comparatively short.[5]

There seems to have been an old-standing variation in the methods of housing cattle between the east and the west. In the Eastern and Central Highlands, already in the eighteenth century, they were kept in separate buildings although, to judge from Burt's account of the hut in which his horses were stabled, these were extremely primitive. In the west there has been a persistent custom of housing the cattle at one end of the dwelling house, which was generally built on a slope with the end in which the cattle were at the lower end. This custom has, of course, entirely gone out, but one of the last people whom I met who

[1]W. Marshall, *Agriculture in Central Highlands*, pp. 37, 38. Sir John Sinclair, *Northern Counties*, p. 114.

[2]I. F. Grant, *Old Highland Farm*, p. 61.

[3]W. Marshall, *Agriculture in Central Highlands*, p. 61. J. Walker, *Economical History of the Hebrides and Highlands of Scotland*, Vol. II, pp. 56, 60 (henceforth noted as *Economical History of Hebrides*). E. Burt, *Letters*, Vol. II, p. 132.

[4]A Scots pint, however, was equal to two English pints See E. Burt, *Letters*, Vol. II, p. 163.

[5]J. Walker, *Economical History of the Hebrides*, Vol. II, pp. 59–60. Actual farming accounts kept by Old Balnespick and by Colonel Sutherland of Evelix fully bear out these figures. I. F. Grant, *Old Highland Farm*, p. 61.

housed his beasts at the end of his house and whose cattle were particularly fine told me that he attributed this to the fact that the light and heat from the human end of the house made the beasts feed for a longer period. In a few byres the old way of fastening the heads of the beasts between vertical wooden bars that slipped between rails can still be found. It was a method that saved the use of iron. The care of the milch cattle, including milking and dairy work, was in charge of the women. Even now, on small farms and crofts, the woman of the house does the milking and the cows are her special charge.[1]

In the East and Central Highlands the keeping of cattle had its influence on the great agricultural changes that transformed the lay-out of the holdings. The two most outstanding innovations then introduced were the growing of turnips as a field crop and the sowing of hay. These changes led to agrarian developments especially the enclosing of the fields and the introduction of a regular rotation of crops, but they are animal feeding crops and mixed farming with an increasing emphasis on cattle raising is characteristic of the normal Highland farm. With better home feeding the need for the yearly migration to the shielings was no longer necessary and, to the great enrichment of the farm, the animals are pastured in the fields all summer and housed at night in the winter. The crop of oats is mainly used for feeding them.

On the west, the loss of the hill-pastures brought severe suffering to the people,[2] and the stocks of the all-important cattle had to be drastically reduced.[3] With the improvements in the cultivation of the crofts the keeping of cattle has approximated to that of other districts in the Highlands.[4] But although, encouraged by financial aid from the Government, the stocks of cattle in the Highlands have been increasing during the last few years, there has been a decline in many of the crofting areas. To meet modern requirements the raising of cattle needs a good deal of arable farming. The less progressive of the crofter communities now tend to concentrate more on the more pastoral raising of

[1]See Chapter IX.
[2]As the Crofters Commission of 1884 brought out, see, pp. 141, 330, 467, 489.
[3]See summaries of holdings and stocks in Appendix B, *Crofters Commission, 1884,* p. 522 onwards.
[4]All the cattle in the crofting counties are now within the Scottish Attested Area, *Industry and Employment in Scotland, 1957,* p. 13.

sheep.[1] An example of survival of old ideas and aptitudes involving a change in the animals kept.

Nowadays with winter feeding and a ration of oil-cake a very ordinary cow would be expected to calve every year and to give at least 2 gallons of milk a day, and a bullock, almost finished on the farm, should be ready for the butcher by the end of the second winter. First the steamships and railways and now motor lorries have simplified the problem of transport and the beasts are sent direct to the auction marts, especially at Oban, Inverness, Dingwall and Perth.

The main emphasis on mixed holdings, with the exception of the long established dairying districts of Kintyre and Coll, has always been the production of beef cattle for sale, but during the last few years there has been a steady reduction in the numbers of milch cows kept on the farm for the use of the people and for sale of milk to near neighbours. This reduction is very marked upon the smallest holdings.[2] Improved transport has encouraged the buying of milk from specialized dairy farms. From low-lying districts, Inverness, Beauly, Dingwall, etc. motor vans take bottled milk into the surrounding hill-country. Stornoway imports 1,000 tons of milk from the mainland and some children in Wester Ross have to be given dried milk under the Milk for Schools Scheme.[3] This is a change from the old dietary of the people and it marks a great alteration in the habits and tastes of the women. From happy memories of cows that were also friends, I know that a cow with her calf are fascinating creatures to look after although the regular hours of milking are a serious tie and, in my young days, it was not only the pride and pleasure of most Highland country women but also a definite sign of social status to keep a cow.

With all these changes the old breed of cattle has survived. In the droving days cattle from the Highlands were generally known as 'kyloes' or 'black cattle'. But, as a matter of fact, the colours of the animals in the Central Highlands varied a good deal although black, dun and 'brandered' predominated and there were

[1]*Report of the Commission of Enquiry into Crofting Conditions, 1954*, p. 51. See also Chapter IV, p. 81.
[2]'In the North-West there is not an average of one cow per croft', *Report of Committee on Crofting Conditions, 1954*, p. 60.
[3]Ibid., p. 48.

some 'hummle' or hornless beasts.[1] But, especially in Skye, Kintail and Argyll, the agricultural reformers of the late eighteenth century noticed the existence of a distinct 'hardy, industrious and excellent breed of cattle'.[2] They were said to be 'short in the legs, round in the body, straight in the back' but small in size—24-30 stone was said to be a good weight for a bullock. They were generally described as black in colour, although reddish-brown was also common. As time went on, the descendants of these little cattle-beasts, with their long coats, sweeping horns and gay carriage, became very fashionable as the ornamental inhabitants of rich men's parks. Black was bred out in favour of brown and dun, and the more utilitarian qualities of breed tended to be sacrificed. Their worst fault was, and still is, that they are very slow to mature and in the Highlands other breeds, such as Shorthorns and Aberdeen Angus cattle, became predominant, so that for a time pure-bred Highland cattle were seldom seen about the farms and crofts. But there has been a revulsion in favour of the Highland breed and the Scottish Board of Agriculture, in its work of supplying pedigree bulls to improve the crofters' stocks, has re-introduced Highland cattle and nowadays the handsome Shorthorn-Highlander cross is becoming much more common.[3]

## SHEEP

The raising of cattle had been the mainstay of the Highlands and the rhythm of the people's lives had been set to the needs of their herds. The keeping of sheep has entirely disrupted the old way of life. Sheep are the synonym for inoffensive innocence and yet they have caused wider devastations and changes in the Highlands than all the feuds, civil wars and other disturbances of the past. And they have now become one of the mainstays of Highland rural economy.

The old breed of Highland sheep is virtually extinct. I tried very hard to obtain a live exhibit for Am Fasgadh, my little

[1] I. F. Grant, *Old Highland Farm*, p. 62.
[2] Geo. Culley, *Observations on livestock*, 1807. See Appendix A. R. B. Haldane, *The Drove Roads*.
[3] Since this chapter was written an admirable account of one of the last of the drovers was published by Mr. E. Cregeen in *Scottish Studies*, Vol. 3, part 2, p. 143.

Highland Folk Museum, and failed.[1] They are described as small; they weighed only about 15–20 lb. They were sometimes white, dun, or parti-coloured and had four to six horns and pink noses. Like the Shetland and the Soay sheep they had short tails and prominent eyes and, like the Shetland sheep, they were the descendants of the ancient sheep of neolithic and the iron ages, although sixteenth century allusions to their four horns show that they had been crossed with another breed. They were not so closely related to the wild sheep still living on the island of Soay off St. Kilda.[2] They were delicate little beasts, housed at night in 'sheep cotes' and often tethered by day.[3] They were largely kept for their milk; in *Old Balnespick's Accounts*, from which I have quoted so often, he mentions twenty-four 'milk sheepes'.[4] This was very hard on the lambs and the ewes only lambed every second year. They had a very fine but rather scanty fleece with a great deal of kemp in it. Their wool was spun into yarn used in making the old, fine Highland 'hard tartan'. Unlike the cattle, which were the main source of what money the people received, the sheep were mainly kept for their own use. From individual figures I think that the people generally kept about the same number of sheep as of cattle.

About the middle of the eighteenth century it was discovered that the hardy, black-faced or Linton sheep of the Borders could spend the winter on the Highland hills. These are the sheep familiarly seen in the Highlands. They have long fleeces of coarse wool, well adapted for carrying off the wet, and are horned. They look thoroughly at home in their Highland setting and are extremely active and enterprising. Watching an old ewe, the ends of her long fleece floating like graceful draperies, the sun glinting on her golden eyes as she snorts and stamps and, if need be, gives a hard biff with her horns, to ward off anything molesting her

[1]Occasionally the modern sheep of Lewis produce specimens that throw back to the old breed and they are known as 'Sassenachs' = English: 'Tolsta bho Tuath', *Stornoway Gazette*, 31.8.51.

[2]For a good description see R. Forsyth, *The Beauties of Scotland*, Vol. IV, p. 261. For theory of origin see J. Ritchie, *The Influence of Man on Animal Life in Scotland*, p. 40.

[3]The Registrum Episcopatus Dunkeldis has entries that show how heavy was the mortality among them. See I. F. Grant, *Old Highland Farm*, pp. 66–67.

[4]They were occasionally milked in Skye so late as 1884. *Crofters Commission, 1884*, 'Minutes of Evidence', Vol. I, p. 55.

lamb, I always think of a description I read long ago in a book on agriculture. 'The black-face' it ran 'is a stylish sheep'. The story was that a drunken inn-keeper in Perthshire bought a few of these sheep and through his neglect they were left out all winter and to his surprise were found to have survived. This is only a tradition, but it is a fact that by 1762 Annandale sheep-farmers were leasing large tracts of land in Perthshire and Dumbartonshire. Then the movement spread to Argyllshire, Inverness-shire. Ross-shire (1794) and to Caithness and Sutherland by the end of the century.[1] The Hebrides were not affected till later, the Long Island not until the middle of the nineteenth century. It has been estimated that at the height of the movement nearly one-third of Scotland was under large sheep farms.[2] The largest sheepwalks were mainly found in the hill country of the north and the west.

This new kind of sheep farming was a complete break with the past. It was not a development by local people. Both the flock-masters and the shepherds they employed were incomers from the Borders. From the very start it was a large-scale type of farming. Large tracts of land were required to provide shelter and good grass for the ewes and young stock in order to utilize the high ground for the adult wedders and large stocks of sheep had to be carried. To import the new breed and to market the product required capital.

For more than a hundred years the new form of sheep farming went from strength to strength. There was a growing demand for wool and mutton in the south and means of transport were developing. From the start it was a highly profitable form of farming. Sinclair estimated that land worth $2\frac{1}{2}d$ per acre under cattle would be worth $2s$ per acre under sheep.[3] The flock-masters flourished and were able to pay greatly increased rents. The hardy wedders could be pastured on hill country of which only the more sheltered glens had been used for short periods in the summer by the cattle. In 1817 a great wool fair was started at Inverness to meet the convenience of the dealers from the south and sheep were sold by the tens of thousands at the old cattle trysts at

[1]*Conditions of the Highlands*, p. 13.
[2]M. Gray, *Highland Economy*, p. 87.
[3]For other figures see M. Gray, *Highland Economy*, p. 194.

Falkirk.[1] About the end of the eighteenth century the demand for a type of wool finer than that of the black-faced led to the introduction of another Lowland breed—the Cheviots—into the Highlands, and in the north one also sees a few of the great Leicesters—locally pronounced as Lycesters.

Something has already been said of the disastrous effects of the introduction of large-scale sheep farming into the Highlands, what John Knox calls 'the devilish custom of ejecting fifty or a hundred families at a time to make room for a flock of sheep'.[2]

The Highland country people were, however, most courageous in learning the new technique of sheep keeping. Eighteenth-century writers said that the Highlanders were poor shepherds and did not understand the keeping of sheep. Knowing how important to a modern crofter or farmer are his sheep, this seemed to me an example of blind prejudice. It was when I kept a few of the cousins of the old Highland sheep, the ancient breed of Soay sheep, at Am Fasgadh, that I learned to appreciate the difficulties that the people had to overcome. The Soays do not bunch together into a flock and follow each other as do the black-faced and Cheviot sheep; instead, when they are startled, they each take their own individual course and it is impossible to herd them with a dog. Other people who have kept them, and also the St. Kilda sheep, have had the same experience, and my own method of controlling them was by slavish bribery. The country people had to learn new ways of managing their sheep and they also had to acquire entirely new stocks, because crosses between the old breed and the new were unsatisfactory. Moreover, to keep sheep in the new way was only profitable if considerable numbers were kept.

Nevertheless, learn they did. By using their common grazings they were able to own joint flocks of an economic size and in some cases they combined to form considerable club farms with up to 2,000 sheep.[3] As Doctor Fraser Darling has pointed out, Highlanders with their 'delight in pastoral husbandry' now take more

[1]As many as 200,000 at the peak of the sales there about the middle of the eighteenth century, A. R. B. Haldane, *The Drove Roads*, p. 200.

[2]John Knox, *Tour through the Highlands of Scotland and the Hebride Isles*, p. xxvii (henceforth noted as J. Knox, *Tour*). See Chapter III, p. 50.

[3]For an interesting and sympathetic account of such farms in Sutherland, see statement by W. Mackenzie, *Crofter Commission, 1884*, p. 284. He said the people had taken up the modern method of sheep-farming 'within the last forty years'.

readily to sheep farming than to the modern methods of bullock fattening.[1] On the sheep or mixed farms a good shepherd, generally the son of a shepherd, has a sense of vocation to his calling. He generally takes little interest in other livestock or in the crops. In heavy snow he will take great risks to find and rescue his flock. He is intimately acquainted with each beast of the 300 or 400 that are in his charge, its looks, health and character, and in his off-time his talk will run endlessly on the ways and vagaries of sheep. Moreover the management of sheep requires something of the co-operative effort that was once required on the old run-rig farms. On all but the largest sheep-walks—on the farms of the east as well as the crofts of the west—the neighbours combine to help each other when the sheep have to be dipped (or in the old days, smeared), clipped and gathered. All the neighbouring shepherds come to lend a hand and are helped in their turn. On a farm a grand spread of food is provided with a dram from the host, and the occasion is one of friendly meeting and good fellowship.

Something may be said of the main activities in shepherding. Sheep are the victims of many insect pests, especially the horrible 'fly' (maggot), and it used to be the custom to smear each animal with a mixture of tar and butter; the fleece was parted again and again and the mixture rubbed in, a laborious process and very detrimental to the value of the fleece. After about 1880 smearing was replaced by dipping the sheep in a chemical wash. By Statute this must be done twice a year, in spring and summer, and the whole body of the animal immersed in a tank of the medicated dip. When the sheep are sheared in the early summer the shearer in some districts uses a special wooden stool, so long that the body of the sheep lies on it in front of him,[2] but in others a mound of turf is used and in others the sheep lies on the ground. After shearing the animals are given their owner's mark, either a specially placed dab of raddle or blue or a mark made with an iron dipped in heated tar.[3] In the autumn all the sheep are

[1] C. F. Fraser Darling: *Crofting Husbandry*, p. 146.
[2] In Harris, for instance, shearing stools are not used, but I acquired a very old one and was told that they had been used for smearing.
[3] In early youth the lambs had been marked by a specially placed notch on the ear. There were special words for the different places on the ear of these notches: Father A. MacDonald, *Gaelic Words*. Ed. J. L. Campbell.

brought down from the higher ground and are sorted out at the Gathering. Strays from other flocks are claimed—although sheep quickly learn the limits of their rightful walk they can also appreciate more sheltered and better pasture! The breeding ewes are kept on the more sheltered ground for the winter but, on hill farms, the young stock has to be sent for wintering on the turnip fields of the coastal districts. The lambs and cast ewes are sold off at the autumn sheep sales. The sheep sent to market and for wintering had to be driven to their destination, perhaps for miles, and in autumn and spring the roads would be full of flocks of sheep, and on that walk, weary for flock and shepherd, more and more would go lame and hirple slowly along, urged on by the shepherd and his dogs. Now the sheep travel in motor lorries.

There have been other changes. The mature wedders that were the hardiest part of the flock are no longer in demand and young, quickly maturing animals are required. This is particularly hard on the farms on the higher hills.[1] For many years the value of the black-faced sheep depended, more and more, upon its meat so that its coarse wool was almost at a discount.[2] Except for the Harris Tweed industry, which uses the wool of the localized breed of sheep, the people have practically given up using it themselves. There was, therefore, a deterioration in the quality of the wool. It is now receiving more attention by the breeders. One no longer sees numbers of animals with some black wool about them and even the distinctive black face is giving way to one freckled like a spaniel's nose. Since black-faced sheep were first introduced into the Highlands about 200 years ago, considerable local variations have been developed. The smaller long-legged Island type with the softer wool so valuable for the local tweed industry is the most distinctive.[3]

Hill sheep farming, although it is so important to Highland rural economy, is not a prosperous industry.[4] When the Govern-

[1] *Report on Scotland's Marginal Farms, 1947*, p. 45.
[2] Before the First World War it sold at about 1*d* a pound.
[3] C. F. Fraser Darling, *Crofting Economy*, p. 146.
[4] *Report on Scotland's Marginal Farms, 1947*, p. 45. In the *Report* dealing with the Highlands, *Report VI*, the large number of farms classed as 'marginal' in Inverness, Ross and Cromarty and Sutherland was noted (p. 4)—and 3,370 'potentially marginal farms were said to be in the Highlands out of a total of 9,800 in Scotland', p. 11.

ment threatened to withdraw the Hill Sheep Farming Subsidy this spring there was general consternation.[1] On the higher ground the losses in a bad season make the raising of sheep a speculative form of farming and, unless sheep are acclimatized to the ground, the losses through disease always tend to be very high. This has led to charges for acclimatized sheep stocks on a farm which complicates the sale of sheep farms. Furthermore, sheep cause more deterioration than other kinds of stock to the pasturage they are kept on by constantly eating out the finer grasses so thoroughly that they do not regenerate themselves, and it is a bad sign in those crofting areas where the ratio of sheep to cattle has increased, because sheep not only take more out of the grazing, but in the more clement west, they do not require the growing of so much of green crops (the great incentive to good husbandry) to sustain them.

It is a sign of the loss of the people's old artistic heritage that, although the keeping of sheep in the modern way has become so important to the Highlanders during the past 200 years, I do not think that they have produced any working songs nor do they figure in many stories.[2]

### OTHER ANIMALS

*Dogs:* With the Lowland sheep came the Border collie dogs. It used to be the custom (and still is in Skye) for Gaelic-speaking men to work their dogs with English words. My grandfather, in the days when Strathdearn (in eastern Inverness-shire) was still mainly Gaelic-speaking, asked a man why he did not speak to his dog in the Gaelic and the man replied: 'Och, he would be too wise altogether if he understood the Gaelic.'

The Highlanders, however, have always had dogs. Watchdogs come into the great Cuchullin Saga and are legislated about in our most ancient code of laws—attributed to the reign of David I (1124–53).[3] Greyhounds, generally described as black, come

[1] *The Report on Scotland's Marginal Farming, 1947*, quotes convincing figures.
[2] The old tale of 'The White Pet'—J. F. Campbell, *Popular Tales of the Western Highlands,* Vol. I, p. 194, belongs to the older ways of keeping sheep and a modern version of the story of the Dunvegan Cup that I have heard has merely substituted a shepherd for the old watch on the cattle.
[3] *Acts Scottish Parliament,* Vol. I, p. 13.

into several of the clan tales. Landseer has many pictures of the great shaggy, grey Highland deer hounds that in his time were used for tracking down wounded deer.

The increase in the value of sheep led to the regular employment of district foxhunters all over the Highlands.[1] Besides making him a yearly payment, the farmers were expected to feed his dogs when he was working on their land. Such dogs are the ancestors of the game little terriers who are still used for going into the cairns of stones in which Highland foxes so often take refuge. Although such little, rough-coated dogs, low in the body, sharp in the nose, of very variable appearance, still do this work in the Highlands, the dog fanciers have derived from the breed the silky-haired Skye terrier, the white West Highland terrier and the Cairn terrier, this last one of the least transmogrified of the products of the show bench. Anyone who has had the privilege of the companionship of a Cairn knows that he has to the full a heritage of dash, courage and single-heartedness from his hard-working ancestors.

*Horses:* Like the stories of cattle and of sheep, that of horses illustrates great changes in the social life of the people of the Highlands. In the case of the horses, however, the developments are modern and are still going on. The traditional breed of Highland horses and ponies, known as garrons (*gearrons*), sturdy beasts with lovely heads, wonderfully sure-footed and often dun or grey, is still with us. On the mainland, where they have been more extensively crossed with larger breeds, they may be 14 or 14½ hands high and are heavier than the smaller types of the islands. The Barra ponies are particularly good. In the old days Islay and Kintyre were famous for their horses and in Gaelic poetry of the Middle Ages the many allusions to grey horses show that that colour is ancient in the breed.[2] It then tended to die out but has now been recovered.

Under the old, unreformed methods of farming, the number of little horses, who were largely expected to fend for themselves, was enormous. For instance, on the farm of Balnespick at the end

---

[1] For instance in careful accounts kept by MacNeill of Carskey, the tenants contribution to the salary of the foxhunter does not appear till 1739. T. F. MacKay, *MacNeill of Carskey*, p. 108.

[2] There is, however, a fine poem on a dun mare: *Book of the Dean of Lismore* (1802 ed.), Tr. by T. MacLauchlan, Ed. W. F. Skene, p. 112.

of the eighteenth century, the tacksman kept six horses and six carts and, as part of their rent, had the part-time work of the twelve more horses belonging to his sub-tenants.[1] The work on this particular farm, after the introduction of the improved iron plough, could be done by two pairs of Clydesdales. Burt, who writes more sympathetically of horses than of Highlanders, gives a heartrending account of the wretched little local horses, dying on their feet of starvation after a bad season. But, later on, after he had ridden Highland garrons through the roadless Highlands of his day, he was full of praise for their activity and staying power. It was a reproach that in the Hebrides harrows were sometimes fastened to the tails of the unfortunate ponies.[2]

The sturdier type of garron was well suited for farm work in hilly country and on the lighter soils of many of the Islands and the local ponies are still invaluable for carrying peat and seaware where roads do not reach. But for many years Highland ponies have largely been replaced by horses of the heavy Clydesdale breed. When the earliest farm machinery, reapers and binders, came into use in the second half of the nineteenth century[3] horses still formed the motive power. In the twentieth century machines began to displace horses. From the beginning of the century motor cars had steadily replaced the horses upon the roads, although up till the 1930s, it was unusual to see a farm tractor at work in the Highlands. It was the drive for agricultural production and the labour shortages of the Second World War years that brought the motor tractor and all the other mechanical aids into increasing use. In many glens and straths horses have virtually disappeared and even on those crofts that are energetically cultivated mechanization is largely coming in. Many small men own the new equipment; if not, and for special purposes, it can be hired. I was told last year that in Skye practically no ploughing was now done with horses. Much the same thing is true of the other islands. There are no separate figures for crofters but the following are the figures for the counties of Inverness-shire, Argyllshire, Ross and Cromarty and

[1] I. F. Grant, *Old Highland Farm*, p. 70.
[2] E. Burt, *Letters*, Vol. I, pp. 76–78, 81, 139, 146. The harness, creels and carts can most conveniently be dealt with under 'Transport' in Chapter XIII.
[3] See Chapter V.

for Sutherland: between 1944 and 1959 the number of tractors increased from 882 to 4,887 while the number of work-horses fell from 11,001 to 1,897.[1] It was thanks to the increased use of mechanization that, in spite of the increased cost of and shortage of labour, the area under cultivation in the Highland counties has almost been maintained.[2]

One of the pleasures in travelling through the islands used to be to watch the many groups of ponies browsing on the moorland. Now one may go long distances without seeing any. Some are still however being bred for there are still uses for the Highland pony in carrying dead stags in deer-forests, between the shafts of milk vans in large towns and as mounts for the pony trekking that is becoming so popular in the Highlands.

*Swine:* The keeping of pigs is still but little carried on in the Highlands. The taboo that existed in some districts has not died away.[3] In Lewis, where swine used to be extensively kept, pig-keeping has almost gone out and the old breed has disappeared. At North Tolsta the last one was killed in 1912 without regret for they were described as 'voracious and destructive'.[4]

*Goats:* Large numbers were kept in the Highlands in the old days. In the lists of animals in claims for compensation for raids they were often more numerous than the sheep. They must have been responsible for much of the deforestation and, with the introduction of planting and the improvements in agriculture, they became unpopular and in estate regulations their keeping was sometimes forbidden. In some parts of the Highlands, for instance in Strathnairn and on Jura, survivors of the old breed have gone wild and many of the billy-goats carry magnificent heads.

*Poultry:* There seems to be no information about when and how the domestic fowls arrived in the Highlands from their original home in Asia. By the time for which we have records the numbers that were kept were extraordinarily large. It was customary to deliver a certain number of fowls to the landlord as

[1]Figures most kindly supplied to me by Mr. Gibson, Secretary to the Advisors Panel on the Highlands and Islands, and Mr. O. J. Beilby, Department of Agriculture.
[2]In 1944 it was 404,111 and 1959 397,178.
[3]See p. 7.
[4]'Tolsta bho Thuath', *Stornoway Gazette*, 31.8.51.

part of the rent in kind and on the MacLeod estates about 1744, when fowls were valued at 3s 6d a dozen, it has been calculated that 8,952 were yearly delivered as part of the rental.[1] These hens were known as 'kain hens' and were a byword for toughness and stringiness but, before the winter feeding of the cattle, all the laird's supplies of meat had to be killed in the autumn and salted, and the hens were a valuable addition to his dietary. The word 'kain' is a corruption of Cain, the ancient Gaelic due of a proportion of the product of the land, and it thus takes us back to the twilight of history when the Gael first came from Erin to Alba.

No doubt the poultry, like all other living things upon the old holdings, had very short commons, but they lived in some comfort, sharing the people's homes and roosting in the rafters, as is described in many of the old tales. The cock, according to Carmichael, was sometimes known by the beautiful name of '*Fear bheannachaidh na Maidne*'—'he who blesses the morning'.[2] But, unfortunately for the poor bird, his magical associations made him the victim of a cure for epilepsy. A black cock was buried alive at the place at which the first attack had taken place.[3]

[1]Canon R. MacLeod, *Book of Dunvegan*, Vol. I, p. 271.

[2]A. Carmichael, *Carmina Gadelica*, ed. by J. Carmichael Watson, Vol. IV, p. 7.

[3]A. Mitchell, op. cit., p. 166, said that he knew of several instances of the carrying out of this cure.

# V

## THE ARABLE LAND—
## THE PEOPLE'S FOOTHOLD

ALTHOUGH cattle and sheep have exerted such powerful influences on the Highlanders' way of life, we know from tradition and story that from the times before written records the people had already reached the stage of living in settled, agricultural communities. Although it is not until the eighteenth century that we get detailed descriptions of their agriculture, it was then identical with the older methods all over Scotland— Sir John Skene in *de Verbum Significatorum* wrote—'In every part of the Kingdom the plan of alternate ridges prevailed'—and was similar to vestiges of early agriculture in Ireland, Wales, Norway and many parts of England.[1] It was therefore evidently of very ancient origin. Land under this system was held in intermixed strips, periodically re-allocated among groups of joint cultivators, and the pasture was grazed in common. As eighteenth century writers on the Highlands said, the farms were 'all interwoven',[2] the land being 'like a piece of striped cloth with banks full of weeds and ridges of corn in constant succession.[3] Where land has gone out of cultivation the old curving ridges into which the land had been ploughed up can still be traced under the grass and heather.

In earlier times these intermixed strips no doubt were always

[1] I. F. Grant, *Social and Economic Development*, pp. 101, 103. 107. J. H. Clapham, *A Concise Economic History of Britain*, p. 48. Sir J. Sinclair, *Northern Counties of Scotland*, p. 263. See also the series of 'Reports on the Agriculture of Scotland to the Board of Agriculture' made at the end of the eighteenth century. I am also indebted to Professor Sigurd Erixon, Institut for Folkslivs Forsking, Stockholm.

[2] Andrew Wight, *Present State of Husbandry in Scotland*, p. 34.

[3] J. Robertson, *General View of the Agriculture of Southern Perthshire*, p. 64.

periodically re-allocated but, by the eighteenth century, in most parts of the Highlands, they had come into the continuous possession of a joint tenant and did not change hands. In some places, however, on the Long Island, the periodic re-allocation lingered on till the middle of the eighteenth century,[1] and a very few traces of it are said to survive even to the present day.

Carmichael and others have derived run-rig, the word used in Scotland for joint cultivation, from a Gaelic term *Roinn-Ruith*, division run, but he admits that the word generally used in the Long Island was *Mor Earann*, great division, or *Mor Fhearann*, great land.[2] In Breadalbane the agricultural terms used were *Croit*, infield and *Roer*, outfield.[3] I have generally heard individual rigs called *Imirean* and the nearest equivalent to 'Infield' and 'Outfield' were *Talamh Traibhta*, ploughed land, and *Talamh Ban*, fallow land. On the other hand *rig*, a ridge, was a common Scots and north of England word, as for instance in the song 'the lea rig'.

A peculiarity of the Scots system was that the arable land was treated in two ways. The best land and that most accessible to the joint homesteads was known as 'infield' and was under a constant succession of grain crops and on it was spread all the available manure. Land less good or less accessible was known as 'outfield' and a portion of it was yearly brought under cultivation and 'wasted by a succession of crops' until its fertility was exhausted. The only manuring it received was by the laborious one of 'tathing', that is, by confining the animals within temporary folds of sods that were moved so as gradually to enrich the whole ground. The number of years during which it could be cropped varied with the quality of the soil.[4] In addition, each joint cultivator had the right to a share in such patches of natural meadow as existed, to pasture a quota of his animals upon the common grazings and at the shielings in the summer. The proportion of

---

[1]For good descriptions see A. Carmichael's statements to the *Crofters Commission, 1884*, pp. 213, 461–7, nineteenth century. M. Gray, *The Highland Economy*, p. 19 for Nether Lorn in 1785.
[2]Statement to *Crofters Commission, 1884*, p. 451.
[3]M. MacArthur, *Lochtayside*, p. 18.
[4]J. Donaldson, *General View of the Agriculture of the County of Banff*, p. 12. For a good general summary of Infield and Outfield, see Sir J. Sinclair, *Northern Counties*, p. 265.

infield and outfield varied very much according to the lie of the land.[1]

The custom of continuous cultivation is a very primitive one and even more so is that of cropping the land to the point of exhaustion and then making fresh intakes. Both of these are to be found in many parts of the world and among very backward peoples. Adam Smith in his *Wealth of Nations*[2] compared the cultivation by periodic intakes in Scotland and America. The combination was probably partly due to the lie of the land but the contrast between the well-organized three-field system of England and the infield and outfield method of cultivation of Scotland is bound up with the entirely different social and economic development of the two countries.

For the intermixing of the peoples shares, so that each joint tenant had more than one little piece of land, there was very good reason. The primitive implements they used required a large seasonal labour force and the lack of transport made each cultivator so far as possible depend upon his own produce and, before the introduction of improved drainage, wet and dry land varied very much even within a small area. Under such conditions it was most important that everyone should have a share of the wet and dry so that, whatever the season, he should get something of a crop. One of the tenants on one of the last run-rig farms in Wester Ross gave me this need as one of the reasons why the joint tenants preferred their intermixed holdings.[3] It was probably for the same reason that in old rentals one often finds the names of men with portions of land in more than one farm.[4]

The size of the individual shares in the holdings varied very much, even before the changes of the late eighteenth and early nineteenth centuries. The shares of arable might not be more than 2 acres, they might be 13 acres, but the amount of grazing

[1]The accounts of the individual parishes in the *Old Statistical Account*, show great variation. Lochtayside was rather exceptional in having a larger proportion of Infield to Outfield, see M. MacArthur, *Lochtayside*, p. xlvi, and in the most fertile districts of Easter Ross and the Black Isle there seems to have been no Outfield, see Sir J. Sinclair, *Northern Counties*, p. 9. In parts of South Uist the valuable machair land was treated as a kind of Outfield and periodic intakes of it were made.
[2]P. 222 in edition edited by E. Cannan.
[3]See also W. F. Skene, *Celtic Scotland*, Vol. III, p. 385 for other examples.
[4]I. F. Grant, *Old Highland Farm*, pp. 2, 3. I. F. Grant, 'Development of an Estate in Eastern Inverness-shire', *Estate Magazine* (pub. by E.S.A.), May 1924, p. 823.

might be on the inverse ratio,[1] and the dependence on cattle was more marked.

In comparing eighteenth-century rentals for the same farms over a number of years one finds that the shares held by the individual tenants varied in size. For instance, on a typical Harris joint farm there were six tenants, two each had a $1\frac{1}{2}d$ share, two each had shares of five-eights of a penny, one at a quarter of a penny and one a holding of $2\frac{1}{4}d$. Moreover a few years later the proportions had been much altered.[2] As the various tenants contributed beasts to the communal ploughing and the traditional Highland plough team was four horses[3] the allocation of the different shares must have been difficult.

When the reformers began to describe Highland agriculture towards the end of the eighteenth century they were very critical. The non-professional tacksmen and the minute subdivisions of land with their 'load of tenantry' were condemned. The lack of winter feeding-stuffs for the stock was rightly considered to be one of the most serious faults. During the summer, as we have seen, the beasts fed on the grass, but natural hay is poor in the Highlands and all land suitable for growing corn was devoted to producing food for human beings[4] while the farms were held in intermixed, unenclosed strips. The great new innovations of sowing turnips and artificial grasses could not be introduced, and in winter the only feeding for the beasts that were housed was the straw of the grain crops—unsuitable food for cattle if nothing else is given—and even this was not available when the lazy and wasteful process of 'graddaning' the grain was carried on. Occasionally a more enlightened tacksman seems to have let the cattle have the last crop taken off the exhausted portion of the outfield. The animals outside had to subsist upon what they could pick up from the shrivelled winter herbage and on the bare stubbles until 'the land was gnawed to the quick'.[5]

The reformers were equally critical of Highland methods of husbandry. As the result of cereal crops grown year after year on

[1]M. Gray, *Highland Economy*, pp. 7, 24. See Chapter IV.
[2]I. F. Grant, *The MacLeods*, pp. 350, 549.
[3]Cf. *Old Statistical Account*, Vol. III, p. 641 (Farr, Sutherland), Vol. VII, p. 125 (Glenshiel, Wester Ross).
[4]See p. 75.
[5]W. Marshall, *Agriculture of the Central Highlands*, p. 31.

the infield and the ineffectiveness of the primitive implements of agriculture the arable land was never cleaned. Marshall, who had described 'the most desolate and distressing picture' of the winter farmlands with 'not a blade of pasturable herbage' and emaciated and dying animals, wrote that by May the colour of the country had changed from a 'sickly hue' to 'the most vivid assembly of tints; beautiful to the traveller but destructive to the occupier and disgraceful to the country. Oats universally were hid under a canopy of weeds in blow'; after specifying the worst of the weeds he wound up, 'husbandry never appeared in a lower state than that in which it is here found'.[1]

A fault that the local Baron Courts constantly complained about was the wasteful use of feal, i.e. turf that was skimmed off for use in building, in making dykes, such as those made for tathing, and for adding to the manure.

The agricultural improvers, however, have not proved themselves to be infallible. The higher returns from the land that they foretold from the introduction of new methods have not been attained. For instance, Sir John Sinclair confidently stated that eight or twelve returns for every boll of grain sown might be expected. As a matter of fact, in a fairly suitable district a return of six is about all that the modern farmer is likely to get.[2] Much money has been wasted on drainage schemes that have proved useless—the upper course of the Spey has many examples—and the wholesale substitution of sheep for cattle, besides its social effects, has led to a great deterioration of the hill pastures.

On the other hand the old system proved itself to be wonderfully adapted to the conditions of the past. In the old days of clan warfare, when it was essential that the utmost man-power should be built up, under the fluid run-rig system shares of the precious arable would be cut down and down to accommodate as many people as possible, everyone getting some share of the dry and wet land. Under the greater stresses of the early nineteenth century this ability to increase the population on the holdings was even more remarkable.

A special way of cultivating the land is found on the Long Island and known as *Fiannagan* or lazy-beds, which was parti-

[1] W. Marshall, *Agriculture of the Central Highlands*, p. 37.
[2] I. F. Grant, *Old Highland Farm*, p. 75.

cularly suitable for the local conditions. The term 'lazy-bed' is a misnomer, for to make them was a laborious process. The manure, or more often the sea-ware which had been brought from the shore and spread out on the grass to decay, was laid in a thick strip on the surface of the growing sward down the centre of what was to be the lazy-bed which had been marked out and was about five feet wide. The ground on each side was then turned over the strip of manure or seaweed, making a sandwich with a nourishing filling of fertilizer and of the decayed vegetation on the original top of the sward. Then another fiannagan was made parallel to the first so that the earth turned over each of them left a 2-ft. ditch between which provided drainage. Grain was originally sown on the lazy-beds but, when the cultivation of potatoes came in, it was for this crop that they were found to be pre-eminently suitable. One can trace the lines of long, low mounds of the old lazy-beds where the land has gone out of cultivation, and I saw them being made about twenty-five years ago. But this method of cultivation has now almost entirely been given up. They were particularly suitable for use in peaty land that cannot be drained or for the narrow veins of soil between the rock faces and they gave depth when the skin of land over the rock below was thin— all conditions liable to occur on the Long Island.[1]

The old varieties of oats have held their own in a few districts, in spite of all that was said against them, because of their special suitability, and one may marvel at the way in which the patches of infield were maintained, year after year, in a state of fertility. There are reliable contemporary accounts which put the returns of grain sown in exceptionally favoured spots as high as sixteen or even thirty fold.[2] Such high returns were, however, exceptional, and under the old system the average was said by the reformers to be only three seeds for each one sown for oats and rather more for barley and bere. There were moreover recurring years of dearth. The people's sufferings in the worst of the famines

[1] C. F. Fraser Darling, *Crofting Agriculture*, p. 8, describes the special suitability of fiannagan in boggy soils. See also M. F. Shaw, *Folk Song and Folk Lore of South Uist*, p. 8. A. Carmichael, *Evidence before Crofters Report of 1884*, p. 467.

[2] M. Martin says that the returns of barley on the most fertile land of Bernera was twenty-four to thirty fold—M. Martin, *Western Islands*, p. 138. Dr. John Walker says that the returns of bere on specially favoured spots on South Uist was twenty to twenty-five fold. J. Walker, *Economical History of the Highlands*, Vol. II, p. 313.

were so severe that traditions about them were handed down. A famine of 1680, when the people of Strathspey had to eat nettles, was remembered more than a hundred years later.[1] Others long remembered were in 1766 and 1772, in both of which the cattle suffered severely, in 1782–3, known as the year of the White Peas because the import of this foodstuff was the salvation of some districts, and a bad one in 1796.[2] Apart from such famines, years of scarcity might come as often as every third year.[3] T. Pennant happened to visit the Highlands after the failure of the harvest of 1769 and he has left eye-witness descriptions of the misery of the people in Islay, Canna and Skye and of seeing them gathering shell-fish.[4] This was an old resource in famine years. Sir Norman MacLeod of Bernera (fl. seventeenth century) was remembered long after his death as 'A Man of Wisdom and Understanding', because, in a famine, he arranged that the tenants on one of his farms which had not shores so well-stocked in shell-fish as the rest of the Bernera farms should be dispersed among the other tenants.[5] In Strathspey the people were said to flavour the nettles they ate in time of scarcity with mugwort; on the Long Island the standby was Silver Weed (*Potentilla Anserina*), but nettles and wild spinach and mustard were also eaten.[6] The introduction of the potato was of special and enormous benefit in the famine years.

The changes in the crops grown in the Highlands have deeply affected not only the people's methods of farming but their whole lives. Under the old system of agriculture in the Highlands two kinds of grain were sown in uninterrupted succession upon the infield land. They were oats and bere. Two varieties of oats were cultivated; white or great oats were grown all over the Lowlands and on the better land in the Highlands, but on the outfield and the higher ground a variety called small, grey or black oats (*corc beag*) now known as Bristle-pointed, was grown.[7] The grains of

[1] *Old Statistical Account for Duthil*, Vol. IV, p. 316.
[2] *Old Statistical Account*, Vol. XVI, p. 192. I. F. Grant, *Old Highland Farm*, p. 54.
[3] J. Knox, *Tour*, p. xci.
[4] T. Pennant, *Tour*, Vol. I, pp. 251–2, 261–2, 311–2.
[5] I. F. Grant, *The MacLeods*, p. 343.
[6] L. Shaw, *The Province of Moray*, p. 36. A. Goodrich Freer, *The Outer Isles*, p. 190. See also Chapter XIV.
[7] W. M. Findlay, *Oats*, pp. 17, 18.

the black oats were so much smaller that a measure of them was calculated as equal to half that of great oats.[1] Sometimes, to make sure of a crop of sorts, a mixture of the two kinds was sown. Both the black oats and the white were very slow in ripening. With the improvements in agriculture many generations of new oats have been introduced and have spread to the Highlands, and the North of Scotland College of Agriculture continues to experiment in finding varieties that will best suit the conditions of the north. The old black oat however is not extinct.[2] It is still grown to some extent in the Hebrides because it is the more suitable for some of the machair land and will stand up to the high winds, and all over the north it stoutly persists as a weed among crops of the newer varieties:[3] an unappreciated link with the past.

The other most important cereal crop was of bere—an early and inferior variety of barley—and barley itself. The account book of my own old ancestor shows that in Badenoch, at the end of the eighteenth century, the tacksman himself was steadily increasing the proportion of barley to bere that he sowed and that he was selling small quantities of barley seed to his lesser neighbours.[4] Bere has now become entirely obsolete.

In the Lowlands, by the eighteenth century, beans and peas had been introduced as a field crop and they were beginning to make their way into the more accessible Highland districts. Small quantities of rye also were sown and occasionally a mixture of rye or bere with oats. Old people have told me that they had heard that rye and bere used to grind more economically than oats, and the device was due to the poverty of the people. Those of us of the older generation can remember the unpalatableness of the 'war bread' of the First World War which was made of a mixture of grains.

The proportion that was sown of bere or barley to oats varied. Sir John Sinclair stated that it was generally one-third.[5] But where the soil was more suitable for bere and barley, as for instance in many parts of the Hebrides, these were the predominant crop.

[1] I. F. Grant, *Old Highland Farm*, p. 42.
[2] W. M. Findlay, *Oats*, p. 18. About 500 to 600 acres of it were grown in 1956.
[3] W. M. Findlay, *Oats*, p. 162.
[4] I. F. Grant: *Old Highland Farm*, p. 49.
[5] On 'Old Balnespick's' farm in Badenoch this was the proportion. I. F. Grant, *Old Highland Farm*, p. 48.

The seasonal cycle of agricultural work followed and still largely follows the span of life of the grain crops, but before dealing with the changes that have come about in their cultivation one may notice how the introduction of three more crops have had a fundamental influence on Highland agriculture and the lives of those who depended upon it. One of the drawbacks to farming in the Highlands in the old days was that natural hay was very scanty and of inferior quality. Yet because of the shortage of winter feeding stuffs it had to be carefully gathered where it grew on boggy ground or among bushes. Marshall describes how 'after the scythe has gone over the free patches, the sickle is used to hook out the remainder from among the bushes, and to clear round and between stones, and to shave the sides of hollow ways' until every handful was gathered. Grass in woods was cut and carried out to the open to dry.[1] The marshy land where 'Old Balnespick' cut his hay crop is full of rank grass intermixed with rushes and would make poor feeding indeed. In one entry he described hay as being cut 'among the bushes'.[2]

Something has been said of how in the Eastern and Central Highlands the introduction of sown hay and turnips, two of the great innovations of the agricultural revolution, transformed the whole lay-out of the farms, and the social organization of the population.[3] As part of a regular rotation, these crops helped to clean the land, which under continuous cereal crops was infested with weeds, and also improved its fertility and led to the enclosure of the fields. They, especially the turnips, provided the much needed winter feeding for the livestock. This, in the Highlands, was of vital importance, for under the modern mixed farming the emphasis on the production of animals is even more marked than in the old days and, for as long as a hundred years, the produce of the arable cultivation has entirely been for the feeding of the livestock.

The cultivation both of turnips and of hay spread to the west and to the small holdings as well as the large ones. Turnips have encouraged the fencing of the strip-cultivation of the crofts. The methods of making hay at the present day show great variation.

[1] W. Marshall, *Agriculture of Central Highlands*, p. 41.
[2] I. F. Grant, *Old Highland Farm*, p. 56.
[3] See Chapter II.

97

On the smallest holdings the hay, after cutting, is allowed to dry in swathes and when quite dry or when rain is threatened it is lightly heaped by means of the fork and the hands into small 'coils' (little hay cocks). Until it is absolutely dry it has to be spread out and regathered, perhaps many times. In wet years a modern wire fence may come in handy over which to hang the hay to dry. Finally, the small coils are piled with the fork into larger ones and securely roped. On the west coast and on the Islands these final coils are made very high and narrow and built round a tripod of timber on a foundation of stones. Such a way of making hay shows little change from the time when sown hay was introduced as a field crop. Not so long ago it was sometimes a communal effort that reminds one of the old days of joint farming. A Skye shepherd's daughter has told me of her happy memories of how her father's hay was made. All the neighbours helped to carry the hay on their backs and the children, as a treat, were allowed to tramp it into place in the stack—they tramped it 'so hard it would tear the flesh off your hands if you tried to pull it apart'. The helpers, who were unpaid, received a series of meals of bread, jam, cheese, tea and whisky while they worked.[1]

On larger holdings, one can see, or could see till lately, the use of the mechanical aids that came in during the nineteenth century, such as the horse-drawn rake, a device for couping over the hay popularly known as a 'tumbling Tommy', and the horse-drawn reaper, but these have now been largely succeeded by the reaper drawn by a tractor and, latest of all, the machine that gathers and bales the hay. (This latter is hired on all but the largest farms.) But even with all the mechanical aids the wit of man can devise, in hilly districts and above all in the west, it is generally a nightmare to get in the hay dry.

In dealing with hay I have followed out the long sequence of changes. The third new crop that deeply affected the life of the people was the potato and its greatest influence was exerted in the west. It did not lead to great agricultural changes but it made possible the survival of the people under the increasing severity of their conditions. The cultivation of potatoes in rigs was quite compatible with the run-rig system and they grew particularly well on the lazy-beds (*fiannagan*) and travellers during the late

[1]Told me by Mrs. M. Grant.

eighteenth century were nearly all struck by the extent to which potatoes were cultivated. The crop flourished under west coast conditions and its returns were not so variable as those of cereals. T. Garnett, writing in 1800, said that before its introduction the people 'pined away near half their time in want and hunger, the country being so little adapted both from soil and climate to the growth of grain'.[1] During the kelp boom potatoes helped to feed the people who crowded along the shores to gather the seaweed and in the direr distress that followed the collapse of that industry, in the words of Sir John Sinclair,[2] the cultivation of potatoes was 'the last remedy'. The subdivision of the crofts upon the shrinking land available to the people made the potato even more essential, as was painfully revealed by the total failure of the crop in 1847, when 75 per cent of the people of the Hebrides were said to be destitute.[3] Nowadays, where the crofts have been improved, potatoes are grown as a field crop.

The implements used in the Highlands have changed with the methods of agriculture. The following is a list of those used by a small farmer about the end of the eighteenth century in the Eastern Highlands compared with the equipment that a man in a similar position about 1930 told me that he considered essential. It emphasizes the difference:

| End of Eighteenth Century[4] | £ | s | d | 1930 | £ | s | d |
|---|---|---|---|---|---|---|---|
| 1 plough, mounted | | 5 | 0 | 1 Plough and ambles | 4 | 4 | 0 |
| 2 pairs harrows 3/- | | 6 | 0 | Harrows | 1 | 10 | 0 |
| | | | | Chain Harrows | 2 | 0 | 0 |
| 1 spade | | 2 | 6 | | | | |
| 4 wooden shovels, ironshod 8d | | 2 | 8 | | | | |
| 2 cabbies or small half-size mattocks | | 2 | 6 | 1 grubber | 4 | 0 | 0 |
| 4 kellocks or carts 2/6 | | 10 | 0 | 2 carts | 16 | 0 | 0 |
| 4 ditto with rungs or rails for carting hay 2/6 | | 10 | 0 | | | | |

[1]T. Garnett, *Tour*, Vol. I, p. 116.

[2]Letter from Sir John Sinclair to MacLeod of MacLeod, 1827, at Dunvegan Castle.

[3]R. N. Salaman, *The History and Social Influence of the Potato*. Pp. 360–76 gives a detailed and well-documented account of its cultivation in the Highlands. See also Chapter III.

[4]Sir J. Sinclair, *Northern Counties*, p. 76. These implements all had to be renewed every two years.

| | £ | s | d | | £ | s | d |
|---|---|---|---|---|---|---|---|
| 4 horse collars of straw 1d each | | | 4 | | | | |
| 4 hair halters 2½d each | | | 10 | | | | |
| 4 crook saddles, 6d each | | 2 | 0 | | | | |
| 4 pairs of hempen rope for traces | | 2 | 6 | | | | |
| 3 yokes and wooden bows 4d each | | 1 | 0 | | | | |
| 2 flails 2d each | | | 4 | 1 *barn fanner | | 3 | 10 | 0 |
| 2 sieves 1/- each | | 2 | 0 | | | | |
| 2 sieves 4d each | | | 8 | | | | |
| 3 riddles 4d each | | 1 | 0 | | | | |
| 6 shearing hooks 5d each | | 2 | 6 | 1 reaper | | 14 | 0 | 0 |
| | | | | (This would not include a binder and would be an old-fashioned, very simple machine) | | | | |
| 2 flaughter spades 6d each | | 1 | 0 | | | | |
| 2 wooden corn forks 2d each | | | 4 | | | | |
| iron chain or soam for oxen plough | | 6 | 0 | | | | |
| sundries | | 3 | 6 | 8 small implements | | 5 | 0 | 0 |
| | | | | 1 scuffler | | 1 | 9 | 0 |
| | £3 | 2 | 8 | 1 roller | | 1 | 10 | 0 |
| | | | | 1 turnip sower | | 5 | 0 | 0 |
| | | | | | £58 | 3 | 0 |

Most of the implements in Sir John Sinclair's list have long been entirely obsolete. They were mainly of wood with the minimum of iron. The chain of the plough is the most expensive item in the list and in poorer districts was replaced with a rope of twisted root fibres or a strip of seal-skin. They were of local construction and were very cumbrous, as one visitor wrote: 'Here everything is done by rude strength and perseverance.'[1]

There were several variations in the ploughs used. In the Lowlands the 'twal ousen plough', an extremely heavy yet inefficient wooden plough drawn by twelve oxen, was in use. The working of oxen was found in the more accessible districts of the Highlands, for instance in Strathspey, and sometimes teams of mixed

[1] R. Heron, *General View of the Natural Circumstances of the Isles adjacent to the North West Coast of Scotland which are distinguished by the Common Name of Hebudae or Hebrides, 1794*, p. 89 (henceforth noted as R. Heron, *The Hebrides*).

animals, cows and horses were pressed into the service.[1] In the hill-country the plough used was very small and light. Doctor Walker called it 'a very singular and feeble instrument', its whole length 'about four feet seven inches'. He was writing of the Hebrides and said that it had only one stilt. This peculiarity, only found in the Long Island and in Orkney, is of Scandinavian origin. Walker, however, also noticed that the plough team consisted of four horses yoked abreast.[2] This was a Gaelic feature usual all over the Highlands and the subdivisions of the joint farms were called horse-gangs (in the Lowlands where oxen were used, such divisions were called ox-gangs).[3] The plough was made of wood, the various parts of it fastened together by wooden pins or leather straps, the only iron about it being the coulter, which was said to be more valuable than the whole of the rest of the plough. (See Fig. 3.) It did not turn a share but 'made rather a triangular

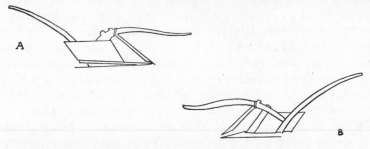

FIG. 3. Diagram of old wooden plough; right and left.

rut in the ground than a furrow, leaving the soil for the most part, equally fast on both sides of it'.[4] So feeble was it that sometimes the ground had to be ploughed more than once or the sward cut in front of it by a horse-drawn, sickle-like implement called a ristle.[5] Three men were required to drive the plough. One of

[1] E. Burt, *Letters*, Vol. II, p. 261. I can remember seeing in my youth very small farmers ploughing with a cow and a horse. I was told that it was very hard on the horse, as the pace of the cow, the stronger beast, was slower.
[2] J. Walker, *Economical History of the Hebrides*, Vol. I, p. 122.
[3] See Chapter I.
[4] J. Anderson, *General View of the Agriculture and Rural Economy of the County of Aberdeen*, p. 45.
[5] J. MacDonald, *General View of the Agriculture in the Hebrides*, has an illustration of this implement.

them walked backwards in front of the horses, as one description
says singing or whistling to encourage them and by another as
'making a hideous Irish noise'; the reason for walking, backwards was said by Burt to be in order that he might look out for
rocks close to the shallow soil.[1] About the middle of the eighteenth century greatly improved ploughs with mould boards that
could turn a share and drawn by a pair of horses came into use in
the Lowlands and spread to Highland farms. In 1785 two tenants
were using two-horse ploughs on Lochtayside,[2] and many people
in the Highlands must have experimented with improved wooden
ploughs for, to my knowledge, three different examples, all with
mould boards, survive. One has a double mould board and was
apparently designed for ridging turnips. It originally came from
near Inverness but ended its working days at Abriachan, a little
settlement high above Loch Ness which is reached by a road with
dizzily steep gradients.[3] A leading Berwickshire ploughmaker,
James Small, eventually made his ploughs of iron and these came
into wide use in the Highlands and I saw an old one made by him
still being used in Easter Ross. Iron ploughs went on being improved and soon superseded the wooden ones although, during
the First World War, very short and simple iron ploughs with
wooden handles and drawn by one horse were much imported by
the crofters of the Long Island (see Fig. 4.) and also elsewhere.
During the Second World War the horse-drawn plough itself
tended more and more to be replaced by the more powerful forms
drawn by tractors. It is necessary progress, but it is a sad lack
that in many a strath one can no longer hear the whistle of the
ploughman, or watch the skill with which he made his lines of
furrows with the precision of an etching or the rhythm of the
slow progress of his team.

Primitive as was the obsolete wooden plough, yet more primi-

[1]E. Burt, *Letters*, Vol. II, p. 144. Burt added 'many of their Methods are too well
suited to their own Circumstances and those of the Country to be easily amended by
such as undertake to deride them'.

[2]M. MacArthur, *Lochtayside*, p. xl.

[3]A rather similar Highland plough with a mould board is illustrated in the
*Encyclopaedia Britannica*, 1771. It had a coulter and sock of iron but was otherwise
made of slight pieces of wood skilfully fitted together to give the maximum effect
in the intractable ground on which it was used. For a well-documented and full
account of the old Scots plough see article by Ragner Jirlow and Iain Whitaker,
'Scottish Studies'. 1 January, 1957, pp. 71.–94.

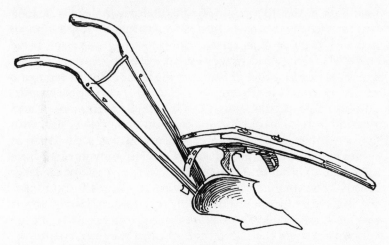

FIG. 4. Plough with wooden stilts; in recent use.

tive and laborious implements survived it because of their special
suitability for the tiny holdings and the difficult terrain of the
west, and these have only entirely gone out of use within the
present century. The best known is the *cas chrom* (crooked foot)

FIG. 5. Man using cas chrom.

(see Figs. 5 and 6B), made of a piece of wood about 5 ft. long with a naturally curved end fitted to a flat piece tipped with an iron sock like that of an ancient plough.[1] A peg was fitted at the angle where the head curves into the shaft against which the worker pressed his foot as he thrust the point of the sock into the earth and with a jerk turned the clod. He worked backwards, turning a succession of clods into a beautifully even share. A man working from January till April was said to be able to deal with five acres, but he might expect a return of five seeds whereas cultivation by the old plough would produce only three.[2] I have seen the cas chrom being used to turn the peaty soil of the lazy-beds in Lewis, on the precipitous slopes of Coigeach and Kintail and in the narrow veins between the rock-faces of Harris. It was also much used in Skye. Sometimes when crofters could not keep horses because of the loss of hill grazings they reverted to the cas chrom.[3] One assumes that the cas chrom is a very ancient implement: a report written about 1549 says that in Harris there was 'twiese mair of delving in it nor of teilling',[4] and one supposes that this was done with the cas chrom. It was, however, superior to the old plough in that it turned over the sward instead of scratching a mere furrow, and it is therefore rather surprising that a share or some similar device was not used much earlier on the native plough.

About Moidart a different form of digging implement was used, the *Cas Dhireach*. It consisted of a single piece of wood about the same length but less sharply bent than the cas chrom and it had a similar iron tip, although examples I collected were rather wider (see Fig. 6F). Either a peg was fixed in the shaft or a step cut in it for the user's foot. I have never seen this implement in use although about fifteen years ago I was told that it had only lately gone out of use near Loch Ailort. I was told that it was

[1]The shape rather depended upon the natural curves of the wood. A specimen found under a layer of peat was made of one conveniently-shaped piece of wood. This ingenious use of the natural curves of wood is seen in many examples of Highland handiwork. An old man who I thought was asking rather a high price for a piece of primitive work told me that it might not take long to fashion something out of naturally curved wood but that to find such a piece might take a whole day and to know how to use it a lifetime.

[2]I. Walker, *Economical History of the Hebrides*, Vol. II, p. 127.

[3]*Crofters Commission, 1884*, 'Minutes of Evidence', Vol. I, p. 44.

[4]Printed as Appendix to W. F. Skene, *Celtic Scotland*, p. 111.

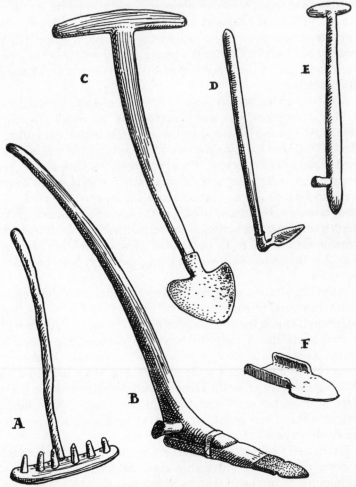

FIG. 6. Ancient agricultural implements. (A) Racan. (B) Cas chrom. (C) Flaughter spade. (D) Croman. (E) Potato dibber. (F) Blade of cas dhireach.

used like a spade to turn over the earth in front of the digger.

In the south-west another implement, now entirely obsolete, the *Ceaba* was used. Descriptions of it sounded much like illustrations of the Irish Loy. It had a stout wooden handle expanded into a footrest on one side and an iron-sheathed tip. I was told that, sometimes at least, a row of diggers would plunge their ceabas into the ground at once and turn a large and deep furrow. The ordinary spade, however, is widely used in the Western Highlands for field work. This cannot be a modern practice because the Gaelic version of the word—*spad*—is the component of many other words.[1]

After ploughing and sowing, which took place as late as April or May, the ground was and is harrowed. The ancient harrows were entirely made of wood and were 'little better than rakes'. Martin describes harrows with wooden teeth in front and heather fixed in place of the last row. The cruel custom of fastening horses to the harrows by their tails has been fairly widely noted in the Western Islands (an accusation also made against the Irish). It must, however, be remembered that the harrows on small crofts, even twenty-five years ago, were very small and the frame and sometimes even the teeth were made of wood and they were so light that they had often, within living memory, been pulled by the women.[2]

In the Highlands and on the north-west coast two other implements were, and to some extent still are, in use for breaking up the ground. One is the *Croman* (see Fig. 6D), an implement with an iron blade like a pick (perhaps the 'cabbies' mentioned in Sinclair's list were of this type). The other is a wooden implement like a clumsy rake called a *Racan* (see Fig. 6A), and used for breaking the clods of earth. There is considerable variation in the shape of these racans. Those I saw in Barra had a short, heavy head with about four wooden teeth. In Coigeach the head is wider and there may be as many as twelve teeth.

The cycle of cultivation of the corn culminates in the harvest. In some districts the incredibly lazy and wasteful method of pulling up the corn by the roots and burning the straw was usual. Duncan Forbes, who visited Tiree in 1737, wrote that barley was the main product of the island but that 'There never was one sheaf

[1] See E. MacDonald, *Faclair Gaidhlig*. In Farr, in Sutherlandshire most of the cultivators were said 'to delve' their land, but we do not know what implement they used. *Old Statistical Account*, Vol. III. p. 541.
[2] In 'Tolsta bho Thuath' there are anecdotes in which the women did so (*Stornoway Gazette*, 5.8.51). For general account see Iain Whitaker, 'The Harrow in Scotland', *Scottish Studies*, Vol. III, Part 2, especially pp. 150, 158–9. For illustration of a primitive triangular harrow see *Scottish Studies*, Vol. III, Part 1, Plate II.

of barley cut in Tiree since the beginning of the world'.[1] The cattle were thus deprived of one of the few sources of winter feeding and the soil of the humus from the decaying roots. The same practice was common on the estates of MacDonald of Sleat and in Lewis.[2] But the corn was generally sheared with the hook or sickle. Sometimes toothed sickles were used in the old days[3] but those I have come across were of the ordinary type with rather narrow blades (see Fig. 7D). The work of bending down to cut armfuls of the corn must have been most toilful and a longer stubble was left than when the scythe is used. The hungry beasts on the stubbles must have been thankful for this. The sheaves were smaller than those cut with the scythe. Shearing was a communal activity on the joint farms and on the tacksmen's holdings where the sub-tenants were obliged to give so many days to shearing and leading the corn. The women made the sheaves and stooked them and sometimes did the actual cutting. To lighten their work they sang. Burt described how 'they all keep time together, by several barbarous Tones of the Voice; and stoop and rise together as regularly as a Rank of Soldiers when they ground their Arms. Sometimes they are incited to their Work by the Sound of a Bagpipe; and by either of them they proceed with great Alacrity, it being disgraceful for anyone to be out of Time with the Sickle.'[4] Miss Frances Tolmie collected a reaping song in Skye in which women represented a MacLeod and a MacDonald, clans whose old rivalries have by no means passed from present-day memory, and they 'flyted' each other with a rousing chorus. This song was said to work the women up to a frenzy of activity.[5]

In Sinclair's list of East Coast implements was a wooden corn fork. A few specimens survive. That such a clumsy and easily broken implement should be used for the exacting and arduous

[1]Report by Duncan Forbes to the Duke of Argyll, printed in the *Crofters Commission, 1884*, p. 382.
[2]Report among Forfeited Estate Papers (Sleat). H.M. Register House, Edinburgh. For further details see p. 112.
[3]One was exhibited at an exhibition at Inverness in 1931.
[4]E. Burt, *Letters*, Vol. II, p. 149.
[5]Printed in *Journal of Folk Song Society*, Vol. IV (1910–12). See also John Leyden, *Journal of a Tour in the Highlands and Islands of Scotland* (1820), p. 93. He said singing at reaping had gone out in the more accessible parts of the Highlands, but likened it to the screaming of sea-gulls.

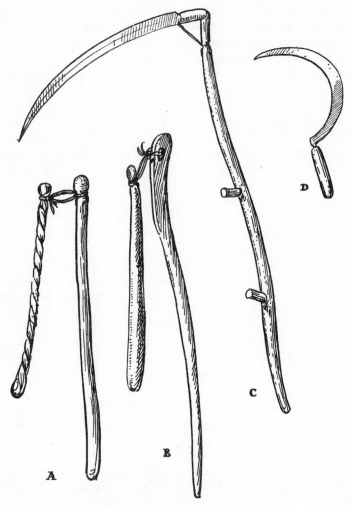

FIG. 7. Ancient harvesting and threshing implements. (A) Island flail. (B) Mainland flail. (C) Scythe with single sned. (D) Sickle.

work of pitching the sheaves on to the stack shows how precious was iron even in the comparatively flourishing parts of the Highlands. The width between the two prongs was said to be 5 in., which was supposed to be the width of a sheaf, and in the Central

108

and Eastern Highlands the 'birley men', the men chosen to adjust the complicated transactions of the joint farms, were expected to use it to see that the workers did not make their sheaves too small.[1]

The sickle gradually gave place to the scythe. Although I came across one scythe with one long straight sned with two grips like that illustrated by Professor Estyn Evans, who said that it was the one preferred in Ireland[2] (see Fig. 7C), that commonly used in the Highlands in the old days had a single sned with a pronounced curve. Nowadays a scythe with a shorter, double sned is used. Scythe blades were not a local or even a Scots manufacture although the sneds are made by Lowland firms.

Not a hundred years ago it was usual for a team of three to work with a scythe; a man with the scythe and two workers, generally women, one of whom laid the corn in bundles and twisted the bands and the other who bound the sheaves and stooked them. The bands consisted of two handfuls of cornstalks the tops of which were knotted together. The bundle of corn was laid across them and the lower ends of the band were crossed and tucked under each other. As a tyro I found the job very hard on the skin of the wrists and forearms! To stook the corn a couple of sheaves were plumped down on end and leaning against each other and three more pairs were added to make a stook of eight sheaves. As in so many seemingly simple agricultural operations, considerable knack is required to make the sheaves stand up firmly. On the West Coast and the Islands the sheaves often have a second band fastened high up round the ears of corn. Reaping with the scythe continued to be a communal activity by neighbouring crofters or the whole staff of a larger farm. The line of reapers, swinging their scythes in wide rhythmic sweeps, advanced in echelon, each with his assistants behind him.

The scythe is still, of course, used for cutting rough patches of grass or weeds and also, only too often, to cut the corn itself when autumn wind and rain has laid patches of it and mechanical means of reaping are not possible. There is great beauty in the measured

[1] I. F. Grant, *Old Highland Farm*, p. 53. For fuller details of the birley men see Chapter VI.

[2] Professor E. Evans, *Irish Folk Ways*, p. 156.

109

swing of a scythe and considerable skill in shearing the crop close to the ground. The long-drawn-out swish of the blade as the darker herbage topples before it, leaving a pale green track, is a most satisfying sound.

By the second half of the nineteenth century the clatter of the horse-drawn mechanical reaper was being heard upon more and more Highland farms, working round and round the lessening patch of standing corn. At first the machine was followed by a train of workers who bound as well as stooked the corn. Binders have now, of course, long been in use and all but the smallest arable holdings are equipped with them. Since about 1940 the tractor has tended more and more to take the place of the horses and, on large farms, the combination harvester carries the work on to yet a farther stage.[1]

Highland cornstacks are round with a conical top. This is evidently the traditional shape in Scotland because they so appeared in old engravings. In the Braes of Angus, a district with easily worked stone, the stacks are built on six 'stackle stones'. These consist of dressed round stones of about 2 ft. in diameter, set on squared plinths about 2 ft. high, the whole effect being like angular toadstools (see Fig. 8). The object is to keep the base of the stack dry and ventilated and to prevent attacks by rats. These stackle stones are very like the straddle stones of the Cotswolds which served the same purpose.

FIG. 8. Stachle stone.

In the Highlands, as in most other countries, the harvest, the supreme moment in the agriculturist's year, was observed by special rites going back, as Sir James Frazer in *The Golden Bough* has pointed out, to ancient pre-Christian beliefs. The Spirit of the Corn was symbolized by the first or the last sheaf to be cut; observances varied. In some districts, especially in the southwest, the first sheaf to be reaped was called the Maiden. Some-

[1]For disappearance of horses and increase in mechanization see also Chapter IV.

times the privilege of cutting it was given to a chosen girl, and
the sheaf or a few ears of it were dressed up or ornamented. It
was later given to the plough-horses in spring. On the other hand,
the cutting of the last sheaf, which was known as the *Cailleach* or
Old Woman, was to be avoided. This belief was held in most of
the Western Isles and parts of Argyllshire. Reaping or shearing,
to use the old-fashioned word, with the sickle was a communal
affair and each reaper tried not to be left to cut the last sheaf. To
do so was considered to be of ill-omen as well as a disgrace. If,
however, a neighbouring group was still at work, the last sheaf
could be passed on to them. The *Cailleach*, like the Maiden, was
generally given to the horses when they began the spring ploughing. In some districts there were both Maidens and Old Women
and occasionally one or other of them was cut by all the reapers
throwing their sickles.[1] In Easter Ross the last sheaf was called
the *claidheag*, evidently a variant of or perhaps the original of the
Klyock sheaf of the eastern Lowlands.[2]

These old harvest beliefs are not yet forgotten. In Barra the
disgrace of reaping the *Cailleach* is still remembered but there
'little private *cailleachs*' were made voluntarily and kept till next
spring. In Skye people have told me that they can remember the
*Cailleach*, the last sheaf reaped on a farm or croft, being passed on
to any neighbour who was still reaping as a reproach but that,
sometimes, the last sheaf to be built into a stack was carefully
arranged at the very top and was called the *Cailleach* and was
thought to protect it.

In the old days the late-ripening grain was apt to be still damp
when it was harvested and it was also liable to smut so that kilns
had to be built for drying it. The sheaves or threshed grain were
dried over a fire of peat. I have seen the remains of kilns in the
outer Islands. The fire was built to one side of a building and the
heat conveyed by a sort of horizontal flue to the other under a
platform of sticks and lathes on which the corn was laid. The process is said to have taken about twelve hours while the corn was
turned several times to ensure even drying.[3]

[1]M. MacLeod Banks, *Calendar Customs of Scotland*, pp. 68, 69  70, 71, 72, 73, 75,
77. Sir James Frazer, *The Golden Bough*, p. 403.
[2]M. Banks, *Calendar Customs of Scotland*, p. 65. Mrs. Banks also describes other
practices, but I have not found reference to them in the Highlands.
[3]For good account see W. M. Findlay, *Oats*, p. 168.

A great deal of tradition was connected with these drying kilns. The fire there was sometimes alluded to as *Aingeal* instead of by the commoner word *Teine* because, as an old man told Father Allan MacDonald, fire was a dangerous thing, especially in a kiln, and if he called it *teine* it might put the kiln in a blaze, and therefore he also always blessed it.[1] To what a remote past does such an idea carry us! The kiln sometimes played a part in the divination rites of Hallowe'en and a girl would throw the end of a rope over it and ask who held the other end. Her future husband was supposed to answer.[2] We know from a good many clan anecdotes that the kiln was a convenient place in which to accommodate surplus visitors. For instance, Angus Og, son of the last Lord of the Isles, gave mortal offence to Kenneth, son of Mackenzie of Kintail, by putting him and his followers in the kiln when he came to visit him.

After reaping, the grain must be threshed. This operation and that of separating the kernel from the husk has followed a long process of change and variation. The wasteful system of pulling the corn up by the roots (see p. 107) was generally followed by burning off the husk. This was known as graddaning. Martin Martin, writing of the seventeenth century, says 'A woman, sitting down, takes a handful of corn, holding it by the stalks in her left hand, and then sets fire to the ears, which are presently in a flame; she has a stick in her right hand . . . beating off the grain at the very instant when the husk is quite burnt, for if she miss that she must use the kiln. The corn may be so dressed, winnowed, ground and baked within an hour after reaping from the ground.'[3] The meal was said to have a distinctive flavour which some people described as delicious but it was less saleable. Rents in kind on the estate of Macdonald of Sleat in Skye were said, in 1720, to be less valuable because of this practice.[4]

As a rule, however, the grain was threshed and winnowed.

[1] The word *Aingeal* was also occasionally used for the household fire Father Allan MacDonald, *Gaelic Words of South Uist and Eriskay*, ed. by J. L. Campbell, p. 22.

[2] M. F. Shaw, *Folk-Song and Folk-Lore in South Uist*, p. 237. In a Lewis Tale a girl who adventured in this form of divination was answered by an icy voice which said 'I am Death'. The girl rushed out shrieking and died soon after. N. Morrison, *Mythology and Folk Lore of Lewis*, p. 24.

[3] M. Martin, *Western Islands*, p. 244.

[4] Forfeited Estate Papers (Sleat), H.M. Register House, Edinburgh.

Kintail is a wet district and much shut in by the precipitous hill slopes rising straight from the sea-lochs and this was probably the reason why special arrangements were made to ensure ventilation in the threshing barns there. Panels of coarse wicker-work were built into the sides of the humbler barns but, in finer specimens, the whole of the sides were made of wickerwork. There is, or there used to be, a good example of such a barn just below the road between Dornie and Kyle of Lochalsh. To thresh the corn the sheaves were loosened and laid in a row and beaten by a flail, an instrument consisting of two pieces of wood joined by a leather thong. It takes some skill to whirl the longer staff so that the swiple, or striking part, hits the corn with a thump and not the thresher's head!

Simple as the flail looks it is one of the most interesting of the old Highland implements. It is still occasionally to be seen. In out-of-the-way places, at least, it is still used for its legitimate office of beating out corn or turnip seed required for sowing, but in more sophisticated districts an old flail is occasionally brought from its last resting-place in the rafters of the barn by some spring-cleaning housewife to beat the rugs which it does to admiration. There are two types of such flails. I used to collect them and I found that the ones found in the Central and Eastern Highlands, the districts in which Gaelic place-names are pre-dominant—but also of course those where there was a wider choice of timber—the staff of the flail was made of ash-wood carefully shaped and smoothed with a slightly bent end with a hole through the top of it through which the sheep-skin thong that fastened the two pieces of the flail together was threaded. The swiple or striker was of hazel-wood with the bark left on to prevent it from splitting. The thong, fastening it to the staff was secured by a bit of sheep-skin tied over the end. The staff was at least a third or more longer than the swiple (see Fig. 7B). In the Islands, on the other hand, the two pieces were of almost equal length. They were made of any kind of wood and indeed some-times the swiple was made of a short length of thick rope; this was generally used for threshing oats. The sheep-skin thong that connected the two pieces of the flail was held in place by being looped round grooves cut round the ends of the swiple and staff (see Fig. 7A). Thus, in this simple implement, live on traditional forms dating from the times when the Gael and the Norsemen contested for the ownership of the Highlands. (It may be noted that in Lowland districts a different method of fastening the two pieces of the flail is found.) Although the use of the flail lingered on on small holdings, on larger farms in the nineteenth century more elaborate methods of threshing were introduced. On many older farms the flat round platform where a couple of horses went round and round working a simple form of mill can be traced. In Perthshire, especially, a rounded extension built to the steading often contains this horse-drawn mill, and on still larger farms water-driven machinery was used. But in the flatter parts of the country itinerant threshing mills, drawn by traction engines, went round the country.

When the grain had been threshed the most primitive way of getting rid of the husks was by winnowing. The operation was performed on a hillock or between the doors in the barn. The grain was tossed up from a wecht or *crerar* so that the wind blew away the chaff. The wecht was a home-made implement made of thin wood or a rod bent into a circle and covered with a calf-skin. A deeper wecht, more carefully made and with holes pierced through the skin by means of a hot iron, was used for separating the sids from the oatmeal after grinding. I had one of these made on a small farm in Strathdearn with a very beautiful pattern of holes. It had been carefully mended. Wechts were used in two forms of divination. At Hallowe'en an intrepid girl going into the barn at midnight carefully leaving the doors open and 'winnowing a wecht of nothing' might ask and be told the name of her future husband by a Something passing behind her, and a wecht swinging from a pair of sheds by its swaying might answer questions, but in both cases the power invoked was more than questionable and the procedure was liable to ecclesiastical censure. In Arran, in 1709, a woman, had up before the local Kirk Session, admitted that she used a riddle for discovering a thief, and 'confessed that she did say "by Peter, by Paul, it was such a person" and that the riddle turned when the name of the thief was mentioned. When it was pointed out to her that, if the riddle was not turned by herself or by the woman who held the other side of it "it behoved to be either God or the devil and she replied that she did not think it was God and she hoped it was not the devil".'

114

. . . She was condemned to make public repentance on three Sundays in church and referred to the civil authorities to be punished 'either corporally or pecuniarily'.[1] From the end of the eighteenth century mechanical 'fanners' came into use on the farms, but the number of wechts still to be found among the lumber on crofts shows that the older method lasted for a long time.

The actual grinding of the grain has a long history of development. The earliest, prehistoric, method of grinding was by a 'saddle quern', a hollowed stone in which the husk was rubbed off by means of a shaped stone[2] (see Fig. 9A). The circular quern

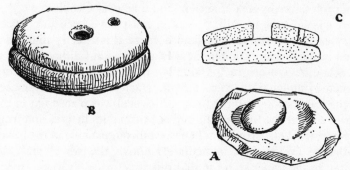

FIG. 9. Querns. (A) Prehistoric. (B) Rotary. (C) Section of rotary.

(see Fig. 9B) is generally said to have been introduced into Britain by the Romans. In Gaelic it is called a *Brath*. It consists of two flat, round stones with a hole in the middle of the upper one into which the grain to be ground was poured (see Fig. 9C). A hole, sometimes two holes, in the upper stone received pegs by which it was turned. In the old days the woman, or two women, who worked the quern squatted on the ground but later on it was generally placed upon a shelf. In a well-made quern the grinding faces of the stones were slightly slanted from the middle to the rim. So late as 1876 'thousands' of querns were still said to be in

[1] *Old Statistical Account*, Vol. V., p. 58.
[2] Miss Goodrich Freer, who visited Eriskay at the end of the nineteenth century saw grain being bruised in a very similar stone by means of a mallet and was told that the implement was called a 'cnotag', the Gaelic term for a 'knocking stone', but she added that rotary querns were generally used on the Island. A. Goodrich Freer, *The Outer Isles*, p. 199. She illustrates the cnotag, p. 421.

use in the Highlands and the older ones to be much better made.[1] There is certainly a great difference in the workmanship of surviving querns. Grinding was monotonous work and was often done by some poor old woman. It has entirely gone out although I have spoken to a woman who had worked a quern and it was still in use on St. Kilda less than fifty years ago. The words of a sixteenth-century working song for helping the drudgery of grinding have been preserved. The strophic form shows the tentative beginning of the beautiful new metres which, in the seventeenth century, led to an upsurge of poetry by all ranks in the Highlands and which gradually superseded the old, highly stylized metres of the professional poets of ancient and medieval Gaeldom.[2]

A special type of mill, however, must have been introduced very early into the Long Island because it is exactly like those used in the Orkney and Shetland Islands and in Caithness, and is of Scandinavian origin.[3] A simple, drystone building was constructed immediately over a stream which ran through apertures in the foundations and the little mill-wheel was placed flat in the water so that the force of the current turned its flanges and from it a perpendicular iron spindle passed through a hole in the lower millstone (which was immediately above the wheel and was bolted to the upper stone so that this was turned by direct drive. By an ingenious arrangement of levers the stones could be adjusted to grind fine or coarse meal and the grain was trickled into a hole in the upper stone by a wooden hopper. Although such mills have gone out of use a few in Lewis were still in a fair state of preservation a few years ago (see Fig. 10).

In the Eastern and Central Highlands mills are mentioned in early charters and in clan traditions. There is a tale about the struggle for the possession of a mill between Mackintosh and Grant of Rothiemurchus. One finds remains of numbers of them. I found abandoned mill stones of not more than 3 ft. in diameter lying beside a burn in a glen in the Monadh Liath where all the land has long since gone out of cultivation. The remains of mill lades show that such mills were worked by means of an over-shot

[1] A. Mitchell, *The Past in the Present*, pp. 35–38 has a good description. See also T. Garnett, *Tour*, Vol. I, p. 155.

[2] See p. 131.

[3] Such a mill is mentioned in *Kintyre* in the Instructions by the 5th Duke of Argyll to his Chamberlain *c.* 1775. I am indebted to Mr. E. Cregeen for this information.

wheel and not on the Hebridean principle. Mills, evidently of this type, were being built by MacLeod of MacLeod in Skye and Harris in the eighteenth century. The possession of mills was a

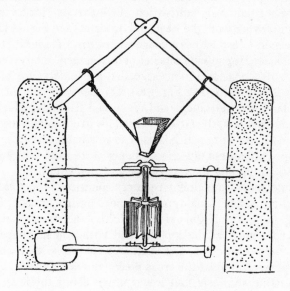

FIG. 10. Clack mill.

valuable source of income to proprietors. Tenants were 'astricted' to grind their corn at the local mill and the use of querns was sometimes forbidden.

To shell the barley it was browned before the fire and then put in a hollowed stone, the *Cnotag* (or *Eornachan*) in some of the Islands), water was added and it was stirred with a stick (the *Maide Cnotaig*) till the kernels were freed from the husks. A cnotag was often the common property of a hamlet. The *Maide Cnotaig* has appeared in many tales, for instance, a witch is said to have flown on one from Moidart to Lochaber.

The cnotag was also sometimes used to bruise whins for feeding the stock in winter. On the larger farms of the East Coast whins were sometimes specially grown for this purpose and they were threshed by means of special flails with swiples of iron or bruised in a primitive mill. On the East Coast instead of the stone cnotag a special iron implement was used for removing the beards of the barley.

Special implements were individually evolved by the people for use in their small-scale cultivation of root crops (for an unusual device for sowing from the Eastern Highlands see Fig. 42D), and I have seen in Wester Ross a board with a row of holes in it which an old man used for sowing pinches of turnip seed. A large wooden dibbler with a peg for a footrest, called a *Pleadhag*, for planting potatoes is still used (see Fig. 6E). On the western sides of the Long Island, on the sandy land reclaimed from the Machair, a special kind of hook, the *Grocan* is used for grubbing up the tatties or gathering sea-ware which is used as a valuable fertilizer on the fields. Special baskets of various shapes were used for gathering the tubers or holding them when they were planted.

Yet one more implement requires mention—the *Cabar Lar* or flaughter spade (analogous to the English breast plough) (see Fig. 6C). The Highland form of this consists of a long shaft with a cross piece at the top end and with a heart-shaped iron blade at the bottom end. The shaft was curved so that when the worker pressed against the cross piece (not with his chest as the English name suggests, but lower down about the level of his tummy), the blade entered the ground almost horizontally so that a layer of turf was peeled off. The Baron Courts constantly fulminated against this habit of skimming off the turf because of its ruinous effect on the soil.[1] But turf was used for making dykes, for the inner layer of the roofs of the houses, for a considerable part of the walls of the smaller houses and outbuildings and, after burning, for adding to the manure heap. The flaughter spade was also used for preparing the peat faces for cutting. For this last purpose the spade is now used and the flaughter has become obsolete, but not very long ago to judge by the numbers of the blades that can still be picked up.

The narrative of how one agricultural implement after another was superseded by something that was more efficient gives a

[1]The best Jacobite commander in the 1715 Rising, Brigadier Mackintosh, while a prisoner in Edinburgh Castle, wrote *An Essay on Ways and Means for Enclosing and Fallowing* (1729) under the pseudonym of 'A Lover of his Country' and has much to say of the 'fearful Havock and Ruin of our best Meadow Ground' wrought by the flaughter spade, p. 56–57.

general idea of the sequence of the changes that have taken place in Highland agriculture, but it does not tell quite all the story. The changes in the lay-out of the holdings show the effects of the great innovations of the Agricultural Revolution.[1] Another great mutation is now going on, and although in this chapter and in the section of Chapter IV dealing with horses, the present fundamental change in the motive power employed has been mentioned again and again, its effects are not writ large on the face of the land. They have largely been conservative, in enabling the decreasing and often ageing labour force available in the Highlands to maintain the tillage of the land. The greater speed of machines, all important in beating the changeable weather at critical moments, and their introduction is a welcome change to most Highlanders because they are generally mechanically minded, and on the whole they do not have the same long tradition of high skill in arable farming that one finds in the predominantly corn-growing districts. As pastoralists they watched their grazing livestock collect their own foodstuffs! Since the beginning of the Second World War the use of the tractor and of mechanical power for a vast variety of agricultural operations, ploughing, reaping, draining, etc. has spread over the Highlands with great speed, not only to the larger farms but to quite small holdings. It has been estimated that that maid-of-all-work, the farm tractor, is not beyond the means of a crofter and a suitable model might cost about £600[2] and in Lewis alone, at the present time, there are 103 cultivators of the tractor type.[3] The machines for specialized purposes can be hired and so serve a comparatively wide district. One finds mechanization in remote, upland straths of the mainland and on Skye, Mull and most of the islands.[4]

[1]See Chapter III.

[2]*Report of the Commission of Enquiry into Crofting Conditions, 1954*, p. 68.

[3]Information given by Dr. D. MacDonald of Gisla.

[4]The number of farm tractors in Scotland increased from 6,250 in 1939 to 20,518 in 1944, *Scotland's Marginal Farms*, 1947, p. 47. Since then, in the Highland Counties of Inverness, Argyll, Sutherland and Ross and Cromarty the increase has been from 882 to 4,887. Between 1944 and 1959 the total increase in mechanical appliances in these counties and also in the Orkney and Shetland Islands (the district known as the 'Crofting Counties') was from 10,726 to 28,825. After tractors the greatest increases were in electric motors and disk harrows. Information kindly supplied by Mr. J. S. Gibson, Secretary to the Advisory Panel to the Highlands and Mr. O. J. Beilby of the Department of Agriculture.

Another change in the management of the land has taken place. In the old days manure and, in districts near the sea, seaweed, were the home-produced fertilizers. Nowadays the laborious process of gathering and spreading the seaweed to let it decay has almost gone out and chemical fertilizers have become available to supplement the manure and for wider uses. The sight of a man throwing even handfuls of fertilizer as if sowing broadcast, or its distribution by mechanical means and of the film of grey powder on the soil are significant signs. For in the general picture of Highland folk ways the use of these imported 'artificials' and the duffusion of the knowledge of how to use them is a mark of the change from isolated farming for subsistence to farming for the market and as one small mesh in the great modern economic network that brings world supplies to the service of the Highland farms and which involves the people who work them in the general movement of prices, a factor as wholly outside their control and sometimes as frustrating to their efforts as the vagaries of Highland weather.

# VI

## THE PEOPLE WHO LIVED
## ON THE LAND

UNDER the clan system folk life in the Highlands had not
consisted of a separate peasant culture. On the contrary,
all ranks of Highland society had been closely co-ordinated. In
material matters, while the clans had flourished, there had been
a strong sense of obligation between all ranks. As Mr. Gray
points out, although poverty was the common lot, the individual
had been shielded 'against the sharpest ravages of misfortune'.[1]
During the eighteenth century, in spite of the great changes that
were taking place, the dissolution of the old interdependence had
been gradual among those clans that were fortunate in the circumstances of their chiefs. The ability of some of the chiefs during
the great wars at the end of the eighteenth century, to raise regiments on their estates that were mainly officered by members of
the old cadet families—although economic conditions had something to do with it—is an illustration of a chief's surviving powers
to call out a following.[2]

It had been 'the use and wont' among Highland chiefs to remit
their tenants' rents in bad years[3] and to supply them with grain

[1]M. Gray, *Highland Economy*, p. 21.

[2]Between 1757 and 1778 nine line regiments were twice raised in this way. When
war again broke out with France in 1783, leading to the great contest with Napoleon,
many chiefs once more volunteered to raise regiments and by 1793–4 eight Highland
Regiments of the Line, besides many more Fencible and Militia battalions were
raised. A. R. Murray, *History of the Scottish Regiments in the British Army*, pp.
245–58. I. M. Scobie, *An Old Highland Fencible Company*, pp. 4, 6. See also the
Appendix to Maj.-Gen. D. Stewart, *Manners of the Highlanders*.

[3]Burt said that this averaged about a fifth of their entire revenues, *Letters*, Vol. II,
p. 160.

in times of famine.[1] On some estates, such as Breadalbane, Glen Urquhart and Strathspey, the landlords made great efforts to adjust changing conditions for the benefit of the lesser folk.[2] Moreover, even with new landlords, many of the crofters of the west were left for years upon years on their holdings with little hope of paying off arrears of rent and repayment for foodstuffs.[3]

Nevertheless, of the three main classes in Highland society (the chiefs, the cadets or tacksmen, and the sub- or joint tenants and cottars),[4] most of the chiefs or lairds were responding to the 'drain south' by the eighteenth century. Their close participation in and support of the old culture of the Gael was ending and the family seanachies, harpers, and, lastly the pipers were no longer employed. Deeply involved in debt more and more of them had to sell their land.

The gentlemen of the clan, the descendants of collaterals of the chiefs, who had acted as lieutenants in the days of clan warfare and who had obtained leases (tacks) of land and were therefore generally known as tacksmen, retained their close links with the land and the people a little longer. Their younger sons entered the professions or took military service and they were well educated and bi-lingual. Boswell and Johnson have left in their journals of their tour to the Hebrides accounts of the piping, fiddling and the singing of Gaelic songs in the tacksmen's houses in Skye.[5] Boswell's account of his visit to MacKinnon of Corriechattachan gives a vivid picture of the simplicity, good-breeding and homely hospitality of a tacksman and there are many other descriptions.[6]

The tacksmen were much concerned in the cattle droving trade. Bishop Forbes has a delightful picture of the younger sons of

[1]M. Gray, *Highland Economy*, p. 17. The papers at Dunvegan Castle give details of how these and other services were continued during the eighteenth century.

[2]M. MacArthur, *Lochtayside*, p. lxxviii; W. MacKay, *Glen Urquhart*, p. 443; Sir W. Fraser, *Chiefs of Grant*, Vol. I, pp. 447, 459.

[3]M. Gray, *Highland Economy*, pp. 194, 220–1.

[4]For a nineteenth century account of these three classes see 'Anonymous Report to James VI' printed as an Appendix to W. F. Skene, *Celtic Scotland*, Vol. III.

[5]A much finer example is the *Fernaig MSS.*, a collection of poems made by a group of small lairds and tacksmen of the seventeenth century notable for the high quality of the verse and the spiritual outlook. Printed by A. Cameron, *Reliquiae Celticae*, Vol. I.

[6]Those by Mrs. Smith, *née* Miss Grant of Rothiemurchus, *Memoirs of a Highland Lady* (henceforth noted as *Memoirs of a Highland Lady*), are outstanding. See also Bishop R. Forbes' *Journals*, p. 297.

tacksmen spending the night with their cattle as they drove them south.[1] But otherwise most of them were not very active farmers. They sublet a large part of their land and cultivated the farm that they kept in their own hands partly by means of the labour dues of their sub-tenants and cottars,[2] and after the newer ideas of agricultural organization came into vogue, they tended to bear a bad name.[3] The account book of a forebear of my own shows that a well-intentioned tacksman fulfilled useful services for the small tenants, importing seed corn and also other grain in bad years and retailing it at cost price, buying the smaller men's beasts for inclusion in the droves of cattle sent to the trysts, organizing such services as the employment of the fox-hunter, acting as a useful and influential friend.[4]

By the end of the eighteenth century the old families of tacksmen were disappearing all over the Highlands. Like the lairds, they were now coming into contact with the south, their means were becoming insufficient to keep up contemporary standards of living and they nearly all plunged into debt. At the same time the impecunious lairds were raising their rents. Moreover, more and more opportunities in the Services and in India were becoming open to them. In the south-west and the Eastern and Central Highlands, where the lairds were re-arranging their farms, these gentlemen farmers did not fit in and, as their leases ran out they were replaced by professional farmers.[5] Unfortunately, especially in the west, there was sometimes a break with the old traditional tacksmen and large farms were let to incomers who were apt to acquire a very bad name.

[1]Bishop R. Forbes, *Journals*, p. 236.
[2]Cf. a 'Report on Islay' made to the Duke of Argyll in 1776 printed in G. Gregory Smith, *Book of Islay*, p. 470.
[3]For instance, Duncan Forbes, in his report of 1737 to the Duke of Argyll of a visit to Mull and Tiree has not a good word to say for them, printed in *Report of Crofters Commission, 1884*, p. 380, but see also Duke's comments, p. 384. A still severer attack on them, that by George Lane Buchanan in *Travels in the Western Isles*, a book that, because of its sensationalism, has been widely quoted is suspect, because the rev. author was dismissed on account of repeated grossly immoral conduct and the people bringing him to book are the individual tacksmen that he pilloried. See Presbytery Records, N. Uist. J. Walker, *Economical History of the Hebrides*, p. 180, writing of the same districts at about the same time has a different account of them.
[4]I. F. Grant, *Old Highland Farm*, p. 155. Also *The MacLeods*, p. 548.
[5]Clan histories show the various causes of their disappearance. C. F. Fraser Mackintosh, *Minor Septs of Clan Chattan* is a good example.

Although the old type of tacksman has entirely disappeared, something of their influence survives. In collecting for the Museum it was interesting to find in small houses pieces of old and fine furniture that had come down from the old tacksmen, and even more fascinating to see their influence in traces of the great styles of furniture, Queen Anne, Georgian, Regency and others on more crudely made local pieces. This is a concrete example of the close interdependence of classes in the old days that is also responsible for the distinguished manners of Highland country people and their extraordinarily acute social flair, especially among the older people.[1] (See Fig. 11.)

The greatest grievance against the old tacksmen was the obligation on their dependants to perform labour dues. These were onerous and tending to become more so. They varied: the humblest class of the people, the scallags (west coast term) or farm servants were expected to work for the tacksman four days a week. In return they generally had a bit of corn or potato land, the grazing for one cow at least and her followers, a weekly allowance of meal, food while at work and four pairs of shoes a year and a yearly wage of £1.[2] There was also a considerable number of cottars or acremen, who in return for small pieces of land for cultivation and grazing worked for the tacksman or even the sub-tenants. The sub-tenants themselves were expected to give work with their horses at harvest and in carrying corn to the mill, in ploughing, dunging and labouring the ground, in the cutting and leading of the peats, by performing a specified number of 'long-loads' i.e. a day's journey with a horse on necessary errands and often extras such as help in bringing home a new millstone, repairing a dyke or delivering a load of 'fir candles'.[3] The cutting of peats often lingered on after other services had fallen into disuse. I know of a case where this due was inserted in leases in the second half of the nineteenth century. Labour dues belonged to

[1]Although it has long been obsolete (the latest example I have heard of was in the early eighteenth century), the old Gaelic custom of fosterage, the entrusting by men of position of one of their children to the care of an adherant, is an example of the close connexion between all ranks of society. Stories of the devotion of the foster parents to their 'dalt' are among the most beautiful of Highland tales.

[2]For financial position of nineteenth century cottars see *Crofters Commission, 1884*, 'Minutes of Evidence', Vol. I, p. 111.

[3]I. F. Grant, *Old Highland Farm*, p. 71 for list of labour dues from various sources.

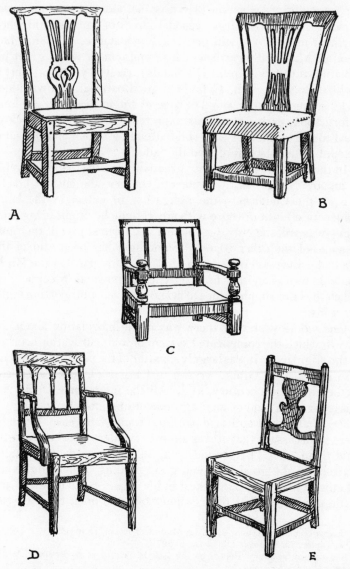

FIG. 11. Chairs of superior quality. Copied by local craftsmen from furniture in current styles.

125

earlier conditions when the primitive methods and implements of agriculture required large seasonal forces of workers and when payment in kind was still general. For instance, in 1686, Mac-Leod of MacLeod's gardener (his employment was a great innovation at that time in the Highlands) received yearly 60 merks, 8 ells of country cloth, 12 bolls of good oatmeal, 2 cows' hides and 2 stones of butter and 2 of cheese[1] and in Braemar, not long before 1869, each farmer was expected to contribute 1 peck of meal to the teacher for each child attending school and the same amount to the blacksmith and the tailor.[2]

In the same way, rents only gradually became mainly payable in money. So late as the sixteenth century, the ancient Gaelic due of 'the Cuddiche'—the obligation to entertain the landholder for a night or more with any retinue he might bring with him—was still the only due in Sleat and formed part of the rents in some of the other islands.[3] Something has been said of the gradual conversion of rents in kind. In many parts of the Highlands there was another form of tenure, known as 'Steel bow' in which the laird supplied the stock and received a proportion of the proceeds.[4]

One would wish that there was more information about the way in which the complicated system of joint cultivation worked in the Highlands. It was largely a matter of the people's own clannish spirit. Mrs. Grant, writing of Laggan (Upper Badenoch) in the eighteenth century, said, 'All the intercourse of life was carried on by a kind of tacit agreement and interchange of good offices that would appear extravagant anywhere else. Yet here were so necessary that it was almost considered a crime to withhold them. . . . The ground being all unenclosed, it depended entirely on the good faith and good herding of his neighbour, whether a man ever put a sheaf in his barn. . . .' 'The sheep and cattle too, wandering promiscuously on the hills, the integrity

[1]The agreement is preserved in the Muniment Room, Dunvegan.
[2]E. Taylor, *The Braemar Highlands*, p. 327.
[3]See sixteenth-century 'Report on the Islands' printed as Appendix to W. F. Skene, *Celtic Scotland*, Vol. III.
[4]For a steel-bow contract see Mackay, MacNeill of Carskey, p. 101. It was an ancient Lowland form of tenure, see *Liber de Calchu*, Vol. I, p. xxxi. Cosmo Innes, *Scotch Legal Antiquities*, p. 265. I have come across allusions to it in Ross-shire, Central Perthshire and Kintyre.

of a man's neighbour was all that he had to depend on for their return.'[1]

In the Eastern and Central Highlands, as in the Lowlands, a system of 'birleymen' or 'Proofmen' had grown up. The word has been derived from 'Byrlawman', i.e. chosen by common consent.[2] He was jointly chosen by the people of a joint farm and by the laird or tacksman to arbitrate on all questions regarding the assessment for improvements, the amount of a 'stent' to be performed as a labour due, the value of unthreshed corn, etc. and to dispute his decision was considered to be disgraceful in the highest degree.[3] Of course when the holdings were reorganized the need for birleymen ended.

In the west there are most interesting survivals. Under the old Pictish Kingdom, the rulers of the seven provinces were called *Mormaers*. In the feudalized Scotland of the Middle Ages the official in charge of a district of an estate was known as the Maer.[4] On the crofter townships of the west, in the middle of the eighteenth century there was a dual method of control. The ground officer, an official appointed by the factor, was called the *Maor Gruinnd*. There was also the Constable, an official elected by and representing the crofters in all dealings with the factor, and who also organized the life of the community—marking out new peat banks and the joint shares of land the people drew lots for under the old system of run-rig, supervising the peat roads and the work of the communal shepherd and the management of the stock. Carmichael describes the solemn ceremony in which the newly elected constable swore to be true to his trust.[5] This organization is very like that described by M. Martin when he

[1]Mrs. Grant, *Superstitions of the Highlanders*, p. 27. Surviving records of the Baron Courts of Glenurchy, printed in the *Black Book of Taymouth*, show that all was sometimes far from peace among the joint tenants and the Land Court at the present day is often called upon to deal with the squabbles of neighbouring crofters.

[2]*Northern Notes and Queries*, Vol. VII, p. 82.

[3]Cosmo Innes, *Scotch Legal Antiquities*, p. 524. For an example of an important arbitration made by birleymen see I. F. Grant, *Old Highland Farm*, p. 113.

[4]The accounts submitted by these officials appear not only on Crown land but on other estates that had come temporarily into the King's hands. See earlier volumes of *Exchequer Rolls*. These officials survived in the Earldom of Moray down to the sixteenth century. E. Dunbar, *Documents relating to the Earldom of Moray*, has many mentions of them.

[5]Evidence by A. Carmichael, *Crofters Commission, 1884*, pp. 214, 452-6. As the word Maor appears in some place-names it would seem to be old.

visited St. Kilda in 1697. The proprietor, MacLeod of MacLeod, appointed a steward for the Island, who visited it yearly and besides other perquisites, had to be maintained by the inhabitants during his stay, with the retinue that he brought with him (a survival of the due of *cuddiche*), but there was also 'an officer', chosen by the people, who 'is obliged always to dispute with the steward for what is due to any of them' until he gains his point or puts the steward into a passion. The officer also had the right to go to MacLeod himself to complain against the steward 'upon extraordinary occasions'.[1] Martin, however, described this arrangement as if it were exceptional, so that it is interesting to find something resembling it on the nineteenth century Hebridean townships, many of which were formed after the great changes of the late eighteenth century. The Constable is still recognized in the regulations for crofter townships made under present-day crofting legislation, and there is generally another, modern, communal official, the secretary to a township, who does the filling-up of forms and the book-keeping under the modern system of Government grants. It is unfortunate that the old spirit of working in close association has not developed into any successful co-operative enterprises like those that are such a feature of Danish rural economy.

Under the old agricultural system the people had a life of alternating hard work and of comparative leisure. Not until the weather permitted it in the spring was the land laboriously tilled and the seed sown and harrowed in. This would not be finished till the end of May. In summer the peats, upon which the community depended for their fuel, had to be cut, dried and led and meanwhile, early in May, the cattle had been sent up to the shielings (*airidhean*). The huts were put in order, there was a simple feast and a blessing was invoked. Then many of the girls and women, with lads for herding, were left to take care of the cattle and make the supplies of cheese and butter upon which the people so much depended. Descriptions of life at the shielings have a particular charm.[2] In my young days old people in the Central

[1] M. Martin, *The Western Islands* (1934 Edition), p. 449.

[2] A. Carmichael gave a description of the poetry of shieling life in the Roman Catholic Islands of Barra and South Uist, *Crofters Report, 1884*, pp. 469–72. The movingly simple piety of life on the shielings of Lewis is described in 'Tolsta bho Thuath', *Stornoway Gazette*, 24.8.51.

Highlands could still recall hearing their parents tell of the bustle when the start was made 'for the Glen'. Blankets, foodstuffs, churns and dishes were loaded onto carts with old women and spinning wheels set on top of them and with lowing of cattle and barking of dogs, more than half the community would set off up the rough track that wound over the shoulder of the hill for their summer sojourn at the shielings.[1] The minister's wife at Laggan described how she saw the people going up, driving their cattle before them: 'The people looked so glad and contented for they rejoice at going up, but by the time that the cattle had eaten all the grass and the time arrives that they dare no longer shoot or fish, they find their home a better place, and return with almost as much alacrity as they went.'[2]

When they came down at the end of July there was constant herding until the late-ripening grain could be harvested and to get it in before the weather broke required the entire efforts of the community. During the winter a time of agricultural stagnation set in, filled with many indoor jobs and also by the people's own wonderful resources for mental recreation.

The poverty of the people and the primitive conditions under which they carried on their agriculture and other occupations can be paralleled elsewhere. But these are not the heritage which is still a cause of pride to Highland folk. The small simply-built houses and the unproductive land was the background to a mental life, proud, vigorous and beautiful, which has existed in continuity from the days of the supremacy of the lordly Gaelic society. No attempt to describe the more material setting of the folk-life of the Highlands can ignore the intellectual life of the people—impossible though it is to do justice to it in a short space.

Nearly every visitor to the Highlands was equally struck by the poverty and simplicity of the people's lives and by the distinction of their bearing, their beautiful manners and their courtesy to each other. One of the earlier ones wrote in 1688: 'There appeared in all their actions a certain generous air of freedom and contempt for those trifles, luxury and ambition, which we so servilely creep after. They bound their appetites by their necessities, and their happiness consists, not in having much

[1] In more primitive times and districts everything had to be carried.
[2] Mrs. Grant, *Letters from the Mountains*, p. 136.

but in wanting little.'[1] Burt noticed a 'kind of stateliness in the midst of their poverty'.[2] He sneered at the family pride of lesser folk and said that they were 'all genealogists'.[3] But Miss Grant of Rothiemurchus, describing how everyone danced together at her father's harvest feast added . . .'a vein of good breeding ran through all ranks, influencing their manners and rendering the intercourse of all most agreeable'.[4] A knowledge of their own pedigree and of the family ramifications of all their neighbours is still very usual and characteristic of Highland country people.

The country people had, and to some extent in the remoter districts still have, a wealth of stories and traditions handed down by practised story-tellers, a few of whom have survived the reading of cheap print, so deadly to oral recitation, and even the disembodied voice of the wireless.[5] These tales are the inheritance from many phases in the Highlanders' past. There are the strange wonder tales—the *Ursgeulan*—some of which, by their strong affinities with the early stories of other peoples, show that they have evidently had their origins from some central source and spread by word of mouth in the days when the peoples of Europe were young.[6]

The noble epics of ancient Gaeldom, conceived and polished when Erin was a kingdom with a magnificent flowering of the arts, were the delight of the Highland society that flourished during the Lordship of the Isles and although the Feinné Cycle gained in popularity compared to the Ultonian Cycle, these stories formed the everyday background of the people's lives.

---

[1]W. Sacheverell, *Account of the Isles of Man with a voyage to Icolmkill*, pub. Manx Society, Vol. I, p. 98. See also a Frenchman Louis Simond, *Journal of a Tour and Residence in Great Britain during the years 1810–1811*, p. 398.

[2]Burt, *Letters*, Vol. II, p. 26.

[3]Burt, Ibid, Vol. I, pp. 69–72.

[4]*Memoirs of a Highland Lady*, p. 196.

[5]A considerable corpus of the old stories has been collected by devoted folk-lorists from the middle of the nineteenth century onwards. One of the earliest of them, J. F. Campbell of Islay, inspired a team of workers, including Alexander Carmichael. The work is now being carried on by the School of Scottish Studies.

J. F. Campbell has wonderful word pictures of the homely interior of the home of a practised story-teller and of his spell-bound audience, laughing at the amusing passages, almost moved to tears by the sad ones. J. F. Campbell, *Popular Tales of the Western Highlands*, Vol. II, pp. xxix, xxii.

[6]For instance, there was a Hebridean version of the tale opening *The Arabian Nights*. Father Allan MacDonald, *Gaelic Words*, ed. J. L. Campbell, p. 218.

General Stewart of Garth, writing in the early nineteenth century of his boyhood in Perthshire, described how: 'When a stranger appeared, after the usual compliments, the first question was, *"Bheil dad agad air na Fheinn?"* (Do you know anything of the Feinné?) If the answer was in the affirmative the whole hamlet convened and midnight was usually the hour of separation.'[1] More and more episodes were added to these tales of Finn Mac Coul and the Feinné but the characters of the principals were faithfully preserved although, in later versions, the Feinné became giants. The stories were localized all over the Highlands. Moreover, so shot through were the people's thoughts with these tales that in their own verse allusions were constantly made to the attributes of their characters—to the beauty of Deidre and Grainne and the valour of Cuchullin and Osgar, etc. A Lament for my own great grandfather, written in Badenoch, brings in Ossian and Osgar.[2] Every district also had its own clan traditions and there evidently always were and certainly still are numbers of drily humorous stories about local worthies.

The people were intensely creative. Mrs. Grant wrote of Laggan: 'In every cottage there is a musician and in every hamlet a poet.'[3] This was no figure of speech and behind both their poetry and their music lies their own long history. Till the sixteenth century poetry was written by highly trained professional poets in the elaborate, highly stylized metres of old Ireland. The well-known *Book of the Dean of Lismore*, begun about 1512 by James MacGregor, was a collection of the songs and poetry of 'the strollers', the wandering bards, and the pieces are nearly all in the classical metres; so one must assume that these were widely appreciated.[4] By the seventeenth century the highly skilled trained poets were gradually decreasing[5] and new, simpler and more tuneful and extremely singable metres came into use and there was an upsurge of poetry-making in the High-

[1]Gen. David Stewart, *Manners of the Highlanders*, p. 114.

[2]T. Sinton, *Poetry of Badenoch*, p. 500.

[3]Mrs. Grant, *Letters from the Mountains*, p. 73.

[4]W. J. Watson, *Introduction Scottish Poetry from the Book of the Dean of Lismore*, p. xvii. This collection is localized in Perthshire. The 'Turner Collections' and the 'Fernaig MSS.' pub. in *Reliquae Celticae* are other local collections and suggest the wealth of poetry that once existed.

[5]The old Gaelic script was disappearing more quickly.

lands. These new poets came from every rank in life, the kinsfolk of chiefs and tacksmen, ministers and schoolmasters, a cattleman, a slater, crofters. They included men and women and some, even among the most distinguished poets, were illiterate. They were to be found all over the Highlands. Between 1645 and 1830 there were 130 Highland poets whose work was considered by so great an authority on Highland literature as Professor W. J. Watson to be 'really good and some of it outstanding'. The movement reached its peak in the middle of the eighteenth century and it has not entirely passed away.[1] But unfortunately the Gaelic-speaking local gentry, who were once the patrons of the poets, have long since disappeared. Another of the factors that has depressed the culture of the Gael is that so little of this literary output has been printed. The market for writing on the Highlands, all too limited as it is, is almost confined to works in the *Beurla* (English). Almost no Gaelic prose, apart from a few religious works, has been published and only a fraction of the wealth of local poetry and most of this in very small editions.[2]

Moreover the people had to a high degree the gift of improvising verse. There are many anecdotes about this talent. A story not yet quite forgotten in Strathdearn tells how the Earl of Mar, flying from his defeat at the second Battle of Inverlochy (fought in 1421), wandered starving in the Monadh Liath until a compassionate herdsman gave him some meal and water mixed in the heel of his brogue. Mar declared in verse that it was the best food he had ever tasted.[3] The aptitude survived till the nine-

[1] M. F. Shaw, *Folk Song and Folk Lore in South Uist* (henceforth noted as *Folk Song and Folk Lore*), p. 71 mentioned the names of four living bards in Glendale, South Uist.

[2] A good example is Thomas Sinton's *Poetry of Badenoch*, a well annotated collection coming down to the second half of the nineteenth century. *Orain Chaluim*, which has just been published is a collection of the verse of Malcolm Macaskill, a crofter poet of Bernera who died in 1903. The introduction shows how intimately the poems were associated with the life of the poet's neighbours. It is by Mr. Alick Morrison.

[3] The words are said to be:

> Is math an cocair an t'acras
> Is mairg a ni talcuis air biadh,
> Fuarag eoin a sal mo bhroig
> Am biadh is fhear a fhuair me riamh.

> Hunger is a good cook
> Woe to him that would despise food,
> This barley gruel in my shoe heel
> Is the best I've found in all my time.

teenth century at the Hebridean custom of the 'Luadhadh'[1] of the cloth (fulling it by hand), and part of the fun was the making up on the spur of the moment of couplets about the company and their friends.[2]

In the Highlanders' music also one can trace the influence of a more spacious past. The Highlanders' use of a special form of the bagpipe, the great war pipe, seems to have developed during the sixteenth century. The clans were growing in manpower and required a more resonant martial instrument than the harp or the voice of the poets which had been used of old for the recitation of the *Brosnachadh* (the incitement to battle).[3] The MacCrimmons, hereditary pipers to MacLeod of MacLeod, are credited with evolving the *Ceol Mor* (big music) or *Piobaireachd*, the classical music of the Highland pipes. The playing of the air is followed by a number of variations according to strict rules of composition and the music is very elaborate and stylized. The themes mainly consist of Laments, Gatherings and Salutes. This was the form of composition that was almost universally played down to the nineteenth century,[4] and although for relaxation pipers might play a few lighter compositions, it was considered derogatory to use the pipes for such frivolous purposes as accompanying dancing. Every self-respecting chief in the seventeenth century had his piper, and had been expected to take a discriminating interest in the quality of his playing and such music was evidently appreciated by the country people. MacLeod of MacLeod employed three pipers, one for each of the divisions of his estates.[5]

But meanwhile the playing of the harp lingered on until the end of the seventeenth century while the viol and then the fiddle were coming into wider use all over the Highlands. In Strathspey, during this century, characteristic dance tunes were beginning to be composed for the fiddle and the movement spread to

[1]See M. F. Shaw, *Folk Song and Folk Lore*, p. 6, for survival of custom in Glendale, South Uist.

[2]For a nineteenth century example of witty improvisation see *Orain Chaluim*, p. 16.

[3]A smaller and more sweetly toned bagpipe had long been in use in the Lowlands for recreation by the country people.

[4]Following the suppression of the Rising of '45 the art was in danger of being lost but was then revived.

[5]I. F. Grant, *The MacLeods*, pp. 165, 489–91.

central Perthshire. These Strathspeys are still used for the four-some reel, the most popular Highland dance, and the sound of them will set the feet of any Highland audience tapping to their rhythm. The fiddlers enjoyed the patronage of the lairds and chiefs, some of whom had their family fiddlers, and by the end of the eighteenth century their music became extremely fashionable south of the Border.[1]

In the nineteenth century the music of the pipes underwent a great change. Apart from the competitions organized at the most important Highland Games and the concourse of local pipers who gather at the Games in South Uist, one hears very little of the Piobaireachd nowadays on the pipes, and the art of composing them has been lost. After about 1844 the pipers have mainly played reel and strathspey tunes, slow marches and the quick-steps or Regimental Marches, introduced when pipe-bands took the place of the fifes and drums in Highland Regiments.[2] Some of them, like the well-known *Pibroch of Donald Dhu*, are founded on older tunes. In spite of such changes, in peace and in war, in times of joy and of sorrow, the pipes are still played by Highlanders of all degrees and can grip our emotions like no other kind of music. Playing them, however, like other forms of music, is much curtailed in certain areas where the most austere sects of the Reformed Church have a predominating influence.

Religion plays an important part in the life of the people, and the service of the Presbyterian Church produced a special way of singing the Psalms that in its complexity and elaboration had close analogies to the interlaced patterns, the old poetic metres, the conventions of the piobaireachd and the setts of the Tartans. Although it has almost gone out of use, it may therefore be worth while to say something about it. In parts of Inverness-shire and in Ross and Cromarty and in Sutherland the precentor used to give out, line by line, an elaborated version of certain of the psalm-tunes used in the Church of Scotland for the congregation

[1]W. Forsyth, *In the Shadow of the Cairngorms*, p. 275. M. Martin, *Western Islands*, p. 200. D. W. Dalyell, *Musical Memoirs of Scotland*, pp. 238, 248. J. Stoddart, *Scenery and Manners in Scotland*, Vol. II, p. 5. A. Mackintosh, *History of Strathspeys and Reels*, p. 280.

[2]I. Mackay Scobie, *Pipers and Pipe Music in a Highland Regiment*, p. 1. For much of the information in the foregoing paragraphs I am indebted to Colonel Iain Grant of Rothiemurchus.

to sing after him. On the few occasions when I have heard this complex way of singing I found it extremely difficult to make out the tunes although they were ones familiar to me.[1]

The Highlanders also played on a humbler instrument—the Jew's harp—generally called 'the trump'. The earliest allusion to it that I have met with is in the record of a trial at a Justice Court held at Inveraray in 1677. A certain Donald McIlmichall, vagabond, was accused of stealing a cow and consorting with evil spirits. Donald told the Court that one Sunday evening he had noticed a lighted opening in a hill in Appin, and, on entering, he had seen a crowd of men and women dancing in a place having many lighted candles. He said he did not know who they were but judged them 'not to be worldlie men'. He admitted that he had returned to meet them in various shians (fairy mounds) 'on ilk Sabbath nights and that he played the trumps to them quhen they danced'. To reward him they told him of stolen cattle so that he might claim the 'Tascal Money' (the reward paid to an informer). Poor Donald was found guilty on both charges and hanged.[2] I have heard that a trump, being of metal, had been considered a safe thing to play on entering a fairy mound. I do not know where the trumps were made but I have seen beautifully carved little wooden boxes specially shaped to hold a trump and evidently of local manufacture.

Sometime in the nineteenth century the accordion made its welcome appearance at Highland dances. Known as 'the Box' it admirably renders the rhythm and snap of Scots dance tunes. In addition *Peurt a Bial* (mouth music) was used for dancing.[3]

But, perhaps most outstandingly of all, the Highlanders have expressed themselves in singing. Mrs. Campbell says with authority that thousands of songs still exist in the Hebrides.[4] Some of these songs were working songs created to help the people through laborious tasks, and in those that have come down to us, the rhythms of the toilsome pull at the oar, the jerk of the loom, the drudgery of the quern, the rising crescendo of

[1] J. Mainzer, *The Gaelic Psalm Tunes of Ross-shire* (1884), pp. IX, X, XI. H. E. Campbell, *Highland Church Music*. Trans., Gaelic Society of Inverness, 1924–5, p. 202.
[2] *Highland Papers*, Vol. III, p. 86.
[3] For dancing see Chapter XV.
[4] M. F. Shaw, *Folk Song and Folk Lore*, p. 71.

activity at the Luadhadh of the cloth, still live on. Boswell has the beautiful passage: 'As we came to the shore (Raasay), the music of the rowers was succeeded by that of the reapers.'[1] An English servant, who accompanied his employer to Skye in 1782, wrote scornfully that the people were so underfed that they could not work well but added that they wasted much time 'telling idle tales and singing doggerel rhymes' and that 'all kinds of labour is accompanied with singing: if it is rowing a boat the men sing; if it is reaping the women sing. I think that if they were in the deepest distress they would all join in a chorus'.[2] Besides working songs there were love songs, humourous songs, laments—songs for every occasion.[3] Some of the songs are traditional, handed down and perhaps gradually evolved by many singers. Others are by the greatest Gaelic poets from the seventeenth century onwards.[4] In their older forms, although there was generally a soloist and chorus, the songs were invariably sung in unison. There was no accompaniment. In the eighteenth century we read that when groups sang they often held handkerchiefs between them which they flapped up and down and people whom I have met still remember this custom. Miss Amy Murray, who had the privilege of visiting Father Allan MacDonald on Eriskay, described interesting personal variations in the singing of the songs,[5] but Miss Shaw wrote of how punctilious the people were in teaching the songs rightly.[6] Although singing is far more closely woven into the life of the people of the Hebrides, some of the songs belong to the Highlands as a whole, for instance, *Crodh Chailein* the favourite milking song of the Eastern Highlands is also sung in the Islands.[7]

The Gaelic songs are still sung all over the Highlands but

[1] J. Boswell, *Tour*, p. 131.

[2] J. Barron, *The Northern Highlands in the nineteenth century*, p. 390–1 reprints his diary. Mrs. Murray in *A Useful Guide to the Beauties of Scotland* (1799), p. 365, said that the people's working songs 'seem to invigorate every nerve in their bodies'.

[3] For an example of the wealth of variety of the songs collected in a single locality see M. F. Shaw, *Folk Song and Folk Lore*, p. 7.

[4] A fascinating example is *Coire Cheathaeth* by Duncan Ban MacIntyre in which the air is modelled on the form of the piobaireachd.

[5] Miss A. Murray, *Father Allan's Isle*, p. 87.

[6] See also Miss Broadbent's account of collecting in Moidart *Journal of the Folk Song Society*, Vol. VIII, Part 5, p. 280.

[7] In M. F. Shaw, *Folk Song and Folk Lore*, there is also 'Mackintosh's Lament'.

there are changes. The words used to be considered of great importance and many verses were sung, now the air is the most important thing, few verses are sung and, apart from the chorus, an English translation may be used. Very often the voice is supported by a piano accompaniment and conventionalized renderings of the songs given. There have been fashions in the limited numbers of songs usually sung. Those most popular twenty years ago are quite different to those one generally hears today.[1] Much of this is perhaps inevitable if the songs are to continue to be part of the people's wider living heritage. In 1891 An Comunn Gaidhealach was formed and has organized local and National Mods (very much on the pattern of the Welsh Eisteddfod) and has done a great deal to make good forms of the songs available and known. The Mods enjoy great popularity among the people of the Highlands and there is keen competition.

The idea of *Celtic Gloom*, which we owe to James Macpherson, is as spurious as his 'translations' of the old epics of Gaeldom; there are many light-hearted songs and stories, there was and is much gaiety and conviviality, the reels and country dances go with a rousing swing and the witty retort is and always has been much admired. Nevertheless, in the past there was a strong element of fear in the people's lives. The fairies of the Highlands, politely spoken of as the *Daoine Sith* (Men of Peace), sometimes said to be fallen angels, were generally inimical to the human race. Among their malpractices were the carrying off of new-born babies and replacing them with changelings, and shooting cattle with elf bolts. No good came of dealing with them. In 1845 it could be seriously written in the *New Statistical Account* that a late Principal of Aberdeen University had contributed 'by his benevolent exertions in an eminent degree to the expulsion of fairies from the Highland Hills'.[2] Not only tales of the fairy folk, but also the 'Shians' they lived in can be found all over the Highlands. There were many other unchancy beings. Among them one of the most widely believed in was the Water Horse (*Each Uisge*, Kelpie), who lured people into the piece of water that he haunted and devoured them. He was sticky all over and

[1] M. Macfarlane, *Half a Century of Vocal Gaelic Music*. Trans. of the Gaelic Society of Inverness, 1924–5, p. 253.
[2] *New Statistical Account, Inverness-shire*, p. 82.

anyone who touched him could not withdraw and was inevitably dragged under. There can hardly be a district in the Highlands that has not the haunt of a Kelpie. I met someone whose keeper forcibly tried to prevent a guest from entering a lochan to rescue his spaniel because it was haunted by a Kelpie. The lochan was found to contain a particularly treacherous form of water weed. And I have seen the name of a man in a rent-roll, who, according to another local tale, resisted the wiles of a Kelpie successfully. In many of the older stories the Kelpie transformed himself into a beautiful young man and the maidens he was attempting to entrap discovered his identity because he had sand or weed in his hair. In the Hebrides there were the *Fuath*, the Spirit of Terror and also the *Sluagh*, the Hosts of the Dead who drifted through the air in the darkness and might carry off a living person for the night,[1] and there were many others such as the *Gruagach*. Ghost stories of many kinds are widely distributed, and the haunted place that one has to pass is how infinitely more frightening than the unlocalized tale!

Human beings might also have dread powers. The Evil Eye was strongly believed in. Sometimes its possessor was a malevolent person, sometimes he was entirely innocent and unable to control his power for bringing misfortune even on his own cattle. Less formidable was the power some people had to charm the substance from the milk of other people's cows.

The Second Sight is an unwelcome gift. To whoever has it, visions come not of his own seeking and their significance is almost invariably tragic, such as the grey mist, called the Winding Sheet, seen round someone about to die, or the simulacra of a funeral that will soon pass that way. Second Sight is still firmly believed in, in many districts, and I have, of course, met people who have this gift although it is difficult to get them to speak of personal experiences. Premonitions of death also come to ordinary people. They might see lights moving along the route that would be taken by a funeral—(a most matter-of-fact woman told me she saw this within a village on the main North Road)—or the boards or sheets that would be used might be heard to move.

For stories of eerie experiences, the country people are now

[1]For the Washerwoman see Chapter X.

apt to refer one to printed and often conventionalized accounts and are inclined to express themselves as sceptical—although this attitude may be modified on such occasions as passing a churchyard at midnight! I have heard a young woman who prided herself on her modern outlook, mutter, when a cow she had bought was not thriving, that it was *buidseachd*, witchcraft, because the wife of the man she had bought it from was grieved to the heart that he had let her go. The feeling of the uncertainty of life as well as the fear of presuming against Providence makes many Highland people chary of saying that they will do this or that. We tend to say that we hope to do it or add the phrase 'if all's well' or, more piously, 'God willing'.

It would be tempting to speculate whether the preoccupation with death that comes into so much of Highland folk lore derives back to our remote predecessors who devoted such immense labours to making their megalithic tombs, or if it is due to the influence of the land we live in, a stern setting for human endeavour with its long drawn-out winters with the nightly darkness that lasts almost two-thirds of the twenty-four hours, its constant gales and rain or heavy snowfalls, and with seas, hills, rivers and lochs that can so quickly become inimical. And, in the same way, if the great heritage of music and poetry was fostered by a luminous twilight of summer nights and the sudden, transient moments of a shining loveliness that come at all seasons and compared to which, the beauties of all other lands to us seem dim.

The social life of the old Highland communities had its centre in the *Ceilidh*. It was very different to what now often goes by that name—an informal concert in the village hall or school. In the Hebrides, till the turn of the century, the men and lads, and to a lesser extent, the women, would gather during the winter evenings in a favoured house where they would be sure of a welcome. The *Fear an Tigh* (Man of the House) would be well able to take the lead and to tell the first tale and everyone else was expected to contribute to the night's entertainment. There might be some singing or playing, but the time was generally mainly spent in the telling of stories and personal anecdotes, the asking of riddles and quoting of sayings (of which from ancient times the Highlanders have been fond) and in a great deal of discussion upon topics of all kinds from the Supernatural to the practical.[1] Ceilidhs now are no longer frequented. In Bernera the custom died out fifty years ago. At Tolsta, in Lewis, the last Ceilidh house was burnt down by its owner's wish as the emigrant ship that was taking him from Lewis sailed past the township.[2] In other parts of the Highlands as well as the Hebrides the oldest people can still remember how similar gatherings used once to be held.

[1]For good descriptions of Ceilidhs see A. Goodrich Freer, *Outer Isles*, p. 6, who gives accounts of the actual conversation at several Ceilidhs. M. F. Shaw, *Folk Song and Folk Lore*, p. 7. A. Carmichael, *Carmina Gadelica*, Vol. I, p. xxiii.

[2]A. Morrison, *Orain Chaluim*, p. 19. 'Tolsta bho Thuath', *Stornoway Gazette*, 27.7.51.

# VII

## THE HOMES OF THE PEOPLE

### THE STRUCTURE OF THEIR HOUSES

THE old-fashioned Highland house was the essential setting for a ceilidh. Such houses are becoming few and far between and although the local modern houses in many parts of the Highlands have a certain individuality, little of the age-long traditions of house-building has survived in them.

The old houses were built for a different sort of life. They were evolved by a people 'of immense ability' to withstand the severe local conditions by means of the limited local materials that were available to them and their own unspecialized skills.[1] They gave the nightly warmth and shelter that was craved by men and women who spent their days largely out of doors, had few worldly possessions and were used to living in close association.

Most of the eighteenth-century travellers who describe them found nothing to admire in our traditional houses. They were dismissed as dark and dirty and were often referred to as huts. Seen from the outside they were likened to a 'smoking dunghill'. Their interiors were said to be scenes 'of nastyness and simplicity'.[2] Yet the poets, Coleridge and Wordsworth, with Dorothy, who had perhaps the keenest observation of the three, sat in such a little Highland house, taking quiet pleasure in 'observing the beauty of the beams and rafters gleaming between the clouds of smoke. They had been crusted over and varnished by many winters till, when the firelight fell upon them, they were as glossy as black rocks on a sunny day cased in ice'.[3]

[1]Article by A. C. Miller in *Scottish Mothers and Children* (Carnegie Trust), p. 427.
[2]R. Heron, *The Hebrides*, p. 221.
[3]Dorothy Wordsworth, *Recollections of a Tour made in Scotland (1803)*, p. 103.

141

I had an illustration of how skilfully local materials were turned to account. At my little Folk Museum at Kingussie, Mr. Alexander MacDonald, then 80 years of age, built for me a little house exactly in the way he remembered from his youth in Glen Urquhart. Almost the entire building was constructed of materials gathered on my own less than three acres of land or from close by. It was at the end of the war, when the housing shortage was extremely acute owing to lack of modern building materials and labour, and at that very moment a housing scheme at the nearby village of Newtonmore was being held up until the iron guttering required for the houses could be delivered. But at Am Fasgadh I watched Mr. Macdonald carefully arranging a frill of heather to project from under the edge of the thatch, which perfectly carried the drip from the roof free of the walls.

The variations in the three main types of old Highland cottages can indeed be largely traced to what local supplies of materials were available and to the presence or absence of shelter. In the Hebrides there was an earlier tradition of circular building formed by over-lapping stone courses and known as bee-hive houses. It has been suggested that they go back to the pre-historic 'wheel houses'. Shielings were still being built upon this pattern so late as the early nineteenth century.[1] But during the ages the Long Island has evolved another distinctive type of house construction, streamlined to offer the minimum resistance to the wind while giving maximum protection achieved with the utmost economy of timber and well adapted to those wind- and rain-swept and treeless islands. The drystone walls were low and built with a pronounced batter and were double with an intervening core of sand or earth (see Fig. 12A, B). The width of these walls would be at least 6 ft. in Lewis in a house the inner dimensions of which might be 12 ft. wide. The corners of the ends of the house were rounded. The timber was by far the most valuable part of the building. Outgoing tenants used often to take the timber of the 'couples' of their house with them and, if compensation for the house were paid by a landlord it was only on the roof.[2] In the days of wooden ships, driftwood was an im-

---

[1] A. Mitchell, *The Past in the Present*, p. 69. Colin Sinclair, *Thatched Houses*, p. 52.
[2] See *Crofters Commission, 1884*, 'Minutes of Evidence', Vol. I, pp. 46, 85, 188, among many examples.

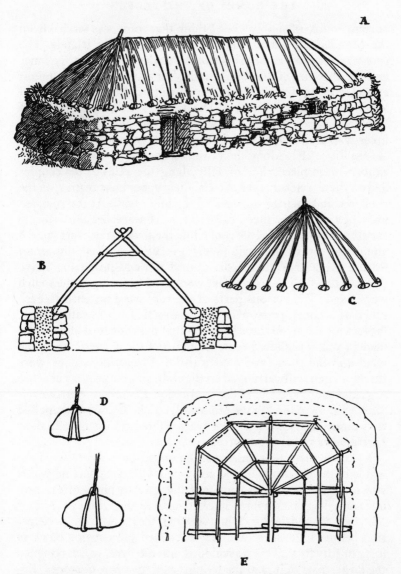

Fig. 12. Long island type of house. (A) General view. (B) Details of construction. (C) Method of roping thatch at the end. (D) Stones that weight roof ropes. (E) Detail of timbers at end.

portant source of supply,[1] but I think that some was ferried from the Mainland as was certainly done to the nearer islands. The roof was very low and the ends of the timbers rested on the inner and not the outer of the double walls. Contrary to what one might expect, the rain from the roof ran down through the core of sand leaving the inner wall dry. The timbers consisted of sets of 'couples', pairs of pieces of wood resting on the edge of the inner wall and with their tops tied together to form an inverted V (see Fig. 12B). Along their tops the roof tree was laid. Lighter timbers were placed horizontally along the sides of the couples and on these a closer layer of rods, their upper ends resting on the roof-tree and their lower ones on the inner wall. At the rounded ends of the house, the tops of the rods were brought closely together at the apex of the roof while the lower ends were spaced along the top of the wall (see Fig. 12E). A most important feature was a stick, tied to the central rod and projecting above the roof to which the ropes that were used to tie down the thatch were fixed. The various parts of the roof were fastened to each other by wooden pegs or in some cases tied with heather rope. A pleasant feature of these houses is that the wide tops of the walls made a warm sheltered seat, for the roof gave shelter from the wind and the thatch radiated warmth. Projecting stones were therefore generally arranged on the walls to give easy access (see Fig. 12A). In South Uist the expression *Piobairean nan Tobhtaichean* (pipers of the tobhta=four walls of the house) was applied to women who stood on the walls of the house to call their husbands or to harangue other women in a quarrel.[2]

In Lewis there was sometimes an unusual arrangement of the whole of the building being constructed within connecting walls, which rather puts one in mind of the ground plans of the pre-historic villages excavated in Shetland and the Orkneys. Arthur Mitchell, who visited such houses when they were in full occupation before 1876 says that they consisted 'of a major block of forty or fifty feet'. This was divided into the byre, which occupied the larger part of it, and the living-room by a row of stones. En-

---

[1]One still finds bits of old ships in use. I saw an old door with fastenings partly wooden but partly taken from the door of a ship's cabin. A brooch from St. Kilda of the traditional round shape was made from the base of a brass cabin door knob.

[2]Father Allan MacDonald, *Gaelic Words*, p. 244.

closed within the same walls was a porch-like wing in front called the *fosgalen*. The entrance into the house was through this little building which often held the quern and a stall for calves or lambs, and it gave on to the byre part of the main building. Behind the main building, built on to the back wall as a wing, was the barn, which was entered through the byre[1] (see Fig. 13). There are

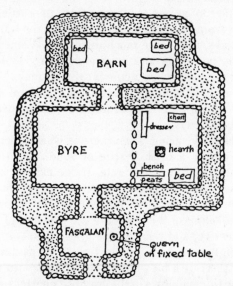

FIG. 13. Ground plan of older Lewis house. After Mitchell.

still, or were recently, a certain number of remains of old houses in Lewis which show that they once consisted of connected buildings, although not so primitive. They had four divisions, the byre, the living-room, the sleeping room and a barn. The house was, if possible, built on a slope with the byre at the lowest end and it was separated from the living-room by a partition of turf or wood not carried up to the roof. The bedroom was also partitioned off. The barn was built on to the back wall of the house and its only entrance was from the living-room, but a small aperture was made in its farther wall that could be opened to make a draught for winnowing. A special feature of Lewis

[1]A. Mitchell, *The Past in the Present*, p. 50.

houses, that I have often seen, is that the end of the byre was broken down when the accumulated manure was carried out. Earth had to be added periodically to the accumulated muck to keep the cattle dry. As one goes down the Long Island one notices how the association of the outbuildings with the living quarters becomes less close and separate byres become common and the walls not quite so thick.[1] Primitive as the keeping of the cattle under the same roof as one's self may seem the cattle are said to derive benefit from the association, especially the warmth when, in the older days, they were much underfed. Women who have had to flounder out in the dark in a snowstorm to look after their beasts during the vigil when a cow is calving, may think that the plan sometimes had its advantages! Tiree is exceptional because although the buildings are separate, the walls appear to be as wide as those of Lewis.[2]

On a day of early spring when there is what a local man once described to me as 'a brisk brattle of wind', and to the mainlander seems to be a howling gale, if one calls at some of the modern houses, perhaps planted upon a knoll so that 'summer visitors' may enjoy the view through the large prefabricated windows, the feeling of the impact of the pressure of the roaring wind is oppressive, and then, if one goes on to some surviving old house, snugly nestling in a hollow, the wind passes unfelt over its low roof, there is a blessed feeling of *shelter*. In spite of the mud floor, the tiny windows in the cramped quarters, one realizes that advantages are not all with the dictates of the Health and Housing Authorities and one may regret that in necessary improvements, all the old traditional building lore has been ignored.[3]

The traditional type of house in the more wooded and more sheltered districts of the Eastern and Central Highlands is en-

[1]See also *Scottish Mothers and Children* (Carnegie Trust), p. 428.

[2]Old houses on the Long Island are sometimes called 'Black Houses'. It is a modern derogatory term—apparently to distinguish their drystone walls from the later masonry houses. Black House in Gaelic would be Tigh Dubh and Doctor Sinclair suggests that it is due to a confusion with Tigh Tughadh = thatched house. (C. Sinclair, *Thatched Houses*, p. 18.) I think, however, that most of the people who talk about 'Black Houses' have not got the Gaelic.

[3]For praise of the traditional houses where improvements had been evolved in them, see M. F. Shaw, *Folk Song and Folk Lore*, pp. 5, 17.

Although many survive as byres or hen-houses there are few if any 'black houses' now in human occupation on the Long Island.

tirely different and the old people took full advantage of such conditions to build higher houses with steeper roofs to carry off the rain. (See Fig. 14A, B, E.)

The old Lochaber tale of the *Glaistig Lianachan* describes the building of such a house. To shorten it—The Big Black Gillie Mac-cuaraig was crossing the ford. A Glaistig (a mythical being of rather dubious disposition) hailed him to give her a lift behind him on his horse over the ford. He, however, swung her in front of him and tied her firmly with the holy belt of St. Fillan.

She begged him to let her go and offered him a full herd of speckled cows, black- and white-faced, but he said that he had that already and that he would not let her go. Then she offered to raise him in a single night a big house, well built, into which spells of fire, or water, or arrow of iron could not penetrate and that he would get it dry, sheltered, and with a blessing upon him against armed men and the fairies. 'Fulfil your oath,' said he, 'and you will get your leave from me.'

Then she let out a scream that would be heard over seven hills and the sound of it was like that which the prime horn of Finn would let out, and there was no shian or hill that did not waken and give back an answer, and they (the fairies) gathered on the other side of the river flat and she put orders on them that they should make haste quickly, regularly and in order. And they brought flags and stones from the Fall of Clainaigh, and they were passing them from hand to hand. And on the inch they were cutting cabers and the taobhan—the long rafters, smooth and flat from the Wood of Caoranach. And she was saying without pause, 'One stone on the top of two stones. Two stones on the top of one stone, sharp sticks, turves, wattle, pins from every tree but the wild cherry.'

'And in the graying of the day, there was turf over the ridge and smoke out of it.' And the Big Black Gillie, knowing of the wiles of the fairies, put the coulter of the plough in the fire. When the house was ready and she had fulfilled every covenant, he let her loose and 'it was not slow she was in putting more than his arm's length between them'. Then she reached out her two claws to him 'that she might be taking her farewell' but he held out the hot coulter and 'the skin of her palms followed it'. Then she put a curse upon him that he should wither like the brackens

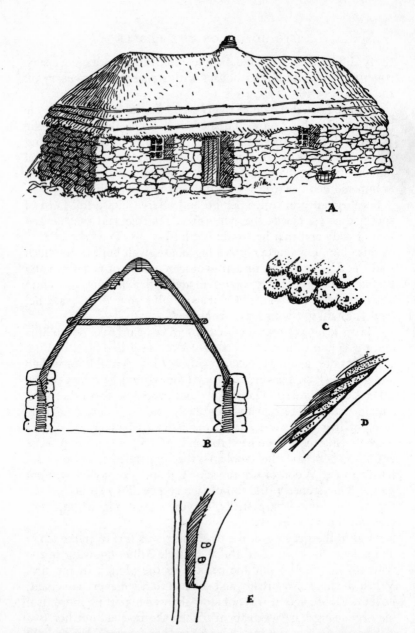

Fig. 14. House typical of Eastern and Central Highlands. (A) General view.
(B) Detail of construction. (C) Roof covering of divots. (D) Method of thatching.
(E) Pegged addition to couples.

148

and grow old like the rushes and that his children should grow grey and that he should have no sons in his own place. And it is still told in that country that this curse came true indeed.[1]

The passing of stones from hand to hand by a chain of people appears in several other tales and traditions. It has been said that when a township united to help build a house it could be finished in a day. I have never been able to discover why the Glaistig would not use pins from the wild cherry.

In these eastern mainland houses, the couples were formed of the naturally bent limbs of trees and they were planted in the foundations of the drystone walls. Their tops were then pinned together and strengthened with a cross piece, and an upright piece of wood fixed between it and the tops of the couples. Four or five pairs of these couples were usual. The walls of drystone walling with a little clay, if it could be had, were then carried up round the couples to a height of 6 or 7 ft., the top layers being sometimes of turf instead of stone. The roof-tree, and the horizontal and vertical rods were added, as in the Long Island houses, but the whole wooden structure is much higher and more massive. The roof-tree is especially so ('To your roof-tree' was an old Highland toast). The rods were covered with a layer of carefully pared divots and then of thatch. The ends of these houses were square. They were carried no higher than the side walls and the roof ended in hipped gables, slanted back from the walls to the end pairs of couples. This form of construction is very ingenious because the main weight of the very heavy roof is carried by the couples, firmly planted in the foundations and not by the drystone walls. It could be developed considerably. If the timber to be used for the couples happened to be straight instead of naturally curved, or if it was rather short, posts might be sunk in the foundations of the walls, and the lower ends of the couples, having been trimmed to a convenient slant, were fixed on to these posts with stout wooden pegs (see Fig. 14E). This method was also used in the making of larger buildings, when the walls might be built with a certain amount of lime, and in that case the upper ends of the couples, instead of being crossed at the tops, were connected by a piece of curved wood, pegged to their ends. The old barn at Corriemonie, in Glen Urquhart, is a fine example.

[1]Told me by the late Mrs. Ryan, born a MacDonell of Keppoch.

There are several good, eighteenth-century descriptions of the type of house in the eastern mainland,[1] and although I do not know of any such houses now being lived in, one can see the construction in many of the outhouses about old farms. At Dunachton, where the account book of my old forebear has preserved so many details of the life of the people, one pair of couples still stands amid the ruins of the old joint farm. The style of houses built on a wooden framework, alluded to in books as 'cruck houses', is, of course, widely distributed in Wales and parts of England and also in the Lowlands. It would be tempting to think that the folk who gave the dominant British elements to the Pictish civilization taught them to construct the wooden framework of their houses. In many parts of the northern mainland the cattle seem of old to have been housed separately. In Skye they were generally under the same roof.

In Skye and the north-western mainland, the houses showed a modification of these two types of houses. The ends were rounded as in the Long Island houses, but the walls were single[2] and the roof sprung from the top of the wall so that the thatch slightly projected as in the Central Highlands. The timbers are shorter and slighter than those of the inland districts. I have seen the roof couples pegged to posts sunk in the ground but usually they only rest on the top of the roof and are beautifully joined

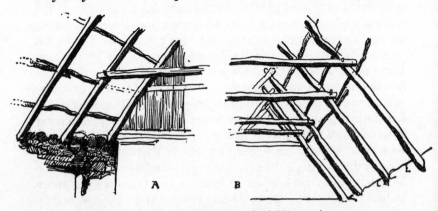

A          B

FIG. 15. Details of roof timbers of North-Western house.

[1]That by Burt (1726) is particularly good. *Letters,* Vol. II, p. 59.
[2]Martin alludes to some double-walled houses in Skye.

together with wooden pins. Below the high road, between Loch Ailort and Arisaig there are some ruined cottages where the surviving woodwork shows the skill and durability of such workmanship (see Fig. 15).

In the south-west, in Kintyre, Knapdale, and on the mainland as far inland as the Trossachs and up the coast of Argyll, with the neighbouring islands, the traditional type of building was quite different. The ends of the cottages were square and the gables were carried up as high as the ridge of the roof. The roof timbers rested upon the sloping walls of the gable ends. The appearance of such old cottages was much like a modern cottage, but it had the important difference that there was no flue in the gable-end (see Fig. 16). In Mull there still are a number of cottages of a hybrid type, with one end rounded and the other with a square gable (see Fig. 16D). An old man told me that they used to be likened to a cow with a crumpled horn. These cottages stand in isolation but, farther south, a long building with cow byre, living-room and sleeping-room joined to each other seems to have been usual. The partitions would be carried no higher than the walls.[1]

The distribution of this south-western type of cottage largely coincides with the area where the local laminated stone is particularly suitable for drystone dykeing and this may explain the style. But when one remembers that it almost covers the area of the old Gaelic kingdom of Dalriada one is tempted to attribute it, at least partly, to racial traditions.[2]

All these types of primitive houses were open to serious criticism. Among their faults was the dampness of their earthen floors, their darkness and that the roof was not entirely watertight. As the rafters and divots lining the roof were thickly coated with peat soot, in the event of heavy rain drips of inky black water were liable to fall on the inhabitants. There was a special word—*snighe*—for rain coming through the roof of a house. On the other hand, the drystone walls admitted a little diffused air, so that even cramped and crowded houses with the

[1]D. Wordsworth, *Recollections of a Tour made in Scotland*, p. 104.
[2]It must, however, be admitted that near Laide, in Wester Ross, there are a number of old cottages with similar gables. They seem to be built of a granite-like sort of stone and no one could tell me the reason for the style.

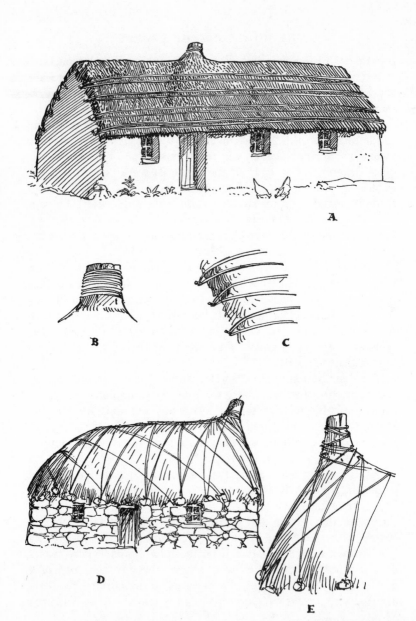

FIG. 16. South-Western type of house. (A) General view. (B) Detail of chimney in middle of roof. (C) Fastening of thatch to square gable end. (D) Mull type of house. (E) Detail of chimney at end of house.

minimum of ventilation (or draughts) are extraordinarily free from stuffiness, and the roof of divots and thatch makes them both cool in summer and warm in winter. Am Fasgadh is at Kingussie which is in a very cold district and in the severe winter of 1947 my own, substantially-built house was glacially cold every morning before the fire was re-lighted, whereas, if I lighted a fire in the reproduction of the eastern mainland cottage, an appreciable warmth remained for two or three days, and, in my reproduction of a Lewis cottage, for a week.

In the eighteenth century a new type of cottage began to appear. Its spread was closely associated with the movement for agricultural reform[1] (see Fig. 17). Superficially it resembled a late

Fig. 17. The later type of house.

example of the Dalriadic cottage[2] for it had the same square ends and triangular gables, but it had the great difference that there were chimney flues in the gable ends. It was built more or less with mortar and although many examples were thatched it was often slated. In a smaller cottage of this type the door opened on to a vestibule into which the two main rooms, which were built at each end of the house, opened while between them was a

[1]Cf. the introduction of the new type of house on Loch Tayside. M. MacArthur, *Lochtayside*, p. xxviii.
[2]Which easily merged into it.

narrow slip of a room often merely screened off by a curtain and which might contain an extra bed, a meal kist and many other things. There might be an attic upstairs.

It is rather curious that the very useful wooden porch was so often a later addition to such cottages. With it a charming feature that one often finds is a little table close to the door, with perhaps an ornament upon it or a vase of flowers—a welcome to all who visit the house. This is surely a survival of the spirit of hospitality, always so strong in the Highlands. We are told that in the more ancient houses a large block of stone or wood was set close to the door which was called the *Clach an t'seabhdail* the wanderer's stone and was for the use of any passer-by or stranger. Snug as these little houses appear to be, the size of their windows and the amount of cubic space inside does not generally conform to modern national health regulations and they have to be altered. A more justifiable criticism is that they had no damp-courses.

The surviving houses built in the traditional styles all belong to the lesser folk. In fact it is rare to see well-kept specimens in use, because the more active and go-ahead people have moved to later types of dwelling houses. But it is evident that in older days they were lived in by all classes.[1]

Although the more powerful chiefs generally had castles, some of them also lived part of their time in more homely houses. There is a wonderful description of the house of a chief of the MacGregors who lived towards the end of the fifteenth century. The poet bands were wont to feast there and for them it was never too crowded 'though narrow it be for all its household'. It was alight with wax candles to the door posts and wine was drunk there and: 'Thus did the masons leave aright the coupled house (*Bruidhean-Chaplach*) of MacGregor.'[2] From their nature the traditional types of houses were not long lasting, and none survive of those that were lived in by the heads of cadet branches. There are no descriptions of them in the seventeenth century, but the following tale is illuminating. Sir Norman MacLeod of Bernera was the younger son of a chief and had been knighted for his services in the Civil War. In his old age he built himself a

[1]C. Sinclair, *Thatched Houses*, p. 29.
[2]By Fionnlaidh Ruadh, *Scottish Verse from the Book of the Dean of Lismore*, ed. by W. J. Watson, pp. 149–50, 238.

new house in Harris. The house-warming feast was prepared. A member of the MacMhuirichs, the famous family of poets, was invited to pronounce the Blessing on the House. MacMhuirich began to recite his poem but he stuck after the first word which was 'tower'. A wag in the crowd at once called out an improvised couplet which has been translated:

'Tower, calling a house a tower
When it has only couples and beams.'

MacMhuirich began to recite his poem twice more and became stuck and was interrupted and he then retired in a dudgeon. An old woman then prophesied that Sir Norman would not live to occupy his new house, which actually came to pass. It was hardly a successful social occasion![1] By the eighteenth century the tacksmen were building themselves slated houses of masonry but some of them continued to live in simpler ones. The Highland Lady (writing of the early nineteenth century) described the house of the last of the Shaws of Dalnavert. This family had occupied Rothiemurchus before the Grants acquired it in 1556 and were of very ancient lineage. The house 'was a mere peat bothy', it had four rooms, each of which had windows but not made to open. The kitchen fire was on a stone on the floor with a hole in the roof. But when the old man died, the two local companies of Volunteers turned out for his funeral and amid a great concourse of people he was carried in state to rest by the old lairds of Rothiemurchus.[2] A family of MacQueens had had a feu of Corrybrough (in Strathdearn) which they only gave up in the middle of the nineteenth century. In 1774–83 the house was said to be 'a stone and turf house having one floor'.[3] When it was rebuilt about the middle of the nineteenth century I have been told that it was very simple and thatched.

Such houses might be extended to contain several rooms. For instance, in 1728 the minister of Carron (Easter Ross) lived in a house built 'with couples but about 100 ft. long'. First there was a room called 'the chamber'. It had a fireplace, glazed windows

[1]A tradition collected by the late Mr. Hector McKenzie, Dunvegan.
[2]This description is not given in the latest edition of *Memoirs of a Highland Lady*. See p. 193 in earlier edition. See also I. F. Grant, *Old Highland Farm*, p. 90.
[3]See Sir Eneas Mackintosh, *Notes*, p. 3.

and a box-bed which formed the partition between it and the next room. In it the family sat and took their meals and any guests slept in the box-bed. The next two rooms were bedrooms for the family. Beyond that was the room used by the servants with the fire in the middle of the floor and the byre was beyond that.[1] Accommodation was very limited. Johnson and Boswell told how at Corriechatachan the ladies used Doctor Johnson's bedroom as their sitting-room and that the house of MacLeod of Raasay had eleven rooms and that besides the family of parents, three boys and ten girls, twenty-five visitors stayed there at one time.[2]

Within the last hundred years new housing ambitions have developed among the country-people. Houses are not only mason-built with slated roofs but there has been a general desire for an upper storey with dormer windows. Under agricultural leases the provision of farm-houses and steadings is the responsibility of the landlord but the crofter provides his own house. Since the 1880s the crofters have made determined efforts to build houses that are not below the generally accepted standards of comfort. The building of such houses spread up the north-western mainland, even to the poorest districts.[3] In Lewis changes in housing were particularly active about the beginning of the twentieth century. The money for building is said mainly to have come from the earnings of people who went away to seasonal work or from remittances from members of the family in the Forces and especially, from those who had gone oversea. Pointing this out, someone well acquainted with local circumstances remarked of Lewis: 'Labour is one of the exports, houses are one of the imports.'[4] The crofters have also received an increasing amount

[1]Donald Sage, *Memorabila Domestica on Parish Life in the North*, p. 13. Hugh Miller's description of the house of his great-uncle on Loch Shin was very similar, *My Schools and Schoolmasters*, 1909 ed., p. 95.

[2]Boswell, *Tour*, p. 134. *Letters of Doctor Samuel Johnson*, Vol. I, p. 327.

[3]Cf. *Scottish Mothers and Children* (Carnegie Trust), pp. 399, 455. The rather critical *Report of the 1954 Commission of Enquiry into Crofting Conditions* pointed out how good was the general standard of crofters' houses, p. 20. In Barra there are a number of particularly pleasing cottages of masonry but thatched and built more in the traditional style. I was told that the building of these cottages was due to the great success of the local fisheries about the middle of the nineteenth century. This is confirmed by *Scottish Mothers and Children*, p. 425.

[4]Report by Mr. Miller in *Scottish Mothers and Children*, p. 432.

of help from the Department of Agriculture and the Local Authorities. Within the last forty years some 5,000 houses have been
built or improved by such loans and grants.[1]

Most of the components of the houses, such as window frames
as well as iron-work, were supplied prefabricated from the south.
A great deal of concrete is used and wartime and post-wartime
shortages have encouraged the use of building substitutes, and a
very alien type of bungalow is all too prevalent in some of the
newer townships sponsored by the Board of Agriculture.

But, on the whole, the plain yet sturdy-looking little two-
storied houses that one sees scattered over the crofting areas
have achieved a definite local character. They fit well into their
background and when, as is generally the case, they have been
given a coat of dazzling lime wash, they look out, like kindly
faces, from the brown hillsides.

## THE THATCH

Something has been said of the roofs of the old traditional types
of Highland houses. Above this framework was a layer of sods
and then of thatch and there were two distinct local methods of
covering the roofs in this way, one belonging to the Eastern and
Central Highlands, the other to the Long Island, and their dis-
tinguishing characteristics merged into each other in the nearer
islands and along the north-western coasts.

The houses of the Eastern and Central Highlands, as we have
seen, had higher and more massive roofs. The outer layer of
vertically placed branches or rods, arranged closely side by side
and sloping from the roof-tree to the tops of the walls, was
entirely covered by layers of hard, heathery divots (see Fig.
14C). In cutting these divots the spade was held at a slant so as
to taper the nearer edge and curve it into a scallop. It is fascinating
to watch how evenly a skilled man can cut them. These divots
were arranged in rows upon the roof, beginning from the
bottom, the lowest layer having straight and not scalloped
edges. The scalloped ends were arranged pointing downwards

---

[1] *Report of the 1954 Commission of Enquiry into Crofting Conditions,* p. 20. The
Acts responsible for this help are the Housing (Rural Workers) (Scotland) Act of
1938 and the Housing (Rural Population) (Scotland) Act of 1938.

and with each divot placed so that its centre covered a joint between the sods in the layer beneath it. The scalloped ends were then pegged down by small twigs of heather trimmed with a knife. At the eaves a thick fringe of heather was arranged to project under the lowest layer of divots in order to carry the drip from the roof clear of the walls. The thatcher then gathered the material that he was thatching with into bundles and tucked one end of each bundle under the edges of the overlapping divots and then flattened the thatch as he went along (see Fig. 14D). This sometimes completed the operation but, in exposed districts and especially towards the south and west, a few slats or rods might be laid along the roof. The whole roof might even be covered by rows of these rods evenly spaced out. In the western districts where the cottages were tending to have rounded ends, the thatch was carefully secured in this way. The rods, often of hazel, were held in position by loops of split and twisted hazel twigs, the ends of which were thrust under the thatch much as one secures a rope that has been thrown over a stack by means of a wisp of straw pushed into the stack. When neatly done, the effect of these lines of rods curving round the ends of a cottage was very decorative.

In the south-west, where the ends of the cottages were formed by gables, the thatching was finished off by a row of divots laid along the edge of the gable over the thatch.[1] In very windswept places and on the southerly islands, the thatch was secured by ropes weighted by stones, as in the Outer Hebrides, but as the ends of the cottages were gabled not rounded, an additional rope was carried backwards and forwards along the roof between the gables and at each end it was looped over projecting stones or iron hooks built into the gable wall a foot or so below the edge (see Fig. 16C). The joint between the chimney and the thatch, was made watertight by bringing the thatch up round the base of the chimney and securing it by a rope wound round and round (see Fig. 16B and E). In the old days the rope used for this purpose was made of straw (*Sugan*—straw rope) but coir rope is now used.

Barley straw (of course threshed by hand) was a material

[1]At Mellon Udrigil, near Laide where, as I have already noted, there was an outcrop of the gabled cottages, the thatch was finished by a row of large stones instead of peats along the gable, suggesting 'crow-steps'.

much favoured for this more lasting kind of thatching. Heather thatch was sometimes used but, although more durable, is said to be very heavy. I have been told that in ancient times churches were generally thatched with heather.[1] The late Father Diekhof, who conducted missions far and wide in the Western Highlands from the Benedictine Monastery at Fort Augustus, once told me that he had occasionally seen old thatching made of differently coloured materials arranged in ornamental scallops and that its effect was like that of feathers. It is curious to remember that in the highly imaginative description of the House of Cael, an old Irish tale embodied in the *Colloquy of the Ancients,* the roof is said to have been covered with feathers.[2] Other materials used for this type of thatching were moor grass (often used in Skye), broom, rushes and bracken, the last three of these were not so durable as straw.

An entirely different method of thatching was used on the lower, more slightly built roofs of the houses of the Long Island and to some extent in adjacent districts. The sods used for its foundation were less carefully prepared and were often of tough grass turf. The thatching material, generally straw or bent grass or a mixture of the two, was placed loose on the roof and raked into a regular covering as one would do in thatching a stack and it was then secured with ropes. This was an amusing process to watch. A man stood upon either side of the cottage and the ball of rope was tossed over the roof from one to the other. The man who received it deftly hitched it round a stone which was allowed to rest upon the roof where it sprang from the inside of the wide walls in the Long Island type of house, or to dangle at the edge of the roof in Skye and elsewhere (see Fig. 12D). The ball of rope was then tossed back and the man at the other side secured it by a stone in the same way and threw it back until the whole roof was regularly roped. It will be remembered that the cottages of the north-eastern islands and coasts had rounded ends and that

[1]There are many traditions of how an enemy clan surrounded a church while the congregation was worshipping inside, set fire to the thatch and burnt those inside. It is told of at least six clans. In the case of the MacDonnells of Glengarry the piper is said to have marched round the church of Kilchrist inside which the MacKenzies were being burnt, and drowned their screams by the tune that is now a famous pibroch.

[2]Translated by Standish O'Grady, *Silva Gadelica,* p. 101.

in making them the rod at the apex of the curve was lengthened by a stick tied to it and allowed to project above the roof. This was called the *Maide Feannaig* (raven's stick). The rope was given a twist round the projecting stick and then brought down and hitched round a stone at the bottom of the roof and the process was repeated until the whole rounded end was secured (see Fig. 12C). I was told that a mischievous person once came to a house that happened to be empty and pulled out these sticks so that the whole thatch blew away before the owners returned. As a finishing touch, an additional rope was generally run right round the roof just above the row of stones and two others were fastened on each side to cross slant-wise from the *Maide Feannaig* to the base of the roof. The rope for Long Island thatching used to be made of heather but imported coir rope has long since come into use.[1] Sometimes, however, instead of the arrangement of ropes, the thatch is secured by fishing nets weighted by stones.

This type of thatching was not expected to last for more than a year. Every summer it was taken off and used as a fertilizer on the land and it must have been quite valuable for this purpose in the days when the fire was in the middle of the floor and there was no chimney or only a very primitive one, for then it was impregnated with the peat soot from the smoke passing through it.

I have never seen or heard of any special implements used for either of these types of thatching but in a third kind, which one finds along the north-east coast, especially in the fishing villages, I have seen a short wooden or iron rod in use and secured specimens. The roof was covered with a layer of clay into which the ends of wisps of the thatching material were thrust with the help of this implement.

WITHIN THE HOUSES

The heart of the house is the fire and the more primitive the house, the more this is so. In the earliest houses, with the hearth in the middle of the floor, the people's lives literally revolved round the fire (see Fig. 18A). It was sitting in a circle round the

[1]In Lewis it used to be known as *Sioman Thearlach* (Charles' rope) because it was supplied by a Stornoway merchant named Charles Morrison. *Stornoway Gazette*, 27.7.51.

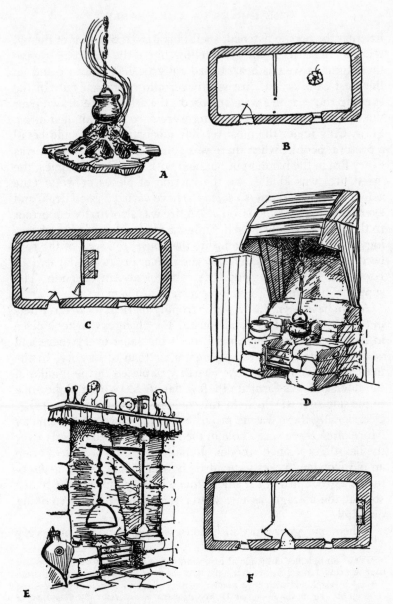

Fig. 18. Details of hearths and fireplaces. (A) and (B) Hearth in middle of floor. (C) and (D) Hearth built against middle partition. (E) and (F) Fireplace under chimney flue.

161

fire that the people listened, spell-bound, to the telling of the old tales or took part in the good fellowship of the Ceilidh.[1] It gave them light as well as heat. It had a mystical significance and, in the west at least, the fire was never allowed to go out. In the evening the peat fire was 'smoored', the ashes were drawn over the embers which in the morning were once more kindled into a glow. Only under the most terrible misfortune that could befall a pastoral people, when there was a murrain on their cattle, was every fire in the hamlet put out, and with special ceremonies, the 'need fire' was kindled by the friction of pieces of wood (the actual method of doing so seems to have varied a good deal) and every fire was rekindled from it.[2] A fire was also vitally important to the primitive house itself. Unless a constant fire is kept burning to dry the atmosphere inside the house, the sods of the roof become waterlogged and heavy and sooner or later collapse. (As I found to my cost in my little cottages at Am Fasgadh. The supply of peat for firing was a constant problem.)

As we have seen, there were strongly marked local variations in the structure of Highland houses. The changes that took place in hearths and chimneys were much the same everywhere and were a question of development rather than of locality. In the most primitive cottages the hearth was placed in the middle of the floor and was formed of a few flat stones with a higher one to the side against which the fire could be banked (see Fig. 18B). Occasionally there was no provision for the escape of the smoke. More often there was a hole in the roof, not placed directly over the hearth, or a small wooden chimney might be provided, often an old wooden bucket without its bottom. Under such arrangements a great deal of the smoke found its way through the thatch so that the cottage, as one writer said, looked like a smoking dunghill.

When one goes into such houses—and they are now very

[1]For a word picture of the inn at Inveroran with a group of drovers sitting 'in a complete circle' round the fire in the middle of the floor, each supping porridge from a wooden vessel, and with busy women bustling round on household business and children playing on the floor, see D. Wordsworth, *Recollections of a Tour made in Scotland*, p. 183.

[2]See under 'Cattle'. Lachlan Shaw, *History of the Province of Moray*, p. 15, writing at the end of the eighteenth century of Badenoch, said he had seen Need Fire made. Sir J. Frazer, *The Golden Bough*, pp. 617, 634, 641, summarizes the methods used.

rare—one finds that the peat reek tends to rise and that the air is relatively clear near the ground. The old chairs and stools were very low and so that the people sat below the canopy of smoke. A distinguished visitor, on a higher seat, would therefore come off the worst. This happened to Prince Charles Edward when he landed in Eriskay and 'was lodged in one of the little country houses'. He constantly had to go to the door for a breath of fresh air.[1]

The next stage of development was to build the hearth against the wooden partition that divided the living-room from the sleeping-room (see Fig. 18C and D). A few feet of drystone walling was built behind the hearth and on each side hobs were constructed of rough stones and clay. A further stage was reached when the fire was raised from the floor by a simple iron grate made by the local blacksmith, but the characteristic feature of this type of fireplace was the *Similear Crochaidh*, or hanging chimney. It consisted of a wide wooden hood projecting over the hearth connected by a sort of wooden flue through the roof to the chimney. The whole thing was made quite separately and was attached to the partition.[2] The *similear crochaidh* often had a shelf along the front for ornaments and wooden flap that could be let down if the fire smoked.

When cottages with chimney flues built into their gable ends superseded the 'hanging chimneys', the old hobs with locally made grates continued to be used (see Fig. 18E and F). But whatever form the fireplace took the built-in oven was never evolved as part of the traditional Highland fireplaces. When the older cottages with rounded ends have survived, a more modern fireplace or a cooking stove is now generally added and these are provided with a jaunty-looking little wooden chimney sticking at an angle out of the rounded end (see Fig. 16E) or, perhaps, a regular chimney of mason-work is added.

The cooking pot or girdle was hung over the fire by means of an iron chain (*Slabhraidh*), which was attached by means of an iron bar or a rope to a wooden crosspiece fixed in the roof, when

[1] Bishop R. Forbes, *The Lyon in Mourning* (Scottish History Society), Vol. I, p. 289.

[2] I bought one out of a derelict cottage in Wester Ross and it was sawn into sections and duly arrived at Am Fasgadh.

the hearth was on the floor, or within the *similear crochaidh* (see Fig. 31E). By means of hooks the slabhraidh could be looped up or left to hang straight down close to the fire as the process of cooking demanded. The local blacksmiths exercised much taste in making these chains; some had double links, and very few were alike. Their thinness or massiveness gave a good idea of the owner's financial position because iron had to be bought and its use was a luxury. I had a particularly heavy one from the fertile district of Kintyre. In very poor houses, instead of an iron chain, the pot was sometimes hung from an arrangement of two pieces of wood connected by little pegs (like a ladder) on to which a pot hook could be hung (see Fig. 34C). Although it had, of course, been hung over a peat fire, one in my possession was badly charred.

The slabhraidh had a very sinister character in folk tales. Children were sometimes not allowed to touch it because it was associated with the powers of evil[1] and it could be used for the unlawful purpose of taking the milk from someone else's cow. But if a bit of fir-wood were stuck into its links this would prevent the fairies from coming down the chimney as in more than one tale they are said to have done.

When the flue built into the gable came into use, the slabhraidh was still sometimes used but more often the swee, a lowland implement like a little crane or gallows for hanging the pot over the fire. At its simplest it was a right-angled iron bar, one side of which was fixed upright inside the fireplace and the other swung free over the fire or into the room. More elaborate ones had double swees and some ornamentation. I have seen a swee in use with a modern oven.

Floors of the more primitive little houses were generally of hard beaten earth but clay was an improvement, and they were sometimes sprinkled with sand and I saw one neatly covered with turves. In the more sophisticated cottages cobbles or flags were used. Upon the floors, mats of plaited straw or bent grass or made of rags in the familiar way were laid, or there might be a deer or a sheep skin.

In tidily kept cottages the inside walls were generally lime-washed or they might be covered with old sacks on which news-

[1]Although if they were alone in the house it was a prank to swing on it.

papers were then pasted. In an old cottage in Badenoch I noticed the dates on this kind of 'wall paper'. They were early nineteenth century. On the mainland, at least, a ceiling was sometimes made by nailing sacks to the rafters and treating them in the same way.

Partitions between the living-room, bedroom and byre did not reach to the ceiling. They were often made of rough boards with such wide chinks between them that more than one visitor complained of the lack of privacy.[1] But as the cottages became more comfortable the box-bed in itself would form a partition.

On the mainland a kind of partition was made of rows of stakes covered with a mixture of straw and clay.[2] I was anxious to show an example of this work and I found a specimen in which the clay had set so hard that a piece of the partition could be cut out with a saw and safely conveyed to Am Fasgadh by a lorry. The use of walls of straw and clay mixed is suggestively Celtic. In the Highlands, especially on the western mainland, basket-work was used for many purposes and Boswell mentions two cases where partitions were made in this way.[3] As already mentioned, wicker-work was also extensively used for the sides of threshing barns.[4]

About eighty years ago, on the Long Island, a straw mat or a cow's hide on a frame might be used as a door,[5] and I have heard of, though I was not able to see it, a door made of wicker-work still in use in Wester Ross. Doors made to turn by means of a projection that fitted into a stone socket with a hollow in it like those found at the entrances to iron-age forts, instead of by means of hinges, were once common.[6] I have seen and collected doors from the Long Island in which wooden hinges worked on the same principle (Fig. 19A). A piece of wood was whittled so that a central pin was left sticking up and was nailed to the jamb and a bar with a hole at the end of it was fixed to the door

[1]The Hon. Mrs. Murray, *A Useful Guide to the Beauties of Scotland* (1799), p. 432. R. Heron, *The Hebrides* (1792), Vol. I, p. 225.

[2]Well described by A. Anderson, *Guide to the Highlands and the Islands of Scotland*, (1850 ed.), p. 644.

[3]J. Boswell, *Tour*, pp. 100, 105. By Lochness and in Glenmoriston respectively. Apparently whole houses were sometimes built in this way, see John Leyden, *Journal of a Tour in the Highlands and Islands* (1800), p. 175.

[4]See Chapter V.

[5]A. Mitchell, *The Past in the Present*, p. 54. T. Garnett, *Tour*, Vol. I, p. 159 said that wickerwork doors were common in Mull.

[6]A. Mitchell, *The Past in the Present*, p. 127–8. See also Fig. 19B.

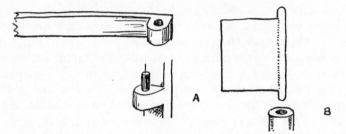

FIG. 19. Details of primitive construction. (A) Wooden door hinge. (B) Shutter turning in socket.

so that the hole fitted on to the pin. The door latches and snecks were also of wood. The latch was placed inside and a string fastened to it and the other end threaded through a hole in the door so that it could be pulled and the latch from the outside.

These ingenious devices on doors show that iron was a luxury that was often dispensed with. Glass was an even more exotic product and one reads that in the earlier houses it was not used in windows at all. The tiny apertures were closed with wooden shutters or skins were stretched over them, or they were stuffed with peats when the weather was cold. A tale bringing in such a window is told of a famous archer named Cam Ruadh who lived in the seventeenth century in Braemar and who had routed many caterans. One very stormy night seven caterans came to take revenge on him and listened outside the window which was stuffed with peat. They overheard his wife asking him what he would do if robbers came on such a night, and his reply was that he would feed and shelter them. The robbers demanded that he should be as good as his word and peace was made.[1]

The most primitive cottages that I have seen had at least tiny panes of glass, but, in two cases, only the upper part of the windows had panes of glass and the lower part had wooden shutters.[2] In one of these windows, found in a ruined cottage at Onich in Lochaber, the wooden shutters turned on pins like primitive doors (see Fig. 19B). The other had hinges of leather.

[1]E. Taylor, *The Braemar Highlands* (1869), p. 190.
[2]In seventeenth century Edinburgh the same device was common and I have seen an example in an old building in Culross.

# VIII

## FURNISHINGS AND PLENISHINGS OF HIGHLAND HOUSES

### FURNITURE

OLD Highland furniture is a fascinating subject. One can trace (and puzzle over) several local variations in construction. One can see the influence of the supplies of materials that were available but, most fascinating of all, the forms of the old furniture bear witness to the great characteristic feature of Highland civilization, that there were no class distinctions but that, although the clansmen varied in their possession of worldly gear and occupation of land, the theory of kinship was held strongly. Therefore (as in their dress) the old Highlanders evolved no separate 'peasant style' of furniture, such as one sees in Continental folk museums.

From contemporary descriptions and from the heirlooms cherished in many of the families of the lesser chiefs and tacksmen, we know that even when they were still living in thatched houses they imported a good deal of fine furniture, china and plate. Boswell and Johnson were struck by the numbers of books they found in the houses of the Skye tacksmen and mention their elegant tea equipages and we know that Major Alexander MacLeod,[1] who emigrated to North Carolina took with him

[1] Blackwell P. Robinson, *Moose Country, North Carolina*, p. 34. The inventories of possessions lost by the Highland Loyalists of North Carolina show what plenishings they took from the Highlands. See R. D. de Mond, *The Loyalists in North Carolina during the Revolution*. See also A. MacRandle, *The Tacksman and his holding in the S.W. Highlands*, Scot. Hist. Rev. xxv, p. 12. *Memoirs of a Highland Lady* (1911 ed.), p. 195 gives a charming account. Besides the mahogany furniture, the fine glass in a corner cupboard, she mentions the old pistols over the fireplace. For two other inventories see I. F. Grant, *Old Highland Farm*, p. 91.

furniture, napery, and a little plate valued at £86 and 324 books.

Many fine pieces of furniture passed from the vanished tacks-men to lesser folk and one finds many copies by local craftsmen of the fine, french-polished mahogany or laburnum wood furniture made by the craftsmen of Perth, Edinburgh or even London that the gentry of the Highlands imported. Thus, locally made by craftsmen in the lesser burghs were the elegant fiddle-backed chairs of unveneered beech or ash that must have been very common in the Highlands for so many examples have fortunately survived. They are generally of the Chippendale type, but I was able to collect examples with the curved edged splats reminiscent of William and Mary chairs, although probably made much later, and even a ladder-back chair from a tiny house in Wester Ross (see Fig. 11). Regency influences are strong even on very roughly made country chairs.[1] Many of these elegant chairs have obviously been made for houses with the fire in the middle of the floor and billowing peat smoke, for they are often very low and, from standing on earthen or clay floors, one quite frequently finds that the bottoms of the legs are decayed. The families of the tacksmen went very far afield and one still finds in the Highlands oriental punch bowls and hangings such as Dr. Johnson found in Ulva. He and Boswell[2] were obliged to spend the night with MacQuarrie of Ulva, one of the most ancient families in the Isles. He described his house as a 'hut' and said that after 'a liberal supper' he was taken to his room where he found 'an elegant bed of Indian cotton, spread with fine sheets', but the floor was only of mud, that had become wet through the windows being broken 'and he felt his feet in the mire'.

Beds show how the country people's furniture developed as did their houses. George Buchanan, writing in the sixteenth century, said that the Highlanders slept upon heather, arranged with the brush upwards and, when visiting in the south, would not use ordinary beds. In the eighteenth century the humblest folk still often slept on heather with blankets,[3] and at the shielings people continued to sleep on heather. But a mattress of sacking filled

[1]Wheel-back chairs were sometimes used in the Lowlands and I have even seen a few examples in the Highlands but they may have been imported.

[2]J. Boswell, *Tour*, footnote, p. 312.

[3]J. Boswell, *Tour*, p. 100. E. Burt, *Tour*, pp. 116, 117, describes people sleeping on straw.

with chaff became usual in the houses. In South Uist and Eriskay, sea-grass carefully washed and dried was used instead of heather and after a death was always burnt.[1] In Badenoch, in the eighteenth century the same custom was observed and care was taken that no animal should come near the discarded bedding. In Lewis a more primitive form of bed was a hole contrived in the thickness of the wall. It was still remembered about the middle of last century, but I have never seen a specimen, even in a ruined cottage.[2]

But by the eighteenth century box-beds were common in the servants' quarters in the larger houses and in inns and were coming into general use[3] even in smaller houses.[4] In simpler houses or where there was not much timber, they were constructed like bunks and enclosed by a curtain. (I had some fragments of such old curtains, some of which were of handblocked linen and had no doubt come down in the world.) The drystone wall against which they were constructed was covered with a bit of sacking. In such beds there was generally a mattress stuffed with chaff. In Sinclair's list of the plenishings of a cottage in the Black Isle the cost of a bed was put at 4s,[5] and it was probably of this kind. But besides a bed in the kitchen, most descriptions of the houses mention several beds in the *Culaisd* (bedroom).[6] The curtains, however, as one writer said gave some privacy and made each bed into a miniature bedroom.[7] These simple box-beds long continued in use in the little middle room of the later type of houses. I have seen many of them. In the Long Island such beds had wooden roofs covered with divots to keep the bedding dry when the roof leaked.[8]

In districts where timber and woodworkers were available, the box-bed in the kitchen was entirely enclosed in deal panelling and was a handsome piece of furniture (see Fig. 20). One that I found in an old cottage in Kingussie had the date 1702 carved

[1]Father A. MacDonald, *Gaelic Words*, p. 179.

[2]A. Mitchell, *The Past in the Present*, p. 51.

[3]R. Heron, *The Hebrides*, Vol. I, pp. 219, 220.

[4]When Prince Charles Edward landed at Eriskay, he was given a bed with sheets. Bishop R. Forbes, *The Lyon in Mourning*, Vol. I, p. 289.

[5]Sir J. Sinclair, *Northern Counties*, p. 76.

[6]Cf. D. Wordsworth, *Recollections of a Tour made in Scotland*, p. 104.

[7]*Stornoway Gazette*, 10.8.51.

[8]A. Mitchell, *Past in the Present*, p. 51. *Scottish Mothers and Children*, p. 431.

upon it. These well-constructed box-beds often formed the partition between the living-room and the next room in houses where
the fireplace was in the gable of the house. About 1860 such box-
beds were in the living-rooms of all the small farmhouses of
Strathdearn and my mother said that when, as a small child, she

Fig. 20. Panelled box-bed.

accompanied her mother on calls she was always afraid that the
doors would open and some grim face look out at her. They have
long disappeared.

On the larger farms in Perthshire and Inverness-shire, about
that time, very handsome bedsteads of polished birch were
fashionable, but long since iron bedsteads have become universal
and one wonders how people managed to get on without them,
so useful are the ends of old ones for stopping gaps in fences,
forming the gate of a calf's pen and for many other purposes!

Besides finer chairs (see Fig. 11) there were several kinds of
home-made ones with local characteristics. In Ross-shire and

FIG. 21. Country chairs. (A) Sutherland type. (B) Unusual chair made on Inverness-shire principle. (C) 'Seise'. (D) Stool of bog wood. (E) Inverness-shire and Ross-shire type of chair.

171

Inverness-shire such chairs generally had their seats formed of a slice of a large tree, or of the elbow of a branch forming a U, with pieces of wood fastened across it to make the seat. The backs of these chairs were made of spars of wood, with a curved rail along the top (see Fig. 21E). Their resemblance to Windsor chairs is strong but this is probably accidental. To make these chairs it was necessary to find pieces of wood naturally curved in the suitable shape and the chairs are often made of several kinds of wood. The legs and the spar backs were fixed into the seats by means of holes burnt in the wood. The most interesting example of this type of chair that I collected came from Strathspey. It was partly made of pear-wood. The seat was formed of the bent branch of a tree. Its peculiarity was that it had an ornamental stretcher like a restoration chair and, like a restoration chair, the stretcher was fixed at an angle (see Fig. 21B).

In Sutherland country-made chairs were made quite differently. The sides of the back and the seat were made by two branches each forming a natural right angle. The back was connected by spars and the seat by flat pieces of wood (see Fig. 21A). In a very simple one I had there were two branches of birch naturally bent to form the shape of a lyre, which was strongly reminiscent of Empire chairs.

In the islands the frames of the chairs were largely made of driftwood and the seats of interwoven cords of bent grass. In these chairs the interlacing was like basket-work from side to side and from front to back. In Kintail and farther north on the coasts of Wester Ross the seats of chairs were also sometimes made of a cord of bent grass but it was interlaced diagonally from the corners. And in the west and also in Skye wicker-work chairs were made (see Fig. 43).

Stools were made for milking the cows and for sitting by the fire, sometimes with four peg legs cut from branches and sometimes with short pieces of board nailed to form end supports. Such stools were sometimes round and sometimes oblong and considerably longer. In Skye and the Outer Islands pieces of wood from the bogs were also used and pegs of wood were added to make them sit steadily on the ground (see Fig. 21D). If they were well chosen they made quite comfortable stools. A chair was sometimes made by cutting out half the side of an old barrel, or a plank placed on stones might do duty or a pile of peats.

Whatever the seating accommodation might be, the man of the house always had his special seat by the fire while his wife occupied a lower one or a stool on the opposite side. I have never heard that the right or the left side was specially appropriated to either partner.[1] A charming feature is the number of very small children's chairs that one finds, some of them elaborate, craftsman-made chairs with arms (see Fig. 11), others replicas of the local types.

Kists were an important part of the plenishing of the little houses. Even the most primitive would have one for meal and one for storing the clothes and blankets, but there were generally several, kept in various parts of the house. To ensure the keeping of the meal in such a kist it had to be packed very tightly and was generally tramped with the bare feet. In a *Lament* printed by Carmichael occurs the line 'thy little chests of meal had been pressed by thy feet'.[2] There might be a row in the *culaisd* along the wall opposite the box-beds and the milk dishes or other things might be kept upon them. In the living-room I have seen them made quite ornamental with a white cloth spread on the top on which could be displayed a few little treasures. In the Islands, with their damp climate, clothes were often hung over a rope looped on the wall.

Dressers are not mentioned in earlier accounts of the furniture of the simplest houses.[3] It was not until the nineteenth century that crockery came into wide use but they have long been a *sine qua non* in any Highland cottage. They are generally made of deal and have four shelves and a plate rack above. The tops of the dressers show some variation. Those from the Central and Eastern Highlands are square while in the islands and in the west they are slanting and slightly projecting (see Fig. 22A). No doubt the reason for this is the lower walls of the houses in these districts. Upon them are displayed the bits and pieces of china that Highland housewives took a pride in collecting. Occasionally one finds examples of the oldest dark blue and white Prestonpans

[1] But see A. Mitchell, *Past in the Present*, p. 52. High Miller, *My Schools and Schoolmasters*, p. 96.

[2] A. Carmichael, *Carmina Gadelica*, Vol. V, p. 343.

[3] J. Leyden, writing in 1800 calls one a 'beisail', *Tour in the Highlands of Scotland*, p. 41. Sir J. Sinclair does not include one in his list of usual furniture.

pottery and there seems to have been a definite preference for
blue willow pattern or for brown and white designs, although
the pale blue oriental scenes made by Bell of Glasgow about the
middle of the nineteenth century are very common. I have found
a few pieces of German pottery and was told that occasionally

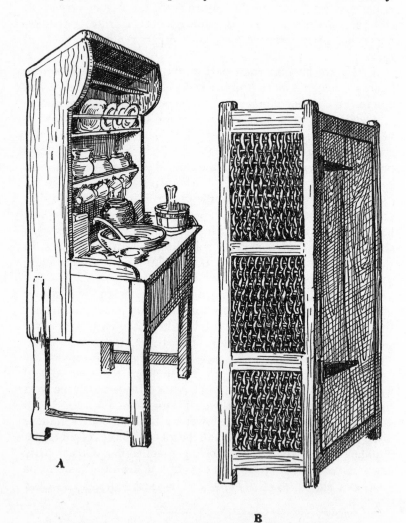

FIG. 22. Furniture. (A) Dresser. (B) Cupboard partly of wickerwork.

shiploads of German ware were sent to the western sea-lochs for retailing. The charming, gaily patterned milk bowls, some of them made in Perth, were till quite lately peddled round by tinkers and exchanged for rabbit skins and old rags.

All over the Highlands and Islands the *seise* or *seisach*, often Anglicized into 'sofa', is characteristic of the sociable habits of the people[1] (see Fig. 21C). It was a sort of settle or bench with arms at each end and a back. It was evidently made by local craftsmen and if people could not afford one they made do with a plank supported by stones at each end. Its shape varied according to the supplies of timber and the woodworking abilities of the district. I bought a *seise* from Wester Ross, from a district with little timber, that had only one horizontal bar at the back, but in most cases there were short perpendicular bars to form a back. A very fine one from Aberfeldy, in Perthshire, a district rich in timber, had a panelled back and the seat formed a long box for holding blankets; another from Strathspey, also a district famous for its timber, had a back formed of closely set vertical spars beautifully turned on a lathe. These *seises* were generally placed against the wall, facing the fire. I have often thought that even the simplest house looked richly furnished when a row of country people sat talking and laughing on the *seise*.

Cupboards and presses were widely used and held foodstuffs, milk vessels and many other things. They were generally square (Mrs. Murray likened them to box-beds),[2] and they were the most expensive item in Sinclair's list of the furnishings of a small farmer, being priced at £1 10s when a bed or a kist could be bought for 4s each and three chairs for 5s.[3] There were local variations. In the east, where the square gable with the chimney flue was early introduced, corner cupboards were common and in the Highlands of Perthshire, a land of timber, very fine panelled cupboards on the top of chests of drawers were called aumbries and were a local feature. But in the west, the land of scrub and bushes and of the most skilful basket-workers, cupboards were often made with wickerwork sides on wooden frames. They were

[1] J. Leyden called it a 'deish' and said it was the most honourable seat in the house.
[2] Mrs. Murray, *A Useful Guide to the Beauties of Scotland* (henceforth noted as *Useful Guide*), p. 263.
[3] Sir J. Sinclair, *Northern Counties*, p. 76.

used for keeping milk, butter and food and were called 'larders' (see Fig. 22B).

Cradles might be very simple with a hood made of a piece of wood bent into shape, or they might be panelled (see Fig. 23).

FIG. 23. A cradle.

There were always two knobs at each side and a length of plaited wool was carried across the cradle and twisted round these knobs to hold in the baby. Cradles used to be handed down and the women would boast of how many babies had been reared in them. One could see how the edges of the sides were polished by the mothers' hands as they rocked the cradle. A hundred babies are said to have been reared in a very fine specimen that I had much admired. Then, one day, it was not in its accustomed place and I was told that it had been broken up for firewood. Cradles have so completely gone out that a local child-visitor to the Museum asked what they were used for. I told her they were used for holding babies. The child asked if the baby would not drown and, when I exclaimed, she went on: 'Oh, I thought that they were little tanks.'

Such was the usual furniture of a Highland cottage, but it would contain many other things. Each little home was in some sort a universal workshop and everyone was to a certain degree a craftsman or craftswoman. There would be much gear and many implements. The milk cog was probably by the door and the churn under the dresser. Baskets of many kinds and creels hung from the rafters. Cooking utensils were by the fire. Very often there was a gun over the fire-place, and in the west I have seen it wrapped in a bit of tarpaulin to preserve it from the damp. On the shelf over the fire-place, on the sills of the windows and on the ledge where the roof springs from the walls, numberless small possessions would be stowed. Rag rugs gave a touch of colour. Any little wall shelves and that above the fire-place might be ornamented with strips of newspaper cut into scallops and on the latter might be a couple of 'china dogs' or other figures in Staffordshire or Prestonpans ware. Twice I have seen a bit of broken mirror fitted into a carefully shaped home-made wooden frame to serve as a looking-glass.

In the more primitive cottages tables do not seem to have been used. The people ate sitting round the fire, but tables have long been an essential part of the furnishings. It was when a much later type of cottage could boast of a best parlour that the table really became important. It might be a round Empire table, come down in the world, but it would be shrouded with a table-cloth, and on it reposed the large family Bible and perhaps a photograph album. On the walls there might be crayon enlargements of family photographs (a great trade was done by wandering agents in supplying these). In the windows indomitable geraniums bloomed behind Nottingham lace curtains.

The old types of furniture have almost disappeared and have no place in the modern way of life of Highland people. I have been in a cottage in the Long Island that still had its fire in the middle of the floor, but none of the furniture was traditional; two of the chairs were made of bamboo in a style reminiscent of the turn of the century. It would be out of keeping with the people's attitude of mind to cling to the archaic and the folksy. Like their forebears they adopt the current styles. One often sees in modern Highland houses the mass-produced three-piece suites so widely sold all over Britain and if there is more comfort and not room for quite so many, the row of Highland folk sitting on the sofa is by blood and attitude of mind the same as the men and women who once sat on the old *seise*.

## PLENISHINGS

The smaller possessions in Highland houses, old and less old, tell their own stories of gradual changes and of local variations. When dealing with the dressers in the section on furniture it seemed to be simplest to describe the crockery displayed upon them at the same time. When transport was primitive and money was scarce, such imported objects must have been hard to come by. The Highlanders themselves were deficient in the art of making their own pottery. Only in favoured spots in some of the islands did even a simplification of the primitive skill of prehistoric potters survive. In the Long Island, Tiree and in Skye home-made jars, known as *Cnaggans* (pronounced craggans) used to be made (Fig. 24). The workmanship is extremely rough. The jars are without ornamentation and were moulded by hand and not thrown on a wheel. The last place where this primitive craft lingered till within living memory was Barvas, in Lewis. Mrs. Quiggin, the widow of the distinguished Celtic scholar, described to me how, in her youth, she saw such pots actually being made at Barvas. It was a woman's craft. After the

FIG. 24. A cnaggan.

pots had been shaped by hand they were set to dry for a few days, then they were baked on the household hearth, burning peats being heaped round them and some placed inside; then, while still hot, they were plunged into milk in order to make them less porous.[1] By the 1880s the women had also begun to make tea-sets of the same crude ware for sale to visitors. The cnaggans were used for holding oil, milk and other liquids and as cooking

[1] For a similar description see A. Mitchell, *The Past in the Present*, pp. 27, 236.

178

vessels and churns. A specimen found in a cottage that had long ago been overwhelmed with sand was of considerably better workmanship than other specimens I came across. In Tiree cnaggans had once been made for ordinary use and, after this had been given up, cows were still sometimes milked directly into little ones and the milk was drunk as a cure for consumption. The one given to me was of a fine red clay.

To make up for the lack of pottery the people had an abundance of wooden vessels of many kinds. Small quaichs (a Scots rendering of the Gaelic *Cuach* drinking cup or bowl); flat little bowls standing on a rim and with two or more ears, were sometimes whittled out of a block of wood and perhaps ornamented with incised, interlaced patterns by the country people themselves (see Fig. 25). Larger bowls for mixing meal were sometimes

Fig. 25. Examples of quaichs.

made in the same way and so were ladles in great quantity, and also drinking vessels with bottoms of sheep-skin. But many people must have been able to work a simple lathe, because numbers of turned cuachs and mixing bowls can still be found. Turned wooden platters were also quite common at least in some districts. In the brief list of the possessions of a joint tenant in

Breadalbane, dated 1596, four 'treen plates' were included,[1] and on Prince Charles Edward's wanderings in the Western Islands, the boatman who was his guide, used a wooden platter for his simple cookery. Although they probably came in much later, turned wooden egg-cups in great variety are still common all over the Highlands. The most usual pattern is in the form of a double ring, one of which was smaller than the other to fit a pullet's egg. Most of the surviving examples probably came from water-driven mills that made a variety of small wares.

Staved vessels were also largely used for many purposes. The simpler ones, I understand, were made by local wood-workers who had a lathe. In the early census returns there were few local coopers except in fishing districts.[2] Kegs for salting meat and herring were essential for the winter economy, milk cogs with their single handles (see Fig. 47F), butter tubs, 'cheesers' and churns (see Fig. 47A, B), were used for dairy work. Before pails came into use, staved wooden vessels were used for carrying water. Washing in the old days was done at the burn or river-side, but there were tubs. In the houses, porringers, with one high handle like a little milk cog, often had a double bottom filled with a few dried peas to rattle as a signal for a second helping (see Fig. 26C). They were probably in use in the more sophisticated establishments or were a later introduction. Such porringers were bound either with wythes or iron bands and the staves were feathered. Simpler vessels were staved drinking beakers. Those I have seen were unfeathered and bound with wythes; one stave on each side was carved into a handle (see Fig. 27). The tinkers are said to have made the smaller staved vessels and to have had the skill of joining the staves by 'feathering' them (see Fig. 26B).

A more carefully finished type of bowl or quaich was made of alternate staves of light and dark wood and was bound with cane (see Fig. 26A). One little quaich in my possession had a glass double bottom and within it a lock of golden hair, so that the owner could drink to his lady-love. Staved quaichs must be fairly ancient because, when silver quaichs began to be made in the

---

[1] *Black Book of Taymouth*, p. 418.

[2] In Sir J. Sinclair's list the small farmer was estimated to require four dishes and cogs costing a total of 5s, the same price as three chairs and three stools. The former were evidently boughten while the latter were home-made.

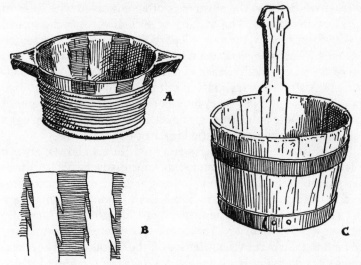

FIG. 26. Staved vessels. (A) Fine example. (B) Example of 'feathering'.
(C) Porringer.

FIG. 27. Staved vessel with handles.

181

seventeenth century, the silver was often engraved with lines to represent the staves. The making of such silver quaichs spread from Edinburgh to Inverness but they would, of course, be treasures. A more ancient and simpler way of taking a dram was out of a scallop shell. Other common examples of the wood-workers skill were the cylindrical salt boxes that hung on the wall beside the fire in many farm-houses (sometimes jars were used instead), and the polished egg-stands made to hold a dozen eggs were also fairly common in the larger of the old farms.

The gaily coloured red, black and gold Russian bowls, always called 'sugar bowls', are common in some districts. When I first met examples in Sutherland, I thought they were chance im-portations, but on going on to South Uist, I found that they were part of the plenishings of almost every old-fashioned cottage in the district of Eochar, and I was told that where it was usual for the men to take part in the fisheries off the Orkneys and Shetland Islands (as so many Highlanders did, because they hired them-selves to the fishermen of the Caithness ports), they often bought these bowls from the Baltic fishermen there. Since then, I have learnt that these bowls are generally to be found in fisher com-munities all over Scotland.

It must be admitted that the lighting arrangements in the old days in the Highlands were very poor. When one's eyes become accustomed to it, the glow of the fire throws a certain amount of light. To supplement this, various devices were used. Cruisies are the best known (see Fig. 28A, B). They were mainly used in the islands and the coastwise districts because fish oil was the usual illuminant (although mutton fat might be used). The cruisie consisted of two leaf-shaped vessels, the upper one fixed on a ratchet above the lower one, so that the drip should be caught and the cruisie could be tilted forward to use every drop of the oil. I have been told that peeling the rushes which were used as wicks, was one of the children's jobs. A thin sliver of the outside was always left to prevent the pith from breaking. Occasionally square cruisies were made with four lips and I have been told that these were used by craftsmen (see Fig. 28C).

To make cruisies a thin plate of iron was hammered into a mould and some Highland blacksmiths had such a mould in the corner of their anvils, but I had a cruisie-mould made of stone

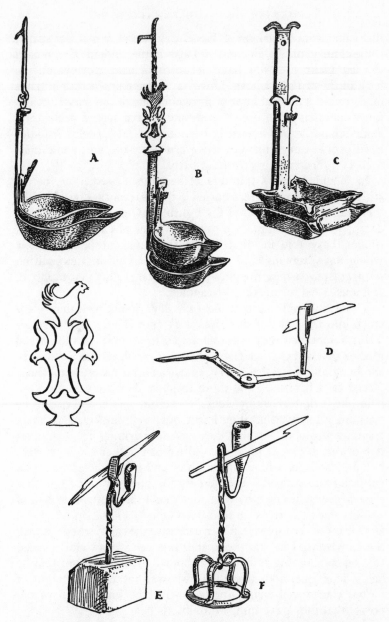

FIG. 28. Lighting devices. (A) and (B) Cruisies. (C) Square, craftsman's cruisie. (D) Clip for holding a 'fir candle'. (E) and (F) Rush light holders.

that came from the island of Tiree. Cruisies vary much in shape, some clumsy, others elegant, and also in the amount of iron used in their making. A few have decorative curley worleys on the back of the cruisie. I have, however, twice come across cruisies made out of a natural knot of firewood, one of the many devices for economizing the use of iron, and I have seen a prehistoric stone lamp that had evidently been used in later times. Middle-aged people can remember when cruisies were still sometimes used to light byres or threshing barns.

In inland districts splinters of resinous fir-wood or, better still, knots from pine-trees buried in the peat mosses, were called 'fir-candles' and were used for lighting.[1] Old people in Strath-dearn, which is a high-lying strath where birch is the natural timber, have told me that their fathers and mothers, in their young days, remembered taking part in an autumn expedition to Strathspey, where the pine-trees flourish, to lay in a supply of resinous wood for making fir-candles.

These fir-candles had to be very dry. Sometimes they were stuck into the links of the *Slabhraidh* (pot chain) (see Chapter VII). Sometimes they were arranged in a circle on the barred girdles that are characteristic of Inverness-shire and Perthshire and hung above the fire to dry. In use a number were sometimes placed on a flat stone and more frugally they were more often held like little torches by a child or an old person and had to be constantly renewed as they burnt out very quickly. A woman traveller wrote in 1799 that they gave 'a charming light' and that it was a pretty sight to see an old woman, in her snowy curtch, holding the light while her daughter and grand-daughters spun and sang and danced.[2] The homely fir-candles remind one that the use of torches held by retainers round the banqueting hall of a chief comes into two clan traditions (the MacLeods of MacLeod and Grant of Glenmoriston). In each case the chief, when visiting the Lowlands, was shown a handsome candelabra and taunted that he had nothing to equal it at home. He laid a wager that he had a finer one, and, when his visit was returned the sight of picked clansmen bearing torches, with the implication of the power that they gave him, won him his bet.

[1]They are fully described by Sir Eneas Mackintosh (1774–82), *Notes*, p. 14
[2]Mrs. Murray, *Useful Guide*, p. 265.

Various devices were also used for holding the fir-candles. Small iron clips were used, with a sharp end that could be poked into a crack in the drystone wall, and in eastern Inverness-shire the clip was even fixed to a jointed bar so that the light could be adjusted (see Fig. 28D). Or the clip might be stuck into a hole at the top of a stick of about 3 ft. high that was itself stuck in a stone with a hole in it. This was known as the *gille dubh* (the black boy) because, standing near the fire, it became covered with soot. Peermen (iron stands for rushlights or candles) were more characteristic of the Lowlands although I have come across a few.[1] Rushlight holders were used in the Highlands (see Fig. 28E).

In the nineteenth century the fir-candles were replaced by primitive naphtha iron lamps, known as 'oilie bubbies'. In Perthshire I have even picked up old miners' lamps. Then, all over the Highlands, came the ordinary paraffin lamps, superseded by Tilley lamps.

Candles and candlesticks must have been used by the gentry from early times, but they do not figure in early accounts of humbler cottages and only gradually came into use. By the nineteenth century, at least, brass candlesticks, of course bought from outside the Highlands and probably much come down in the world, were a usual ornament for the mantelshelf. Wooden candlesticks often have features of special interest. A most ingenious one that could be raised or lowered by means of a loop working on a ratchet, seems to be of local manufacture. Another was carved in a double spiral. This motive of the double spiral I have also seen on the shanks of several ladles, some of which I know were locally carved. It seems to be a survival of the underlying idea of the ancient interlaced patterns. The candles themselves were made of mutton fat and the tin moulds for making them are one of the things that seem most easily to survive. They vary from moulds for half a dozen fat candles to humble ones for two candles, one of them very small. Old people have told me that they could remember seeing candles being made by pouring the mutton fat into such moulds or by dipping the wicks into the

---

[1] The word 'Peerman' is said to be derived from poor man as pronounced in the Aberdeenshire dialect. It was usual for a wandering beggar to earn his night's shelter by holding the taper or fir candle, but the stand dispensed with his services.

boiling fat. For carrying a light outside the tinkers used to make tin lanterns punched all over with holes in order to admit air and with a small pane of glass. One can only rejoice that nowadays in the Highlands electric light is coming into so many small homes. By 1951 it was estimated that one out of every six crofts had electric light and great progress has been made since then.[1]

The humble, much battered, clothes beetle represents the old custom of washing clothes by beating them on the shore of the burn or river. This is associated with a very ancient and widespread superstition. The Fairy Washerwoman was said to be seen before a battle, washing the shirts of those who were to be killed. She appeared to Osgar, the grandson of Finn MacCumhal in a very old epic tale of the Feinné and again to Ewen of the Little Head, a chief of the MacLaines of Lochbuie, in the sixteenth century. The custom of treading the blankets with the bare feet by two girls standing in a wash-tub is mentioned by Burt, writing in 1726 and can still be seen today (see Fig. 29).

Goffering irons, for laundering the frills of the mutches, seem to be of all old plenishings, the most indestructible (see Fig. 30). Made of cast iron they consisted of a tiny poker in a socket. The

Fig. 29. Girls treading blankets. After Slezer (1693).

[1]*Report of Commission of Enquiry into Crofting Conditions, 1954*, p. 20.

poker was made red-hot in the fire and was then put into the socket, and the frill was bent over and under it until the whole was neatly fluted. Mutches do not seem to have come in before the

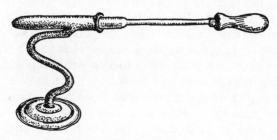

FIG. 30. A goffering iron.

nineteenth century, and so goffering irons must be of comparatively recent introduction, and also the minute irons for finishing the backs of the mutches. But whether the old Highland women wore the mutch or the older curtch, nearly all the visitors seem to have been struck by their exquisite whiteness.

Among the old plenishings there are many things that illustrate how local crafts turned local materials to account. In the Long Island and the more windswept parts of the west coast one finds that bent grass was much used. *Ciosans* (see Fig. 44E), are vessels about a foot high, used for holding meal, grain, or anything dry. To make them several strands of the grass were coiled round and round.[1] Larger vessels of the same kind used to be made but I have never seen a specimen. Bent grass was also woven into bags for holding meal and grain and, with a different weave, into pads that were put under pack saddles, and it was also fashioned into the most excellent brushes.

In these districts of the west where brushwood abounds, basket-workers were particularly skilful. Plates were, and occasionally are still made and also flat baskets for holding oatcakes. This seems to have been an old and more general custom. Sir Rory Mor MacLeod of MacLeod (Fl. end of sixteenth and early

[1]Bowls of similar construction but with curved instead of straight sides used to be made in the Faroe Islands.

seventeenth century) is said to have had his meat and bread served in baskets,[1] and in a MacKenzie yarn of a feast in the sixteenth century the food is said to have been served in baskets.[2] A dish with the sides of wood and the bottom of wickerwork has several times been described to me as usual in the old days on the west coast and in the Islands. It was used for serving potatoes, with perhaps a relish of herrings. The potatoes were tipped into it from the cooking pot and the water they had been boiled in was allowed to run on to a bundle of fodder, which served as a nourishing bite for any cow that needed special attention. The dish was put on a stool, and the company helped themselves out of it.

Spoons used by humbler folk were made of wood or, more often, of horn (see Fig. 32F). Sinclair's list of a small farmer's plenishings included ten spoons of horn valued at a total of 2s. The making of them was a tinker's craft. Tinkers also made horn tumblers and ladles.[3]

Some of the plenishings, long since obsolete, remind one of the difficulty of providing meat in the winter in the days before the introduction of turnips, when the animals had to be killed in the autumn. The catching of fish also was seasonal. I have mentioned kegs for pickling the meat among the staved vessels (see Fig. 33D). I have known the wives of shepherds and keepers in out-of-the-way places who used to salt down supplies of mutton and fish in this way. Salt, owing to the duty upon it which pressed so heavily on the Highlanders, was beyond some people's means and I have heard of meat being put to soak in the sea. The salted meat was so unpalatable that much spice was used. The spice grinders were elegant, tall objects made of turned wood and consisting of a grinder and cup to hold the spice. Mustard was ground in a turned wooden bowl with a lid and the grinder was often a cannon ball. These utensils no doubt once belonged to the more affluent people and are not distinctly Highland. The general need for spice to make the meat palatable was a prime cause of the trade of the Venetian Republic and of the great markets of the Netherlands to which the raw produce of Scotland mainly went;

[1] J. Boswell, *Tour*, p. 184.
[2] Applecross MSS. printed *Highland Papers II*, p. 31. A. MacKenzie, *History of the Clan MacKenzie*, p. 110.
[3] See Chapter XI.

it was a factor in the rise of the sixteenth-century Joint Stock Companies, the beginnings of the present capitalistic system. So far into European economic history do some of our homely plenishings take our thoughts!

Highland textiles are so important and fascinating that it is better to deal with them separately, although ill-supplied would a little house seem without them.

An important household article was the pair of tongs. It is essential for tending a peat fire and it was evidently made by the local blacksmith, the two pieces being connected by a joint and not a spring. It had its ritual significance for when the bride was brought home, her husband handed her the tongs as a symbol that he made her the mistress of his house.

Cooking utensils have a long history. As the grains locally grown were oats and barley or bere and the use of white bread, even in the eighteenth century, was a luxury, ovens were practically unknown in the Highlands. (By the end of the eighteenth century white bread was occasionally baked in a pot oven.)[1] One reads that in prehistoric times meat was cooked in holes filled with hot stones. I have never come across any later allusion to this very practical device. But a primitive way of boiling was in skins or paunches of an animal, suspended over the fire on sticks. So long as there was liquid within the skin it did not burn. This was also an Irish custom[2] and it was still sometimes used in the Islands so late as the end of the eighteenth century.[3]

Cauldrons made from plates of bronze riveted together, had been used by the Gael from early times and they come into the epic tales of feasts. They were so precious that in the old stories they were often credited with magical properties. In the old Irish tale of the Battle of Magh Rath the King of the Scots is said to have had a cauldron that always supplied the right food, no matter what was put into it, or the rank and the number of people for whom the meal was being prepared. This convenient utensil was kept in the King's stronghold of Dunmonadh—a bleak hill-fort now known as Dunadd.[4] In the later times the important

[1] In castles ovens were occasionally installed. For instance in the ruins of a Mackintosh's old stronghold on an island on Loch Moy there were traces of more than one.
[2] See illustration, Major H. McClintock, *Old Irish and Highland Dress*, p. 41.
[3] J. L. Buchanan, *Travels in the Western Highlands*, p. 106.
[4] Translation printed *Proc. Soc. Antiq.* (Scots), 1878, p. 33.

people in the Highlands had cooking utensils in great variety. From the sixteenth century umpteen numbers of pots, pans, spits, ladles, etc. are listed in the old inventories.[1] But lesser people, even if their belongings were meagre, almost always seem to have had a cooking pot. The possessions of two joint tenants in Perthshire, which happen to come into a document of 1596, each had a pan and one also had a kettle.[2] The Museum was presented with a cooking pot by the man who had found it under some stones in the ruined shieling of 'The Lady of Lawers'. Her name appears in recorded history at the end of the seventeenth century and traditionally she was credited with the second sight. A tragic tale is attached to her shieling, for her daughter is said to have trysted a lover of humble birth there and the lady to have got word of it and to have sent some of her followers who pursued and killed the youth. This pot was made by a method of casting now obsolete and instead of the three short legs of the later type of pot, it stood on a sort of base. At the top it was not contracted into a short neck (see Fig. 31A). I was able to collect a similar pot from Strath Glas, in Easter Ross and also the base of another, used as a teapot stand, which came from the remote island of Heiskir, off the coast of North Uist. When the making of cast iron was introduced at Falkirk and the first great Scots iron industry started, pots must have become much more easily come by, and three- or four-legged pots of cast iron were the usual complement of a housewife's cooking implements (see Fig. 31B). In Sinclair's list, the small farmer had three pots valued at 10s and a pan worth 2s.[3] But he was said to live in the Black Isle and in remoter places pots may have been scarcer. Some lucky people had outsize pots, used for boiling water for washing blankets or for dyeing. By the end of the eighteenth century, large, flat-sided pots with lids,[4] had come into fairly wide use for sinking in the embers and for baking in. These pots were generally used for baking meat and an old woman who had tasted some said that it was more flavoursome than any roasted in an ordinary oven. I

[1] There are very full ones of the Breadalbane family, see *Black Book of Taymouth;* see also W. Forsyth, *In the Shadow of the Cairngorms*, p. 151, for a sixteenth-century tacksman's inventory.

[2] *Black Book of Taymouth*, p. 418.

[3] Sir J. Sinclair, *Northern Counties*, p. 96.

[4] Known as Pot ovens or Dutch ovens.

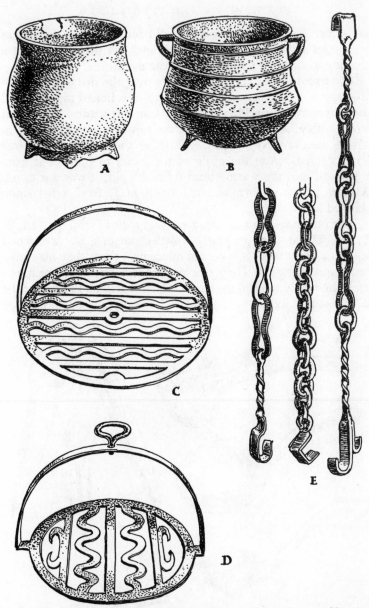

Fig. 31. Cooking utensils. (A) Seventeenth-century cast-iron cooking pot. (B) Later cast-iron cooking pot. (C) and (D) Barred girdles. (E) Pot chains.

asked her how the housewives could tell when the meat was ready and she said that they 'just knew' and that a little extra cooking in such a pot did not spoil the meat.

The handles used to hang the pots over the fire were detachable and were formed of two pieces of iron linked together and the pots were covered by wooden lids, simply made of a round of wood with a batten nailed across the top by which to lift them. There was, however, a skill in making these. The batten was always fixed across the grain of the wood to prevent it from warping as, in the warm steam from the pot, it was apt to do. A more primitive form of pot lid was made from a flat stone chipped into a round.

With the pots are associated wooden ladles (see Fig. 32A, B, C, D). These were generally whittled out of a block of wood and, as a heart was often carved on them, I think they may have been betrothal gifts. Their size and shape varied very much, but they almost always had the end carved into a hook to fix over the lid of the pot and prevent the ladle from slipping down into the

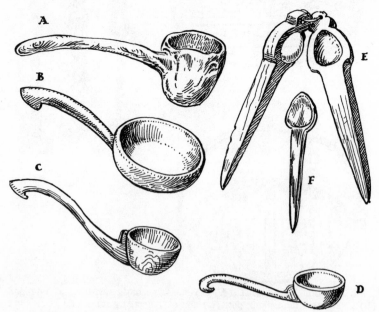

FIG. 32. Cooking utensils. Wooden ladles. Horn spoon and mould.

contents. A few were elaborately carved and horn ladles also were used.

Of course the pots were largely used for cooking potatoes upon which the people came so largely to feed and tattie mashers of many different sizes and shapes were in use (see Fig. 33A, B, C).

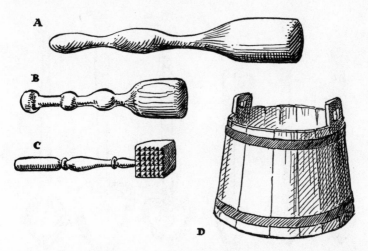

FIG. 33. Cooking utensils. (A), (B) and (C) Potato mashers. (D) Wooden pickling keg.

They and the spurtle for stirring the porridge were probably often home-made, but sometimes they were turned.

The girdle was universally used for baking either scones or oatcakes. From about the beginning of the nineteenth century heart-shaped iron bannock spades were used in the Lowlands for turning the bannocks on the girdles and some found their way into the more accessible parts of the Highlands (see Fig. 34).[1] In Inverness-shire and Ross-shire, as a variation to the flat iron plate of the ordinary girdle, girdles were formed of narrow bars of iron bent into pleasing designs (see Fig. 31C, D). Old people have said that these barred girdles were used sometimes for drying the 'fir-candles' so much used in these districts, and that fish grilled on them were very tasty, and that if a very stiff dough

[1]J. Muir Haddow, 'What is a Spurtle', *Scots Magazine*, August 1958, p. 385.

were baked on them, the mixture formed delicious crusty
nubbles. There is a local story that the last wolf in Strath Errick
(south of Loch Ness) was killed by a woman, whom it was preparing to attack, with a girdle that she had gone to borrow and
was carrying home. (Told by the late Major Neil Fraser Tytler

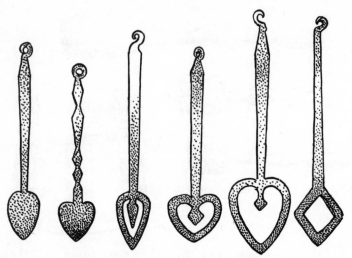

FIG. 34. Cooking utensils. Bannock spades.

of Aldourie.) This suggests that an earlier form of girdle with a
flat handle instead of the half loop of iron bent over the plate was
then in use. On the west not everyone had a girdle and the bannocks were baked on a stone. Prince Charles Edward, when a
fugitive in the Islands, 'birstled' his bannocks in this way.[1]

It is quite evident that the Highlanders liked their food well
browned, for the variety of devices for toasting and brandering
were endless. When the fire was on the hearth bannocks were
browned by propping them against a flat stone and better-off
people had very finely dressed stone bannock toasters (see Fig.
35B). Humbler folk, as well as stones, used simple wooden supports made out of a naturally curved piece of wood supported by
little struts (see Fig. 35A). But I also had an iron bannock toaster,

[1]Bishop R. Forbes, *Lyon in Mourning*, Vol. I, p. 109.

and one made of iron and wood which came from the fertile districts of Morayshire and Perthshire.

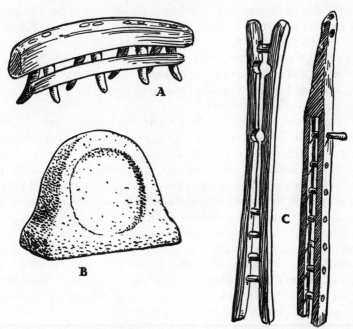

FIG. 35. Cooking utensils. (A) and (B) Bannock toasters. (C) Wooden rack for
hanging pot over fire.

When the fire was within a grate between hobs, the devices
for toasting bannocks or fish became even more varied. The
simplest was a sort of rack that hooked on to the top bar of the
grate, and in Perthshire and also in Kintyre people could afford
to embellish these toasters with elaborate scrolls of iron. A
severely practical tin brander from Wester Ross, evidently
tinker-made, had a little channel at the bottom to save the fat
with which the fish had been smeared. Other branders were designed to rest over the fire between the hobs. The most sophisticated of all, and certainly an importation from the south, was
made of brass and on a flat plate a little toast rack had been made
to revolve by means of a cogged wheel and a ratchet. One also

comes across roasting jacks, but they seem to have come from inns or more sophisticated houses.

Dairying utensils properly belong to a section of their own, but the *Loineid bheag* or *fro-stick* or milk whisk was used to prepare a dish known as broken milk (see Fig. 47E). The *Loineid* was a stick about 1½ ft. long with a cross-piece at the end and round this a circle of twisted cow's hair. It was rotated between the palms and either cream or the top of the milk was frothed up and a sprinkling of oatmeal might be added. This little stick is found all over the Highlands.

To preserve small fishes they were dried upon a hake which hung outside. It consisted of a triangle of wood with little hooks on it on which to hang the split fish. In my young days one constantly saw hakes hanging outside the cottages but they seem to have disappeared. The preservation of fish was important because even on the coasts the herring shoals only came seasonally and in winter storms line fishing for white fish was not possible. In inland districts supplies were even more spasmodic. After roads were made, when there had been good catches, the fish was hawked round by cadgers in carts. They might bring it 20 or 25 miles inland and it might become very 'high' by the time it reached its purchasers. Nowadays, with motor transport, the distribution of fresh fish is much easier.

A most interesting thing about collecting was that even the simplest house nearly always contained some treasure that had been handed down—perhaps a silver toddy ladle with a stem of twisted whalebone, perhaps a lacquer snuff box or a bit of fine china or an engraved wineglass or two, but more often it was something exotic. I have again and again been told that the people in some cottage had something really interesting, only to find such things as an ostrich's egg, a carved coco-nut or an Eastern dagger. Comparing notes with someone who had collected for a similar Museum in England I learnt that to find so many things from remote parts is peculiar to the Highlands. It is indeed characteristic of our far-wandering race that although all the old plenishings may vanish from their houses I think there will always be found there things sent from the ends of the world.

One more form of decoration may be mentioned. One often finds white rounded stones on the window-sills or round the

cottages. Some of the houses in Bohuntine in Glenroy had quite
a little border. Such pebbles are no doubt put there because they
are attractive, but it was a liking that the remote ancestors who
built the chambered cairns and decorated them with little white
pebbles seem to have shared.

# IX

# THE PEOPLE'S DAILY ROUND
# AND COMMON TASKS

APART from the general work on the land or the fishing grounds, men and women performed a vast variety of tasks. As Sir Frederick Eden wrote: 'Everyman . . . is Jack of all trades —so convenient in general, and so well adapted to all really useful purposes in their cloaths, furniture and implements, that the want of regular tradesmen and mechanics seems to be but little felt.'[1] The men threshed the grain, the women ground it. The men built their houses, constantly had to renew and re-thatch the roofs, made and mended the furniture of the house and often made and mended their shoes.[2] The women, as well as their housewifely tasks, did the dairy work and also the more important part in making textiles. They were also said to 'assist in various tasks in which the chief task is performed by men'.[3] As a matter of fact they seem to have done many of the more laborious jobs. So late as 1823, Hugh Miller wrote that in the district round Gairloch the men dug the land with the *cas chrom* and sowed it while 'the wife conveys the manure to it in a square creel with a slip bottom, tends the corn, reaps it, hoes the potatoes, digs them up, and carried the whole home on her back. When bearing the creel she is also engaged in spinning with the distaff and spindle'.[4] On the crofts where the men are obliged to undertake subsidiary work often away from home a great deal of the cultivation of the croft still falls upon the women. The men can do the heavy work

[1]F. M. Eden, *State of the Poor (1797)*, Vol. I, p. 559.
[2]W. Marshall, *Agriculture of the Central Highlands*, p. 24.
[3]R. Heron, *The Hebrides*, p. 77.
[4]Peter Bain, *Life and Letters of Hugh Miller*, Vol. I, p. 116

of cutting and floating the seaweed in February, before they go to the fishing, and can dig the ground. The women do much of the carrying of the seaweed and the planting of the potatoes.[1] In May or June the men are available to do the peat cutting, but much of the harvest work falls on the women, and they also help with lifting the potatoes.

*Peat cutting:* The winning of the peats is a family or even a communal affair and the old spirit of co-operation comes into play. Several families will often join together and will combine to cut peats for one household one day and for another the next.[2] It is hard work but, in many districts, people are still dependent on their supply of peats for their fuel. In the old days peat was universally used. The duty on coals made their cost prohibitive and there was often the difficulty of lack of transport. In places where there was little or no peat people had to make great efforts. I was told that on Iona, the people used to cross to Mull to cut their peats and then ferry them back. The following are the careful provisions for his widow, written in 1792, the year before his death, by a forebear of my own in Badenoch. He enjoined that his son 'shall cast and make ten faces of good and sufficient peats for firing to her in the ordinary peat moss . . . and carefully cause win and dig them and that he shall lead and build the said full ten faces of Peats in the most convenient part of the Green of Dunachton' (near her house), 'and Each face of the said peats to consist of and contain therein Seventy Sack loads of well filled creels she being alwise Bound to pay one Peck of meal for each face of the said Peats yearly to the workers.'[3]

The cutting of the peats begins about the end of April. The surface along the top of the peat bank is skimmed off with a spade (in the old days with a *cabar lar* (see Fig. 6), and the peats are cut along the face of the bank in oblong cubes, the shape of which varies according to the quality of the peat and the district. This work is done by two men, one cuts the peats and the other lifts them to the bank above. They frequently change places as peat cutting is hard work. The implement they use is a peat iron made by the local blacksmith (see Fig. 36). The usual form has a small

[1] M. F. Shaw, *Folk Song and Folk Life*, p. 4.
[2] M. F. Shaw, *Folk Song and Folk Life*, p. 4 has good account.
[3] Papers in possession of my brother.

flat blade, like a minute spade with a flange at one side. The length of this flange varies from district to district. Those used by the people of the Long Island to cut their beautiful peats have very long flanges. At Am Fasgadh I had about fourteen peat irons

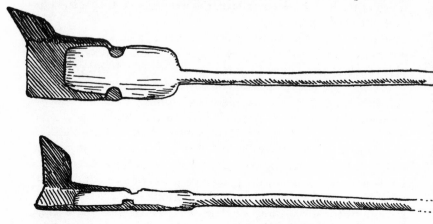

FIG. 36. A peat iron. Back and side view.

from almost as many districts and it was amusing to find that invariably a Highland visitor picked out that coming from his own district as the best one. The blade is fixed to a wooden haft by bending its upper edges round the haft. The top of the peat iron is often ornamented with a sheep's horn.

The newly cut peats are very soft and they have to be carefully spread to dry and this part of the work is done by women and children. For the latter it is a glorious time. They get thoroughly begrimed with the peat; they enjoy the open-air meals and, in some districts, this was the one day in the year that they had the treat of jam.[1] If the weather is not unkind, the peats are dry enough in about two weeks to be made into *cas bhic* (little feet) —three peats are set up tentwise with a fourth one laid on top. The pattern of these is the same all over the Highlands. Later they are gathered into heaps and then built into stacks and are then ready to be carried in sacks or creels or on peat barrows (see

[1]*Stornoway Gazette*, 10.8.51.

Fig. 37),[1] to the point where carts, or nowadays sometimes motor lorries, can be got to carry them home. The whole process takes about a month and, in a very wet season, the peats never dry properly and great discomfort is entailed upon the people.[2]

FIG. 37. A peat barrow.

Doctor Fraser Darling calculates that about 15,000 peats are needed by an average crofter family and that it takes a good man to cut a thousand a day, after which of course all the rest of the work of winning the peats has to be done. He also points out that the month or so taken up by this work comes at what is generally the driest time of the year when the crofter should be working his ground and cleaning it.[3]

Peat cutting is carried on extensively by the distilleries for use in the making of whisky but, in many districts, the nearer and better mosses are worked out and labour to work the peats is not available because, at just about the same time, the very important turnip crop has to be singled. Therefore coal is being more and more used and is brought to inland districts by rail or by lorry. On the west coast it is brought by 'puffers', small steam vessels that can be beached at low tide so that the coal can be loaded directly on to the people's carts or lorries. A community will often club together to buy a cargo of coal and it used to be a sight to see the concourse of carts gathered from far and near to collect a share of the coal. (Fig 38.)

[1]The peat barrow made of wood, but nowadays with a cast-iron wheel and shaped rather like a porter's hand-barrow but often with more curved handles.
[2]For theories about seasons for cutting peats see Chapter XV.
[3]Dr. Fraser Darling, *Crofting Agriculture*, p. 5.

FIG. 38. A 'puffer'.

*Home carpentry and harness-making:* Something has been said about the home-made furniture and household utensils. In the old days the people also made their own harness. In roadless districts pack ponies were used, as they still sometimes are, for carrying home the peats. The wooden pack-saddle was carved with a hook on each side, upon which the paniers could be hung. A pack-saddle at the Museum that came from Rannoch and was at least over eighty years old, was very skilfully carved out of one piece of fir-wood. But I also had a good many examples from the Islands, where the use of pack-ponies was only just declining, and these pack-saddles were made of as many as six or eight separate bits of wood nailed together. In the Islands, even at the present day, the pack-saddle is placed upon a home-made pad woven of bent grass (see Figs. 39, 40). In the old days the bridle was made of twisted twigs or even honeysuckle.[1] Instead of a crupper, a stick about a yard long, was put under the pony's tail and fastened with

[1] It will be remembered that the old Scots word for a rope was a 'woodie'.

twisted birch twigs or hair ropes. I had a halter and tether made of twisted twigs and a pair of 'branks', a device consisting of two pieces of wood, connected at the bottom by a piece of iron that went under the horse's chin and at the top by a bit of rope that

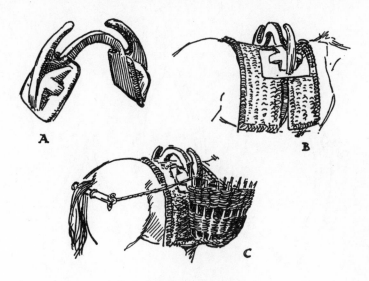

FIG. 39. Pack saddle and pad.

FIG. 40. Pack pony. Long Island.

203

went over his head. Horse-collars are said to have been made of straw in the Eastern Highlands, but I have never seen a surviving specimen. But examples of haims made of two pieces of carved wood, very like those still occasionally to be seen in Norway,

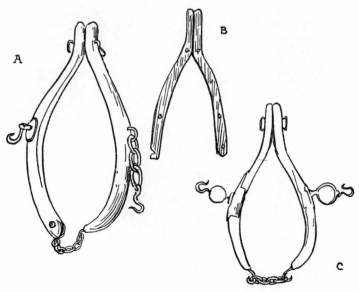

FIG. 41. Wooden haimes. (A) Probably for an ox-collar. (B) For a pony collar.

have survived (see Fig. 41). I was told that in the few Highland districts where oxen were used such wooden haims persisted after they had gone out for horses. On the Long Island very shapely horse-collars of bent grass have only gone out of common use within the last fifty years. They were made of several rings of the plaited grass, sewn edge to edge and of course did not open (see Fig. 44A, B). But, with the agricultural reforms, the use of iron ploughs and of modern carts, craftsman-made, leather harness came into use and gradually spread over the country.

Sleds and carts more properly belong to transport but it may be mentioned that slypes, primitive sleds (Fig. 65) made from a forked tree trunk and a few rough planks, were used till quite lately for dragging large stones from fields. Field gates, of course, only came in with enclosure. Old-fashioned ones were generally home-made. They consisted of undressed spars of wood morticed into the uprights of the gate[1] or merely lodged in niches cut in the gate posts. I have been told that to close a fank or cattle fold the bushy top of a tree was sometimes used. Such gates in the Islands were sometimes made of wickerwork.

*Rope making:* A great deal of rope of different kinds had to be made at home. Rushes were twisted into ropes for tethering animals. They were quickly made but were not strong. Straw rope was used in the thatching of stacks and many other purposes, but for holding down the thatch of the houses of the islands and the west coast, heather rope, which was much stronger and more durable, was used. Even greater strength was needed in the ropes used for drawing the plough and they were made of the twisted fibres of roots. I have seen small fragments. Hugh Miller described how he saw a man stripping a piece of moss fir into filaments with a pocket knife. The filaments were twisted into rope of great strength and flexibility for use as hawsers, the baulks of herring nets and the lacing of sails.[2] Horsehair rope was valuable because of its lightness and strength but the supply was limited. I was told that if a man who had a pony with a fine tail stabled it at an inn while he attended market or other diversions, he was apt to find that all the hairs had been plucked out when he returned to fetch his beast. Fine horsehair rope was often used to hold the tops of drift-nets in position. Twisted into a thick cable, horsehair was used for letting fowlers down the cliffs. A young man on St. Kilda was not supposed to marry until he had a horsehair fowling rope wherewith he could supply the needs of his family. This must have been a consideration because, within recent times, there have been no horses on St. Kilda. Much thinner ropes of twisted horsehair were also used to snare the seabirds and in Martin Martin's day the marriage portion of a St. Kilda woman was expected to bring her husband was 1 lb. of horsehair for the purpose.[3] Twisted strands of horsehair were also used for fishing casts and snoods. (See Chapter XV.)

[1]For account of similar English 'Hurdle Gates', much used in sheep country, see *Country Life*, 14.9.58.
[2]Hugh Miller, *My Schools and Schoolmasters*, pp. 268, 283.
[3]M. Martin, *Western Islands*, p. 317.

Heather rope was twisted by hand, but for making other kinds of rope various devices known as thrawcocks were used (see Fig. 42 A, B). Normally they consisted of a piece of wood with a

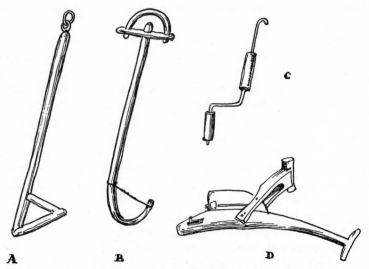

FIG. 42. Rope twisting devices. (A) and (B) Varieties of thrawcocks. (C) A more modern device. (D) Turnip seed sower.

cross-piece at one end and an iron swivel and hook at the other to which the end of the rope was attached. But I had a rope twister from Benbecula entirely of wood without any iron. One man turned the stick, another fed the straw or rushes to him. The same method was used with a later implement made of bent wire with wooden grips (see Fig. 42C). Professor Evans likens its shape to that of a carpenter's brace. He said it was more tiring to use but required less skill.[1] I have seen such implements in the Highlands but for a long time now imported coir rope has entirely taken the place of home-made rope about the crofts.

*Drystone dyking:* To split large stones required for building, a fire was sometimes lighted on the top of them to crack them with the heat. I have seen a snapshot of this being done in South Uist, or holes were bored and filled with wooden wedges which were

[1] E. Estyn Evans, *Irish Folk Ways*, p. 202.

wetted and, as the wood swelled, the stone was split.[1] The actual building of the walls was not originally a separate trade although, when enclosing began, a man good at drystone dyking might take on outside jobs. I have spent many happy hours watching Mr. MacDonald, an expert at this fascinating craft, selecting his stones, and fitting them into place as he built my cottages.

*Home shoe-making*: According to a letter to Henry VIII by John Elder, a priest in the Highlands, the ancient Highlanders generally went barefoot, but if, in specially inclement weather, they required footgear, they simply cut a piece of undressed hide to fit their feet, punched holes round the edges, so that it could be tied round their ankles and made additional holes to let the water out.[2] Even within living memory, footgear almost as primitive and known as 'rivelins', were occasionally still worn in Sutherland and the Hebrides. They were made of untanned calf-skin worn hairy side out, roughly shaped to fit the feet, the edges of the toes and heels were drawn together by overcasting, holes were punched along the tops and laces threaded through. They are said to have given a better foothold on the slippery seaweed covered rocks than any other kind of footwear. By the eighteenth century the people of the west coast were also said to be tanning leather with the roots of tormentil to make their own shoes. The labour of collecting enough of this small plant must have been enormous. In some districts this custom lasted till the end of the eighteenth century,[3] and there were many local shoemakers.

*Basket making*: Certain districts used special skills in turning their chief available resources to account. Something has been said of the use of bent grass in treeless areas and of some of the special uses of basket-work on the west coast where scrub abounded.[4] Another was the making of coffins of wickerwork. An old man who had been employed in the restoration of Iona Cathedral told me that in the crypt they had found numbers of the remains of wickerwork coffins. Another old man in Moidert had a grim tale of a badly made wickerwork coffin out of which the corpse tumbled during the funeral procession. I did not

[1]Alexander Carmichael, *Carmina Gadelica*, Vol. IV, p. 32.
[2]*Collectanea Rebus Albanicis*, p. 23.
[3]W. Marshall, *Agriculture of the Central Highlands*, p. 24. (See Chapter XI.)
[4]See Chapter VIII.

attempt to add a second-hand wickerwork coffin to my collection! Wickerwork was used in threshing barns in Kintail and on the Long Island, where timber was even more precious than bushes, the gates to the cattlefold seem originally to have been made of wickerwork for Carmichael states[1] that it was called *Cadha-Chliadh na Cuithe*—the Gorge or Pass of Wattle. Doors were also sometimes made of wickerwork and in some districts, chairs. (See Fig. 43.)

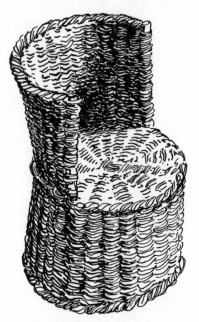

Fig. 43. Wickerwork chair.

Baskets, were, however, made all over the Highlands for many purposes such as bait-baskets for line fishing and the crans which herring drifters still use to land the fish, and by which a catch is estimated, baskets for planting potatoes, panniers for ponies and creels for carrying peats or tangle (see Fig. 44C, D). In older times, larger creels were made with hinged bottoms for emptying their load of manure upon the land and specially shaped ones for

[1]A. Carmichael, Memorandum in *Report of the Crofters Commission, 1884*, p. 454.

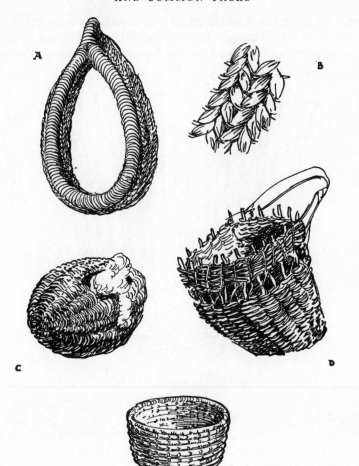

FIG. 44. Examples of wickerwork and bent grass work. (A) Bent grass collar. (B) Detail of work. (C) Wool basket. (D) Creel. (E) Ciosan.

placing in a wooden frame in a kind of primitive cart. Creels from the west coast are more shapely than those made elsewhere. It is fascinating to see one being made. The thicker rods of willow or hazel that form the framework are planted in the ground and lighter rods are woven in and out of them round and round to build up the sides of the creel (see Fig. 45). As the work proceeds the frame of upright rods is gradually drawn inwards until the ends overlap and are bound together and the creel is complete.

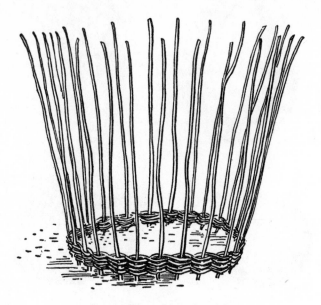

FIG. 45. The making of a creel.

'Windows', gaps in the sides, are left to give a grip in lifting. I watched the process on the island of Scalpay in Harris and afterwards saw a picture of the very same way of making a creel in an eighteenth-century print.

Woodwork was more extensively carried on in inland and eastern districts where the natural woods of birch and other small trees supplied plenty of timber. Besides making a great many articles for their own use, small wooden vessels were made and sold by the country people at local markets, such as Inverness. The splendid fir-trees were much used for deal panelling, but that of course must have been a craftsman's job.

*Kelp making*: Kelp making was carried on within a limited area and is now almost confined to a few places in the Long Island. Something has been said about the great boom in kelp making that ended so disastrously in the 1820s. Since then the use of kelp for making iodine instead of alkali has been introduced and although the Hebridean industry has never regained even a fraction of its earlier prosperity, it has struggled on in a small way, fluctuating according to movements of world supply quite outside the control of the Islanders. In spite of attempts to improve it, the process of making kelp is little changed. In the old days the seaweed had to be carried from the shore and the descendants of some of those who worked at the time of the great boom still remember stories of the acute rheumatism caused by the constant wetting. Nowadays carts lighten the labour. The seaweed was and still is collected, then dried on the machair and then burned so that it melts into a kind of slag. Kilns in the form of long narrow trenches used to be dug for this purpose, now the weed is burned in heaps. But the implements used for stirring it described in a report of 1811 are just the same as those recently used when I visited South Uist in 1937 (see Fig. 46). They consisted of 9- or 10-ft. poles with a 3-ft. rod of iron at the end with its tip bent into a hook.[1] In 1911 kelp making was still being carried on in North and South Uist and in Barra and since the Second World War Alginate Industries has been developing the use of seaweed for new purposes. In 1952, 133 seaweed collectors in South Uist and Benbecula earned more than £4,500.[2] The processing of the seaweed is however done elsewhere.

*Dairy work:* A very important part of the women's work was the care of the milch cows and the making of the butter and cheese upon which Highland economy so greatly depended. Much of the work was done at the shielings when the cows recovered from their winter starvation,

FIG. 46.
A kelp iron

[1] See Appendix XIII, W. R. Scott, *Report to the Board of Agriculture in Home Industries in the Highlands and Islands (1914)* (henceforth noted as W. R. Scott, *Report in Home Industries*). See also M. Gray, *Highland Economy*, pp. 156–8.
[2] *Report of Commission of Enquiry into Crofting Conditions, 1954*, p. 72.

had calved and were in full milk. The milk of goats and sheep was also used for the making of cheese.

The cows had their own names, *Magan, Blarach* (Dun one), *Sealbhach* (Fruitful one), my own dearest cow was Kirstie. They were sung to as they were being milked and it is said that if the song stopped they would not let down their milk and even that they had their favourite songs. I am bound to confess that the modern Highland cows seem to have lost their ear for music. I endeavoured to revive the old custom of singing (for which crouching on a milking stool is a very bad posture) but no cow I ever had paid the least attention! When they were milked outside, the hindlegs of the animals were tied together with a *buarach*, a fetter of hair plaited in a particular way and fastened with a wooden button. These fetters had to be kept very carefully, because if anyone with malign powers got hold of one, she could steal the goodness of the milk.[1] There was generally a hollow stone near where the cows were usually milked and the women were careful to pour a little milk into it as an offering to the Brownie or Gruagach who looked after the cattle.

While the crops were ripening the cows were generally kept up the hill and women had to go up to milk them. They used wooden, staved vessels with one upright handle (see Fig. 47F). In earlier times these were bound with wythes, in later times with iron bands. They were known as a *Cuman* or coggs, and in many districts they used to have a blessing said over them. For instance, an invocation of the protection of Peter, Paul and Bride was said over them in the Braemar Highlands about the middle of the nineteenth century.[2] It is only comparatively lately that coggs have gone out of use. An old gentleman was extremely scornful when he saw that I had collected some milk coggs at the Museum and said that in his young days they were as common as blackberries in his native Perthshire glen. I could not point out that this cannot have been yesterday but I asked him to find me one, and he never did. As in all staved vessels, unless they are very skilfully feathered, the staves shrink if they are allowed to become too dry and the whole vessel collapses.

[1] For examples of stealing the goodness of milk and precautions in Lewis, Norman Morrison, *Mythology and Folklore in Lewis*, pp. 13, 16.
[2] E. Taylor, *The Braaemar Highlands* (1869), p. 213.

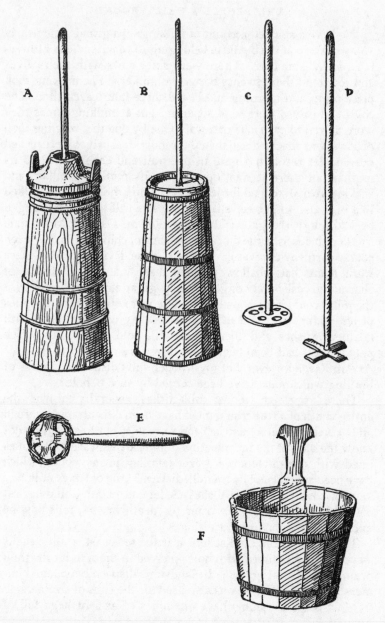

FIG. 47. Dairying implements. (A) and (B) Types of plunger churns. (C) and
(D) Their plungers. (E) Milk whisk. (F) Milk cogg.

213

We have a spirited account of milking on a grand scale nearly 156 years ago at the big farm belonging to MacKenzie at Flower-burn in Wester Ross. There were sixty cows with their calves and to attend them twenty herds and milkers. The milking took place night and morning and lasted three hours each time. The cows and calves were kept separate, but at milking times they were driven to each side of a wall. One by one the 'bawling mob of cows' was shackled and then their individual calves were picked out and let through a gate in the wall and each dashed to its mother but there it was 'opposite to its mother's milker, and sucking away like mad for its supply, while the milkmaid milked like mad also to get her share of it'. The calf was then dragged back through the gate and another let in. Osgood Mackenzie goes on to describe the dairy. 'No finery of china or glass or even coarse earthenware was ever seen in those days; instead of these were many flat, shallow wooden dishes, and a multitude of churns and casks and coggs, needing great cleansing, otherwise the milk would have gone bad.' There were of course no supplies of hot water and to clean the vessels they were scrubbed with heather brushes and then filled with cold water into which pebbles that had been heated in a fire were dropped to heat it.[1] At Am Fasgadh several of my wooden milk dishes had marks of burning which must have been caused by such pebbles.

These large, flat, wooden milk dishes, generally cut from the entire width of a tree trunk, must have been difficult to procure in all but well-timbered districts and were very apt to split. I do not know the date of the introduction of the earthenware milk dishes lined with cream-coloured glaze, familiar in my youth, which have been superseded by tin milk dishes. In the old days milk was kept in covered wooden dishes. A legend of St. Columba, recorded less than 100 years after his death in 597, tells how he exorcised a demon lurking inside.[2]

To skim the milk, in districts near the sea coast, scallop shells were used, sometimes with holes pierced in them to let the milk drain away (see Fig. 48). In landward districts wooden skimmers were used. Wood was also used for the rims of strainers. Most Scots museums have examples of ancient kegs full of

[1]Osgood Mackenzie, *A Hundred Years in the Highlands* (1949 ed.), p. 25.
[2]St. Adamnan, *Life of St. Columba* (Historians of Scotland Series), p. 48.

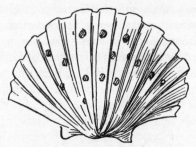

FIG. 48. Shell milk skimmer.

what was once butter, which are found buried in peat mosses. Many of these are thought to go back to prehistoric times and Professor Ritchie dated one found in Skye to the early Christian era.[1] But a strange practice is referred to in a seventeenth century history of the MacDonalds, in a narrative of events that happened in the time of John, 1st Lord of the Isles (fl. mid-fourteenth century). Lachlan and Hector, the two brothers who founded the fortunes of the MacLeans, came to the Lord of the Isles in quest of their fortunes, and MacKinnon, who was MacDonald's 'Master of Household' was bitterly jealous of them. He set before them bread and 'gruthim', 'consisting of butter and curds mixed together, which is made in harvest and preserved until time of Lent'. The story says that the gruthim was so brittle that the men could not take it up on their long knives and MacKinnon ejaculated that if they could not eat the meat as it was they should put on the nebs of hens. The sequel was that the MacLeans murdered MacKinnon.[2]

The late Mr. Francis Cameron Head, so well versed in the ways of life of his native Loch Ailort, told me that old people had told him that butter was sometimes made by shaking a leather bag. In districts where cnaggans were made, large ones were used as churns and when Carmichael was in the islands (towards the end of the nineteenth century) the wooden plunger churn was said still to be an innovation.[3] The plunger churn however had long been in wide use in other districts (see Fig. 47A, B, C, D). It consisted of a cylindrical staved vessel with a top with a hole in it through which the plunger, a stick with a disk at the lower end, projected. The butter was made by working the plunger up and down. Churns varied very much. The earlier ones were bound

[1]J. Ritchie, *Proc. Soc. Antiq. Scots*, No. 75, p. 5.
[2]History by Hugh Macdonald, printed in *Collectanea Rebus Albaniois*, p. 295.
[3]A. Carmichael, *Carmina Gadelica*, Vol. IV, p. 82.

with wythes and the tops were often whittled out of a block of wood. Later ones were bound with metal hoops. They varied in size from the tiny churn of a cottar with one cow made of deal, to the large churns of teak used by farms with fine stocks of cattle. I came across one square churn, which must have been very difficult to keep clean, although there would not be the trouble of keeping the staves from drying out and starting. The disk at the end of the plunger also varied. It was sometimes a ring of wood with a cross-piece. Sometimes a circle of solid wood pierced with holes in different patterns. The plunger churn was still in use on smaller farms less than fifty years ago but various other devices have superseded it. A box-like implement with paddles inside turned by a crank came in later than the plunger churn but has become obsolete and the glass and metal churn, supplied by shops, is now used.

Flat shallow tubs were used for washing the butter and one finds quantities of butter stamps, some ingenious ones made with a cone under which the stamp could be pushed down. The large quantity of butter that was made in the old days is surprising. Butter used to form part of the rents in kind and it was one of the few products that could be sold in order to pay for necessaries that could not be home-produced. In the eighteenth century there was a serious shortage of currency in the Highlands and in Kintyre (a great dairying district) and probably to some degree elsewhere 'cheese and butter provided this to some extent, holding value in local transactions as steady as coin and interchangeable one with the other at a fixed rate.'[1]

Cheese making was universally carried on. I have been told how it was made on smaller holdings in the days of older people's grandmothers—about fifty years ago. The curd, wrapped in a cloth, was put in the top half of a cheeser, a round staved vessel with a partition with many holes bored in it about two-thirds of the way down. A heavy stone was put on top and the whey drained away through the holes. On larger farms the cheeses were put into cheese presses, consisting of heavy blocks of stones in an iron frame which enabled them to be lowered by a wynch as the cheeses were pressed down (see Fig. 49).[2]

[1] F. F. Mackay, *MacNeill of Carskey*, p. 35.
[2] There is a modern cheese-making factory in Islay. The industry in Coll, once flourishing, has died out.

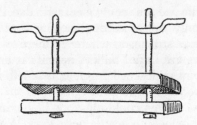

Fig. 49. A simple form of cheese press. On larger farms blocks of stone screwed down upon the upper board.

Things have changed much in the work of the dairy in the Highlands. The emphasis is strongly upon the production of beef stock and the cows are generally allowed to suckle their calves. In the crofting areas, on summer evenings, one may still see women going up to the edge of the pasture, where the cows come to meet them to be milked just as their forebears used to do, although a little covered tin milk pail has taken the place of the cuman (see Fig. 50). But, as already noted, fewer and fewer people keep their own milch cows. Only on very few farms is butter still made and no cheese is made in the Northern and Central Highlands. The industry lingered on in Coll till after the First World War. A little may still be made in Islay and Kintyre

Fig. 50. Milking a cow on the summer grazings.

217

where, before the war, one could meet with excellent home-made cheeses. The only substance approaching cheese still made is crowdie, which is still made wherever there is a surplus when home-kept cows are in full milk. The milk is either allowed to stand till it becomes thickened or rennet is added. It is then heated but must not be allowed to boil. I was told that the right temperature was when you could dip your finger in *very quickly*. If rennet has been added no heat is necessary. When the curd has coagulated sufficiently, it is lifted out of the pan, squeezed in a net cloth and salt and a small piece of butter added and it is ready.

So far as the very beautiful and interesting Highland textiles are concerned, the main part of the work was done by the women at home as part of their daily round of work, but weaving became a separate craft and, beside production for the use of the family certain sections of the textile industries from time to time became commercialized. The subject is so large that it deserves a chapter to itself.

Writing of the old handicrafts as a whole, although in many cases, the work was simple, even crude, one is constantly struck by the individuality of almost every object made. No two are exactly alike and the shape is usually adapted to take advantage of what one might term the idiosyncrasies of the actual material of which it was made. Surely it was a fine thing to go out and select one's own material and then to fashion it to one's own design. Although home crafts are no longer carried on in the Highlands in the old way, something of the same originality and gift of improvisation is shown in making-do and mending. It may be ingenious running repairs to a motor-car with a bootlace or plumbing operations with a bit of bent wire. A friend is making a collection of photographs of the most incredibly odd materials she has seen used for fencing. Most men and many women can cobble a shoe or do a bit of carpentry. Some natural genius will generally be found to tinker successfully with any mechanical device that goes wrong. In the same spirit of improvisation I saw a polished stone axe-head being used as a hammer, and very efficient it was.

# X

## HIGHLAND FABRICS

THIS was, I think, the most beautiful of the old Highland crafts and its development is closely associated with Highland history. When one is lucky enough to come across a woman sitting at her spinning wheel, one is apt to think that one is seeing something that has survived straight out of the misty past. As a matter of fact, one is watching a process that is the penultimate link in a long story of change and development.

Several different fabrics used to be made in the Highlands, linen, 'hard' woollen fabrics and blanketing and also the less important 'drugget' and 'cloutie'.

The making of linen fabrics entirely went out in the Highlands considerably more than a hundred years ago. But the history of the industry has its special interest. The wearing of saffron-dyed, closely pleated linen shirts, the *Leine Chroich*, was the defensive battle-dress of the Gael in medieval Ireland and Scotland. Besides written descriptions, one can see the carved effigies of warriors wearing the Leine Chroich on fifteenth century Highland tombstones. And linen contined to be made and used by the people till cotton took its place. The women's snowy curtches are often mentioned and everyone who could afford it had a wealth of napery.[1] Many Highland families, my own amongst them, still have beautiful hand-spun and woven linen sheets made 150 or more years ago. The servant girls of the lairds and tacksmen used

[1] A well-off laird's son of the sixteenth century had twenty-four pairs of sheets. W. Forsyth, *In the Shadow of the Cairngorms*, p. 151. Later inventories show equal quantities of napery and shirts and the critical Burt admitted that in supplies of 'sheeting and table linen people are much better furnished in that particular than those of the same rank in England'. E. Burt, *Letters*, Vol. I, p. 18. No doubt the habit of keeping the soiled linen for a great periodic wash was partly responsible.

to spin the yarn for sheets, table-cloths, bed-curtains and worka-
day shirts,[1] and it was woven by itinerant or local weavers, except
for some of the more elaborate table linen which were woven at
Musselburgh or, later, at Dunfermline.[2] I was able to collect
many pieces of linen, fine and coarse, made in many parts of the
Highlands. A beautiful diaper towel, made in the Isles of Lewis,
has the bird's-eye design that was such a favourite with Highland
woollens. I had another example of skilled weaving, given to the
museum by the direct descendant of the weaver, William Jack,
who wove it at Tain about 1800. Deer, goats, sheep and swans
with flowers and foliage were woven into his tablecloth.

This wealth of linen illustrates bygone standards of living.
The industry was closely connected with the developments in
agriculture and it was for making linen yarn that new devices for
spinning were introduced into the Highlands. It must be remembered that during most of the eighteenth century linen was the
most important Scots industry. (In 1771 13 million yds. were
stamped as fit for sale as required by Act of Parliament.) To
keep a weaver occupied the work of three or four spinners was
needed. But, as the agricultural reforms made their way up
Scotland, the supply of women seasonally employed upon the
land diminished and the spinning industry was pushed farther
and farther afield. It had become important in Perthshire by the
middle of the eighteenth century and, in 1803, that county was
described as 'enriched by raising flax and spinning it into yarn,
which is the people's chief support and staple business, for afford-
ing them cash to pay their rent, buy meal, pay their servants'
wages, etc.'.[3]

Apart from Inverness and the district around it, spinning for
the market did not spread much farther at this time in spite of
various attempts to introduce it. In 1753 a Government grant of
£3,000 payable for nine years for 'civilizing and improving the
Highlands' was largely devoted to this purpose and the Commissioners for the Forfeited Estates (forfeited in the Risings of
the '15 and the '45) set up centres in Glenmoriston, in Athole and

[1]Cambric for the fine shirts was imported.
[2]See account dated 1756 to Mrs. Ross of Pitcalnie, a Ross-shire Laird's wife.
R. Ross Williams, 'Letters from the Highlands', *Blackwood's Magazine*, November
1917.
[3]Essay, Angus MacDonald, *Transactions of the Highland Society*, No. 2.

on Loch Carron,[1] and many public spirited lairds also tried to foster it. Among their activities was the establishment of spinning schools to teach the women to use the spinning wheel. But, apart from Athole, the efforts were unsuccessful. No doubt the lack of transport was largely responsible. This was the chief difficulty the manufacturers complained of, when, at the end of the eighteenth century, the increasing demand for yarn and the dwindling supply of workers in districts where the agricultural reforms were spreading, obliged them to try to develop spinning in the Highlands. They organized it up the roadless but less mountainous coastal regions of Easter Ross and then in the north.[2]

Although flax spinning machinery had been introduced in 1793, the agricultural reforms affected the supply of the workers in the spinning districts before the demand for their work seriously declined and there is little record of unemployment or distress for this reason. In Sutherland, where agricultural reforms were later than the slackening of demand, the surplus women were employed on straw-plaiting and net-making for the booming herring industry. The contrast between the lot of the rural spinners and the urban hand-loom weavers who were ruined by the introduction of machinery is striking. The inter-relation of the circumstances of the workers and outside factors was to play a definite part in the revival of Highland crafts in the nineteenth century.[3]

The preparation of flax, which has long been a dead industry, may be treated briefly. Flax will grow well in the Highlands (to prove this I grew some at Am Fasgadh). It was regarded as a troublesome crop, exhausting the ground and requiring hand-weeding (a woman's job). An old man told me that the very large gardens, the traces of which one sees attached to the remains of many old cottages in the Eastern Highlands, were partly used for growing flax. The flax, after being pulled up, was soaked to rot the softer part of the haulms, a smelly process, known as retting. In several places I was told that the local retting pool

---

[1] W. R. Scott, *Report on Home Industries in the Highlands, 1914*, p. 564.
[2] Essay by James Mill, who did much of the work, published by the Highland Society, 1799.
[3] See p. 237.

had been a favourite place for concealing anything the people had not wished the Excise Officer to investigate. In districts where linen spinning was for home use the dusty job of freeing the fibres was done by beating by hand (a man's job). I had two wooden implements like thick toy-swords which had been used for this purpose in Deeside but sometimes a sort of mallet was used. The lint was then combed with iron combs (see Fig. 55B, also used for finest woollen cloth), but from Perthshire I had a formidable set of spikes arranged on a stand (and provided with a wooden cover), and in that old centre of spinning, water-driven machinery for preparing the lint was early introduced. Farther north, where commercial spinning was introduced much later, the flax was supplied to the spinners ready dressed.

The oldest implement for spinning is the spindle *(Fearsaid)*— (of course used for spinning wool as well as linen). Spindle whorls dating back to the Iron Age have been found all over Scotland. The process was a simple one. The thread was twisted and lengthened by the dangling spindle which was sufficiently weighted to spin when it was given a twirl by the finger and thumb. Spindles exist in infinite variety—a straight rod weighted by a stone with a hole in it (a whorl),[1] or shaped so as to have a wider lower end (see Fig. 51). The spinner wound the lint or wool round a longer piece of wood, the distaff, which she could carry in the crook of her arm so that she could spin as she moved about, herding cattle or walking to market, etc. Spinning with the spindle is, however, a slow process and wherever attempts to introduce spinning for the market were made, every effort was made to teach the women to use a wheel. Spinning wheels seem to have become very general in the Eastern Highlands by the end of the eighteenth century. Two spinning wheels valued at 8s for two are included in Sinclair's list of the plenishings of a small Black Isle farmer. But in more out-of-the-way districts women continued to use the spindle. In 1820 there was not a spinning wheel in Gairloch and in the Hebrides in 1850 most of the women were still using the spindle.[2] Yet, by 1884, very few women were said

[1]These carefully made whorls are evidently very ancient but within living memory a small potato might be used for the same purpose.

[2]H. Miller, *My Schools and Schoolmasters*, p. 284. G. and P. Anderson's *Guide to the Highlands and Islands of Scotland* (1850 ed.), p. 645.

to be still using it.[1] In South Uist, in 1937, I saw an old woman who still used the spindle. She was very poor and gathered wool from heather and fences and used a very crudely formed distaff and spindle. I also had similar ones which had been used by the last woman to spin with the distaff in Applecross. She had lately died.

Although spinning with the spindle has gone out comparatively lately, like so many obsolete artifacts, spindle whorls were often used as charms in the Highlands. I had two, made of deer's antlers, which were found in the thatch above the door of the donor's cottage in Glenurquhart and which she said had been put there by a witch.

Two kinds of spinning wheel (equally suitable for spinning wool and flax) were introduced into the Highlands. The muckle-wheel was a very simple implement that could almost be home-made (see Fig. 52A). A band connected the wheel with the

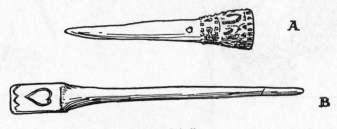

Fig. 51. Spindles.

spindle, which consisted of a thin rod of iron (see Fig. 52B). The Sleeping Beauty in the fairy tale must have pricked her finger on the spindle of such a wheel, for neither the hand-spindle nor that of the modern spinning wheel ends in a metal point. The spinner turned the muckle-wheel by hand, drawing out and twisting the thread as she stepped backwards. Then she reversed the wheel, so that the spindle wound what she had spun. It is said that a woman walked 20 miles, backwards and forwards, in a day's spinning. The muckle-wheel was common in England by Tudor times and was widely used in the Lowlands and made its way

[1]Evidence before *Crofters Commission*, 1884, Vol. I, p. 145.

A

B

FIG. 52. The muckle wheel. (A) Woman spinning. (B) Detail of spindle.

into the Highlands, but, when the flax spinning industry was being developed commercially, it was evidently the more sophisticated 'saxony wheel' that was provided (see Fig. 53). Everyone

FIG. 53. The 'cocked up' type of Saxony wheel.

is familiar with what we now think of as the old-fashioned spinning wheel, either in the 'cocked up' form with the wheel and spindle on the same level or with the spindle directly above the wheel. Both varieties were used in the Highlands. Such wheels were made by craftsmen and the earlier ones sometimes had their makers' names carved on them. There is a great deal of variation in the details of the construction, but I do not think these were due to local causes but to the idiosyncrasies of the individual maker, the earliest of whom were generally incomers. A skilled maker at Bunessan in Mull, who died a few years ago, used to embellish his wheels with a scalloping round the edge and some wheels had ornamentally turned legs. Although spinning wheels have come only comparatively lately into use in the Highlands, they have become closely integrated into the life of the women. In Father Allan MacDonald's collection of the Gaelic words of South Uist and Eriskay one is struck by the number of Gaelic terms for every part of the spinning wheel. Miss Shaw (Mrs. M. F. Campbell) included in her collection of South Uist songs some for spinning.[1] Spinning wheels have also been incorporated into fairy lore and it was considered inadvisable to leave the band on the wheel when the household retired for the night for fear that the fairies might then use the wheel. This was perhaps a cautionary tale, for if the band is left in position round the wheel the tension may be loosened, and if it is turned the thread is snapped and has to be untangled and re-threaded through the eye of the spindle.

These spinning wheels are quite elaborate machines. The wheel is turned by a treadle and the woman sits at her work. There is a double band connecting the wheel and the spindle and by means of a bobbin running loose on the spindle and a hake that controls the winding of the yarn, it winds and twists at the same time (see Fig. 56B). The improvements in these spinning devices are in speed and convenience. It is possible to spin as fine a thread upon the old spindle or the muckle-wheel as upon the Saxony one.

With the improved spinning wheel was introduced the jack reel for winding the yarn (see Fig. 54A). It, also, is familiar. It consists of a stand and a sort of rimless wheel—a series of radiating spokes with cross-pieces on the ends over which the yarn was wound. Generally there were mechanical devices for counting the number of threads. This jack reel took the place of a simple device consisting of two pieces of wood, one of which could be slipped through a slot in the middle of the other so that they formed an X. A hole through both of them at the crossing fitted on a pin fixed in an old tree stump or block of wood and upright pegs fixed in the two cross-pieces enabled the wool to be wound on them (see Fig. 54C).

The earliest looms (used for woollens as well as linen) were upright, like those still used in Finland. A fanciful description of the terrible loom of the Nornir made of weapons and parts of human bodies, as seen in a vision presaging the slaughter at the

[1] M. F. Shaw, *Folk Songs and Folk Lore*, p. 202.

Battle of Clontarf by someone in Orkney, comes into the 'Saga of Burnt Njal' and was evidently upright.[1] The weights for these upright looms, flat stones with holes through them, are found on

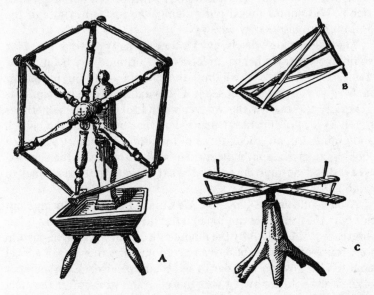

FIG. 54. Winding implements. (A) Jack reel. (B) Crois iarna. (C) Primitive wool-winder.

old sites all over the Highlands but I have never heard recollections of the use of anything except a simplified form of the present loom with its horizontally placed web. In the earlier form, the shuttle had to be passed from side to side of the web by hand and therefore only a narrow width of cloth could be woven. For this reason old Highland blankets have a seam down the middle and the belted plaid, the ancient dress of the Highlanders, was made of two widths of fabric sewn together.

In 1733, the fly-shuttle, which could be thrown across a double width of the web, was invented in England. It only made its way slowly and partially into the Highlands. In the Museum I had shuttles from Perthshire dating back at least 150 years that were made of turned birch-wood, polished and with metal ends and

[1]Translated in *Everyman's Edition*, p. 325.

little rollers that made easier the throwing of the shuttle. The bobbins that were used with them were also turned and well finished. But I also had shuttles from South Uist that had only just gone out of use, which had been whittled out of one piece of wood. The bobbins used with them were formed of bits of the hollow stem of the cow-parsley.

The old muckle-wheels, even after they had gone out of use for spinning, continued, and indeed still continue, to be used by domestic weavers for winding the bobbins (although simpler devices were sometimes used). The winding of the bobbins was generally the task of the weaver's children and was sometimes given as a punishment. A man who was an elder of the church and eminent in all good works in his local community was once looking at my bobbin winders. He said that he was the son of a weaver and he murmured 'and what a lot of bobbins I had to wind'.

A tale collected in Barra by Alexander Carmichael brings out not only the processes used in making linen at home but has other interesting allusions.[1] By the nineteenth century it was the custom for groups of the men of Barra to combine together to sail a local boat to Glasgow once a year to sell their produce.[2] Each member of the crew sold his own goods there. In the story, after the start of one of the boats, the mother of a member of the crew saw the Fairy Washerwoman[3] washing her son's shirt. In recognizing the shirt that she had made, she gave a list of all the processes she had used, 'Is that the linen I planted' . . . plucked, shrank, beetled, softened, heckled, combed, spun, steeped, sewed and bleached. Unlike the sequel to most encounters with the Fairy Washerwoman, the son whose shirt she had been washing eventually and after many delays, found his way home with a bride.

Apart from the weaving, the making of Highland woollens, like the linen made for the women's own use, was a part-time occupation. Although many of the implements were the same as those that they used for linen, it had its own processes which are of particular interest.

The first process, after washing the wool, was to dye it. The

---

[1] A. Carmichael, *Carmina Gadelica*, Vol. IV, p. 273.
[2] See Chapter XII.
[3] See p. 186.

quality of the colouring of Highland textiles largely depends upon the fact that the raw wool is dyed and not the woven fabric as was always the custom with the urban woollens. This was partly a matter of convenience, because there were no large vats in the Highlands and the dyeing had to be done in comparatively small quantities. It was quite impossible to match different batches of wool exactly, which may explain partly why checks, in which comparatively small quantities of the different colours were used, were so usual from oldest times.

As a rule the wool to be dyed and the dye plant are put into the dye pot in layers of about equal quantities and, if necessary, each layer is sprinkled with a mordant. Then the pot is filled with water. (Peat soot, nettles, heather and a few other plants are first boiled separately and the liquor is used with the wool). The brew is then boiled and the worker stirs it with a stick and every now and then raises a bit of the wool to see if the right shade has been reached. The dyeing is often done in the open air. There are no formal receipts and the worker goes by experience, taking handfuls of wool and dye plant and pinches of the mordant as she fills the pot. The work is very skilful, for the stage of development of the plant as well as the proportions of the ingredients has to be considered. Some women can get exquisitely clear dyes while others only achieve muddy ones—(or only too often in my case, a dirty grey or no colour at all). Several books have lists of plants used for dyeing and the colours they make. For instance, Professor Scott, in his authoritative *Report on Home Industries*, gives a list of forty-eight (Ref. Appendix XXIII). But for success one has to know what mordant to use and which part of the plant. For instance, to dye red with yellow lady's-bedstraw the bark of the root had to be used. The age of heather makes all the difference to the colour obtained. Flag should be used when the flower is over.

The easiest dye of all is crotal, a coarse rock lichen which gives a reddish-brown very familiar in Harris tweed. Many other lichens very readily give different shades of brown. A dullish yellow is easily got from birch leaves or bog myrtle or heather. The colour is much improved by the addition of alum as a mordant, but, unless very little is used, the texture of the wool is hardened. The real expert can get a brilliant clear yellow from heather in flower. Another easy dye is greyish-blue from the roots of yellow flag, but the expert is said to be able to get black from this or from alder or the roots of tormentil; this latter will easily give a dark grey. Peat soot boiled in a bag was much used for a yellowish-brown. Red or reddish-purple are most troublesome colours to get. I often think that it was for reasons of swank that red appears so prominently in so many of the dress tartans! Besides lady's-bedstraw (which is botanically related to madder) two kinds of lichens will give reds of different shades. The lichen is soaked for days in a warm solution of ammonia—in the Highlands what a tactful woman called 'home solution' was used.[1] The wool was then boiled in the solution. I have tried this dye with a bottle of ammonia bought from the chemist and have got a lovely rose crimson, but the colour faded as the wool dried to a warm grey. The red in a good many specimens of old tartan, however, is the distinctive shade dyed by madder and the dye may have been imported. Indigo for dyeing blue was certainly imported and was much used for the blue checked blankets so common in the Highlands and for the women's skirts. The process of dyeing it was very similar to that used for red from lichen. Mixed with a yellow vegetable dye plant, indigo gives green. I have read that both blue and green could be got from native dye plants but I have only once come across an instance. The white water-lily root was used for dyeing black but I was told that it had been used in a beautiful but fugitive blue in a tweed that I once bought. The lochans of the Islands are spangled over with this lovely plant but what a labour it must have been to grub up the roots! Many of the other dye plants in common use were troublesome to procure in quantity or to prepare, and it is very remarkable that although some of the early plaids collected by Carmichael in the Islands had a background of yellow or of the undyed wool of a black sheep, they had brilliant over-checks, and that so many of the old fabrics that have come down to us—the utilitarian checked blankets and colourful bed-covers as well as the fine 'hard' tartans—were not dyed with the easy browns and yellows but with red, green and blue. This is surely a tribute to

[1]To keep it warm the receptacle containing it was sometimes to be found in the closet against the wall of the kitchen living-room, *Scottish Mothers and Children*, p. 399.

the hard-working women who not only spun and dyed the wool but who settled the proportions of the different colours in the web. Spinners have often told me that the dyeing of the wool was the most troublesome part of their work.[1]

I have been told that staghorn moss was used as a mordant before the introduction of alum and other chemicals, but imported mordants have evidently been used for a considerable time. About twenty years ago a very old lady told me that in her young days her father had kept a little shop on Tiree and that he had stocked dyeing mordants and indigo. That would take one back about a hundred years. There is also a tale about a woman who was dyeing with indigo and alum. A lady dressed 'in ruffled green', whom she suspected of being one of the Good People, came and asked her for a drink and she gave her unwelcome visitor some of the unappetizing brew. The lady vanished.

In the eighteenth century a small professional tartan weaving industry sprang up in the outskirts of the Highlands to supply the stuff needed for the many Highland Regiments formed at that time, and the descendant of one of the weavers kindly allowed me to copy some of the old formulas for dyeing. Imported vegetable dye-stuffs were used and the same is largely the case in the modern commercially organized Lewis and Harris tweed industry. But women working on their own still use the old native dyes although they may sometimes fall for easier substances. I took a handicraft enthusiast to visit an old lady who spun and dyed her wool in Strathdearn. A rather pleasant purplish tone in her yarn intrigued her visitor and she was asked how she had got it. 'Out of a packet of Twink' was the disconcerting reply.

Once dyed, in the old days the next process determined the nature of the fabric. To make the old, very fine 'hard' fabrics the yarn was combed to remove the short, fluffy fibres (the noils). The iron combs that were used for preparing the lint were used for this purpose (see Fig. 55B), but a comb with whalebone teeth, now in the Museum of Antiquities, was probably an earlier form.[2] The combed fabrics from the Hebrides were said to be especially fine. Martin said that the best of them could be drawn

[1]See also p. 238.
[2]Similar yarn could be spun from carded wool if only the long fibres were used. Father A. MacDonald, *Gaelic Words*, p. 237.

through a wedding ring. I have seen beautifully fine fabrics but none quite so fine as that. In an account of payments of rent in kind upon the MacLeod estates in 1754, linen was valued at 11*d* and 1*s* 1*d* an ell, tartan plaiding and 'coarse grays' at 1*s* 1½*d* but some other stuff called 'Caeldos' at 1*s* 7*d*. Some of the women's plaids, woven with a white ground and with red, blue and green overchecks were specially beautiful. They also served as bed coverings by night and sometimes as their owner's winding sheet. A much coarser combed fabric, dyed dark blue with indigo, was used for the women's petticoats in Barra till within living memory. It was practically waterproof.

Because of their fineness, their colouring and the complexity of weaving them, the old checked plaids were articles of value. In the sixteenth century there are instances where rents were partly paid in such plaids[1] and in 1596, in an interchange of gifts between MacDonald of Islay and Tyrone, the Highlander's contribution was plaids. In 1621 the Baron Coirt of Glenurchy fixed the rates of charges that weavers might make. For 'a guid hard plaid', 1 firlot of meal, for a grey plaid 'of half heus', 2 pecks of meal and 2*s*, for a grey plaid 'that hes bot ane spraig of hewes' 1 peck and 2 lippies of meal and 2*s*.[2]

The making of fabric of combed yarn has long gone out in the Highlands.[3] So entirely is this the case that when a hank of combed yarn was discovered in an old cottage in North Uist, about twenty years ago, although a good deal of spinning and weaving is still done in the Island, no one knew what it was and wondered if it were linen yarn.

The wool, however, could be spun uncombed and when all the shorter fibres were left in it, it made a softer, fluffier fabric. Uncombed yarn was used for blankets, bed-covers and, no doubt, the cheaper plaiding. The blankets sometimes had wide coloured borders, sometimes an over-all pattern of large checks. The bed-covers were woven in a small bird's-eye pattern, with a border reversing the colouring. Occasionally they were made with a

---

[1]For a fourteenth century example for lands in Lorne see *Origines Parochiale Scotiae*, Vol. II, Part I, p. 112.

[2]*Black Book of Taymouth*, p. 262. 4 lippies = 1 peck, 4 pecks = 1 firlot.

[3]'Hard Tartan' made professionally for the use of the Highland Regiments continued until the days of Queen Victoria, who considered that it was too harsh for the men's bare legs and ordered that the Saxony type of wool should be used instead.

linen woof and a woollen weft. Among the dozens I collected all had individuality. The colour schemes varied very much and were sometimes subdued and subtle—two shades of brown or black and grey, and sometimes very daring, as for instance, orange and red. One of my favourites was of reddish- and bluish-purples. The old blankets, although warm, were very heavy and they and the bed-covers are now little esteemed.

For many years the wool has first been carded, but wool cards (see Fig. 55), rather like butter 'hands' covered with small metal hooks with which the wool was fluffed out and then rolled

Fig. 55. Implements used in preparing lint and wool. (A) Wool cards. (B) Combs used for linen yarn or for woollen yarn used in 'hard tartan'.

into *rolagan* ('rollocks') were certainly not of local manufacture, and I know, from experiment, how difficult it is to spin wool that has merely been teased out by hand. Before carding the wool it has to be teased with the fingers and a special basket, a *Mudag*, round, with a hole in it, like a wren's nest is used for holding it (see Fig. 44C). Wool always seems to card most easily in the warmth of the fire (see Fig. 56A).

The woman having dyed and spun her yarn according to her taste employed a local weaver to weave it. She first measured the

Fig. 56. Women preparing woollen yarn. (A) Women carding and spinning with upright type of Saxony wheel. (B) Details of spindle of Saxony wheel.

234

proportions of the colours to be used by winding the required number of threads of each colour backwards and forwards between a series of pegs fixed in the walls of the barn or on a large wooden frame *(the Beart Deilbh)*. Then, for convenience, she looped the assorted yarns over her hand and elbow to make a sort of chain to carry it to the weaver.

Whether made with combed or carded yarn, a web of cloth has to be consolidated by the process of fulling. Water-driven fulling mills had been common in England from medieval tmes and they were the usual process of fulling cloth in the mainland districts of the Highlands in the eighteenth century and probably long before that. In the Islands and some parts of the Western Highlands the process was done by hand.[1] On the Long Island the old process is still often gone through as an entertainment and is well remembered, but there can be few places where it is still carried on as part of the normal making of the cloth. The *luadhadh* or waulking of the cloth (generally written luaching) was a communal function and when a web was cut from the loom about ten women of a township were invited to take part in the process. In the illustration to Pennant's eighteenth century account they are represented as sitting on the ground and working the web with their bare feet, but in nineteenth-century accounts they are described as sitting on each side of a barn door which was placed flat upon supports in the middle of the room or, in later times, on each side of a table, and working the cloth with their hands. Considerable judgement was required in the process and it was always directed by an experienced leader. The new web had been soaking in a solution of ammonia and it was passed round the table sun-wise in a series of Vs backwards and forwards between the women on the opposite sides of the table and rubbed and thumped in time to the women's singing. This singing of special songs for the different parts of the process was a special feature. The women began with slow ones and gradually worked themselves up to a frenzy. Each song lasted about eight minutes and periodically the cloth was inspected by the leader to see if it had been sufficiently shrunk. If not she would estimate that it would take so many more songs. In a final song, while the web was rolled and patted, part of the fun was the improvisation of verses. The

[1]There are still traditions of it in Moidart. Calum MacLean, *The Highlands*, p. 74.

finished cloth was finally stretched and re-rolled tightly, and was then blessed. Mrs. M. F. Campbell, who saw the *luadhadh* of the cloth while she was staying at Glendale in South Uist has pointed out that the process and the method of singing are unique to the Western Islands. She has made a study of them and has published many of the songs with their music.[1]

Carded yarn is also used for knitting. For this purpose two strands of the wool are twisted together. Two pirns of wool are put on a little frame (or in the heels of a pair of shoes) and are run backwards on the spinning wheel or twisted the reverse way in a spindle. This reverse twist gives the knitting wool its elasticity. To make the twisted yarn into skeins it is wound on the *Crois Iarna*, which consists of a wooden bar about 2 ft. long with a small cross-piece at each end. These are set pointing opposite ways, and the wool is brought over the end of one cross-piece, then down to the end of the other piece, then back to the farther end of the first cross-piece and so down to the end of the second one and when the winding is completed one pulls it off as a complete skein. The *Crois Iarna* are generally home-made and are fascinating in their variety. Some have a joint to facilitate the slipping of the yarn. Others have a knob at either end of the cross-pieces to keep it in place. Mainland ones have the cross-pieces nailed on; in island ones the ends of the bar are pushed through slots in the cross-pieces. Some are large, others small. I had about fifty, all individual. (See Fig. 54B).

To make a digression, in the early nineteenth-century Highland women were also very fond of knitting cotton quilts in complicated stitches and also elaborate white cotton stockings. These were the successors of linen ones, of which I had one example.[2]

Other Highland fabrics may be mentioned. The women used to wear a very attractive stuff of dark blue, the weft striped with bright colours, for their petticoats. Originally the warp had been of linen and the weft of wool, later on the warp was made of cotton. This stuff was called drugget (*drogad*) and it was still

[1]See M. F. Shaw, *Folk Songs and Folk Lore*, pp. 71, 206 onwards. T. Pennant, in his *Tour of Scotland and Voyage to the Hebrides*, Vol. I, p. 328 gives an eighteenth-century account. Of later ones that by Miss A. Goodrich Freer, in *The Outer Isles*, p. 254 is particularly detailed.

[2]See also Chapter XIV.

being made in the Islands less than fifty years ago. It seems a pity that the making of it could not be revived.

Another stuff, not peculiar to the Highlands, was 'cloutie', consisting of a weft of thin strips of old stuff woven on a cotton warp and it was used for quilts. I have been told that cloutie was often made by old or infirm weavers.

At roups one comes across so many tiny looms suitable for weaving braid, ribbon or garters, that one imagines that this must have been a favoured pastime among the better-off women.

It will be noticed that I have not mentioned the making of tweed. The introduction of the making of this fabric into the Highlands belongs to the mid-nineteenth century. By that time the people had largely given up making stuffs for their own wearing. In the more prosperous districts the statistical accounts for parish after parish state that under the new system of agriculture there was less seasonal employment and those still working on the land were better off and preferred to buy fashionable clothes —the vogue for cottons did much to oust linens, and men preferred broadcloth to home-made plaiding. In the districts affected by sheep-farming the decline was sometimes for the sadder reason that the people, deprived of much of their hill-grazings, often could not keep sheep. This is a frequent complaint in the evidence before the 1884 Crofters Commission. As the people of the north-west tended, more and more, to supplement the living to be made from their holdings by work away from home, they tended to buy more and more of their clothes (if they could afford to do so).

Meanwhile, upon the Borders, an old manufacture of coarse woollen stuff in white, grey and black (natural colours) known as *tweel* had become fully mechanized. About 1820, as an innovation, wools of different colours were carded together and this caught the popular fancy. According to a tradition it was sheer chance that the name of *tweed* instead of tweel was given to these rough Border fabrics. It was at the time when the fame of Sir Walter Scott and of his writings on the Borders were at their zenith, and the word tweed caught on and the manufacture of tweeds became well established. Later in the century, the writings of Ruskin and the wearisome monotony of perfection that

237

machine work had reached led, as a reaction, to an aesthetic interest in craft work and about the same time the new fashion for shooting in the Highlands had introduced the need for warm country clothes by the well-to-do people who indulged in the sport. Meanwhile the condition of the people in the Western Highlands and Islands through congestion on their holdings and a series of bad fishing seasons was going from bad to worse. Tentative efforts had been made by well-disposed lairds, and still more by their ladies, to develop home industries. Then the destitution caused by the potato famine gave the spur of urgency to such efforts. Stocking knitting, the weaving of plaiding and other crafts were started in many parts of the Highlands. The Gairloch stocking industry was particularly successful, and her descendant presented to the Museum the jack-reel which its founder, Lady MacKenzie, used in measuring out the wool delivered to the knitters. In every case a philanthropic lady revived or initiated these industries, supervised them and found a market for the products among her friends. And in a great many cases the industries tended to decline or to lapse when the founders were unable to continue their active supervision.

There was one significant exception. Harris had always produced a good deal of plaiding. The making is mentioned in sixteenth century reports on the Islands and a good deal of rent was paid in plaiding. In 1844, Lord Dunmore, the new proprietor of the Island, had Murray tartan (his family tartan), woven in the local plaiding and the stuff was worn by himself, his keepers and other retainers. Lady Dunmore then introduced the making of tweed with its characteristic yarn of mixed colours as a handicraft industry, and found a market for it among her friends and it became a mainstay to many of the people. As Professor Scott points out, although the making of Harris tweed only dates from this period, the cause of its success dates far back in the old skill of the workers and their taste in colours.[1]

The making of tweed was taken up by most of the other societies trying to develop Highland Home Industries[2] and the

[1]W. R. Scott, *Report on Home Industries*, p. 33.

[2]Such as the Scottish Industries Association, the Highland Home Industries, the Crofters Agency, The Highland Home Industries issued an interesting account of *Highland Home Industries*.

Government[1] has also helped. In spite of ups and downs the industry has achieved an independent position. In 1911 Professor Scott estimated that the value of tweed sold from Harris, Lewis, St. Kilda, Islay, Orkney and Shetland totalled £83,399, while the sales 'of twenty-four Home Industries Associations operating on the mainland and largely selling tweed totalled £6,292.[1] Although the industry has its roots in the old skills that the people developed in making things for their own use, the nineteenth-century Highland tweed industry is essentially different (and has the serious weakness) that it is in some degree a luxury trade catering for customers very far removed in their tastes and circumstances from the people of the Islands.

As it has developed it has become increasingly mechanized. Fabrics entirely home-made with the old implements are still made but machine-carding and machine-spinning have been extensively introduced. In Lewis, in 1948, there were 800–1,000 hand looms on which was woven wool spun in the mills of Stornoway. The weavers generally work on commission for the spinning mill owners. The Harris Tweed Association has done good work in pushing the tweed industry and keeping up the standard.[3] Over 6 million yds. of tweed were stamped by the Association in 1958. In Harris some tweed is made partly of hand-spun yarn.

[1]Through the Congested Districts Board, later absorbed into the Scottish Board of Agriculture.
[2]W. R. Scott, *Report on Home Industries*, Appendix XX.
[3]*Report of the Commission of Enquiry into Crofting Conditions, 1954*, p. 78.

# XI

## THE CRAFTSMEN

IN spite of the variety of tasks the country people performed themselves there had long been, except in the poorest and remotest communities, a certain number of specialized craftsmen who were employed by people who could afford to do so. During the eighteenth century their numbers were evidently increasing.

Probably the most ancient craftsman was the smith and armourer. He appears in many of the ancient folk-tales, and it is because iron had a magical significance as well as because of the importance of his work in the community and his special skill, that he is so often an heroic or at least a distinguished figure. In the days of the clans the armourer and smith was an adherent of the chief and the office was generally hereditary. Members of the small clan of Maceacherns, for instance, served the chiefs of several clans. The chief gave the armourer a piece of land rent free and he also received certain perquisites—in Lewis, the head of every slaughtered cow. All over the Highlands one constantly finds the place-name Balnagowan, the *Bailé* of the *Gobhainn* or smith.

One can see proof of the skill of the old Highland armourers in the mail shirts that were worn by those Highlanders who could afford them from medieval times down to the sixteenth century and which appear on so many of the West Highland effigies. A traveller to the Highlands in 1800 visited a family of MacNabs who claimed to have been the hereditary smiths of the Breadalbane family for 400 years. He was shown a coat of mail that had been made by one of their ancestors.[1] No doubt the armourers

[1] J. Leyden, *Tour in the Highlands of Scotland*, p. 86. See also T. Garnett, *Tour*, p. 114.

made the blades of the dirks and, presumably, those of the two-handed swords. But those of the best of the beautifully balanced basket-hilted swords, that became a typical part of the fighting equipment of a Highlander in the seventeenth century, were often imported, and one finds the mark of Solingen craftsmen or of *de Ferara* upon them.

When clan warfare came to an end, the importance of the smith as armourer declined, but he had more work in other ways. The use of roads led to the shoeing of horses (the shoeing of cattle for their long journey to the southern markets also became necessary). The improvements in agriculture led to the use and repair of more metal implements. I had in my possession an old hoe with a little patch carefully rivetted to the blade, showing that iron was still precious. Now, with the passing of horses and carts, the work of the smith has long been diminishing, although local repairs are still needed for the more new-fangled implements. As a highly skilled worker in what was a precious metal, the number of smiths can never have been great. In the eighteenth century there were far fewer of them than of other kinds of craftsmen.

Although the smith had a croft as a valuable part of his remuneration, he was probably more of a whole-time worker than the other craftsmen. What was written of the craftsmen of Rogart was true of those in other districts. 'A great many people in the parish call themselves tradesmen and, at the same time, exercise their several crafts as weavers, taylors, shoemakers, millers, carpenters, coopers, etc., but there is hardly anyone in these professions that does not hold more or less land: so that the whole may be said to be farmers and their chief property consists in the number of cattle of different sorts they keep.'[1] Or, as Sir John Clapham put it all Highland craftsmen had 'if not a foot at least a toe on the land'.[2]

Weaving was, of course, a very ancient craft in the Highlands, although it is not clear when the professional weaver emerged. It was certainly so by the seventeenth century because payments to weavers were then being fixed by the Baron Court of Glenurchy.[3] By that time a good deal of weaving was going on in the

[1] *Old Statistical Account*, Vol. III, p. 566.
[2] J. Clapham, *A Concise Economic History of Britain*, p. 215.
[3] *Black Book of Taymouth*, p. 362.

Highlands and the sale of woollen plaiding was the only rural craft there that menaced the monopoly in trades and crafts still enjoyed by the Royal Burghs. Proceedings against such sales were constantly taken by the burgesses of Inverness during the seventeenth century.[1]

Something has been said of the implements used in textiles. The local weavers generally did bespoke work for the women of the district, being largely paid in kind. But sometimes the weaver went to work a loom temporarily set up in a laird's or tacksman's house. Miss Frances Tolmie has a delightful account of the visit of such a weaver and the feast of song that followed. There is a Bernera story about another who adjusted the rate of his work to the amount of refreshment supplied to him by the employers that he visited. In the Islands, the weaver generally was, and occasionally still is, a woman and not a man. Father Allan MacDonald recorded a beautiful tradition that shows how much weaving was regarded as a woman's occupation. He says that a woman's request for yarn to finish the weft on her loom is never refused because a poor woman once came to Our Lady to ask for some yarn for this purpose and, having no wool, Our Lady tore a handful of hair from the left side of her head, and this enabled the web to be finished. For this reason women's hair is said to be thinner on the left side than on the right.[2]

The eighteenth century also contains records of shoemakers. But the professional shoemaker was evidently only gradually becoming general, for we know that in poorer districts people were still making their own shoes and, even in the far-advanced district of Atholl a shoemaker at Kenmore in the 1770s petitioned the Earl of Breadalbane for a rent-free house because he was 'as useful to the country and this family as the smith, the merchant and the bellman, all of whom sat rent free'.[3] This suggests that his regular employment was an innovation.

The shoes made by the early shoemakers were unwelted and consisted of a sole of single leather, stitched to the upper part.

---

[1] These wide monopolies had very serious effects in preventing the development of domestic industries and the rise of villages in the Lowlands. I. F. Grant, *Social and Economic Development*, p. 133. See also W. MacKay, *Life in Inverness in the Sixteenth Century*, pp. 23, 25, 38.

[2] Father A. MacDonald, *Gaelic Words*, p. 151.

[3] M. MacArthur, *Lochtayside*, p. xv.

They were neither durable nor expensive. A tacksman, as part of the pay given to his servants, usually supplied each of them with two pairs of shoes a year, valued at 1s 6d to 2s a pair. I was given a child's shoe made in this primitive way with its tiny last. It had been found near Nethybridge but the story of why it had been treasured had been forgotten. An old Gaelic poem, collected in Barra by Alexander Carmichael runs:

> Awl and last
> Wax and tallow
> Hen's feathers as a point
> To thrust it through the heel.
> Stitches eighteen
> From snout above round about down to heel
> In the Gaelic shoe.

Professor J. Carmichael Watson, who edited and translated this volume of his grandfather's papers, says that hen's feathers were used in place of bristles to push the thread through the thickest part of the shoe at the heel. Leather thongs or laces were sometimes used instead of waxed thread and only one thread or lace was used instead of the two used by modern shoemakers, and therefore each side of the shoe was worked down from the toe so as to make the tension equal.[1]

The home shoemaker originally tanned his leather with the roots of tormentil but, in the eighteenth century, a great deal of tanning was done in Elgin and oak-bark was regularly stripped from the trees in Badenoch and sent there (I had one of the tools used for the purpose). I do not know how widely and when the use of professionally tanned leather spread through the Highlands. The Kenmore shoemaker, already mentioned, stated in his petition, that he imported his leather from Perth.[2]

Properly welted shoes were, however, introduced into the Highlands long ago. From the lonely hamlet of Mellon Charles, on the coast of Wester Ross, I was able to secure a complete set of cobbler's tools. From what I learnt of their former owner they must have been at least fifty years old at the time, but they were

---

[1] A. Carmichael, *Carmina Gadelica*, Vol. IV, p. 100–1, ed. and translated by J. Carmichael Watson.

[2] See p. 207.

exactly the same as those used by the father of the local shoe-maker at Kingussie. From Atholl came a simple wooden vice of a kind said to have been once used all over Britain. It consisted of two curved blades of wood, meeting at the tips like a pair of pincers and fitted into a wooden handle. A screw a little way up the blades could be turned to compress them so that the curved tips gripped anything inserted between them.[1]

That there were so many tailors is particularly interesting and significant of the people's personal pride. One would have expected that, when so many things were made at home, the people would have made their own clothes, but especially in the case of the men, this was not so. They invariably employed a tailor, who used to make the round of the countryside, staying in one township after another to make the people's clothes and generally bringing a welcome budget of news and gossip. This was not an eighteenth century innovation, for the tailor figures in many old folk-tales.

The *Old Statistical Accounts* often give the number of craftsmen in a parish. Weavers are invariably the most numerous, generally nearly as many as all the other craftsmen put together. In Farr, with a population of 386 families, there were thirty-four weavers and in Alvie, with a total population of 1,011 people there were six. Tailors and shoemakers were generally about equally numerous. In Farr twenty tailors and twenty-four shoe-makers, in Alvie four and two. There were seldom more than four smiths in a parish.[2]

The rise of the Highland fishing industry was responsible for the increase in two kinds of craft workers in wood. Coopers were to be found in the many fishery villages that sprang up and were employed in making the barrels for the salted herrings. No doubt they also made many of the staved wooden vessels, coggs, cheesers, tubs and churns, etc., that were so essential to the Highland household economy, although these seem also to have been made by local less specialized craftsmen, and the smaller ones by the tinkers. I had two tools that were a complete puzzle until an

---

[1]See *Scottish Studies*, Vol. II, Part I, p. 119, for the description of a similar vice found in South Uist and details of distribution.

[2]*Old Statistical Account*, Vol. III, p. 540; Vol. XIII, p. 375. In Duirinish, there was said to be a blacksmith in every barony, Vol. IV, p. 132, suggesting his association, as armourer, with the old social organization of the clan.

old man, the son of a long dead cooper, identified them as like those that he remembered his father using. One was a sort of gouge, used for smoothing the inside of a barrel, the other was a wooden implement, with movable arms sliding up and down it, that was used for the placing of the iron hoops. He knew nothing about the feathering on the finer types of staved vessels. That one does not find it on the heavier barrels and kegs explains this. In the earlier days of local fisheries, when small boats were used, there were boat-builders all along the coasts, although they were not always specalists in that particular branch of carpentering. Some few still exist but boat-building belongs to the story of the fisheries.

All over the Highlands, but especially most markedly in the well-wooded areas, there must have been a number of skilled woodworkers who made some of the staved coggs and churns and the turned bowls. Most of the more ambitious schemes for developing textile industries in the Highlands made provision for the introduction of a skilled man to manufacture the spinning wheels. And one hears of wheelwrights who served wide districts, but the craft has died out. A riddle made of split willow rods that I got in Perthshire was evidently the work of a craftsman. It is the only Highland specimen I have seen, but examples of the same work were made in Ireland. The fine fiddle-backed chairs, generally of elm or beech already described,[1] were widely distributed and were evidently locally made, but locally made furniture is not only more plentiful and of better quality, but these are more definitely traditional types in the well-forested districts. Good deal panelling was not uncommon in the better type of houses there and there used often to be fine deal box pews in the local churches. In Duthill Church, they have now been made into an effective dado on the walls. One can see that the planking in some of the older houses was cut with the adze and this tool must have continued to be the favourite implement among the country people for shaping the timbers of their houses, because one finds such a number of old adze heads still lying about in older steadings. Pitsaws were, of course, a great advance on the wasteful process of hacking a single plank out of a tree-trunk by means of an adze. To use these huge saws the tree-trunk was laid across a pit so that the saw could be worked up and down

[1] See Chapter VIII.

vertically. About 1731 in Aberdeenshire, Grant of Monymusk was paying £1 to a man for 'cutting and sawing timber', but by 1754 he was planning to build water-driven saw-mills.[1] Grant, however, was a pioneer in forestry work and the great pitsaws long continued to work in remote districts. Hugh Miller has left an unforgettable character study of his uncle, a sawyer, who lived in the first part of the nineteenth century in the town of Cromarty, and of the beautiful country where he used to set up his temporary saw-pits.[2] I was much surprised to discover an outsize specimen of a pitsaw in the treeless island of North Uist. One must, of course, remember that in the days of wooden ships a certain amount of wreckage must have been washed ashore on the Islands. In Strathspey saw-mills were well established by the early nineteenth century.

The improvements in housing led to a great increase in the demand for joiners and masons. In the late eighteenth and early nineteenth centuries masons generally combined this profession with quarrying, and had their homes in some little town, spending the summer travelling over the countryside and working on the mansions, farm steadings, bridges and other works that were being built all over the Highlands. We have a vivid and most human account of the life of such a mason in Hugh Miller's experiences, when he was employed in this way upon the house Mackenzie of Gairloch was building.[3]

The agricultural reforms also encouraged other specialized craftsmen. Again it is Hugh Miller who describes how another of his uncles carried on the trade of harness-maker, living in the little town of Cromarty and making harness for the farmers over a wide district.[4]

These craftsmen, some of them living in the small towns in or close to the Highlands (in the case of some of the joiners and masons living in the country) are a vanishing race. In my young days, in many little towns and villages, there were renowned shoemakers, tailors and kilt makers, whose handiwork not only supplied local needs but was often taken far afield by shooting

[1] *Monymusk Papers, 1713–1755,* ed. H. Hamilton (published Scottish History Society), pp. 9, 157.
[2] Hugh Miller, *My Schools and Schoolmasters* (1907 ed.), pp. 34, 58.
[3] Hugh Miller, *My Schools and Schoolmasters,* pp. 153, 268 onwards.
[4] Hugh Miller, *My Schools and Schoolmasters,* p. 34.

tenants and other visitors. Now these skilled local workers have all but disappeared and the multiple stores are spreading through the north and supplying their standardized goods. Even the old 'general merchants', whose shops, to my childish eyes, were veritable Aladdin's caves, with their curious aroma, compounded from leather goods, woollens, paraffin, spice, household soap, and apples and dear knows what else, are becoming things of the past.

These modern changes have done much to degrade the status of the tinkers. In the old days the tinkers or cairds, Gaelic *cairdean*, were the wandering craftsmen. They made such things as the handles of the finer dirks (see Fig. 68C), and were silversmiths, making brooches and other adornments out of coins. A Lewis tale that goes back to the seventeenth century described how Tormod MacUrchy, a warrior of great note, was given a pot of silver that had been dug up. He had noticed how a wandering tinker melted metal with his portable bellows and anvil and he was able, himself, to melt down the silver. But he could not make it into anything. So when the tinker next came round, he asked him to show him how to work up the silver. The tinker said that he would do so if Tormod gave him a sixpence each time he saw his face. Tormod accordingly gave him a sixpence and the tinker made off with the silver and never returned to claim another coin. (Told in a manuscript history of the Morrisons.) I was able to buy a silver brooch and was told that the grandmother of the old woman who sold it had been herding cattle by the track that was then the only road to Applecross (in Wester Ross). She found a silver spoon that had probably fallen from the creel of a pack-pony and she took it to the tinkers, who kept the shank of the spoon in payment and hammered a heart-shaped brooch out of the bowl. The shape of the bowl of the spoon was still unmistakable and this was a crude piece of work, but some of the earlier tinker-made silver-work is very good. I had a lovely little heart-shaped brooch with no hall-mark, so presumably it had been made by a tinker. Some of the more skilled ones, however, were registered as silversmiths and had their hall-mark.[1]

[1]Very fine silver-ware was made in Inverness and other burghs on the borders of the Highlands by skilled craftsmen from the seventeenth century onwards. Each burgh had its special mark and the craftsmen turned out beautiful quaichs, brooches, spoons, etc. This was not a rural craft but had been introduced from southern towns.

I had a brooch made by a member of a family of Stewarts. Unfortunately another member got into trouble. A customer had ordered an article of silver-ware, but among the broken silver that the tinker was preparing to melt down to make it, he recognized an article of silver that had been stolen from himself. I once asked a tinker's wife if she could get for me a pair of the brooches connected by a chain that tinker-women once used for fastening their shawls when they had small babies to carry. To make a digression. The shawls were fastened to the woman's belt at the back, the child was then placed pick-a-back in the small of her back and the shawl was brought over him and fastened in front with these brooches, which the woman called 'Skivvies'. Her husband made me a pair using two white metal spoons and a bit of a child's toy watch-chain to connect them.

The tinkers were also the makers of horn spoons. Now that they have given up this craft, it is possible to acquire the spoon moulds that they used (see Fig. 32). They consisted of two pieces of wood with the shape of the bowl of the spoon projecting on the end of one and recessed on the other, and fastened together at one end. The horn, after having been softened in the fire or by boiling (the tinkers' accounts varied) was pressed between the two pieces of the mould. The making of spoons in this way was the tinkers' secret. On two occasions old men have come to see the Museum and been specially interested in the horn spoon moulds because they said that when they were young their fathers had sent them with a horn to the tinkers to ask them to make a spoon and the tinkers had taken the horn and told the boys to come back in a day or two and they would get their spoon.

These tinker-made spoons are very crude and there was also a skilled, urban horn-work industry, but I have often wondered if it was the tinkers, the *cairdean*, who made the beautiful powder horns of the seventeenth century with their interlaced patterns and spirited hunting scenes (see Fig. 69B).

The tinkers still remember their old skills. Many of them used to bring their children to the Museum to see the horn spoons and moulds, the older silver-ware and the collection of tools they used for soldering, and they were punctilious in putting something into the box I kept at the door for contributions towards the upkeep of the Museum. But I never could persuade them to take up the making of horn spoons, although I could have found a good market for their work among other visitors.

After the making of horn spoons went out, the tinkers still turned out very serviceable tin-ware from the sheets of tin that they bought, but about 1890 the import of cheap, mass-produced tin-ware began to kill this trade.[1] They still mend tins, make baskets and fish for pearl-bearing mussels in the Highland rivers. To do so they use an old pot or a box with a bit of glass in place of the bottom—one that I acquired from them had the glass fixed with candle grease. They hold this contraption so that the glass is below the surface of the water in order to do away with the reflected light and enable them to see where the mussels are lying on the bottom. They raise the mussels by means of a long stick with a forked end. Many of them are pipers and nowadays they play on ordinary shop-made, ebony pipes, but I bought from one of them a piece of a very old drone, made of unpolished wood and hollowed out by burning.

I once asked a party of tinkers to make me one of the larger tents in which they spend the winter and which they called 'ghiellies'. They arrived with a bundle of birch wands and, without taking any measurements, and in what seemed the most casual way, they stuck the wands into the ground, tying their tops together and fastening more wands round them. The result was a most symmetrical oval framework. A space had been left in the framework to serve as a door and the whole thing was covered with tattered tarpaulins held down by ropes weighted with stones. A hole had been left in the covering to let out the smoke and a hearth of flat stones was arranged in the middle of the tent. Beds were made up at each end of straw and blankets. The whole thing was about 12 ft. long and I was told that eight people could live in it. To hang the pot over the fire the tinkers use an iron rod, which is thrust into the ground, and the upper end of which is bent into a U-shaped hook.[2]

[1] *Scottish Mothers and Children*, Carnegie Trust, p. 514.
[2] Under the 1908 Education Act tinkers with children are required to remain stationary during the winter in order to send their children to school.

# XII

## SEA FISHING AND BOATS

A GLANCE at the map shows how much indented are the coasts of the Highlands and how large the company of islands. On three sides are formidable oceans; to the east is the stormy North Sea while to the west, for months on end, the gale-driven Atlantic rollers pound the coast, and to the north, the most formidable seas of all pile up where strongly-running currents meet. On the other hand, although the channels between Ireland and the South-Western Highlands and between the Long Island and the mainland (the Minch) can be very rough, land is within sight. And twining in and out between the clustering islands and penetrating far inland in long sea-lochs are narrow but tantalizingly dividing arms of the sea. Even inland, the Highlands are full of freshwater lochs.

Water has, therefore, played a great part in Highland life—it has been a means of defence—the castles of the north, perched on beetling crags above boiling seas are examples—and so are the crannogs, the lake-dwellings, the remains of which can be found on so many lochs or the later castles built on islands. And it was perhaps partly for protection against lesser depredators that the Gael loved to confide their dead to an island sepulture. The sea was, however, also the way by which raiders and invaders only too often came and all along the coasts brochs and hill forts and a long chain of medieval castles were built as refuges and points of defence. In the west, especially, travel by sea, although it was often very dangerous, was generally preferred in the days before roads. Even so late as the '45 sea transport played an important part in strategy in the west.[1] The rich store of food

[1]This is well brought out in Sir James Fergusson's *Argyll in the '45*, esp. Chapters II and VI.

within the seas, the fisheries, seems to have been astonishingly unimportant in the Highlanders' economy until comparatively late in their history, but then through their dire necessity the industry became closely integrated into the life of the people of the west and north. Yet because of the physical setting, in the midst of the great waters, the tradition of seafaring was part of the people's heritage both from their Gaelic and their Norwegian ancestors.

There were three traditional ways of making boats in the Highlands. Like forest dwellers the world over, the mainland Highlanders used to make boats of hollowed out logs.[1] This primitive method like the habit of living in lake dwellings, may have lingered on,[2] but even in the days before written history, a more advanced type of boat building had begun to play an important part in the life of the Gael.

The making of boats of hides stretched on a wooden framework is an ancient and widely spread technique.[3] Such boats were used from Norway to Tibet and are as old as the paleolithic civilization. The Irish were particularly skilled in making large sea-going vessels of this contruction. It was in such ships that the wayfarers of their much loved tales of wanderings ventured forth to find the land of their heart's desire. St. Brendan, the Voyager, however, after many failures, was warned by St. Ita not to seek the Earthly Paradise in a ship made of death-stained hides and built a wooden ship for his last voyage. To quote an illustration dearer to Highlanders, the place where St. Columba landed on Iona is to this day pointed out as *Port na Churraigh* and, although the making of larger skin boats was superseded, small ones continued to be widely used in the Highlands. A curragh comes into one of the best known tales of a Highland prophecy. The Very Reverend Norman MacLeod, who in later life held very high office in the Church of Scotland, recorded that, as a lad, in 1799, he stayed at Dunvegan Castle and saw the unfurling of the Fairy Flag of the MacLeods by the inquisitive family lawyer and he told how the old prophecy by Coinneach Odhar, a sixteenth-

[1] Examples were recently found at Loch Laggan and Loch Treig.
[2] A. W. Brögger and H. Shetelig, *The Viking Ships*, p. 25.
[3] For summary see T. C. Lethbridge, *Herdsmen and Hermits*, p. 31. Brögger and Shetelig, *The Viking Ships*, p. 14.

century seer, that when that was done for the last time the heir would perish, MacLeod's Maidens (rock stacks off Udrigil) would become the property of a Campbell, a fox would have her young in a turret of the castle, and a curragh would suffice to carry all the gentlemen of the name of MacLeod across Loch Dunvegan, all came to pass.[1] Old people of Skye can still remember hearing of the use of curraghs and, on the other side of the country, the men who floated the logs down the Spey in the great lumbering industry of the late eighteenth and early nineteenth centuries used curraghs in guiding the logs down the river and walked home carrying them upon their backs.[2] Even later still curraghs were used for crossing the dangerous River Spey and a specimen is preserved in Elgin Museum.

The Gael of the west, however, took kindly to the clipper-built wooden galleys of the Norsemen who raided and conquered them and who became the ancestors of a mixed race. In Norway the gradual evolution of the Norsemen's beautiful boats was reaching its zenith as they began their worst raids in the ninth century.[3] Ships and boats for use in home waters and far afield, for peaceful occasions and for war and raiding, were evolved. The war-galley, with its high stem and stern, light draught that enabled it to skim over the water, and banks of oars upon which it could rely far more than upon its square sail, is the prototype of the West Highland galleys that have been so lovingly carved upon so many of the tombs and crosses and constantly described in Gaelic poetry and that figure in the traditions and sober histories of the Island clans (see Fig. 57). In their medieval charters several of the Highland chiefs were required,

Fig. 57. Galleys from carvings on West Highland tomb stones.

[1]J. N. MacLeod, *Norman MacLeod of St. Columba's*, pp. 4-6.
[2]Lachlan Shaw, *History of the Province of Moray*, p. 249.
[3]A. W. Brögger and H. Shetelig, *The Viking Ships*, pp. 44, 51, 54, 57, 72.

as their feudal military service, to supply one or more fully manned galeys for the King's service when required. The ships of the Islanders were so formidable that King Robert the Bruce in his dying charge to his son specially warned him against them and English official reports bear witness to their extreme fitness for fighting in the narrow west coast seas. According to an official document, a galley had up to twenty-four oars and a birlinn up to sixteen and in war-time they carried three men to each oar.[1] They are sometimes called lymphads, a corruption of the Gaelic *long fada*, i.e. long ship. According to tradition, Somerled (twelfth century) could call out 160 galleys and, in the official report to the English Privy Council on the landing of Donald Dhu, a claimant to the forfeited Lordship of the Isles, at Carrick Fergus in 1545, he was accompanied by 180 galleys.[2]

From surviving records we know that they were used in the larger expeditions of the sixteenth century; in raids carried out by the leading gentlemen of the clan, who might keep a galley and crew of ten or twelve men 'ready for any enterprise';[3] on piratical expeditions in which the west coast Highlanders excelled—MacNeill of Barra in the sixteenth century was described as a Scotsman who stole when he could; for ferrying the dead to the Island burial places—some rowing songs lamenting the dead man have come down to us; and, of course, still more often for journeying about the Islands. For instance, Iain Garbh of Raasay attended a feast in Lewis accompanied by sixteen kinsfolk and on the way back they were all drowned. There are several versions of a tale that this was brought about by the incantations of a witch but a more sober contemporary historian briefly notes 'drunkenness did it'.

They must, indeed, have been dangerous craft. Tales of losses at sea abound and there was good reason for the special prayers recited by the steersman with responses by the crew that were offered before setting out on a voyage.[4] Their only sail was a

---

[1]Reg. Pr. C., Sc., Vol. X., p. 347.
[2]D. Gregory, *Western Highlands*, p. 170.
[3]See description of John MacLeod of Sanday in 'Ewill Troubles of the Lewis', *Highland Papers II*, p. 273.
[4]A version of these prayers is appended to the Gaelic translation of Knox's *Liturgy* and is repeated in Martin's account of the Islands and in a beautiful metrical form in Alexander MacDonald's great sea-poem, *The Birlinn of Glanranald*.

square lug and, unless the wind was very favourable, the main reliance had to be upon the oars. The labour of rowing was lightened by the special *irrim* (singular *iorram*), or rowing songs. There is, for instance, a Lewis song made by one of three Morrison brothers who were hotly pursued across the Minch by a superior force of MacLeods and who pulled a single oar against the two oars of his brothers and composed this rousing iorram to encourage them.[1]

In the old poems 'the lofty peaked smooth galleys with their speckled bulging sails' of the chiefs are constantly mentioned. From the carvings we know that, although they were very like the early Viking ships, they had a rudder instead of a steering oar (see Fig. 57). Like the Norwegian ships, their sails were of woollen fabric and often coloured although the white sails of a fifteenth century MacLeod chief are mentioned in a poem in his honour.[2]

Stories about the building of their galleys by the chiefs are specially interesting. So early as 1354, in an agreement between John, Lord of the Isles and MacDougall of MacDougall, the latter had the right of building eight vessels of twelve to sixteen oars,[3] and in the story of how Gillespuig Dhu murdered his half-brother, Donald Gallda Macdonald of Sleat in 1506, as part of his efforts to secure the chiefship of that branch of the clan, we are told that Gillespuig went with Donald to inspect a galley that the latter was building and declared that one of the planks was faulty. Donald, who was a skilful builder, was astonished and bent down to examine the plank, whereupon Gillespuig seized the chance to plunge his dirk into his brother's back. According to another tale, a skilled boat-builder was asked to come and advise MacNeill of Barra about a galley that he was building. He did not consider that he was receiving the respect due to him and he composed an extemporary cryptic rhyme about the building of boats and went away. Argyll employed a family of hereditary boat-builders. There are entries in MacLeod of MacLeod's accounts for 1706 for the expenses of building a birlinn. It was

[1]For poem as collected by Miss Anne MacLeod see I. F. Grant, *The MacLeods*, p. 189. Mrs. Kennedy Fraser's *Iona Boat Song* is a well-known adaptation of an iorram.
[2]*Book of the Dean of Lismore* (Professor Watson's Tr.), p. 23.
[3]*Highland Papers*, Vol. I, p. 75.

built of oaken boards caulked with oakum and thirty yards of white plaiding were supplied for its sails.[1]

In the seventeenth century there had been a great decline in the numbers of these Highland galleys. The Scots Privy Council, who wished to prevent the Highlanders from helping each other against the punitive expeditions that the authorities were constantly sending against them, discouraged the use of the galleys by limiting the numbers that a chief might own and by destroying large numbers. The wishes of the Privy Council, however, were not always successfully enforced as, for instance, in their prohibitions against the carrying of arms; and the decline in these formidable boats with their large crews was probably a sign of the social changes that were coming about. The chiefs were being drawn more and more towards the south, and large-scale clan raids were dying out. The birlinn built by MacLeod was probably one of the last that he owned. By the end of the century his successor was hiring boats for conveying goods from one island to another and a little later we find both Captain MacLeod of Harris and MacLeod of Raasay buying Orkney boats. Boats were becoming much smaller. A crew of four to six was the number generally mentioned and the difficulty in procuring boats that both Prince Charles Edward and Doctor Samuel Johnson experienced in their very different travels in the islands, shows that vessels were less plentiful.

We know that boats were used from early times to bring the cattle from the Outer Islands in the all-important cattle trade and that MacLeod supplied farms rent-free to certain families of 'ferriers', who conveyed people from one of his islands to another, but there is little evidence that local boats were much used for fishing.

It seems very remarkable that a potential source of food should, apparently, have been so little made use of. For instance, two reports were drawn up in the sixteenth century about the resources of the Western Islands. They were apparently for the use of King James VI, who wished to exploit the supposed riches of the Hebrides. In these reports the fertility of certain districts for corn and bestial are enthusiastically enumerated and whales, birds' feathers, the pelts of wild animals, the young of falcons are

[1] I. F. Grant, *The MacLeods*, p. 359–60.

carefully listed as sources of revenue, but surprisingly little is said about fishing by the local inhabitants.

The people, however, certainly had one very ancient way of sea-fishing. At the narrow head of many a sea-loch one still sees the tumbledown, semicircular drystone walls of a *caraidh* or *yaire*, how old no one can tell. When the tide was going out the fish were imprisoned by the walls of the yaire and the people were able to wade out and catch them in hand-made nets. Yaires were in use within the last century.[1] They interfered, however, with the inshore netting of the salmon and were declared to be illegal.[2] The spearing of flounders is also probably an old custom and, especially in times of need, people gathered shell-fish. It is said that Sir Norman MacLeod of Bernera (who fought at the Battle of Worcester) made special arrangements on his land that in a bad year the people upon farms without a suitable bit of shore should have access to those where shell-fish were plentiful.

The herring fisheries were the monopoly of the Scots Royal Burghs[3] but were more successfully fished by the Dutch in their better equipped boats. In the seventeenth century, in order to counter the Dutch fisheries, the Crown began to form a series of privileged companies provided with larger boats like those used by the Dutch. The Highlanders were actively discouraged from fishing in their own sea-lochs both by the Royal Burghs and the new companies.

By the eighteenth century the monopoly of the Royal Burghs ceased to be effective. But the Government continued to encourage the use of large fishing boats by means of bounties upon the actual boats and on their catches. The local people were still further penalized by the imposition of a heavy duty on the import of salt, essential for the curing of fish. It was not only the raised prices of the salt that they suffered from but, owing to official red tape, from the difficulty of obtaining it in small quantities and in out-of-the-way places.[4]

---

[1] J. MacDonald, *Highland Ponies*, p. 141. J. Anderson, 1785, in his *Present State of the Hebrides and Western Coasts of Scotland*, p. 338, speaks of them as ancient (henceforth noted as J. Anderson, *Present State of the Hebrides*).

[2] Evidence before *Crofters Commission, 1884*, Vol. I, p. 248.

[3] A class of towns enjoying special privileges by royal charter and liable to special dues to the Crown.

[4] For the hardships of the salt and coal duties see *Old Statistical Accounts*, Vol. I,

It was not until the second half of the century that the possibilities of developing the Highland fisheries for the people themselves became recognized. A report was made to the Government in 1785 by James Anderson emphasizing the need for local fisheries and the difficulties caused by the people's distance from markets, their inability to provide boats and equipment, the fact that they also had to grow their own food and win their fuel.[1] At the same time a traveller, John Knox, in touring through the Highlands about 1787, became deeply concerned over the poverty of the people and wished to help them. In his account he said a good deal about their methods of fishing. As he sailed northwards he described how he saw boatloads of men who had crossed from Skye to Loch Hourn, to which shoals of herring had come, to get fish for their families and how, on the long pull back in the teeth of an adverse wind, the crews were all singing 'in choruses abserving a kind of time with the movement of the oars'.[2] Some sold a little of their catches locally. The people of Waternish in Skye he described as 'all dabblers in the herring and white fisheries, they sold some of their fish to a local trader in exchange for meal.' Fishing was merely a sideline. Another traveller, writing in 1808, who was badly frightened by the inexpertness of his crew, attributed 'the little dexterity' of the people of Mull in seamanship to 'the variety of occupations practised by the same individual'. Each one of his crew of four he said was at once a farmer, a cattle dealer, a fisherman and occasionally a boatman, and, in addition two were weavers and one a shoemaker.[3] It would, however, have been impossible for the people to have depended upon fishing. As MacLeod of MacLeod wrote, about 1780, with 'their execrable tackle and with their miserable boats' they could not

---

p. 500 (Lismore and Appin), Vol. VII, p. 130 (Glenshiel), Vol. XI, p. 427 (Loch Alsh), Vol. XII, p. 333 (Jura), Vol. XVI, p. 228 (Strath), p. 389 (Harris). T. Newte, *Tour in England and Scotland*, p. 106. J. Knox, *Tour Through Scotland and the Hebride Isles*, p. 162, for disastrous effects of salt duties on Captain MacLeod's attempts to develop the Harris fisheries. J. Anderson in his *Present State of the Hebrides and Western Coasts of Scotland* (1785) (to be referred to as *Present State of the Hebrides*), gives examples of the hardship involved, pp. 12, 35–40. See also T. Garnett, *Tour*, Vol. I, p. 149.

[1] J. Anderson, *Present State of the Hebrides*, pp. 18, 252.
[2] J. Knox, *Tour*, p. 91.
[3] J. Stoddart, *Remarks on the Local Scenery and Manners in Scotland*, p. 16. J. Anderson, *Present State of the Hebrides*, pp. 18, 225.

locate or venture out to the good fishing banks and the price of salt was an insuperable difficulty to any attempt to preserve 'the catch'.[1]

How primitive Highland boats could be is shown by Hugh Miller's account of those being built at Gairloch, a very backward district, so late as early nineteenth century. The seams were caulked, he said, with moss steeped in tar, which he was told had been used from time immemorial. The rope for the hawsers and rigging was made of twisted tree roots.[2] The sails were of woolen stuff of a harder and stouter kind than was used for plaiding and had been locally spun on the spindle and woven. This is in the old tradition. The 'Gokstad' ship, excavated in Norway, had woollen sails.[3] The Gairloch boats, however, were far behind their time. We have the account book of an Inverness merchant of the early eighteenth century, who sent cargoes of grain and other materials to the sea-lochs of the west to sell in exchange for salmon, butter and other local produce, and who also supplied various gentlemen with a considerable quantity of cordage and sail-cloth.[4]

By the end of the eighteenth century the Highland fisheries were becoming increasingly important. John Knox, in his resolve to help the people, had been a prime mover in the founding of the British Fishery Society, formed under the auspices of the Highland Society in 1786, which tried to establish local fishery stations along Highland coasts where boats and gear could be supplied and the local fishermen would have opportunities of disposing of their fish. This scheme did not achieve all its good intentions partly because the herring shoals took to swimming farther out to sea and partly because of the oppressive salt tax, which was raised yet higher in 1801. Captain MacLeod of Harris and MacDonald of Lochboisdale also made patriotic efforts to help their people to develop the fisheries, but were thwarted by the salt and coal duties.

Owing to war-time conditions, however, the markets for fish were improving and, at last, in 1787, the Government had

[1]MSS. pamphlet in Dunvegan Muniment Room.
[2]H. Miller, *My Schools and Schoolmasters*, p. 283.
[3]A. W. Brögger and H. Shetelig, *The Viking Ships*, p. 132.
[4]See *Letter Book of Bailie Steuart*, Scottish History Society.

changed their policy and gave bounties for barrels of herring caught by the small local boats as well as by the large Lowland ones. It was not till 1825 that the salt tax was repealed and although in 1830 the bounty system was abolished, the northern fishing industry had by that time become established.[1] The *Old Statistical Account* shows that in 1790 its development had still been sporadic. For instance little was done at Gairloch, where afterwards fishering was considerable.[2] Herring fishing was already important within the burgh of Stornoway (Lewis) where thirty-five larger vessels of a kind known as Stornoway yawls, were employed[3] and especially markedly on Loch Fyne where a number of men were able to make fishing their whole-time occupation. On the whole, however, the development of fishing for white fish preceeded that for herring. In Barra the hardy crofter-fishermen in their open boats—by 1790 they had twenty or thirty—caught and cured the white fish at home and then sailed to the Clyde to sell their catches. This was often a hazardous undertaking. In 1783, a bad year, four out of five boats that made the trip were lost at sea with their crews.[4]

The following tale, told by a Barra raconteur and repeated to me by one of his audience, tells of what happened to one of these Barra crofter-fishermen and gives a vivid picture of the old life and beliefs. As was the custom, he had sailed to Glasgow with salt fish, butter and eggs, to buy supplies, including cordage for his boat. As he was starting from home an old woman had asked him if, while he was away, she might graze her cow upon his grass and he had agreed. He and the men with him had a good voyage back and when they came to the Sound of Mull, he opened a keg of whisky and he and his crew drank in honour of the good voyage they had had. At once the wind whipped round and became so boisterous that they had to land on Coll. The people there received them well and as it was the time of the corn harvest they

[1]For a summary of the Government's measures see M. Samuel, *The Herring*.

[2]*Gairloch*, Vol. III, p. 90. The same surprising lack of fishing enterprise is noted for *Skye*, Vol. XVI, p. 144 (although the men of Ramsay were more enterprising), *Tiree*, Vol. X, p. 467, *Clyne*, Vol. X, p. 301, *Dornoch*, Vol. VIII, p. 3.

[3]*Old Statistical Account*, Vol. XIX, p. 242.

[4]*Old Statistical Account*, Vol. XIII, p. 90. M. Gray, *Highland Economy*, p. 123. J. J. Anderson, *Present State of the Hebrides*, p. 57. See also A. Carmichael, *Carmina Gadelica*, Vol. V, p. 273. White fishing was also beginning at Gigha about 1790, *Old Statistical Account*, Vol. VIII, p. 90.

helped to get it in. Then they helped with the lifting of the potatoes for still the wind was contrary and they could not make for Barra. Then it was the time of the ceilidhs and one night it was so stormy that the horse came into the house and stood with his head to the west and his tail to the east with the snow on him. As beasts turn their backs to the wind this shows that it was an easterly wind. The woman of the house was pitying the horse because the Lady in Barra had sent snow so untimely. The man heard her mentioning the Lady in Barra and asked her what she meant. The woman said that she had wished to tell him that the old woman who was using his grazing would never let him get back to Barra unless he did what she herself told him. Then, at a time when she knew that the old Lady of Barra would be asleep the woman gave him a *sugan* (straw rope) with three knots tied in it and said that if he untied one knot there would be a favourable breeze, if he untied the second knot, a favourable wind, but that he must on no account untie the third knot or there would be a gale. He set forth. He untied the first knot and they had a breeze, the second knot and the ship carried them quickly towards Barra. Then, as the boat entered Castle Bay, he could not resist untying the third knot and at once such a gale arose that the boat was hurled on to the shore. He and his crew scrambled out in safety and when he reached his home the old woman to whom he had lent his grazing came to meet him with soft words of welcome, but he told her to be off and never to come near his grass again. The belief that some women could give or sell favourable winds and that these could be released by the untying of knots is, of course, widespread and appears in other Hebridean tales.

During the first half of the nineteenth century the disparity between the east and the west coast fisheries was far less marked than it was to become. Unlike the English fishermen they all fished from small, open boats and it was their practice to deliver their catches of herring within twelve hours of catching.[1] The east coasters, however, were mainly professionals, fishing almost the year round for white fish and herring in their seasons and, with great self-denial and enterprise, they were gradually improving their boats and extending the range of their fishing

---

[1]*Parliamentary Papers, 1849, Fishing Boats (Scotland)*, p. 3. Jas. Thomson, *Scottish Fisheries*, p. 51. A. J. March, *Sailing Drifters*, p. 225.

grounds and of their markets.[1] On the Western Highlands the fishermen of Loch Fyne and the sea-lochs to the south of it were exceptional; they had the great advantages that the herring were in the finest condition when they reached their fishing grounds and their salted herrings were regarded as special delicacies; that they had conveniently placed markets in the Firth of Clyde towns for their uncured fish and that they fished in less tempestuous waters. Many of them, therefore, also early became mainly whole-time fishermen. Farther north conditions were very different and fishing was carried on by crofter-fishermen.[2] As in the late eighteenth century, individual crofters would combine to make a crew of four to six men and to buy and equip a boat built by a local boat-builder and costing perhaps £35 to build and £5 to £10 to equip.[3] Nets, fishing lines, sail-cloth, cordage, etc., had to be imported and also the timber used by the builders. The relative importance of their fishing and farming activities varied from district to district. Barra, especially, and also Lewis and the district of Gairloch carried on the fisheries vigorously and exported dried white fish. On the other hand, in Skye, Eriskay and many of the other islands of the Inner Hebrides and some mainland districts, the fisheries soon declined or were never developed further than for home and local needs. These, however, were of great importance to the people who largely subsisted upon salted herring during the winter.[4]

By 1841, compared with the tonnage of the east coast boats, that of the Loch Broom boats was one-half, of those of Sheldaig one-third, of those of Dunvegan and Carron only one-sixth. There was the same discrepancy in the nets and other equipment.[5] On the other hand, on Loch Fyne and most of the south-western lochs, boat building was almost keeping pace with that of the east coast. During the second half of the eighteenth century the disparity between the importance of the fisheries of the east and

[1]See P. Anson's, *Fishing Boats and Fisher Folk on the East Coast of Scotland*, pp. 24–34 for the development of their boats.

[2]For examples see *The Old Statistical Account* (Applecross), Vol. II, p. 373, (Duirinish), Vol. IV, p. 132.

[3]M. Gray, *The Highland Economy*, pp. 108. 169.

[4]M. Gray, *The Highland Economy*, pp. 102. 123, 124. A. Goodrich Freer, *The Outer Isles*, p. 92.

[5]M. Gray, *The Highland Economy*, p. 167.

the north-west increased. In the east, right up to Caithness in the extreme north and, outstandingly to their credit, even in the case of a few of the most enterprising of the fisher villages of Sutherland, boats became larger and larger and new types were introduced which could go much farther afield. Such boats were not only too large but, with their upright stems, were unsuitable for pulling up upon the open beaches of the exposed west coast. From about 1880 the larger boats of the east coast were decked. Transport facilities were, of course, better upon the east coast and the advantages of larger harbours, full establishments for curing and barrelling and the increased number of boats delivering their catches reacted on each other and were cumulative.

On the north-west and in the case of some fishing communities on the north there were no harbours and the stormy seas on the open beaches prevented fishing being carried on during the winter months and therefore the people still relied partly upon agriculture for their livelihood.[1]

This combination of occupation was, however, disadvantageous because the main fishing seasons, the spring fishing for white fish and the main summer and autumn local herring season came at the very times when the land required most attention and therefore much of the work in the fields had to be done by the women.[2] Yet, on the other hand, the small crofts were inadequate to support their owners and, in the words of the writer of *Tolsta bho Tuath*, 'the life of the people was bound up in the fishing'.[3] Stories of the daring and skill of the men and of the losses on the sea have become part of the people's heritage of tales,[4] and the pride of the men in their hazardous calling and the anxieties and bereavements of the women have found expression in many of the songs of the Long Island.[5]

[1] The 1884 Crofters Commission recognized this and stated that it was essential that the West Coast fishermen should also have land (p. 127). See also A. Goodrich Freer, *The Outer Isles*, p. 352.

[2] A. Goodrich Freer, *The Outer Isles*, pp. 123, 126, 352. *Stornoway Gazette*, 16.8.51. T. Garnett, *Tour*, Vol. I, p. 180 for hard life of Mull fishermen.

[3] Not only did the relative importance of agriculture and fishing vary from district to district, but from time to time because the herring shoals were fickle in the sea lochs that they entered on their way south. M. Gray, *The Highland Economy*, pp. 169, 215, 217.

[4] 'Tolsta bho Thuath', *Stornoway Gazette*, 10.9.51, has good local examples.

[5] For examples see M. F. Shaw, *Folk Song and Folk Lore*, pp. 85, 87, 209, 221, 225, 245, 261, 263.

After 1850 the importance of the white fishings in the Hebrides had declined and that of the herring fishings had increased. Centres for packing and curing the herring during the season had been set up at Stornoway, Loch Boisdale and Castlebay.[1] Some of the boats of the Lewis men ventured farther and farther afield. They joined in the fishing from Wick to the annoyance of the local men and even went to the east coast.[2]

The Lewis boats by that time were 20–25 ft. long and half decked. There was generally a crew of eight[3]—a skipper, mate, *gille deiridh* who unhooked the fish, four oarsmen and a bowman. The boats were kept pulled high up on the open beach and had to be pushed down into the sea to be launched, which was a difficult operation. To beach one of them, especially in a rough sea, was an even more risky undertaking. The sail, mast and fishing gear were carefully packed away to keep the boat on an even keel. Ballast was placed in the stern to keep this as low as possible because, if the rudder left the water, the boat became out of control and was generally thrown broadside on the beach. The crew then took up their positions and the skipper watched for a suitable moment between the breaking of the waves. Then he cried '*Le sin i*' (with this one) and the four oarsmen drove the boat forwards. As soon as her prow touched the beach the bowman sprang overboard with the painter and waded ashore through the the surf until the helpers on shore took it from him and began to haul. Meanwhile, the crew had jumped into the water, and, with their backs against the boat, were pushing her towards the land. The skipper remained in the boat, urging the men to make special efforts as successive waves broke and helped to move the boat towards the shore. When clear of the worst of the waves, the men emptied the boat of her gear, the women took charge of the catch and she was pushed to safety above the high-water mark. The catch was then divided into shares for each member of the crew and one for the upkeep of the boat. The skipper was chosen by the crew for his especial skill. Such was the usual return from the fishing on those open coasts, but only too often the boats were caught by a gale before they could land and were obliged

---

[1] P. Anson, *Scots Fisher Folk on the East Coast of Scotland*, p. 65.
[2] *Stornoway Gazette*, 17.12.51.
[3] So large a crew for a boat of this size was not needed on the north and east coast.

to lie beyond the breakers all night, while their friends and kins-folk watched and prayed on the beach until, at last, in the dawn, the boats, one by one, ran for the beach and were dragged to safety. There is a tale of how the skipper of one boat sat at the tiller for fourteen hours manoeuvring her in the open Minch before he was able to beach her. His grandfather, father, two uncles, and his brother-in-law, had all been lost at sea.[1]

In the north east and north the fishermen's settlements clus-tered round the creeks and bays on that rock-bound coast. These natural harbours were quite inadequate to give protection in gales and there were disastrous losses in 1839, 1845 and 1848. In an official report in 1849 it was stated that along the 50 miles of the coasts of Caithness the fisheries were carried on by 1,200–1,500 open, undecked boats, manned by 6,000–7,000 fishermen and that there was no harbour that could be entered at all states of the tide or place of refuge in a gale.[2] It is said that the fisher-men's wives used to wade out to the boats, carrying their hus-bands on their backs so that they could set forth in dry clothes on their night's fishing. The boats carried provisions for one night only, a keg of water and one oaten bannock for each man. After the nets were set the men had a meal and then sang part of one of the metrical psalms and said a prayer before beginning the night's vigil.[3]

In Barra we are told that even so late as the end of the nine-teenth century, the fishermen still cast lots for the individual right to fish certain places on the fishing banks as they did in the allocation of their grazings, after which the skippers drew lots for their crews.[4] As elsewhere the emphasis had shifted from white fish to herring and there the fish curers had long set up establishments and Castlebay was full of their private piers. They supplied the boats and bought the catches at a fixed price.[5] The fishermen of the extreme north continued to own their boats but there the curers made agreements engaging a boat at the

[1]This information was mainly gathered from 'Tolsta bho Thuath', a series of articles published in the *Stornoway Gazette* in 1951.
[2]*Parliamentary Papers, 1849, Fishing Boats (Scotland)* Captain Washington's report, p. 12.
[3]A. J. March, *Sailing Drifters*, p. 225.
[4]*Crofters Commission, 1884*, p. 457. A. Goodrich Freer, *The Outer Isles*, p. 121.
[5]A. Goodrich Freer, *The Outer Isles*, pp. 26, 117, 119, 121.

beginning of the season to supply a given number of crans at a fixed price. A bounty was paid at the beginning of the season towards the cost of the equipment and the curer supplied the barrels and salt. At the end of the season the curer would often pay a retaining fee to a successful boat in order to secure her engagement next year. The fishermen could get what price they could for any herring they were able to catch over the stipulated number of crans and might make a good profit.[1]

The rise of the lively fishing ports of the extreme north, some of them, like Portmahomack, Lybster and Helmsdale inhabited by Gaelic-speaking folk, others like Wick, the greatest of them all, by the Scots-speaking men of Caithness, became almost a boom about the middle of the nineteenth century. They had good boats, highly skilled professional fishermen and, because of the importance of the catches they made, curing establishments were set up and a fleet of swift clippers began to carry the cured fish direct to Continental markets.

Their rise opened a new resource, additional to their own more struggling fisheries, to the people of the Hebrides at the very time when the pressure of population on the limited amount of land available was at its greatest. Men from the Western Isles readily found work during the busy autumn season as deck-hands and as porters, packers and gutters about the curing yards and they began to come in their thousands. It has been estimated that in 1845, 10,000 workers, mainly Highland, came to work at Wick alone.[2] People still living can remember seeing the parties of men from the Islands come tramping from the west to work at the herring fisheries. They had also begun to find their way to the east coast fishing ports, and, under the dire pressure of the potato famine, the island girls also began to come to the mainland to work as herring gutters. Such subsidiary earnings, although perhaps not more than £3 or £4, were of such importance to the poverty-stricken people that, although the work clashed with the time of the harvest, all who could tended to go to work at the fishing ports.

The counting of the fish used to be carried on by special

[1] A. J. March, *Sailing Drifters*, p. 242. Information kindly given me by Mr. J. W. M. Gunn.
[2] M. Gray, *Highland Economy*, p. 161.

methods. I could not obtain the special words used in the North.

In the Loch Fyne district three herring counted as a 'cast' and 106 casts were estimated as 'a hundred' and for each hundred a herring was flung into a special basket. Five 'hundreds' counted as a *mease*. The modern estimate is by the cran (a type of herring basket). Within living memory, both in the north and the west, the various shares were divided among the crew by lot in exactly the same way as the old run-rig strips of land had been allocated.

Besides fishing for the pot from the rocks or trolling from small boats, there were three main methods of fishing on the west coast. Until the middle of the nineteenth century all white fish, both on the east and west coasts, had been caught on lines. In small line fishing about 800–1,000 hooks had to be baited with sand eels or shell-fish.[1] This was the women's job, and a smelly and unpleasant one it was, and to bait a line took an hour or more. Each of the hooks dangled at the end of a horsehair 'snood' or 'tipping' attached to the line, and this, when fully baited was skilfully arranged on a special flat basket or a wooden tray (see Fig. 58). Both the snoods and the baskets with their graceful

FIG. 58. A bait basket.

shapes, were home-made in the Highlands. The line and hooks had to be imported. In fishing, the end of the line was fastened to an anchored float and, as the boat was rowed along, the line was gradually thrown overboard so skilfully that there was never a tangle among the dangling hooks.[2]

[1] The collection of bait was always toilful. In many districts, mussel, the best bait, had to be collected from distant bays.
[2] P. Anson, 'Fishing Boats and Fisherfolk on the East Coast of Scotland', p. 91. *Stornoway Gazette*, 17.12.51.

The Great Line Fishing was only carried on in some Highland districts. The little fish caught on the small lines were used as bait and the lines were baited at sea and cast and left for forty-eight hours. Cod, ling, skate and turbot were caught on these lines.[1]

For catching herring drift nets have long been and still are widely used. Long lines of nets are hung in a continuous curtain from just below the surface of the water to intercept the swimming shoals of herring. The fish are entangled in the nets by their gills.[2] In the old days on the west coast the rope along the top of the line of nets used to be made locally of horsehair and the floats that kept it in position just below the surface of the water were also home-made of inflated skins of sheep and sometimes of dogs, that had been peeled off the carcase of the animal so as to be almost whole and bound to a plug of wood.[3] But first imported rope and corks, and then by the twentieth century, floats formed of glass balls enclosed in little nets have replaced such devices. The herring nets from fairly early times were imported, but the fishermen are skilful in mending them with a home-made wooden shuttle. The fishermen 'barked' them in solution to make them resistant to rotting and the brown nets hung up rather like semi-transparent drapery to dry on groups of poles used to be very picturesque. But there was and is another method. Until the middle of the nineteenth century the catching of herring by means of ring nets was forbidden. Nevertheless the fishermen of Loch Fyne persisted in using this method. There are still told traditions of how sometimes the fishermen would start out with their boats equipped with drift-nets while their women-folk secretly carried the ring nets to some agreed spot where the men took them on board. The enforcement of the law led to constant trouble and finally, in 1860, it was repealed.

Fishing for lobsters is still carried on by means of baited lobster pots or creels that are lowered among the rocks off the coasts from small boats, now generally fitted with an auxiliary motor.

[1]'Tolsta bho Thuath', *Stornoway Gazette*, 17.12.51. Peter Anson, 'Fishing Boats and Fisherfolk of the East Coast of Scotland', p. 10, has a full description of the more elaborate tackle used on the East Coast for Great Line Fishing.

[2]For a full description and illustrations see Peter Anson, *Fishing Boats and Fisherfolk of the East Coast of Scotland*, p. 15.

[3]A few specimens were still to be found when I was collecting.

As a child I can remember seeing round lobster pots of wicker-work with an entrance in the middle like that of a patent non-spilling inkwell and such I believe was the older form. Nowadays a creel formed of hoops of hazel or willow wands bent over a rectangular board and covered with fishing net and with an entrance on the same ink-well principle seems to be in universal use and is made by the fishermen themselves (see Fig. 59). The

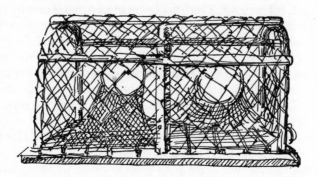

FIG. 59. A lobster creel.

obvious difficulties and losses involved in getting the lobsters, a luxury food, while still alive, to the urban epicures who consume them is very great but by means of 'lobster-pools' and better organized transport efforts are being made to help the fishermen and some of the men, for instance in Barra, are beginning to take up lobster fishing on a large scale. A further development is that crabs, which are very plentiful and used to be thrown away when they got into the lobster creels as the country people seldom eat them, are now being exported or processed at Gairloch and Mallaig and there are great hopes of a prawn industry and of developments in Stornoway across the Minch.

It may be noted that there is no record of eel fisheries, old or new, in the Highlands and that eels have never formed an article of food there.

During the last quarter of the nineteenth century, however, the whole pattern of Scots fisheries began to change with dire effects upon those of the Highlands. The first steam drifters and trawlers were introduced about 1882 at Aberdeen and gradually drove out the old sailing boats. These large and very costly vessels require suitable harbours and, in order to repay the heavy capital outlay required for building them, have to be in use throughout the year. They are almost entirely concentrated at the larger east coast ports,[1] although there were a few locally owned steam drifters based on Stornoway. For instance, the small community of Tolsta for a short time owned one of these steam drifters but she was unfortunately lost[2] at sea. This change spelt the ruin of nearly all the valiant northern ports as well as of the more simple fisheries of the Long Island and north west. The old sailing drifters steadily went out of use and the Highland fishermen tended to go and work as deck-hands on the steam boats, although some combined to buy small motor boats, and lobster fishing survived, although trawlers, and especially the depredations of those illegally fishing within the 3-mile limit, have also ruined the in-shore fisheries. Once so vital a subsidiary to the life of the crofts, the decline of the fisheries has been an irreparable blow to the crofting system,[3] and the people clung to it as long as they could. In 1890 three-quarters of the Highland crofters were still partially dependent on fishing.[4] By 1936 the crofter-fishermen still numbered 10,073, but by that time fishing was no longer an important subsidiary work to crofting. And although *The Annual Scottish Fisheries Statistics* still show a considerable number of crofter-fishermen, only a small percentage of these do more than fish spasmodically in the summer. Things, however, may improve, it is now recognized by the Scottish Home Department that a revival of fishing activity is essential to the Hebridean economy and special measures are being introduced to encourage this. The fleet of steam drifters from the eastern ports in the course of their year-round pursuit of the herring shoals, comes to the northern waters and brings temporary bustle and trade to Stornoway, Castlebay and Mallaig, and a certain amount of white fish, also, is landed at some of the north-western ports, especially at Oban. A small proportion of this is caught by

[1] *Commission of Enquiry into Crofting Conditions, 1954*, p. 72.
[2] *Stornoway Gazette*, 17.12.51.
[3] *Report of the Commission of Enquiry into Crofting Conditions, 1954*, p. 71.
[4] *Commission on the Western Highlands and Islands, 1890*.

local men in Seine nets. But unfortunately since the First World War, the whole fishing industry has been increasingly depressed, owing to the failure of foreign markets.

In the south-west, however, the fishermen of Loch Fyne and the neighbouring lochs have been able to keep their boats up to date and to hold their own with improved methods of fishing with seine and ring nets and power-driven boats.[1] The build of Highland fishing boats has undoubtedly undergone many changes and there have always been local variations. The fishermen of Loch Fyne and the southern sea-lochs early developed their own types of craft. About 1849 two different types were said to be in use there, both built locally or on the Clyde.[2] By the end of the century the typical 'Loch Fyne Smack' resembled in many ways the large and speedy 'Zulus' that were evolved on the Moray Firth about 1880, although they were smaller and carried a different rig—a standing lug and a jib— as more suitable for use in the sea-lochs. The great rake of the mast was very noticeable (see Fig. 60).[3] Boats of this kind of 35–45 ft. were still being built up till 1920, some at Tarbert and Ardrishaig. Since then the introduction of power has profoundly modified the build of the local boats and they may be 50 ft. in length.

There is little information about the early build of the fishing boats of the Hebrides and the north-west.[4] There are illustrations in contemporary prints of various craft. John Slezer's *Theatrum Scotiae* (1693), J. Fitler's *Scotiae Depicta* (1804) and Daniel's prints (1817). All the sea-going fishing craft round the coasts of Scotland are shown with steeply sloping stems and sterns (see Fig. 61B), so perhaps one may assume that this was the normal type. Daniel moreover has several representations of boats in his views of the west coast with very high stems and sterns like the carvings of the ancient galleys and also like illustrations of the

[1]For a vivid account of the men and their methods see N. Mitchison and D. Mackintosh, *Men and Herring*.

[2]*Parliamentary Papers, 1949, Fishing Boats (Scotland)*, pp. xxi, 63–64.

[3]Information kindly supplied to me by Miss Blaikie, whose family is associated with these fisheries and by Mr. Plenderleith of the Scottish National Museum.

[4]*The Handbook on British Fishing Boats and Coastal Craft*, published by the Science Museum, London, on p. 44, points out that in spite of much research no information could be obtained regarding the exact build of West Highland fishing boats before the Government Report of 1849.

FIG. 60. Loch Fyne fishing boats. End of nineteenth century.

contemporary Orkney boats (see Fig. 61A). But, *per contra*, Garnett's illustration of boats on Loch Long are very flat.[1] As we know that boats from the Orkneys were brought to the Western Highlands at the end of the eighteenth century by people who were trying to develop the Highland fisheries and by the British Fishery Company, one may wonder whether there had been an older fishing boat distinct from the galleys. Too much weight must not be placed upon the local correctness of illustrations of boats introduced by the artists in order to enhance their compositions. They may have been taken from their general

[1]T. Garnett, *Tour*, Vol. I, p. 69.

notebooks or even from a book of engravings of suitable objects, for foregrounds such as that by a Mr. Pyne.[1]

Fig. 61. Fishing boats from early nineteenth-century prints. (A) West Highland boat with high stem and stern, after Daniels. (B) Typical fishing boats, after Fitler.

In 1848 a terrible storm played havoc with the fishing fleets of Scotland, especially with those in the far north,[2] and an official report was drawn up by Captain Washington which mainly dealt with the adequacy of the harbours. But the report also contained outlines of many types of the local boats. At Wick and the neighbouring ports a type of boat was built and used, wide in the beam and with curved but almost upright stem and stern. In Captain Washington's words, 'having a form that approximates to a spheroid'. He was very scathing about it (see Fig. 62L). A similar type of boat, in use all down the Scots coasts south of Banff is illustrated. It is surprising that the outline for the district in between—the Moray Firth area—shows a boat that was quite different and was sharply raked at each end (see Fig. 62R).[3]

[1]W. H. Pyne, *Microcosm: or a Picturesque Delineation of the Arts, Agriculture, Manufactures, etc. of Great Britain, in a Series of Several Thousand Groups of Small Figures for the Embellishment of Landscape.* Comprising the most interesting subjects in rural and domestic scenery, in external and internal navigation, in country sports . . . the whole accurately drawn from Nature. 2 Vols., 1806.

[2]At Wick, forty out of 800 boats were lost and neighbouring ports suffered equally.

[3]*Parliamentary Papers*, 1849, *Fishing Boats (Scotland)*, Plates V and VII and pp. xix, 27 and 35.

Unfortunately no illustrations are given of the north-west coast types of fishing boats.

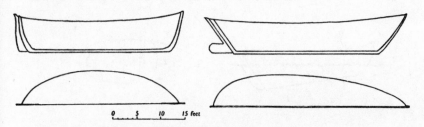

FIG. 62. Outlines of fishing boats from mid-nineteenth-century report.
Left: Wick boat. Right: Moray Firth boat.

It must have been very shortly after this that the typical Moray Firth 'Scaffie' was evolved, a more capacious craft with a bluff stem but retaining the raked stern, and it was steadily improved, enlarged and decked. Farther south the 'Fifie' was developed from the local boats with more upright stems and sterns shown in the 1849 Report.[1] Later on the 'Baldie' was evolved in the south and the 'Zulu', described as 'the noblest sailing craft ever designed in these islands', in the Moray Firth.[2]

During this period (the nineteenth century) a number of east coast boats came to the north-west coasts when the herring shoals were there. The opening of the Caledonian Canal made this much easier and obviated the voyage round the north of Scotland. The influence of the east coast is indicated by the names of some of the fishing boats of the Long Island. For instance, in a poem on the boats of Bernera, out of nine that are mentioned, seven have Lowland names[3] and much the same is the case with the boats mentioned in Tolsta traditions (see *Stornoway Gazette*, 1951). The influence of the Scaffie, especially, with her upright stem and sloping stern, is strong on the general type that exists or recently existed all down the north-west Highland seaboard. I am indebted to Mr. D. J. MacDonald for an expert description of

[1]For details of these various craft see P. Anson, *Fishing Boats and Fishermen of the East Coast of Scotland*.
[2]Ibid., p. 33.
[3]A. Morrison, *Orain Chaluim*, p. 24.

it (see Fig. 63). 'They are 32–34 ft. overall—24–28 ft. keel, drawing about 2 ft. forwards and raking down to about 5 ft. 6 in. or 6 ft. aft with the characteristic stern-post. They are sharp at

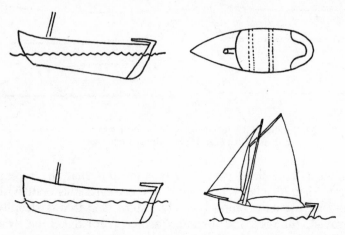

FIG. 63. Outline of typical West Highland fishing boat from sketch by D. J. MacDonald.

both ends with rather a pear-shaped plan section, the wider part aft. They are decked far forrard to provide shelter for the crew with the full width amidships open as a fish hold and for nets. The sails are a standing lug (loose-footed) and a jib hoisted from a short bowsprit. They lie to their nets by the stern, which with its slope gives a "lift" to the seas. They always have a fairly heavy "sheer". The smaller boats used for inshore fishing are somewhat on the same lines, though with not so pronounced a slope from stem to stern. In Loch Broom they were known as *Bata Ghearrloch* and were entirely open with a single lug sail and from 15 to 20 ft. in length.' In Skye I have been told that the yawl or *geola* was 9–12 ft. and the *eather* or *sgoth* 15–20 ft., although larger half-decked boats, said to be like those of Barra, used once to be built there by local builders. Mr. Sutherland and Mr. MacKenzie of Pennefeiler, who still build boats in Skye, told me that the old typical boats had upright stems and raked sterns and the whole boat was built with a slant, the stern being much deeper than the stem. The frames were made of ash steamed into shape and the sides of planks of larch. In the old days the Skye boats were generally tarred but the upper parts of the Bernera boats were painted in bright colours. In the north much taste was shown in the painting of the names of the boats, which were often named after the skipper's wife. A very interesting point told me by one of the Skye boat-builders was that the looms of the oars were squared by pieces of wood being fastened on to them and, instead of rowlocks, the oars were held in position by thole pins, two upright pieces of very hard wood or of iron inserted on each side of the oar. The Orkney and Shetland boats of the earlier types had the same form of oar. The sails of the Skye boats, like those described by Mr. MacDonald, were a lug and a jib. In the days of the prosperity of the West Highland fisheries, local boat-builders lived all along the coasts of the Islands. Now they are few in number and they make more varied craft.

The fishermen have always had taboos upon certain words when at sea. Martin, writing of the end of the seventeenth century, said that when at the Flannan Islands (in the Minch) fishermen never named St. Kilda, Flannan, water, rock, shore, shipping and several other things but used synonyms instead, such as hard instead of rock. When at sea Canna was called Tarsuin and Eigg the Island of the Big Women.[1] In some remote places I have been told certain place-names are still taboo but the Highland fishermen seem to have taken over the superstitions about words of the east coasters. The forbidden words in the north were priest or minister, salmon, pig, hare, rats and rabbits (exactly like the east coast). Rabbits were alluded to as 'little feeties'.[2] In Lewis, Skye and Barra the words forbidden were only minister or priest, rats and rabbits. In Barra it was unlucky to meet a red-haired woman when setting out to fish—in Lewis any woman. There was a widespread belief in the Hebrides that it was unlucky when at sea to wear clothes dyed with crotal because crotal would go back to the rocks. In Barra it was considered undesirable to wear seal-skin at sea and that a woman ought not to comb her hair at night when her menfolk were at sea. There is a story that a sailor who had been drowned appeared to his wife and told her that when he fell overboard he would have

---

[1] M. Martin, *Western Islands*, pp. 98, 301, 304.
[2] Information kindly given me by Mr. J. W. M. Gunn.

been saved if his feet had not been entangled in her long hair in which he and she had taken such pride.[1] An old custom was that a boat on starting out was turned *deasil* (sunwise).[2] In the south-west the bourtrie (elder) was considered lucky.

A quite separate method of riverine fishing may be noted. The rights to net salmon were valuable from medieval times as we know from charters. The simplest way of catching the salmon as they make their way in the spring and summer into the tidal mouths of the rivers on their way to spawn in the higher waters is by means of a seine net. When there is a run of salmon a coble, towing a net, is rowed from the shore and the fish are encircled and drawn to land. Slezer's *Theatrum Scotiae* (1694) has an illustration of it (Plate 43) and I have watched it on the shores of the Ness. But a more usual method is by setting a line of stake nets at right angles to the shore. At the end is a sort of bag net held in position by three stakes. The fish, as they swim towards the river mouth, meet the obstruction of the stake net, swim along it to the narrow entrance of the bag and cannot find their way out. Periodically a coble is rowed out to bring them in. The salmon fisheries are generally operated on licence from the owners of the land. It is a specialized form of fishing and is not combined with ordinary sea-fishing.[3] Seventeenth-century illustrations of the boats used in this type of fishing and farther up the rivers[4] show them as rounded at each end and, in some cases, one cannot be sure if they are cobles or curraghs.

The continuity with the past is more strongly shown in the people of the Hebrides than in their craft. Sea-going rather than fishing has been in their blood for generations and, although few of them still toil at the oars of their little fishing boats, more and more have they become deep-sea sailors. For instance, in 1914 only half a dozen men from Tolsta followed this calling; by 1951 there were more than 200.[5] Many of them serve in fighting craft

---

[1]Information kindly given me by Mrs. de Glehn and Mrs. M. Grant.

[2]M. Martin, *Western Islands*, p. 178. This custom is still remembered by an old fisherman at Carradate (Kintyre).

[3]P. Anson, *Fishing Boats and Fishermen on the East Coast of Scotland*, p. 78.

[4]Slezer, *Theatrum Scotiae*, Pl. 28 (Dunkeld), 38 (Inverness), and 43 (Cromarty).

[5]*Stornoway Gazette*, 17.12.51. In Barra, more than half the male population is or has been deep-sea sailors.

—not the galleys and birlinns of their ancestors but in the ships of the Royal Navy—and the proportion of men in the Royal Naval Reserve is very high. Others are seamen in the Merchant Service on the high seas of the world. It is proverbial how often the man in the charge of a ship's engine-room is a Scot and there, among the men controlling the mighty powers of steam and oil, one can often hear the lilting speech that was learnt in the Hebrides. There is a close connexion between these widely dispersed Islanders and the survival of the crofting system, for it is due to the help that such men send home that many a crofting family still manages to maintain itself on its holding.

# XIII

## COMMUNICATIONS AND TRANSPORT

TRANSPORT is one of the most serious problems that the modern crofter, especially in the western Islands, has to face, and the means, or the lack of means, of travelling about have always exerted important influences on the Highland way of life. The history of transport into and within the Highlands falls into two well-marked periods. In the days before roads (that is, before the eighteenth century) the Highlands were difficult to penetrate and the inhabitants were left to develop their own way of life with comparatively little outside influence or interference, but, within their own country, the people showed a mobility that is amazing when one remembers the hilly nature of the mainland, the many sea-lochs and the high proportion of islands. They raided far and wide: for instance one reads of a foray by the Munros from Easter Ross to the Braes of Angus and of expeditions from the Hebrides to Sutherland and the Orkneys. By the sixteenth century the Highlanders' trade in cattle at Lowland fairs, and of fish to Glasgow was already established, and hides and skins, plaiding and salmon had long been articles of export from remote districts. Glengarry floated his timber to Inverness and by the seventeenth century and probably earlier, chapmen travelled about all over the country and the cairds wandered far and wide. Many chiefs had widely scattered possessions—the Laird of Grant in Strathspey and Glenurquhart, MacLeod on the mainland, in Skye and in Harris, Clanranald had lands on the mainland and in the Long Island. These chiefs and their people moved constantly to and fro across the Minch. The Highland chiefs were now and then obliged to attend before the Privy Council in Edinburgh—generally much against their will—and by their marriages and bonds of friendship had connexions with their fellows all over the north. It is difficult to trace how much the lesser folk moved from one district to another. The use of patronymics and the custom of adopting their landlord's surname makes rentals less useful than one might hope, but, even so, there is considerable variation in surnames and to quote a few examples that are recorded—after the fall of the Lords of the Isles, the MacMillans, who had been their vassals in Knapdale, were largely dispersed and among other places were to be found on the shores of Loch Tay and so far north as the Great Glen. A MacLeod heiress received some farms in Harris in the sixteenth century and a member of her husband's clan, a Campbell from Knapdale, came up to administer them and founded several Campbell families on the MacLeod estates. In 1613 MacLeod got into trouble over the misbehaviour of a man who had been a tenant of Glengarry and had then moved to Skye. A family of Shaws are known to have moved from Strathspey to the MacLeod estates in the sixteenth century.[1] A family of MacQueens from Skye became established in Strathdearn and several branches of Clan Chattan moved from Lochaber to Strathdearn and Strathnairn.

This mobility[2] within the Highlands no doubt helps to explain the considerable degree of homogeniety that existed there. This is surely an outstanding and remarkable fact especially when one remembers how disunited were the clans, how varied were the physical conditions, as for instance, between those of the Long Island and of the Central Highlands and how different was the background of districts once dominated by the Gael of Dalriada, the Picts, even the Britons and by the Norsemen, and that it was not till the thirteenth century that the King of Norway ceded the Long Island and Skye to Scotland. Although there were sometimes local differences in customs, the shape of implements, pronunciation and vocabulary and in songs and traditional stories yet, by and large, there was a predominantly Gaelic culture and similarity in methods of agriculture and in social organization,

[1]For notes of tenants not of his name on MacLeod's estates see I. F. Grant, *The MacLeods*, pp. 126, 225, 351-2, 506.
[2]This mobility and readiness to settle in other Highland districts is still characteristic.

and new developments were widely diffused. A good example of this latter is that of piping. It is generally agreed that the chief centre of the art was in Skye from which the standard of playing and the form of the *piobaireachd* spread over the whole of the Highlands. Another example is the belted plaid, that in essentials was typical of the whole country. Compared to the valleys of Norway, it seems strange not to find more divergence in different parts of the Highlands, often at fierce variance with each other.

Until the eighteenth century—in many cases till the nineteenth century—the country was without roads and the tracks that drovers and travellers followed generally ran along the straths, avoiding the more marshy bottoms and much influenced by the position of suitable fords and they crossed from strath to strath by hill passes. There were many more of these recognized tracks than there are present roads. For instance, a number crossed the Grampians from the central valley of the Garry to Strathspey and Upper Deeside, and there was direct access from the west to the east. One of the best known was the route from Kintail to Glen Affric and Strath Glass.[1]

Strangers required guides for these tracks. Burt described a journey that he took from Inverness to the valley of the Spey before the making of Wade's military road. It took him two days and he piled on the agony in his account to his London friend of his adventures from quagmires, the Findhorn in spate, the excruciating discomfort of the inn that he stayed in and the precipice that he negotiated at Slochd Muich.[2] The same journey by rail or motor barely takes an hour. In the west, travel by open boats was much preferred to that by land as the siting of the castles and principal houses shows. Dunvegan Castle was entered only by the sea-gate and had no door to the landward side till the middle of the eighteenth century.

Something has been said about the boats. In landward districts the most usual way of transporting goods was in creels carried upon the human, especially the female, back. Louis Simond, a Frenchman, writing so late as the beginning of the nineteenth

---

[1]Details of many of these tracks are given by D. C. C. Pochin Mold in *The Roads from the Isles*, see especially pp. 6, 8, 99, and A. R. B. Haldane, *The Drove Roads*, has details of numbers of the drove roads.

[2]E. Burt, *Letters*, Vol. II, Letters xvi and xvii.

century, describes how, going up Glencroe (the pass over the hills on the south side of Loch Fyne) he met 'a troup of Highlanders, mostly women barefooted and bareheaded, with heavy loads on their backs, very like our Indian Squaws in America in appearance and walk; their feet turned in, moving in file. An old woman who led sang a plaintive, melancholy ditty. . . . It rained, but they did not seem to mind it.'[1] Of course the little Highland horses were also much used as pack-ponies and for riding. One of the labour dues exacted by the tacksmen from their subtenants was the performance of a given number of 'long loads' with their horses.

In those roadless days certain primitive vehicles also had been developed, how far back one cannot tell.[2] Sledges were made of two sapling trunks (see Fig. 64C). The thinner ends were fastened to the horse on each side like shafts, while the thicker ends dragged along the ground and slats or boards were fastened between them upon which the load rested. They were so suitable for use on steep slopes that in Kintail and the Gairloch districts they had only just gone out of use about thirty years ago when I was inquiring about them. In earlier times they were also made with a sort of frame for carrying peats,[3] but as roads penetrated the country these sledges went out of use. When Hugh Miller took the newly made road to the west to work in Gairloch in 1823 he noticed two abandoned 'Highland carts' lying beside it.[4] An even more simple vehicle was the slype used for moving boulders from the fields and already described (see p. 204). (See Fig. 65.)

By the eighteenth century, at least in the more sophisticated districts on the edges of the Highlands, very simple and primitive carts called kellachs were used with solid wheels, formed of

[1] L. Simond, *Journal of a Tour and Residence in Great Britain during the years 1810 and 1811*, Vol. I, p. 296 (henceforth noted as *Tour and Residence*).

[2] John Slezer in *Theatrum Scotiae* (1694), illustrates spoked carts (Dundee), sled-cart (Arbroath), pack horse (Culross), horse with panniers carrying harvest (Brechin).

[3] Described by Burt in 1730, *Letters*, Vol. I, p. 75 and in 1876-9 by A. Mitchell, *Past in the Present*, p. 96. See also Osgood MacKenzie, *A Hundred Years in the Highlands*, p. 31 for their suitability.

[4] Hugh Miller, *My Schools and Schoolmasters*, p. 108. But T. Garnett in *Observations on a Tour through the Highlands and Part of the Western Isles of Scotland* (1800), in the picture of Glencroe opposite p. 284, Vol. I, shows a sled-cart on the road.

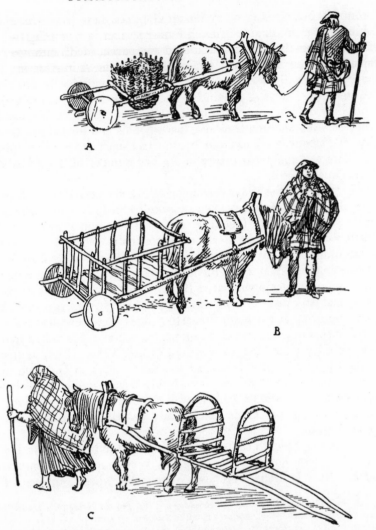

FIG. 64. Primitive means of transport. (A) A version of the Kellach, after Burt. (B) Another version of the Kellach, after Burt. (C) A sledge, after Mitchell.

'three pieces of wooden plank, pinned together at the edges like the head of a Butter Firkin, and the Axletree goes round with the wheel' (see Fig. 64B). The wheel soon became worn unevenly so that it became 'rather angular than round' and made 'a disagreeable Noise as it moves'.[1] Burt has an illustration of

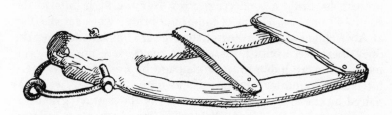

FIG. 65. A slype.

such a cart with a creel set between the shafts (see Fig. 64A), and another with a framework of rough stakes.[2] The rough harness was of twisted twigs of birch and horsehair. He was scathing about the carelessness of the drivers in allowing their horses to become galled by the ill-adjusted cart.[3] So small were the carts that in order to turn one in a narrow place Burt says that he saw the carter 'take up the Cart, Wheels and all, and walk round with it, while the poor little Horse has been struggling to keep himself from being thrown'.[4] But by the end of the century advanced farmers in the open districts were beginning to use wheels with spokes. Even so their loads were about 9 stone. The smallest cart in the twentieth century would hold at least three times as much and two pairs of Clydesdales would do all the work on a farm such as Dunachton, which required six horses and carts with the labour dues of about twelve more in 1770.[5]

There was a *Via Regis* up the Lowland eastern shelf of land even in medieval times, but the Highlands were practically

[1] E. Burt, *Letters*, pp. 77-78. See also L. Shaw, *History of the Province of Moray*, p. 35.
[2] E. Burt, *Letters*, Vol. I, p. 75.
[3] E. Burt, *Letters*, Vol. I, p. 75.
[4] E. Burt, *Letters*, Vol. I, p. 77.
[5] I. F. Grant, *Old Highland Farm*, p. 70.

roadless.[1] The first road-making scheme was not undertaken till
1726–37 as a military measure to control the Highlanders.
General Wade suggested and carried out the scheme. He built
about 250 miles of roads connecting Dunkeld (to which there was
already a road from Perth) and Inverness, then due westwards
to Fort William and finally, as the most ambitious part of the
project, he made a connecting road over the high hills to the
south of Lochness. His most important bridge was over the Tay
at Aberfeldie but lower down that river at Dunkeld and over the
Spey there were only fords and his roads were not very well
made and were liable to much damage by freshets. They were
intended for military purposes and until 1799 they were re-
paired by the army and by the middle of the century great improvements had been made, bridges built and 600 more miles of
road had been constructed under the system.[2]

Although these roads had some effect in opening up the
country, the volume of traffic that they carried was not considerable. Simon, Lord Lovat, tried to drive his coach from Inverness
to Perth in 1740 and told a rueful tale of two breakdowns and
how, at one point, his daughters had to continue their journey
upon the coach-horses.[3] Post vehicles could be hired but so sparse
was the traffic that when, in July 1762, Bishop and Mrs. Forbes
were driving from Blair Athol to Dalnacardoch (a stretch of the
main road carrying now almost a continuous stream of traffic in
the season) and they had made a stop and the lady strolled along
the road, two kindly local women came up to her 'in the greatest
consternation to see a gentlewoman all alone' at that lonely
place.[4] Over the greater part of the Highlands people had to walk
or ride. There were no roads north of Inverness or through the
greater part of the west. Contemporary writings show how inconvenient was travelling. For instance, a lady travelling with her
children in 1784 had to ride from her home in Skye, then cross a
sea-loch by boat, then ride across the island to take boat from

<hr>

[1]A few small attempts to construct roads and bridges were made in the south-west.
[2]The officers in charge were Generals Caulfield and Clayton and Sir John Cope.
[3]Printed in Spalding Club Miscellany, Vol. II, p. 5.
[4]Bishop R. Forbes, *Journal of the Episcopal Visitations*, ed. by J. B. Craven, p. 142.
T. Garnett in the first three weeks of his tour which took him up to Oban, did not
meet a single traveller on horseback or in a carriage. *Observations on a Tour through
the Highlands and Part of the Western Islands of Scotland*, (1800), Vol. I, p. 109.

Broadford to Glenelg on the mainland and thence ride to Fort Augustus.[1] The adventures of Doctor Johnson on his tour to the Hebrides are of course well known. The Highlands were therefore still largely cut off from contact with the outside world.

With the beginning of the nineteenth century there was a marked change. The Government had become disturbed at the depopulation brought about by the Clearances. It was the age of great civil engineering projects and they called upon Thomas Telford, the well-known engineer, for a report. This he submitted in 1805.[2] His recommendations included the making of the Caledonian Canal to encourage the fisheries and agriculture, the reconstruction or making of a number of harbours in the northeast (by which the rising fishing industry greatly benefited), and a well-planned system of roads with the necessary bridges. The work was carried out by Government grants supplementing expenditure by the local authorities and the proprietors and, by 1830, was completed. Nine hundred and thirty miles of excellent roads penetrating to the far north and to the west had been made, and, with them, more than that number of bridges, some of them, like that over the Tay at Dunkeld, very fine. The roads have, of course, been added to, but in essentials were not greatly changed until the era of the motor-car.

The first coach service to Inverness, a two-horse vehicle, had already begun to run in 1811, but, after the improvement in the roads, there was a daily service from Perth direct to Inverness and from there, after 1819, coach and mail-gigs penetrated to Dingwall, Wick and Tain.[3] Post chaises also still ran. About 1840 Lord Cockburn, when he was on his circuit journeys, still hired one between Perth and Inverness and sat on the hood to enjoy the view of the Cairngorms. With coaches and mail-gigs came a great improvement in the postal services. For instance, before 1813, letters from the south for the family at Rothiemurchus (close to Aviemore, now on the main railway line and road to Inverness) were delivered three times a week, going

[1] James Barron, *Northern Highlands in the Nineteenth Century*, Vol. III, p. 393.
[2] H. Hamilton, *Industrial Revolution in Scotland*, p. 229. Also A. Newlands, *The History of Roads in the Highlands*. J. Anderson, in 1785 had already urged the importance of the making of the Caledonian and Crinan Canals and a road up the west, *Present State of the Hebrides*.
[3] Anderson's *Guide to the Highlands and Islands of Scotland*, pp. 48–49.

from Aberdeen to Inverness, from thence by a runner to Grant-town and on from there by another runner.[1] The old, narrow up-and-down roads with steep cuttings were very liable to be snowed up, and one still sometimes sees the lines of sentinel posts set up to mark the course of the older roads through the snow wreaths. Old letters describe the rigours of winter journeys on the outside of Highland coaches.

I do not know what the earliest of these coaches looked like, but those that in my young days still ran in a good many districts to connect railheads were open and rather like the old-fashioned charabancs. On a rainy day, even in summer weather, although tarpaulin aprons were supplied, one got pretty wet. Mail-gigs varied in shape. Those I can best recollect were after the pattern of a double dog-cart. On the long hills the passengers were in-vited to get out and walk and on the steep brae into the valley of the Nairn one can still see the foot-worn tracks where they used to take short cuts. Sometimes a travelling piper or fiddler struck up a tune to cheer them on.

The use of wheeled traffic increased with areas served by the new roads. The first farm carts with spoked wheels must have been simple affairs, but the spread of an improved form of box-cart is made specially interesting by a particular type of ornamentation upon its front, variously described as the 'fiddle' or 'spectacles'.[2] It is thought to have been evolved in Lanarkshire or Stirlingshire in the eighteenth century and then, to have spread to the ex-treme north and to the western islands and it also had penetrated into Ireland and parts of England. Most of those used in the Highlands seem to have been made by specialized firms in the south but there was one maker at Invergordon. These carts were particularly suitable for use in rough country and had extreme versatility. The back let down or the whole body of the cart

[1] *Memoirs of a Highland Lady* (1911 ed.), p. 244. For primitive postal arrange-ments in Gairloch so late as 1840, see Osgood MacKenzie, *A Hundred Years in the Highlands*, p. 32. For earlier difficulties see Jas. Anderson, *Present State of the Hebrides and Western Coasts of Scotland*, p. 199.

[2] The cart is illustrated in *Explanations of the Engravings of the most usual Implements of Husbandry used in Scotland*. Illustrated by A. Gray (1814), Plate VIII and p. 36, but the curious form of ornamentation is not shown. Such carts were gener-ally used in most improved districts of Scotland. T. Garnett quotes figures for the parish of Campsie. In 1759 there were about twenty carts with wheels hooped with iron. By 1794 there were nearly 200 improved carts. Op. cit., Vol. II, pp. 182–3.

would tip backwards to empty the contents and a wooden frame could be placed as an extension to the top to accommodate hay or sheaves of corn. The ornamentation on the front persisted upon these carts; in earlier or better examples it was cut out of the outer board of a double thickness on the front of the cart to form a panel and emphasized by being painted in a contrasting colour—red and blue were the favourite combinations—but in time it was merely painted. There is no definite information about why it was evolved and its persistence seems to have been merely a matter of custom.[1]

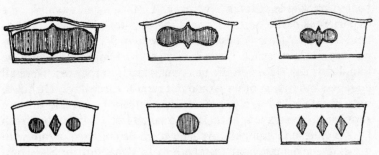

FIG. 65A. Ornamental cart panels (from *Irish Folkways*, p. 179).

These little carts can still be seen in use in spite of mechanization, but the other forms of vehicles that were in common use in the Highlands during the last part of the nineteenth century are quickly giving place to the motor-car. So, although they are not peculiar to the Highlands or indigenous, they are, perhaps, worth describing. Farmers almost invariably had a gig or dog-cart drawn by one of the farm horses or by a pony, and in winter they drove in a sleigh, very simply made of deal by a local craftsman. The spring cart, a light vehicle with no sides or very low ones, was much used by cadgers and tinkers. For more luxurious travel or for hiring, the most usual vehicle was the wagonette, generally referred to as 'the machine'. It was drawn by one horse or a pair.

[1]The foregoing paragraph is based upon an article by C. F. Tebbutt in *Man*, Vol. 55 (1955), p. 113 and E. Estyn Evans, *Irish Folk Life*, p. 178. See also A. C. Haddon, *The Study of Man*, Chapter VI. I have seen carts with both forms of ornamentation in use.

There was a driving box facing the horses but the passengers' seats, two or three a side, were placed sideways to the drivers and facing each other. By the time it was plying for hire from the local inn it had probably come down very much in the world, and it may well have been made originally in Edinburgh where, in the first half of the nineteenth century, there was a very extensive carriage building industry.[1] Last summer I saw an abandoned wagonette on the rubbish dump at Portree (Isle of Skye), probably the last one on the island.

The changes, however, only spread slowly over the country. So late as the middle of the nineteenth century travel off the beaten track was still far from easy. To take as an example, the experiences of the writer of one of the best-loved books on Highland travel—Alexander Smith in *A Summer in Skye*. In the 1850s he travelled by coach from Inverness to Dingwall. There he found that the places on the next mail coach to the west were all engaged and that another would not run for three days. He hired, with great difficulty, a gig with a recalcitrant horse. There were supposed to be six stages to Jane-town on Loch Carron, but fresh horses were unobtainable. At Jane-town he engaged, again with difficulty, a fishing boat to take him to Broadford in Skye but, after a squall, the boat was becalmed and put back to Plockton, only a few miles from where he had started. By the kindness of the local minister, Smith proceeded in a cart to what is now Kyle of Loch Alsh, where he found four people awaiting the ferry to Skye. Thoroughly soaked in a stormy crossing in an open boat, they reached Kyleakin. From thence he had to hire a gig and then, abandoning his luggage, he ended his journey on foot.

On the Long Island roads spread slowly to the lonelier townships (and are still inadequate). With roads, carts made their appearance—the earlier ones although very simple made 'like a box on wheels' acted as carriers for goods and people. It was this introduction that enabled the first local shop to be set up in Tolsta. It was not till 1909 that the first gig appeared there and the following year a 'Coupcart'.[2]

[1] D. Bremner, *Industries of Scotland*, p. 109.
[2] "Tolsta bho Thuath', *Stornoway Gazette*, 31.8.51. The White Paper, *A Review of Highland Policy, 1959*, shows that a special effort is to be made to improve the township roads.

Soon after the early nineteenth century development of the roads came the use of steam in shipping. These great changes were, of course, not of indigenous origin but were the result of outside forces and influences, but they have their essential place in any attempt to describe Highland folk life because of the sweeping alterations they helped to bring about in the people's food, clothing and general attitude. They began at the times of great agrarian changes and the interaction between these two sets of factors is complementary. In the Eastern and Central Highlands the agricultural revolution led to more direct earnings in money, both for the farmer who sold instead of consuming his produce, and to the worker who earned cash wages. Men and women were either entirely dependent on agriculture or earned their living in other ways. The standard of living rose and the home handicrafts declined, and at the same time improved transport brought in supplies of manufactured goods and let in the fashions and standards of the outside world. We read how the girls adopted the widespread vogue of the early nineteenth century for coloured cottons and the men replaced homespun coats by broadcloth. Meanwhile, on the north-western mainland and islands the lesser folk became only partially supported by their holdings and were obliged to seek subsidiary sources of revenue. What little means they had therefore tended to be more in cash though much less in produce, and at the same time the improved means of transport made tea and other imported and manufactured goods available.[1]

More intangible but more fundamental was the disruptive effect of personal contacts with the outside world upon the people's attitude to their own, old way of life. With the improvement in the roads more and more visitors came to the Highlands; sportsmen, family parties who settled down for some weeks, and tourists. And at the same time there was the ebb tide of Highlanders, returning home from work in the south. This kind of impact from the outside has been greatly intensified by the coming of the railways to the Highlands.

[1]*Crofters Commission, 1884.* Report by the Rev. D. Mackinnon, Minister of Strath, Skye, p. 46. A. Mitchell, *Past in the Present*, p. 29, brings out the contrast between primitive conditions and the use of cottons, tea, sugar, etc., from the great manufacturing centres and India, the Indies and China.

In the great railway boom of the 1840s, railway lines began to touch the fringes of the Highlands and different lines reached Perth and Aberdeen about 1848. Although the great North of Scotland railway had been authorized to carry a line from Aberdeen to Inverness, the project was only gradually realized during the 1850s. In the '60s a line was completed from Perth to Forres and the railway from Inverness was gradually carried to Bonar Bridge. In 1865 the companies running most of the northern lines amalgamated to form the Highland Railway. This was a line of great character. Most of the shareholders and directors were people in the north and there was a very real proprietary feeling in its green and gold carriages.[1] The 1880s saw more ambitious projects and gradually the far north and the west coast at Mallaig and at Kyle of Loch Alsh were reached. The actual making of the permanent ways brought great, although transient, local prosperity and work and money became plentiful for a time, although there were no industrial developments and little permanent economic advantage followed.[2] Since then the motor-car has worked still more changes leading to the drastic reorganization of the main roads,[3] and the aeroplane has brought the Islands within easy reach.

Every one of these revolutionary changes in modes of transport has opened the door yet wider between the Highlands and the south. People whose memories can go back to the coming of the railway to their own strath (if not of a road), speak of changes in the whole attitude of the country people far more subtle and fundamental than the disappearance of merely material survivals.

The increased tourist traffic has been of enormous economic advantage to the Highlands. The people's standards of living and requirements have been raised but many local characteristics have been lost; the old language, the Gaelic, has tended to die out and the country people to despise or to degrade to popular standards their own old culture with its magnificent heritage of

---

[1]H. Hamilton, *The Industrial Revolution of Scotland*, p. 250. O. S. Nock, *Scottish Railways*, pp. 12–14, *Handbook of the Highland Railway*, 1894, pp. 1–2.

[2]D. Campbell, *Memoirs of an Octogenarian Highlander*, pp. 531, 532.

[3]And causeways have been built over the inconvenient but picturesque North and South Fords that divided the Uists.

songs and stories. With their flair for social assimilation the Highlanders have adapted more and more their own to the current standards of life outside.[1] In other ways increased transport facilities have not solved Highland problems. Farmers and crofters have increasingly produced for sale rather than for direct home consumption.[2] To keep up with modern requirements and methods of marketing as well as those of actual farming, not only has farm produce to be sent to central markets but feeding stuffs and fertilizers have to be imported. This two-way traffic becomes an increasing handicap to holdings more difficult of access and especially upon the crofters of the north-west and the Hebrides. The Commission of Enquiry into Crofting Conditions (1954) quotes representative figures and states that 'diverse as the conditions are throughout the crofting area there was one complaint that was universal. It related to the high cost of carriage both by land and sea, and to the strain which this imposes on the precarious economy of these remote communities'.[3] The Commissioners agreed with the witnesses that some alleviation of the cost of carriage 'was a matter of life and death for the crofting community'.[4]

Improved transport has not, therefore, brought renewed economic life to the Highlands. If one lives there one cannot but be profoundly thankful for the increased accessibility and supplies of goods. One may regret, even mourn, a great deal that has vanished, yet one must realize that a life deliberately different to that of other people, and lived in a sort of museum case of archaic folksiness would be utterly at variance with the proud and objective attitude of Highland people. The solution of the problem of adjustment between the old and the new is difficult, perhaps impossible, to solve satisfactorily.

It may not be entirely fanciful to see a curiously prophetic touch about the tradition that, when the building of Wade's road through Strathearn endangered Ossian's reputed tomb, the country people petitioned that the course of the road should be

[1] D. Campbell, *Octogenarian Highlander*, p. 591, writes of 'Highland imitativeness'.

[2] *Conditions of the Highlands and Islands of Scotland* (Scottish Economic Committee, p. 189).

[3] *Commission of Enquiry into Crofting Conditions* (1954), p. 69.

[4] Ibid., p. 69.

diverted and that when this was refused, they gathered, opened the grave and raised the stone coffin 'with religious veneration, and, the pipes playing the wail of the coronach, they marched in solemn silence to the top of a neighbouring hill' where they buried it.[1]

[1]J. F. Campbell, *Popular Tales of the Western Highlands*, Vol. IV, p. 241.

# XIV

## FOOD, PHYSIC AND CLOTHING

### THE PEOPLE'S FOOD

IN the old days open-handed hospitality was one of the main obligations on a chief. Of a Lord Lovat (chief of Clan Fraser), who lived at the end of the sixteenth century, it was written: 'It is a rant to speak of the meal and malt spent in his family, for he kept an open table, his hospitality singular, lying in the center betwixt two clans.'[1] He used seven bolls[2] of malt, seven bolls of meal, one of flour a week, besides seventy cows a year, poultry, mutton, venison and game of all kinds. He imported wine 'in great quantities' from France in exchange for his salmon. We have an eyewitness's account of 'the prudent economy' of a later Lord Lovat (the notorious Simon of the '45). His hall was crowded by visitors, vassals and tenants of all ranks, and the table, which extended right down it, 'was covered, at different places, with different kinds of meat and drink; though of each kind there was always great abundance'. At the head of the table the lords and lairds pledged him in claret; the tacksmen drank port or whisky punch; the husbandmen refreshed themselves with strong beer and, at the door, a multitude of clansmen without shoes or bonnets, regaled themselves with bread, onions or a little cheese and small beer. Lord Lovat courteously told each group of guests that he was sending them what he understood they liked best and everybody was well pleased and no one so

[1]With one of whom, the MacKenzies, he was often at feud!—the *Wardlaw Manuscript*, p. 117. Taylor, 'the King's Water Poet', has a vivid account in his *Pennylesse Pilgrimages* (1618), of the *al fresco* catering at the Earl of Mar's hunt. Printed in P. Hume Brown, *Early Travellers to Scotland*, p. 123.

[2]1 boll is equal to 10 stones.

ill-bred as to gainsay his lordship.[1] Sometimes, however, the chiefs were very hard pressed for food for themselves. At the beginning of the seventeenth century during the minority of an Earl of Sutherland, his guardian had to send men out to the hill in April and May to kill deer for the support of the earl's family.[2] Deer killed at the end of the winter would be in miserable condition and most unpalatable. And Burt, when he visited the Highlands in the early eighteenth century, was scornful of Highland cooking and he described the 'inelegant and ostantatious Plenty' at a castle with food become cold, smothered in rancid butter and tainted by cooking in dirty pots. The mutton and the wine were excellent. He added that the host's family probably had to starve for a month 'to retrieve the Profusion'.[3]

The many travellers who wrote of their adventures in the Highlands towards the end of the eighteenth century had high praise for the tacksmen's hospitality and the abundance of cream, butter and cheese, of game, poultry, fish fresh- and salt-water, mutton and beef and also of the tea, coffee, chocolate, wines and spirits and they were especially impressed by the noble Highland breakfasts. Meat and cheese, as well as more usual breakfast foods were served and the Frenchman, Fujas de St. Fond specially noted 'a sort of pap of oatmeal and water, in eating which, each spoonful is plunged into a bowl of cream'.[4] Samuel Johnson, however, in his private letters, was more critical. He said: 'Their tables were very plentiful, but a very nice man would not be pampered. As they have no meat but as they kill it, they are obliged to dine upon the same flesh while it lasts. They kill a sheep and set mutton roasted and boiled on the same table together. They have fish both of the sea and of the brooks, but they barely conceive that it requires any sauce.' Barley broth, however, he said, was 'a constantly well made dish' and he advised any guest to make a point of having some for he might not be able to eat anything else.[5] Root vegetables did not appear

[1]Paraphrased from *Memoirs of Sergeant Donald MacLeod*, ed. J. G. Fyffe, p. 45.
[2]Cosmo Innes, *Scotch Legal Antiquities*, p. 34.
[3]E. Burt, *Letters*, Vol. I, pp. 160–1.
[4]Cf. Pennant, Knox, Johnson and Boswell, Bishop Forbes and especially the Frenchman Fujas de St. Fond. *A Journey through England, Scotland and the Hebrides*, Vol. II, p. 69.
[5]Samuel Johnson, *Letters*, Vol. I, p. 371.

on the menus in Skye as a rule and turnips, boiled with mutton at one place (Fernielea) were said to be 'remarkable'.[1] The tea and coffee, wine and spirits that were served so plentifully had, generally, no duty to pay! White bread was a great luxury only served to guests of distinction. White flour or bread is not mentioned in the household accounts of an eighteenth-century Badenoch tacksman.[2]

Such plentiful hospitality could only have been offered in the summer when home produce was in its short season of abundance[3] and the tacksmen could not have enjoyed such fare in the winter. All meat in those days had to be salted down in the autumn, even now milk and eggs are scarce in the Highlands in the winter and locally caught fish unobtainable. When they were alone the tacksmen probably lived much more simply. We know that the children in the family of a very hard-up tacksman (MacLeod of Ullinish) were fed on porridge and cakes of oats and barley meal, milk and fish but never with salt to season it. An egg was a treat and they hardly ever had meat.[4] Entries in the account book of the old Badenoch tacksman I have often quoted from show that pron and skillings were used in his household:[5] pron was meal mixed with husks and is now only given to hens; skillings, the husks to which some of the grain has adhered, was used for making sowens. He also sometimes mixed rye with the better kinds of meal.

The country people lived much more austerely. Several descriptions comment on the small size of the poorest people and attribute it to under-feeding.[6] Sinclair, writing of the comparatively fertile Black Isle, said that people lived on meal, dairy produce and occasionally a little fish but in quantities that enabled them 'to subsist' but 'hardly in a manner adequate to give spirit or strength for labour'.[7] The menus he gives consisted of: Breakfast: gruel and bread or pottage and milk or flummery and

[1] J. Boswell, *Tour*, p. 212.
[2] I. F. Grant, *Old Highland Farm*, p. 82.
[3] Bishop Forbes, *Journal*, p. 292.
[4] *Memoirs of Sergeant Donald MacLeod*, pp. 3, 8.
[5] I. F. Grant, *Old Highland Farm*, p. 93.
[6] Burt, *Letters*, Vol. II, p. 87. *New Statistical Account for Parish of Alvie*, Vol. XII, p. 85. J. Barron, *The Northern Highlands in the Nineteenth Century*, Vol. III, p. 390–1. T. Pennant, *Tour*, Vol. II, pp. 311–12.
[7] Sir John Sinclair, *The Northern Counties*, p. 73.

milk; Dinner: potatoes and milk, bread and milk or sowens and milk; Supper: potatoes, gruel or kail except in the months of May, June, July and August, when gruel, pottage and milk with some bread constituted their food invariably. Bread would, of course, be bannocks of oat or barley meal, and pottage meant porridge. In less fertile districts and in times of shortage the proportion of dairy food would be higher. Martin says that the people of Skye's 'ordinary diet' was butter, cheese, milk, coleworts, potatoes and brochan (i.e. oatmeal and water boiled).[1] In handwritten notes by MacLeod of MacLeod, written about the end of the eighteenth century, he said that the lesser people's stocks of grain were exhausted by the end of the spring and that they lived on milk, shell-fish and fish until the potatoes were ready.[2] In Badenoch, so late as 1846, a minister wrote, 'Potatoes and milk may be said to constitute the principal foods of the peasantry. For the meal which the small tenants can raise on their farms in their mode of cultivating them would not support their families during one third of the year'.[3] He added that animal food was a luxury that they never indulged in except at times of special festivity. In Upper Dee-side about the same date the people were said to have dined on boiled kail with pron, breakfasted on sowens and milk and supped on sowens.[4]

In these dietaries potatoes had begun to play an important part. Before their introduction there must have been acute shortage of food in bad seasons. Kail—itself apparently a newcomer to upland districts, for my own clan, which inhabited Strathspey, was sometimes described as 'the kail-eating Grants' —appears and also two extremely frugal dishes: (a) *pron*, which consisted of meal mixed with chaff, food now only considered fit for hens, and (b) *sowens, frumerty* or *flummery*, in Gaelic *laghan*, which was made of the skillings, i.e. husks of oats which had some grain adhering to them. These were steeped in water for some

[1]M. Martin, *Western Islands*, p. 242. He adds, 'There is no place so well stored with such great quantity of good beef and mutton where so little of both is consumed by eating.' Among similar descriptions see *Old Statistical Account, Harris*, Vol. X, p. 366; *Edderachilis*, Vol. VI, p. 278. For effect of a famine on the dietary see T. Pennant, *Op. cit.*, Vol. II, pp. 317–18, 351–3.

[2]Preserved in the Muniment Room, Dunvegan Castle. An anonymous pamphlet, *The Highlands of Scotland*, edited by Andrew Lang, p. 94 says exactly the same thing.

[3]*New Statistical Account, Inverness-shire*, p. 90.

[4]E. Taylor, *The Braemar Highlands* (1869), p. 319.

days until the liquid thickened and became sour. This was eaten, if the people were lucky, with milk or beer. Oatmeal itself was often mixed with bere or rye meal.

Porridge and bannocks have a large place in the people's traditional lore. In parts of the Long Island, meal had to be sprinkled over the dough of the bannocks before baking to prevent the fairies from taking them. An alternative precaution was to make a hole with the finger before baking.[1] At Beltane bannocks marked with a cross on one side were rolled down a hill and it was a bad omen if they broke or became stuck on the way down or came to rest with the side marked with a cross uppermost. A slope to the left of the main Inverness road a little to the south of Slochd Muich was pointed out to me as a place where this used to be done. There were several variants of the wonder tale of the final triumph of the virtuous younger son who, on setting forth to find a fortune, preferred his mother's blessing to a bannock. One cure for a bewitched cow was to milk her through a hole that had been made in a bannock. A bannock above the door prevented fairies from seizing a new-born child. On Lewis and on Iona an offering of porridge used to be thrown into the sea to induce a mysterious being called Shoney to send plenty of sea-ware.[2] In Breadalbane the housewife, on the Thursday before Easter, used to stir a special pot of porridge with a stick made of rowan and secretly to hide it in the dunghill in order to encourage the fertility of the manure.[3] Pennant, visiting the Beauly district in the eighteenth century, mentions crosses of sticks that had been dipped in porridge on the same date and placed over the sheep cots, stables and byres. On the first of May (Beltane) they were decked with flowers and carried to the celebrations of that day and then returned to their former positions.[4]

Different varieties of bannocks were made. They might be thick or thin, baked on the girdle before toasting in front of the fire, or merely plastered by hand upon the baking stone. These latter were called *Bonnach Bois*. The most luxurious kind, after cooking, were covered with a thin batter of eggs, milk and butter

[1] Father A. MacDonald, *Gaelic Words*, p. 117.
[2] Gregorson Campbell, *Superstitions of the Western Highlands and Islands of Scotland*, p. 244.
[3] M. MacLeod Banks, *Calendar Customs, Scotland*, p. 33.
[4] T. Pennant: *Tour*, p. 170.

and then baked before the fire. They were eaten as a special feature at certain festivals, but in Lewis, in later times, such a bannock was given to the herd lad who reported that a cow had calved.[1]

In Skye and Barra savoury kinds of bannock named *Bannach Gruan* or *Bannach Donn*, in which a cod's liver and seasoning had been mixed were steamed over a pot and were recently, or are still, eaten.[2] The essential of good porridge is that the meal should be sprinkled slowly into the pot and that it should be well boiled, but a mixture of hot water stirred into raw oatmeal and known as *stapag* is still often eaten. I have been assured that it is more digestible than porridge. It certainly takes less time to prepare! Gruel, *Brochan*, was a regular drink and it has always been considered a good remedy for colds and coughs if taken hot last thing at night,[3] and the Jacobite leader, Lord George Murray, wrote in 1745 that on the retreat from Derby he had caught a bad cold through getting his clothes soaked in fording rivers, and that, having washed in warm water, he had 'oatmeal and water—what Highlanders call a brochin' and was cured.[4]

The milk of goats and sheep (especially for cheese) as well as cows was used and besides butter, cheese, crowdie and whey, the Highlanders used frothed milk. Martin describes how boiled milk or whey was 'wrought up to the mouth of the pot with a long stick of wood, having a cross at the lower end'. He said it was used 'in time of scarcity when they want bread',[5] but whisked cream and meal was a usual festival dish, sometimes, especially at Hallowe'en, a coin was put into it and foretold that the finder would be married. The stick used in preparing frothed milk was called a *Loineid* (in Badenoch a *frohstick*) (see Fig. 47E) and a strand of twisted hairs from a cow's tail was fastened round the cross pieces at the end. It was thought to be a sign of good luck to find a piece of the cow's hair in one's portion. The considerable number of such implements that I was able to collect shows that the dish was widely made. In my young days and in my mother's

[1]'Tolsta bho Thuath', *Stornoway Gazette*, 31.7.51.
[2]F. M. MacNeill, *The Scots Kitchen*, p. 109.
[3]M. Martin, *Western Islands*, notes this several times in his late seventeenth-century descriptions, cf. p. 144.
[4]K. Thomasson, *The Jacobite General*, p. 137.
[5]M. Martin, *Western Islands*, p. 242.

before me, in the Central Highlands 'yearned milk' (curds and cream) was generally given to child visitors to the small farmhouses. An old drink that is still sometimes met with is Athole brose, which is made of equal quantities of heather honey, water in which oatmeal has been steeped so that it is thickened by the floury part of the meal, cream, and rather more whisky.[1]

Something has been said of the historical and economic causes for the increased dependence on potatoes. One gathers that from early times the people did some fishing for their own consumption, drying or salting the fish for winter use, but with the great drive to develop the fisheries and the pressure on food supplies the consumption of fish evidently increased. In Sleat, at the end of the eighteenth century, meal supplies were inadequate, and the people were said to live largely on potatoes and herrings, the shoals of the latter arriving about July so that nature 'seems to have made[2] some provision for the support of the inhabitants of this land, as the fish casts up nearly at the time that the meal is consumed'.

By the middle of the nineteenth century, in all too many of the crofting areas, the people had a monotonous diet of fish and potatoes with some meal but with little milk and few eggs because few cows were now kept and the eggs had to be sold.[3] White fish was cured by drying in the open air. Herring in Martin's day were cured in the reek by hanging them in the rafters,[4] but in spite of the oppressive salt duties, pickling them in barrels came in and eventually became the usual method of preserving them. Salted herring formed an important part of the less well off crofters' winter dietary.

All over the coastwise districts of northern Scotland an economical soup was made by boiling the heads of haddocks and cod with milk and meal and with flakes of fish in the broth. It was known in my family as 'fish and sauce' and was one of the detestations of my childhood. In the Western Isles the heads of haddocks were stuffed with the liver of the fish and seasoning and boiled.

---

[1]Highland regiments have their individual recipes for this drink.
[2]*Old Statistical Account*, Vol. XVI, p. 534.
[3]Evidence before *Crofters Commission, 1884*, Vol. I, cf. pp. 162, 200.
[4]M. Martin, *Western Islands*, p. 200. He said that apart from butter the country people ate little salted food.

This dish was certainly eaten within living memory. In the east it was known as 'crappit heads', in the west as *ceann cropaig*. Cod's gullet was stuffed in the same way. Fishermen often took a sandwich of fish-liver between oatcakes to sea with them as their 'piece'.

Apart from special occasions, hardly any meat was killed for eating but there were casualties in the flocks and herds and in the old days calves or lambs had often to be killed because there was not enough milk to rear them. An account of life in the old days in Lewis describes how every bit of the carcase of a sheep was turned to account. The skin was used for making a crerar or for coverings for jars and pails or as a mat. The blood was made into black puddings and the intestines were used for the skins of black and white puddings. The liver was fried and eaten first and the heart and lungs were used for the next day's dinner. The head and trotters were singed and then made into soup. The meat was salted in a tub and then hung up in the smoky kitchen to dry.[1] Sir Eneas Mackintosh writes in the eighteenth century of goat hams[2] and shepherds' and keepers' wives have told me of how in their young days mutton hams and kegs of pickled mutton were prepared for use in the winter, when their lonely homes were so liable to be snowed up. But the most usual way of cooking meat in the Highlands was, and still is, by making it into broth with barley and vegetables and then eating the meat. Apart from such broth the modern Highlanders are not, as a rule, great vegetable eaters. If they have a garden, and the habit is on the increase, little is generally grown beyond cabbage, curly kail and in sandy districts, carrots. I have seen very tired looking lettuces imported from Glasgow to the Islands to be eaten by visitors. But I do not think that nowadays there is a conscious reaction against the hard days of the past when the people were obliged to eat more vegetable food. Much as salmon was once despised few people nowadays would refuse a cut of it. The tinned variety is bought and tinned peas and beans are very popular.

The people, in their need, turned to many forms of food in the old days. A curious one was the eating of the blood of their cattle. Blood was drawn, either from the yeld (barren) cattle when they

[1]*Stornoway Gazette*, 27.7.51.
[2]Sir Eneas Mackintosh, *Notes*, p. 3.

FOOD, PHYSIC AND CLOTHING

were in good condition in the summer, or, in the case of dire necessity, from the stalled milch cattle in the winter. It was boiled, mixed with meal and eaten as a sort of cake. Unfortunately in some cases people were convicted of bleeding their neighbour's cattle for this purpose.[1] To this day, all over Scotland, 'black puddings' are widely bought. Of course the blood is not drawn from living animals.

On the mainland and in those islands where there were good salmon rivers, salmon was largely eaten 'be or by' the proprietor's consent. Sir Eneas Mackintosh said that the country people killed large numbers.[2] Salmon was so plentiful that the farm servants stipulated that it should not be given them to eat more than twice a week and Burt has a tale of a Highland gentleman who, when visiting London, ordered a beef steak for himself and said that his servant could have salmon and discovered that his own meal cost eightpence and that of his servant as many shillings.[3]

Shell-fish was abundant on the west coast and was much eaten, especially in times of scarcity. Nowadays lobsters have a market value and are exported rather than eaten. I think there is generally a prejudice against eating crabs.[4] Oysters, which used to be common in the bays of Skye and very large, are now a rarity, and if they are gathered they are generally sold. The other molluscs' chief value is as bait, but they are also eaten. Miss F. M. MacNeill has collected several recipes for soups made of shell-fish, thickened with meal and well seasoned.[5] Whale meat and seal meat were also eaten at the end of the seventeenth century.[6]

The people turned to good account the rich variety of seaweed that grow on their coasts. Martin gives a list of four kinds that were used as food and also as remedies,[7] and Miss MacNeill has collected recipes for cooking some of them. Dulse is eaten when it is found but the seaweed still most generally used is *carrageen*

---

[1] Cosmo Innes, *Scotch Legal Antiquities*, p. 34.
[2] Sir Eneas Mackintosh, *Notes*, p. 4.
[3] E. Burt, *Letters*, Vol. I, p. 129.
[4] But they are now being exported.
[5] F. M. MacNeill, *The Scots Kitchen*, pp. 100, 101, 102.
[6] M. Martin, *Western Islands*, pp. 88, 92, 296.
[7] M. Martin calls them linarich, slake, dulse and sea-tangle. *Western Islands*, p. 202.

(Iceland moss). One gathers it where it grows on rocks that are only exposed at the very lowest ebb tides and it is then washed and bleached until it becomes white. To use it, a little of the dried weed is boiled in milk which it thickens into a sort of blancmange which is delicious if lemon juice or jam is added, and is still believed to be a specially strengthening food for delicate people, especially those suffering from chest complaints.

In times of scarcity, seasonal or periodic, the Highlanders also fell back on native herbs. Nettles were sometimes made into soup.[1] I had heard of their being merely boiled and chopped up but when vegetables were scarce during the war and I tried this dish I thought that it was tasteless although a lovely green colour. Miss MacNeill has collected recipes for making nettle broth which might be more tasty.[2] Silverweed, *brisgean* ( *Potentilla Anserina* ) a creeping plant that grows on the shingle, seems to have had considerable nutritive value and was much relied upon in times of scarcity in the Islands.[3] In the old days the places where it grew were allotted among the people to give everyone a share. Charlock and a plant peculiar to the western shores of the Outer Isles and called *shemis* ( *Ligusticum Scoticum* ) were also eaten.[4] In the time of great scarcity during the potato famine the patches of wild spinach, *Blionigean*, growing on Eriskay were marked off into shares for the use of the different families.[5] A plant called *Carmile* or *Cormeille*, tuberous bitter vetch ( *Lathyrus macorrhizus* ) has been well known since ancient times for the property of preventing hunger on long journeys.[6] Plants served other useful purposes. The root of the earth nut is still grubbed up and eaten as a delicacy by children and in the old days the seeds of wild carrot were sometimes used instead of hops in brewing.[7] The ashes of burnt seaweed were used to preserve cheese instead

[1] Lachlan Shaw, *History of the Province of Moray*, p. 36.
[2] F. M. MacNeill, *The Scots Kitchen*, p. 93.
[3] A. Goodrich Freer, *The Outer Hebrides*, p. 190. Father A. MacDonald, *Gaelic Words*, p. 50.
[4] M. Martin, *The Western Islands*, p. 26.
[5] Father A. MacDonald, *Gaelic Words*, p. 44.
[6] Lachlan Shaw: *History of the Province of Moray*, p. 9, quotes more ancient authorities upon this plant. See also F. M. MacNeill, *The Scots Kitchen*, p. 17. Martin says that this plant is useful in preventing people from becoming tipsy, p. 226.
[7] M. Martin, *The Western Islands*, p. 117.

of salt and for scouring flax in Skye.[1] Yeast was preserved in a twig of oak boiled in wort.[2] The use of herbs for medicines requires separate treatment.

The story of Highland beverages would require a book to itself. Apart from milk, the commonest drink in the Highlands in the old days was ale. The inventories that have survived almost always contain the utensils for brewing and in ancient ruins one can often see the remains of the brew-house. MacLeod's accounts for payments to the brewer he employed and for the repair of girnals for his grain are still extant. When rents were partly paid in kind more barley was received than a chief's family would eat and transport would generally be difficult, so it was most convenient to use it for brewing.

Wine, however, was drunk in large quantities in Scotland. In the seventeenth century the Privy Council became much concerned over the consumption of wine by the natives of the Hebrides and they passed Act after Act declaring that 'the great and extraordinary excesses in drinking in wyne commonly usit among the commonis and tenentis of the Yllis, is not only an occasion of the beastlie and barbarous cruelties and inhumanities that fallis oute amangis thame, to the offens and displeasour of God, and contempt of law and justice, but with that it drawis numberis of thame to miserable necessitie and povertie and that they are constraynit, quhen they want from their awne to tak from their neighbouris'. One Act limited the consumption of wine by several of the chiefs—but they did not do badly for their yearly allowance varied from 1 to 4 tuns, i.e. 500–1,000 English gallons.

The constant repetition of such Acts shows that they were not observed, but unfortunately the provisions in one of them—that householders might make as much *aqua vitae* as was needed for the use of their household—was only too well carried out. The drinking and making of *aqua vitae* (whisky) had been coming in during the sixteenth century.[3] There are allusions to it in Kintyre, Ross-shire, Sutherland and Inverness-shire. For instance, a farm in Kintyre paid 6 quarts of it as rent and, in the trial of the

[1] M. Martin, *The Western Islands*, p. 231.
[2] M. Martin, *The Western Islands*, pp. 235, 295.
[3] M. N. Scott Moncrieff, 'Notes on the Early Use of Aqua Vitae', *Proc. Soc. Antiq.* (Scots), 5th Series, Vol. II, p. 266.

murderers of Campbell of Cawdor, a witness said that he had consulted a witch and given her some *aqua vitae* as a present.[1] With the increased consumption of *aqua vitae*, the Highland name for it, *Usque Beatha* (water of life), came into use. For instance, in Clelland's scurrilous poem on the Highland host, a Highlander was said to carry 'a tup's horn filled with usque bay'. It was from *Usque Beatha* that the word whisky was evolved but not for some time. A very early example of the use of the word is in a letter from Inverness dated 1736. By the middle of the eighteenth century the drink was becoming universal in the Highlands. When Prince Charles Edward was hiding in Skye in 1746 he could get nothing but whisky in the inns. By that time ale and beer were said only to be found in gentlemen's houses.[2] But until French wines were penalized by heavy duties and then banned altogether for a time at the end of the eighteenth century, the favourite drink of Highland gentlemen was claret.

Whisky was very cheap. About 1770 the best whisky, brought from Ferintosh and Glenlivat, cost 1s 10d a Scots pint.[3] Large quantities were regularly drunk and whisky was referred to as 'the drink of the country'. The French traveller, Louis Simond, wrote that a Highlander would drink a quart a day and that to be able to bear that quantity of ardent spirits he must have practised much and often.[4] It was often said that the use of spirits in a cold, damp climate like that of Scotland was good for the health. The making of whisky is certainly one of the few things for which parts of the Highlands, in the quality of their water and supplies of peat, have natural advantages. Specially suitable barley was also easily obtainable and the people seem to have had a natural aptitude for the work. The production was also stimulated by the licensing laws. The history of the duties on whisky is complicated and technical.[5] They were imposed from the beginning of the eighteenth century and steadily raised but, owing to the differences in the rates levied in England, the Lowlands and the

[1] A. MacKerral, *Kintyre*, pp. 138, 145. *Highland Papers*, Vol. I, p. 219.
[2] Scott Moncrieff, 'Notes on the Early Use of Aqua Vitae', *Collectanea Rebus Albanicus*, p. 43.
[3] I. F. Grant, *Old Highland Farm*, p. 82. A Scots pint was equal to two English ones.
[4] L. Simond, *Journal of a Tour and Residence in Great Britain during the years 1810 and 1811*, p. 406.
[5] For a summary see D. Bremner, *Industries of Scotland*, pp. 445–50.

Highlands, smuggling became more and more profitable and illicit stills flourished. The traditions of the skill of local men in distilling their spirit and outwitting the Customs officers are among the most vivid, living tales of the past that survive. There can be few districts without them or where the sites of old stills cannot be pointed out. And, had I been allowed to do so, it would have been possible to acquire parts of obsolete apparatus, the great metal pots and the bronze tubes.

The heyday of illicit distilling and smuggling ended in 1823 when the method of levying the duty was changed; a flat and greatly reduced rate was fixed for the whole country and a determined effort was made to stamp out the making and selling of whisky that had paid no duty, and although it may occasionally be carried on, it is a very secret and hazardous occupation. The legal distilling of whisky in the Highlands, however, was for long a flourishing industry and, in spite of the very heavy duties now imposed on it, is still a valuable source of employment and of revenue.

Strange though it may seem, the drinking of tea was at first much frowned on. Duncan Forbes of Culloden, the enlightened patriot who served his country so devotedly in the eighteenth century, was one of its bitterest opponents and he used his great influence to induce the lairds and gentlemen of the Highlands to ban the drinking of tea in their households.[1] Tea-drinking was sometimes preached against as an effeminate habit and I was given a small earthenware jar in which an old lady of long ago in North Uist had kept her supply of tea carefully hidden away in a cranny in the wall. Nevertheless, all through the eighteenth century, it was steadily making its way into the regular dietary of the Highlanders. Tea was, however, still an expensive luxury at the end of the century, for it cost 5s or 7s 6d a lb. whereas port and malaga could be bought for 15s a dozen bottles and a sheep cost from 3s 6d to 8s. As we have seen, tea, coffee and chocolate were offered to distinguished travellers by the hospitable Highland gentlemen, but it would appear from his household accounts that the family of my prudent old ancestor only consumed about 3½ lb. per annum.[2] I have heard two yarns of country women who

[1] G. Menary, *Duncan Forbes of Culloden*, p. 140.
[2] I. F. Grant, *Old Highland Farm*, pp. 69, 82.

had been sent presents of tea from relations abroad and stewed and ate the tea-leaves.

By the nineteenth century, as part of the great changes in the eating habits of the people due to agrarian changes, improved transport and the people's assimilation of general standards of living,[1] tea became a universal drink in the Highlands. In spite of the dire poverty of some of the crofters of the west, by the middle of the century, they managed to buy and drink it. Nowadays, at whatever time one may call at a Highland house, the hospitable teapot is seldom absent from the hob and the visitor is almost invariably regaled with a 'strupach'.

White wheaten flour came in as well as baker-made white bread and all self-respecting housewives became expert in baking scones—drop scones and girdle scones made on the open fires and now, with the almost universal cooking stoves, oven scones. The tin and the tin-opener have taken the place of the pickling keg. Apples and oranges and now tomatoes and bananas appear in country shops and help to supply the lack of home-grown vegetables.

On occasions of formal festivity the country people will buy a bottle of port; on ordinary ones, from motives of economy, the men have reverted to drinking beer, although a good deal of whisky, in spite of its inflated price, due to the heavy duty, is still drunk.

### THE PEOPLE'S PHYSIC

A catalogue of some of the remedies that the country people used for themselves and their animals is specially interesting in illustrating the changes that have taken place in the long story of Highland civilization. Different cures can be attributed to the different stages in the story.

There are some that seem to go back not only to pre-christian days but to the shadowy times of nature worship before the coming of belief in the gods.[2] An example is the widespread belief in

[1] For typical late nineteenth-century dietaries see *Scottish Mothers and Children* (pub. by Carnegie Trust), pp. 400, 455. For references to the changes see *Crofters Commission, 1884*, pp. 27, 39, 43, 46.

[2] G. Henderson, *Survivals of Belief among the Celts*, p. 6.

the powers of certain wells to cure or to foretell the outcome of maladies. Such well-worship is surely one of the most understandable of primitive beliefs for, as one watches the water of a mountain spring bubbling out of the ground, the grains of sand in the little basin it has made for itself, dancing in the flow of water, it is easy to imagine that some mysterious power is immanent within it. The veneration for wells was so strong that the early christian missionaries often came to terms with it and dedicated many of these wells to a saint.[1] All over the Highlands one reads of traditions about the healing powers of wells and belief in their efficacy in some cases lasted until within living memory.[2]

The persistence of older beliefs is also mixed up with the cures for insanity practised as part of the cults of St. Maelrubh at his island in Loch Maree and St. Fillan at his chapel by Loch Earn, for by the seventeenth century, bulls were also sacrificed to St. Maelrubh and the ceremony at St. Fillan's pool took place during the third phase of the moon and offerings of rounded pebbles were laid on a cairn. The actual procedures, in one case towing the unfortunate patient behind a boat round the island and in the other throwing him into the pool and then tying him up for the night within the saint's stone coffin in his ruined chapel, were forms of shock treatment.[3]

The idea of fire-worship is surely at the root of the rite of passing an ailing child through a hoop of iron to which blazing wisps of straw had been fastened.[4] The driving of a newly-calved cow through peat reek and of the flocks and herds through the Beltane fires to safeguard them for the coming year are variants of the same idea.

A cure for 'hectic and consumptive diseases' practised in the Central Highlands is one of many that contain the idea of the transference of the disease. Parings from the nails of the fingers

[1]St. Adamnan describes how St. Columba sanctified such a well. See *St. Adamnan's Life of St. Columba*, p. 45.

[2]For lists of such wells and their properties see J. Anderson, *Scotland in Early Christian Times*, p. 193. M. MacLeod Banks, *Calendar Customs, Scotland*, p. 157. M. Martin, *Western Islands* has many circumstantial accounts.

[3]For an eyewitness's account of the ceremonies at St. Fillan's, see J. Anderson, *Scotland in Early Christian Times*, p. 191. Shock treatment in the form of a heated piece of iron suddenly touching the patient's body was also one cure for jaundice.

[4]For full description see F. M. MacNeill, *The Silver Bough*, p. 65.

and toes of the patient were put in a rag cut from his clothes, waved three times round his head—*deasil*-wise and then buried in some place unknown to him. Lachlan Shaw,[1] who wrote his *History of Moray* at the end of the seventeenth century, said he had actually seen this done.

Among examples of cures containing the idea of sympathetic magic are two recorded in Lewis. To cure a weak heart a small heart was made of lead and thrown into the sea from Tolsta Head, and the remedy for a stye was to point a knife or an axe at the place and repeat the rhyme:

> Carson a thigeadh aon gun a dha,[2]
> Carson a thigeadh a dha gun a tri.
>
> (Why should one come and not two,
> Why should two come and not three.)

Prehistoric artefacts or unusual looking objects, such as fossils, were sometimes supposed to have curative properties.

One of the commonest forms of cure was by the use of 'silvered water', i.e. water taken from a ford or from under a bridge where the dead and the living passed—that is to say on the way to a graveyard—and into which a silver coin had been dropped. Often the person who was performing it was forbidden to speak to anyone in going or coming to fetch the water. A charm was said. Someone I know well has told me his mother had seen this cure practised for the recovery of a sick child and a bewitched stirk. It was often used to counteract the effects of the evil eye. At the museum I had a wooden ladle that came from Easter Ross and I was told that it had been used for bringing home silvered water.[3]

Curative properties were also often believed to be immanent in certain stones or pebbles. Originally no doubt used for the cure of human beings, their use for beasts survived longer. The MacDonnells of Keppoch had such a charm stone.[4] At the museum

[1]Lachlan Shaw, *History of the Province of Moray*, p. 154.
[2]'Tolsta bho Thuath', printed in *Stornoway Gazette*, 17.7.51.
[3]Among accounts of this charm see F. M. MacNeill, *The Silver Bough*, p. 155. A. Goodrich Freer, *The Outer Isles*, p. 252. The latter adds: 'I can personally testify that when silver is put into a bowl of water to work a spell, the wise woman keeps the silver.'
[4]Catalogue of the Palace of History, Glasgow Exhibition, 1911, p. 663.

I had six small water-worn pebbles and five coins so much defaced that they could not be dated, in a little bag netted from hand-spun linen yarn. This charm had belonged to the MacDonalds of Dalchosnie. The last surviving member of the family wrote down how it had been used. Water from between the lands of two lairds and over which the living and the dead had passed was brought by the owner of the animals to be cured and was placed in a wooden vessel with three bands on it and the charm was dipped into it and it was then taken for the sick animal to drink. This charm had been bequeathed to the faithful maid of the last member of the family and by her was presented to Am Fasgadh. I also had a wooden goblet from Mull in which, as its owner remembered from his young days, medicine for animals had been compounded, and a stone with a hole in it from Morayshire which, to the knowledge of the man from whom I got it, had been worn suspended by a thread round the neck as a cure for toothache. Unfortunately, the charms which were said when charmstones were used were repeated in secret and have almost invariably been lost. Even the particular cures the charmstones were once believed to work are all too often forgotten.[1] The power of the seventh son of a seventh son to touch for 'the King's Evil' (Scrofula) was widely believed in in the Islands. Sometimes members of Clan Ranald's family were believed to have the power. In the notes on remedies written down by a bygone MacNeill, Laird of Carskey (in Kintyre) about 1703–43, he states that a snake-skin placed round a woman's thigh would give her an easy delivery in childbed.[2]

Such charms are survivals from very primitive times but it is important to remember that in the heyday of their civilization the Gael had their highly trained physicians. Robert II confirmed a charter granting lands in the extreme north to Ferchard, the King's Leech in 1386,[3] and in 1444 there is an allusion to a 'leche' in company with Sir Colin Campbell of Glenurchie. The 1444 reference probably refers to one of the O'Conacher's, who practised as hereditary doctors in Lorn. The Beatons, the

[1]A. Carmichael in his *Carmina Gadelica*, Vol. I, gives a number of Gaelic charms. Some are printed in John MacKenzie, *Beauties of Gaelic Poetry*, p. 268.
[2]F. F. Mackay, *MacNeill of Carskey*, p. 103.
[3]*Origines Parochiale Scotiae*, Vol. II, pp. 651, 704. For further early references see J. D. Comrie, *History of Scottish Medicine*, p. 93.

physicians to the Lords of the Isles, are better known. The family held land in Islay, the headquarters of the old Lordship, and a charter of 1408 survives written and witnessed by a member of the family. After the fall of the Lordship of the Isles, the Beatons became hereditary physicians to several Highland families—to the MacLeans of Duart, from whom they held lands at Pennygheal in Mull where the remains of their herb garden was until lately still to be seen—to the MacLeods of MacLeod and the MacDonalds of Sleat who, although at bitter feud with each other, combined to support a branch of the Beatons in Skye to the Munros of Foulis (Ross-shire), the Frasers of Lovat and to the Earls of Sutherland. A certain number of the Gaelic manuscripts used by these Highland physicians still survive. They are written in the Irish character and most of them date from the fourteenth to the sixteenth centuries. They are works of great erudition quoting the medical authorities most esteemed by contemporary doctors—classical, Arabic and medieval—from Hippocrates onwards.[1] A work called the *Lilium Medicinae* by Bernard Gordon, Professor of Physics at the University of Montpelier was a famous medical authority and was published in 1305. It was very soon afterwards translated into Gaelic and several copies have survived. The writing of one of them, made for one of the Beatons in Skye, was said to have cost as much as sixty milch cows and it was so precious that when the doctor crossed an arm of the sea the book was sent round by land.[2] Another of the Beatons manuscripts, now in the British Museum, was translated by H. Cameron Gillies. It is known as the *Regimen Sanitatis* and is thought to date from the sixteenth century. It begins by stating that there are three aspects of the Regulation of Health, '*Conseruatiuum*, that is, guarding; and *Preseruatiuum*, that is, foreseeing; and *Reductiuum*, that is, guiding backwards' and he explains that the first is the maintaining of a healthy state which is the right of a healthy man, the second is the taking of proper measures by those in a declining state of health and is a

[1]For a description of these manuscripts see Professor Donald MacKinnon, *Descriptive Catalogue of Gaelic Manuscripts*, p. 5; J. D. Comrie, *History of Scottish Medicine*, p. 93; H. Cameron Gillies, translation of *Regimen Sanitatis*, a manuscript of one of the Beatons in the British Museum.
[2]Professor Donald MacKinnon, Op. cit. p. 270.

duty, and the third is the restoration of those who are ill and is a necessity. Many of the rules of health are admirable.[1] The other old manuscripts deal with such matters as fevers, anatomy, diseases of the heart, methods of diagnosis, *materia medica* and the properties of different plants. But they also contain passages upon astronomy, astrology and metaphysics and a few included charms. On the margins of the pages their owners have scribbled many notes about cases and their conclusions, but it is rather touching that one of them refers to one of the well-known epic tales of Eire, that of the 'Deaths of the Children of Tuirenn'.

The decline of this tradition of medical learning has a general interest in the study of Highland folk life because it is a clear example of the gradual extinction of their old culture that was forced upon the Highlanders in the seventeenth century when the fountains of knowledge became concentrated at the Lowland universities and for political reasons persistent efforts were made to discourage the Gaelic language.[2] The remembrance of the old literature of their people became dependent on an oral folk tradition kept alive by the innate artistic good taste of the country people. By the end of the seventeenth century writing in the Irish character had gone out and Gaelic prose literature had been killed. As we have seen the music and the poetry of the Gael continued to flourish but it was mainly preserved by verbal repetition. A medical family of MacLeans, who had lived upon the lands of the Lamonts (in Cowal) are last heard of in 1568.[3] The last evidence of the existence of the O'Conachers is a fine and learned medical treatise dated 1611 which still survives.[4] Of the different branches of the Beatons, that which had become associated with the Frasers, alluded to in the *Wardlaw Manuscript*[5] as 'the Tolly Molloch', i.e. *an T'Ollamh Muilleach*, the Mull doctor, had occupied a davoch in Glen Conveth 'time out of

[1]H. Cameron Gillies, tr. *Regimen Sanitatis* (Beaton MSS. in British Museum), pp. 8, 31.
[2]For an admirable survey of the measures taken, see J. Lorne Campbell, *Gaelic in Scottish Education*.
[3]*Highland Papers*, Vol. IV, p. 75.
[4]*Miscellany of the Scottish History Society*, Vol. IV, p. 235. Professor Donald MacKinnon, *Descriptive Catalogue of Gaelic MSS.*, p. lx.
[5]*Wardlaw MSS.*, pp. 145, 236.

mind', but by 1622 we are told that a Perth doctor was in attendance on Lord Lovat (who died under his ministrations) and the Beatons are no longer mentioned. In Islay, in 1609, Fergus MacBeath (a variant of Beaton), obtained a charter for land formerly granted to his family 'by the Lord of the Isles', having been 'Legally entered in the office of principal physician within the said island, and for the administration of the said office'. Twenty years later, however, the family disposed of their lands though there was still a Doctor Beaton a few years later in Islay.[1] A member of the Mull family is said to have been on the deck of the Spanish galleon that took refuge in Tobermory Bay when it was blown up, but fortunately escaped. There is a tombstone erected to another at Iona in 1658 on which he is described as 'MacLeanarum Familiae Medicis'. A medical treatise belonging to a member of the Skye family of Beatons has corrections on it dated 1671, but in the eighteenth century they seem to have mainly entered the Church. There was, however, some survival of their old skill, for Martin records that at the end of the seventeenth century there was a Neil Beaton living in Skye who 'although without the advantage of education' worked wonderful cures by means of herbs and said that he had been taught by his father. In 1881 Carmichael met a descendant of the family in Barra and said that he showed great knowledge of plants.[2]

The MacLeods of MacLeod continued the old custom of the family and, during the eighteenth century, organized and helped to provide medical treatment for their people, but this seems to have been exceptional.[3] There were few medical men in the remoter parts. Thus, when Doctor Garnett visited Mull in 1800 he found that there was no doctor on the island and that people who desired medical treatment had to go to Inveraray.[4] While the Highlanders thus lost their own trained medical men, their reputation for uncanny powers of healing survived. For instance, Gaelic was used for the charms mentioned in some witch trials in Bute in 1662 although English was otherwise spoken.[5] The

[1]Gregory Smith, The Book of Islay, pp. 139, 383, 402.
[2]M. Martin, Western Islands, p. 288. A. Carmichael, Carmina Gadelica, Vol. II, pp. 78, 79.
[3]I. F. Grant, The MacLeods, pp. 357, 488, 508, 558.
[4]T. Garnett, Tour, Vol. II, p. 120.
[5]Highland Papers, Vol. I, pp. 165, 167.

fallacy of investing the Highlanders with an aura of glamourie is therefore an old one and it dies hard! Although the charms that the people used are interesting because they suggest a continuity from ancient times, one must remember that their chief reliance for cures was on the natural properties of the agents that they used. Martin truly says of the Islanders that although denied the pursuit of more conventional studies 'they seem to be better versed in the book of nature than many that have greater opportunities of improvement' as was shown by the way in which they preserved their health 'by temperance and the prudent use of simples' in the use of which they first make experiment and afterwards reason upon their effects.[1] After enumerating a number of their cures he wrote: 'They are generally a very sagacious people, quick of apprehension, and even the vulgar exceed all those of their rank and education I ever saw in any other country.'[2] The fact that there had once been highly trained doctors among them must also surely have left some tradition of medical knowledge.[3]

The people had discovered and turned to account the curative properties of their local plants.[4] Many of those that they most used are noted as possessing considerable medicinal value in modern books on British plants, such as C. A. Jones and G. Elliot's, *Flowers of the Field*. As, for instance, in the case of the Greater Plantain (*Plantago Major*), Gaelic *Cuach Phadraig* and the Ribwort Plantain (*P. Lanceolata*), Gaelic *Snaithlus*, the use of which for poultices or dressings to draw inflammation from sores is remembered by people still living; Marsh Trefoil or Buck Bean (*Menyanthus Trifoliata*), Celtic *Tribhileach*, a plant with strong medicinal properties which was used for colic and internal upsets and which, as I have been told by people who had actually used it, was most efficacious; the virtues of Scurvy Grass is shown by its English name but it was used for stitches and other troubles; nettles for nose bleeding and headache; Sorrel, with its distinctive acid flavour; Wood Sanicle, belonging to a

[1] M. Martin, *Western Islands*, p. 63.
[2] Ibid., p. 240.
[3] The extraordinary length of the lists in H. Cameron Gillies, *Gaelic Names for Diseases and Diseased States* is suggestive.
[4] I was interested to compare the lists of plants that they used with those in Culpepper.

genus well known for medicinal properties; Foxgloves, from which in modern times the valuable drug of digitalis is still derived was listed by Martin, but to be used to induce sleep after a fever. Other plants used by the people and known to have curative properties were Scabious, Gentian and Centaury, Gaelic *Teantguidh*, both valued tonics, the latter also used for colic. St. John's Wort, which was perhaps more of a charm; Tormentil, the Crowsfoot (*Ranunculus Sceleratus*) and the more formidable Lesser Spirewort (*R. Flamulus*), which Martin mentions several times for its powers of raising a blister and for use in sciatica. Martin also makes mention of two seaweeds of which the herbals do not treat. One, which he calls *linarich*,[1] he says was efficacious for burns, megrim, sores and sleeplessness, and *dulse*,[2] which was even more versatile, being used for headaches, constipation, skin diseases and certain complications following a confinement. Butter, taken internally and externally, comes into many cures. In Lewis it was spread on a cloth and singed with a hot iron before being applied to a wound—surely an example of an anti-septic precaution. Fractures, Martin says, were treated by a coating of white of egg and barley meal before the splints were applied.[3] In the treatment of consumption great importance was attached to the drinking of milk warm from the stripping of a cow —the richest part of the milk, or, better still, the milk of goats, and the eating of specially nourishing foods, such as marrow, but also snails. A speaker in 1887 recorded that in his youth his chest was massaged to strengthen it.[4] Another member at the discussion that followed told of his successful treatment by a bone-setter for a dislocated shoulder. Scrapings of deers' horns and deers' grease were esteemed. When I was a baby an old man gave my mother a quantity of the latter for her to rub me with. An eel skin used as a bandage on a sprain was elastic and the fat was soothing. Coughs and colds were treated by wearing wet clothes and going to bed and being heaped with blankets to produce a sweat, and although there is no trace of the regular use of 'sweat

[1]M. Martin, *Western Islands*, pp. 145, 224, 225.
[2]M. Martin, *Western Islands*, pp. 22, 225, 229, 230.
[3]M. Martin, *Western Islands*, p. 230.
[4]D. Masson, *Popular Domestic Medicine in the Highlands*. Trans. of the Gaelic Society of Inverness, Vol. XIV, p. 297.

houses', such as one hears of in Ireland, both Martin and D. Masson speak of heating a hole in the ground into which a limb could be thrust, or specially heating the kitchen with burning straw for the purpose. Hot gruel, taken last thing at night, a cure for a cold that our grandmothers still prescribed, was among Martin's remedies. Whisky entered into many of his cures and has continued to be used. A visitor records a Highland prayer for preservation from the disorder that whisky would not cure.[1]

If strange and repulsive things such as snails (which were applied both internally and externally in various cures) were sometimes used, one must remember the extraordinary prescriptions made out by fully qualified medical practitioners in general down to the eighteenth century. The notes on cures for men and animals written down by MacNeill of Carskey, a Kintyre laird of the first half of the eighteenth century, contain a strange variety of ingredients—some native herbs such as tormentil and sorrel (both mentioned by Martin), elecampane and the bark of the alder; spices, such as ginger and cinnamon; butter and honey; some drugs but also a snake-skin, slaters (wood lice), and the fat from a roasted black cat.[2]

We may feel thankful that the people of the Highlands, even in the remotest areas, no longer have to rely upon such remedies as happen to grow at their doors and upon their untutored skill for medical help. The older Highlands and Islands Medical Service and now the nation-wide Health Service covers them and by means of improved transport, latest of all by the air-lift, they are within reach of the most skilled treatment.[3] In the long struggle to extend medical help to people in remote, snow-bound glens on the mainland and on islands severed from aid by raging seas, local stories of acts of courage and of lives of devoted service by doctors and nurses are still remembered and handed down as part of the living folk tradition and are as heroic as the ancient, almost forgotten wonder tales, and epics and traditions of the clans.

[1]James Hall, *Travels in Scotland* (1807), Vol. I, pp. 4–9. Other authorities quoted in this section are Father A. MacDonald, *Gaelic Words*, and M. F. Shaw, *Folk Songs and Folk Lore*, pp. 47–49.
[2]F. F. MacKay, *MacNeill of Carskey*, p. 103.
[3]Hospitals at Stornoway and Daliburgh have also brought enlightened medical treatment to within the Long Island itself.

## THE PEOPLE'S CLOTHES

It is a sign of the liveliness of surviving feeling that certain theories about the old dress of the Highlands still rouse hot controversy. But the clothes worn by the people of the Highlands have a wider interest, not only because they help to illustrate the changes that have taken place in the people's way of life, but, more significantly, because they have the unique distinction of having been the dress of all Highland people and were never merely the dress of peasants.

The early inhabitants of the north of Scotland are of several different origins and there is little to show what they wore. The old stone carvings of the seventh, eighth and ninth centuries and analogies with Ireland suggest that in the Central Highlands at least, it consisted of a long or a short kind of tunic and a cloak or plaid.[1]

It is evident that although the ancient people of Alba carried arms, like the ancient Irish, they did not wear defensive body armour. The tradition of their reliance on the desperate assault of lightly clad men comes out strongly in two contemporary English accounts of the Battle of the Standard (fought between the English and the Scots in 1138). The Scots army consisted partly of the native people, whom the monkish chroniclers allude to as 'barbarians' and partly of the mail-clad Anglo-Norman knights whom the Scots kings were so lavishly encouraging to settle in Scotland. Before the battle, the 'Picts of Galloway' had insisted upon their ancient right to lead the van, much against the wishes of the knights, who declared that they would be repulsed by the armoured English forces and that this would throw the rest of the Scots army into confusion. The chroniclers gloat over the failure of the men of Galloway, in spite of gallantry, to penetrate the English front. The incident is an illuminating illustration of the supreme value of knights in armour in the days before

[1] H. F. McClintock, *Old Irish and Highland Dress*, Chapter I of the Irish section and Chapter I of the Highland section has a scholarly assessment of the little that can be deduced. The passage in Magnus Berfaet's Saga (1903) is well known. It states that when this Norse king came back from a conquering expedition to the Hebrides 'he adopted the costume in use in the Western Lands, and likewise many of his followers'; 'and that he went about barelegged having short tunics and also upper garments, and so many men called him "Bare legged" or "Barefoot".'

gunpowder, and explains the dominating influence of the Anglo-Norman incomers and the introduction of the feudal system over the whole of Scotland. (*See Chap. I.*)

The Gael, however, both in Ireland and Scotland, learnt to adopt protective armour as we know from contemporary accounts and from the effigies carved on many of the Highland tombstones. A few of the more affluent chiefs are depicted

as wearing plate armour, but, as a rule, besides an iron headpiece with a camail and leggings of mail, they either wore a shirt of chain mail or an 'aketon' (haqueton) of quilted leather or linen, both of which were also worn by the Lowlanders of similar degree as ordained by the series of Acts regulating the military service of the lieges from the fourteenth to the sixteenth centuries, or else they wore a garment distinctively Irish, the *Leiné Chroich* or saffron shirt, which consisted of as many as 24 ells of pleated linen (see Fig. 66). It is obvious that the camail and the leiné chroich were somewhat costly garments and they illustrate the fact that in the organization of the rising clans the main fighting was done by the gentlemen, mainly the kinsmen of the chiefs. In a report of the seventeenth century to James VI it was estimated that one-third of the 6,000 fighting men of the Western Isles (from whom the 'labourers of the ground' were expressly excluded) wore coats of mail or aketons.[1] This was the

FIG. 66. Effigy of typical West Highland warrior. Probably that of Roderick MacLeod of Lewis, 7th chief. Fl. End of fifteenth century.

battle dress. What ordinary people wore in times of peace we do not know. On the one hand the figures in a representation of a hunt on the fifteenth century Cross at Kilmorey Knap in Knapdale

[1]This report is printed as an Appendix to Vol. III, W. F. Skene, *Celtic Scotland*.

wear contemporary Lowland dress; on the other, in Elder's letter
to King Henry VIII, written about 1543, he says, as if it were an
old custom, that the Highlanders were known as Redshanks
because they went bare-legged.

The plaid, however, continued to be worn as it probably had
been from ancient times and, as already noted, finely 'hewet'
ones were of some value. In the sixteenth century the people of
western Europe were becoming more dress conscious and there
are nine fairly full contemporary descriptions besides many
allusions to the distinctive dress of the Highlanders.[1] In nearly
all these descriptions the shirt of linen or of mail, and also the
plaid, appear. Bare legs are several times mentioned or implied,
but in one, a list of the garments bought for James V to wear in
the Highlands in 1538, 'heland tartane' for 'hois' is mentioned,
probably for tartan trews. In the Acts regulating the arming of
the lieges during the sixteenth century the mail shirt or aketon
was still ordered for the Highlanders although the battle dress
of the Lowlanders had been changed. By the end of the century
the emphasis in descriptions was increasingly upon the plaid
rather than the mail shirt. This was distinctively Highland and
a break with Irish traditions.[2] For instance, when, in 1594,
MacLeod of MacLeod and MacDonald of Sleat led a force of
their men to Ireland to help Red Hugh O'Donnell, the contemporary Irish writer, Lughaidh O'Cleirigh wrote that 'They were
recognized among the Irish soldiers by the distinction of their arms
and clothing, their habits and language, for their exterior dress
was mottled cloaks of many colours with a fringe to their shins
and calves, their belts were over their loins outside their cloaks.'[3]

This passage gives an early description of the *Feileadh Mor*
(Big Wrap) or belted plaid that was to become the characteristic
dress of the Highlanders during the seventeenth and eighteenth
centuries and even into the early nineteenth century. It consisted
of a double width of fabric,[4] in all about 5 ft. wide and from 12 to

[1]For details of these descriptions see *Collectanea Rebus Albanicis*, and H. F.
McClintock, *Old Irish and Highland Dress*, p. 3 onwards.
[2]By this time the Elizabethan conquest of Ireland was bringing about a general
eclipse of Irish influences.
[3]Life of Aodh O'Domhnaill, *Book of Lughaidh O'Cleirigh*, Irish Text Society
Publication, Vol. XLII, Part I, p. 73.
[4]On the old loom, fabrics only about 30 in. wide could be woven.

18 ft. long. To put it on, the Highlander laid it down on the ground and arranged it in pleats except for a small piece at each end and with his belt below it. He then lay down upon it, with the lower edge level with his knees and after folding the two un-pleated ends across his body so that they overlapped, he fastened the whole thing round his body by means of his belt. He then stood up, the longer part of the plaid hanging down all round him, almost to his feet, and he put on a special short Highland jacket.[1] He could then either bring the whole of this longer part of the plaid up over his shoulders and back so as to be a protection if the weather were wet or, and more usually, he could bring the left side up to his shoulder and pin it there, leaving the rest to drape over his coat[2] (see Fig. 67). Till the seventeenth century the men wore their hair long and uncovered, the flat bonnet then came in.

This dress which formed a covering by night, even out of doors, and a clothing by day was considered essential for the High-landers when they were herding their cattle, and was admirably suited for wear when they went raiding. The former point was strongly argued by Duncan Forbes of Culloden and others who opposed the passing in 1747 of the law proscribing the wearing of Highland dress after the last Jacobite rising—the latter point by the commanders of the troops engaged in enforcing the Act and in putting down cattle driving.[3] Surviving family pictures show that it was a costly and beautiful dress when the plaid was fine and dyed in the brilliant colours that the most skilled dyers could achieve and with it was worn a slashed doublet, richly chased Highland pistols, carved dirk, silver buckles on the belt and brogues, a finely engraved powder flask and, in later times, an ornamental sporran. A targe with tooling and metal embel-lishments besides a gun and a sword were carried. Wade, writing

[1]The ancestor of the modern doublet.

[2]A series of engravings by Van der Guchte (1743) and illustrations to Burt's *Letters from a Gentleman in the North of Scotland* (*c.* 1730) show that the plaid was thus adjusted. They are reproduced in H. McClintock's book. For written descrip-tions see Martin, *Western Islands*, pp. 206–9 and Burt, *Letters*, p. 87.

[3]MacLeod of MacLeod and MacDonald of Sleat raised Independent Companies for service on the Hanoverian side during the Rising. The latter wrote of the diffi-culty MacLeod would have in bringing his company to full strength because 'he does not know that though he has men, they are not Men of War without Plaids'. *Culloden Papers*, Vol. IV, p. 202.

FIG. 67. Method of adjusting the belted plaid. After Van der Gucht.

in 1727, said that arms were 'worn by the meanest of the inhabitants of the Highlands, even in their Churches, Fairs and Markets, which looked rather like places of Parade for Soldiers than Assemblies for Devotion or other meetings of Civil

Society.'[1] The gentlemen, when riding, sometimes wore tartan trews instead of the belted plaid, but otherwise, though its form might be simpler, the same style of dress was worn by all ranks of society.[2] To compare with some of the beautiful clothes worn in the portraits of chiefs,[3] there is Defoe's pen-picture of a Highlandman (apparently a drover) he met in the High Street of Edinburgh. 'They are all gentlemen, will take affront from no man and insolent to the last degree. But certainly the absurdity is ridiculous, to see a man in his mountain habit, armed with a broadsword, targe, pistols at his girdle, a dagger and staff, walking down High Street as upright and haughty as if he were a lord, and withal driving a cow.'[4] Or that of the rank and file of the Jacobite army as it marched into Derby at the point of highest achievement in the '45. 'A crew of shabby, lousy, pitiful look'd fellows; mixed up with old men and boys; dressed in Dirty Plaids, and as dirty shoes, without Breeches; and wore their stockings maid of Plaid, not much above half-way up their Legs, some without Shoes, or next to none, and with their Plaids thrown over their Shoulders.' Had they been unarmed they would have appeared 'more like a Parcel of Chimney Sweeps than Soldiers'.[5]

The belted plaid was particularly suitable for a pastoral life, but not for more laborious work and this is generally given as the reason for the introduction of the *Feileadh Beag* (Little Wrap) or kilt. The story generally told is that about 1720 the manager of some iron-smelting works set up by an English company in Glengarry introduced a garment made of one width of stuff sewed into pleats—in other words the kilt—because the belted plaid worn by his Highland workmen was so unwieldy. In a fuller version a regimental tailor, who happened to call on the manager, is said to have suggested separating the upper and lower part of the belted plaid and to have made the first kilt. The manager

[1] *Historical Papers Relating to the Jacobite Period* (New Spalding Club), p. 160.
[2] See for instance an account of the cattle tryst at Crieff in 1723. (See p. 69.)
[3] There are some fine illustrations of such pictures in an article by A. E. Haswell Miller in *Scotland's Magazine*, November 1947.
[4] Letter from Defoe to Harley, 1736, quoted by R. Salaman, *The History and Social Influence of the Potato*, p. 353.
[5] 'A Plain, General and Authentic Account of the Conduct of the Rebels, during their stay at Derby', reprinted in *Historical Papers Relating to the Jacobite Period* (New Spalding Club), p. 288.

himself wore this tailor-made kilt and MacDonnell of Glengarry was so much taken with it that he had another made for himself.[1] The suggestion that the kilt originated in this way has called forth hot denials but it is possible that a single width of stuff might have been used by poor people as a humble substitute for the belted plaid. The stitching and making up by a tailor would then be the great innovation. In any case, after the early eighteenth century, the kilt is more and more often mentioned and became the undress uniform of the Highland Regiments formed during that century. Like the belted plaid it is wrapped round the body. Great skill is required to make it properly.

Arms were so much part of the people's everyday equipment and, as more than one writer has pointed out, so much helped to account for their belligerence and pride and also for the respect that they paid to each other,[2] that a brief word may be said of them. Almost contemporary with the wearing of the belted plaid instead of the mail shirt, the two-handed *claidheamh mor* (big sword)=claymore, gave place to the basket-hilted sword, still part of the uniform of an officer in a Highland regiment. With this belted plaid and basket-hilted sword were carried a dirk, a targe, a powder horn and, by those who could afford them, a pair of Highland pistols and a gun (see Fig. 68, 69). It may be noted that the use of the belted plaid and the broadsword made possible the furious downhill charge, the most formidable Highland fighting tactic.

In 1747, after the last Jacobite rising, a very severe Disarming Act was passed and, besides prohibiting the carrying of arms, all males except those serving as soldiers in the Forces of the Crown, were forbidden to 'wear or put on cloathes commonly called Highland Clothes this to say the Plaid, Phillibeg or Little Kilt, Trowse, Shoulder-belt, or any part whatsoever of what peculiarly belongs to the Highland garb; and that no Tartan or party coloured plaid or stuff shall be used for great coats or for upper coats'. Under a terrible oath Highlanders were forced to promise compliance and the penalties for contravening the Act were a fine of £15 or six months' imprisonment for the first con-

---

[1]H. F. McClintock, *Old Irish and Highland Dress*, p. 37.

[2]Cf. William Sacheverell, who wrote in 1688, see an *Account of the Isle of Man, with a Voyage to I-Columb-kill*, p. 125.

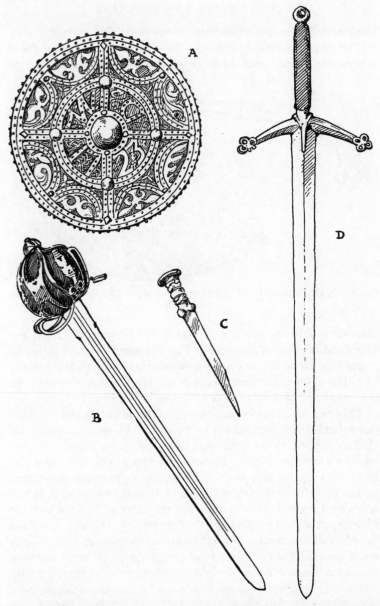

Fig. 68. Highland arms. (A) (B) and (C) Seventeenth to eighteenth-century Targe, dirk and basket-hilted sword. (D) Fifteenth-century two-handed sword.

viction and transportation for seven years for a second one.

The Act was strictly enforced in some districts but in those where there had been little overt Jacobite sympathy it was

Fig. 69. Highland arms. (A) Eighteenth-century pistol. (B) Seventeenth-century powder horn.

allowed to fall into abeyance so far as the wearing of tartan and Highland dress was concerned. For instance, Boswell when he visited the Hebrides, several times mentioned the wearing of the kilt. The splendid achievements of the Highland regiments kept the wearing of the kilt not only in use but in high repute.

This Act was repealed in 1782 and to some extent the old dress came back into general use[1]—no doubt in many cases good clothes tended to be treasured like 'the good Highland coat' which a MacSweyn lent to Boswell when he was in Coll and which had lasted him for fifty years and would pass from one generation to another.[2] The wearing of the kilt, however, was patchy. It was worn by the drovers who attended the sales at Falkirk into the nineteenth century. Among the gentlemen farmers beautiful doublets of fine tartan, cut on the cross, were much worn. They were generally accompanied by tartan trews or more conventional garments.[3] To my delight the museum was presented with

[1] J. Stoddart, *Tour*, Vol. I, pp. 228–9 said that at Luss he began to hear the Gaelic 'and also begins the plaid with all its accompaniments'. See also T. Pennant, *Tour*, Vol. I, p. 173. R. Heron, *The Hebrides*, Op. cit., p. 3.

[2] J. Boswell, *Tour*, p. 293.

[3] Mrs. Murray, *Useful Guide*, Vol. II, p. 230.

a particularly fine specimen in Robertson tartan. Garnett, writing in 1800, noticed in Strathtay that the full Highland dress of kilt of bright tartan, plaid and blue bonnet was more completely worn than in the other districts that he had visited, viz. up the west coast as far as Oban, Mull, down the Great Glen, Inverness and southwards through Badenoch. The dress he said was 'fast wearing out in the Highlands; many dress in the English manner, and still more have a mixture of the Highland and English; for instance, many have a hat and short coat, with kilt and hose; while others have no other part of this dress than the hose and bonnet'.[1] Another visitor, in 1823, noticed that the wearing of the Highland dress had almost gone out in Inverness but that in Glenurquhart at a funeral the men and women were dressed in 'bright, showy tartans'.[2] Doctor Garnett's remarks are interesting because in Strathtay and Glen Garry the provisions of the Act prohibiting the wearing of Highland dress had been strictly enforced, but he had visited districts where a variety of other causes were leading to its disappearance. Southern influences would be effective in a town like Inverness; it also tended to go out in districts where the workers were earning more money wages. In the extreme north, so early as 1793, the people were said to be buying 'fine Stirling plaids if their money can afford them' although they still depended on home-made stuffs for work-a-day use,[3] and in Glen Lyon and Fortingal (Perthshire) by the early nineteenth century the country people were buying 'cheap factory-made goods'.[4] In Farr (Sutherland) where Highland dress had been worn in the 1790s south country cloth and cottons were worn in 1845.[5] Reasons were rather different among the crofters of the north-west, in cases where the people had not enough land to supply wool for clothing as well as produce for food consumption and had to earn money by seasonal work, they bought clothes as well as food.[6] But where the people could obtain wool in the crofting areas they tended to wear homespun clothes

[1]Garnett, *Tour*, Vol. II, p. 88.
[2]I. Spence, *Letters from the Highlands*, pp. 128, 205.
[3]I. M. MacKay Scobie, *An Old Highland Fencible Company*, p. 19.
[4]D. Campbell, *Octogenarian Highlander*, p. 22.
[5]*New Statistical Account, Sutherland*, p. 81.
[6]*Crofters Commission, 1884*, Vol. I, pp. 96, 145; *New Statistical Account Kintail (Ross and Cromarty)*, p. 183.

although these were no longer the fine coloured tartans but stuffs dyed brown or dark blue.[1] In these districts the kilt had tended to go out early because it was unsuitable for wearing when engaged in the increasingly important fishing industry. For instance, in 1790 at Lochgilphead, where fishing early became important, the people were said still to wear Highland dress except those who fished.[2] Due to these combined reasons, as a dress for the country people, the kilt had virtually died out by the 1840s. Lord Cockburn, who was constantly on circuit in the Highlands during the 1840s, in his shrewd descriptions hardly mentions the kilt. For instance, he writes of the congregation attending kirk at Inveraray there was not 'a single kilt or blue bonnet, a plaid or a yard of tartan'.[3]

The wearing of the kilt has survived as part of a new development. By the end of the eighteenth century a number of Highlanders who were in good positions in the towns combined to form Highland Societies. The earliest and most important were founded in London (in 1778) and Edinburgh (in 1780). These societies fostered Highland sentiments and did a certain amount of useful work, especially in the preservation of piping and they encouraged the wearing of Highland dress. The powerful influence of Walter Scott and the visit of George IV to Edinburgh in 1820 led to a furore for the kilt and tartan by Lowlanders as well as Highlanders and the kilt is now often regarded as the national dress of Scotland. The Highland clothes, however, that now came into fashion were made by urban tailors of boughten stuffs and the sporrans, dirks and other accessories were manufactured in towns by ordinary commercial processes. Although it is sometimes worn in the country by Highland lairds, sportsmen and keepers, the kilt has now largely become a ceremonial dress.

The dress of Highland women has also undergone great changes. Apparently up to the seventeenth century women wore the *arisaid*, a checked plaid with a white ground worn with a belt According to Martin's description, it could be a very fine dress, worn with a large jewelled brooch, with silver ornaments on the

[1]Anderson's *Guide to the Highlands and Islands of Scotland* (1850 ed.), p. 645.
[2]*Old Statistical Account*, Vol. III, p. 190.
[3]Lord Cockburn's *Circuit Journeys*, p. 182.

belt and over scarlet sleeves.[1] Later on women of position wore
contemporary dress with a silk or fine woollen plaid 'two
breadths wide and three yards in length' and Burt remarks 'to
a genteel woman who adjusts it with a good air it is a becoming
veil'.[2] But we know from portraits and from two very interesting
examples that survive that women also wore dresses of tartan.[3]

A picture by Waite (c. 1719) of the henwife at Castle Grant
is one of the few illustrations of what the country women then
wore (see Fig. 70). She has a dress of dark checked stuff, a
'curtch' and a round brooch. In a description written nearly a
hundred years later, a woman traveller said that men and women
wore home-made 'thin coarse woollen stuff' dyed indigo blue and
that: 'The form of the women's dress is generally a petticoat and
a sort of bedgown of that cloth, and a white mob cap or an handkerchief wrapped closely round their heads and under their
chins'.[4] But in other accounts and in MacIain's prints the younger
women wore a 'bedgown' of white linen. The *curtch* or *breid* was
a triangular piece of white linen worn with one point hanging
straight down the back and tied by the other ends under the chin.
Unmarried girls went bareheaded except for a snood of coloured
woollen thread or perhaps ribbon. When the bride first put on
the curtch on the morning after her marriage it was an occasion
of some ceremony. Carmichael tells that a woman he met described to him how in Lewis in the old days, on the morning after
the marriage the bride's mother placed on her head the '*breid tri
chearnach*' (the three-cornered kerchief) with a solemn invocation
to the Trinity under whose guidance the young bride was to
walk. When she was dressed, she joined the wedding company
who saluted her with songs and the wedding festivities continued
throughout the day.[5] A poem to greet his bride when she appeared wearing the curtch was composed by Donald MacLeod,
a minister in Skye, and was widely known. Among the virtues
enjoined on the young matron were:

[1] M. Martin, *Western Islands*, p. 247.
[2] E. Burt, *Letters*, Vol. I, p. 87.
[3] In her young days, in the early nineteenth century, as Miss Grant of Rothiemurchus, the writer of *Memoirs of a Highland Lady*, recalls both she and other
young ladies wore tartan when in the country, p. 205.
[4] Mrs. Murray, *Useful Guide*, Vol. II, p. 230.
[5] A. Carmichael, *Carmina Gadelica*, Vol. I, p. xxix.

Be thou hospitable, yet be wise.
Be thou vigorous, yet be calm.
Be thou frank, but be reserved,
Be thou exact, yet generous.

It ended up : 'With thy kertch, to thee a thousand thousand hails'.[1]
By the nineteenth century as Mrs. Murray's description shows,
the curtch was giving place to the mutch.

FIG. 70. Dress of the country-women. Early eighteenth-century henwife at Castle
Grant. After Waite.

[1]It is printed in A. Carmichael, *Carmina Gadelica*, Vol. II, p. 213. The advice is
reminiscent of ancient Gaelic admonitions such as the Maxins of Cormac of which
several versions exist and which are attributed to Cormac MacArt, High King of
Ireland. See D. Hyde, *Literary History of Ireland*, p. 246.

The flat round brooches worn by the women were generally of brass, sometimes of silver, in the seventeenth century occasionally with the design emphasized by insets of Niello work. They go back as far as the sixteenth century or earlier and the designs on them of interlaced foliage and zoomorphic patterns to the Gael's art of the Middle Ages and carry one's mind back to their more ancient predilection for penannular brooches. They were formed of an ingot hammered flat and bent into a round and they were principally worn by the women (see Fig. 71). For instance, in one tale a chief of Clan Donnachie, who had got into disgrace for raiding, managed to reach the presence of James II dressed as his own grandmother in order to plead his cause and we are told he fastened his plaid with a brooch. In a seventeenth century witch trial a woman confessed how she worked a spell to cure a child by putting her brooch over a certain herb and picking it through the brooch. She was burned.[1] By the eighteenth century silver brooches of the 'Luckenbooth' type were made and worn in the Highlands but the round brooches also persisted. Garnett saw several in 1800,[2] and a kind friend of the museum gave to it two specimens bought in St. Kilda shortly before it was evacuated. One of them was made of part of a modern door knob, an extraordinary example of the persistence of women's fashion!

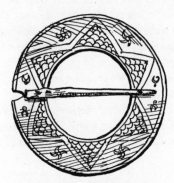

Fig. 71. Seventeenth-century Highland brooch.

I was lucky enough to secure examples of the older women's plaids of fine combed yarn, the overchecks still in lovely clear reds, greens and blues. Such plaids would serve as blankets by night as well as plaids by day and I was told that they were sometimes used as their owners' winding sheets. By the middle of the eighteenth century very fine and beautifully coloured

[1] *Highland Papers*, Vol. III, pp. 5, 6, 9, 19.
[2] T. Garnett, *Tour*, Vol. I, p. 121.

imported shawls of Saxony wool were much worn by those who could afford them.[1]

In older times the men and women wore stockings cut out of fabric. A sixteenth-century St. Kildan, among all the wonders he noticed on a visit to Glasgow mentioned that the stockings were not made in this way. Women sometimes wore stockings without soles (the tops secured by a loop over the toe), called *Osanan* or *Mogans*. One of the prophecies of Coinneach Odhar was that the old wife with footless stockings would drive the Lady Clanranald from Nunton House in Benbecula. And when, in the nineteenth century, Clanranald had to give up the island, a Mrs. MacDonald, who had been one of the last women to wear Mogans, was the mother of the man who rented Nunton House for many years.[2]

By the nineteenth century the crofter-fishermen wore jerseys, trousers and bonnets all made of home-spun yarn. The women took pride in knitting the jerseys in elaborate patterns. On Sundays they wore a sleeved vest or double-breasted jacket of shop cloth with a velvet collar. The women wore long voluminous skirts of dark stuff which they could bunch up at the back to help to support a creel. Above the skirts they usually wore a sort of blouse and they had woollen head scarves, small shoulder plaids called *guail-leags* and, on Sundays, larger plaids. The older women generally wore black clothes and all the married ones mutches.[3] (Fig. 72.)

FIG. 72. A mutch.

When I was young many of the older women in the Central Highlands still wore such mutches. The snowy frills forming a charming frame to the face, and keeping the elder women's hair

[1]M. Martin, *Western Islands*, p. 319.
[2]Told by A. Goodrich Freer, *Outer Isles*, p. 319.
[3]Cf. 'Tolsta bho Thuath', *Stornoway Gazette*, 27.7.51.

beautifully tidy as they went about the byre and their other outside jobs. Mutches varied from very fine ones with insets of lace or embroidered in eyelet work and occasionally with a coloured ribbon put under the open work, to simple ones for everyday use or as nightcaps. Special goffering irons were used to launder the immaculate frills and many women had special boxes in which they could carry a fresh mutch to pop on just before reaching the church or the friends they might be visiting.

In spite of the many changes there was a fundamental continuity in the Highlanders' clothes. General David Stewart of Garth, writing of his young days in Central Perthshire about the turn of the eighteenth century, pointed out that the Highlanders willingly submitted to the simplest food, accommodation and plenishings in order 'to procure arms and habiliments which may set off to advantage a person unbent and unsubdued by conscious inferiority. . .' . And the Highlander's clothes were made by professional tailors when nearly everything about him was of home manufacture.[1] Am Fasgadh was given a good many examples of the country people's best clothes of the nineteenth century that had been so treasured that they had been handed down as heirlooms. Knowing how hard was the old life I was often amazed at their good quality and excellent taste. Nowadays people in the Highlands, whatever their position, tend to wear for best the well-cut country clothes in which Scotland excels—tweeds and woollens, often a tartan skirt for the women. This is surely in the old tradition. I think that it is in noticeable contrast to other countries where, apart from approximations to peasant dress, versions of towny clothes are worn for best.

It is not possible to write about Highland clothes without mentioning tartans but, in a short general sketch, it is not possible to present the opposing views held upon the subject. That such strong feelings should be aroused shows that tartans are a very live issue. I was so often asked to show clan tartans at the little folk museum that I arranged a small collection of samples. One always saw people with Highland blood picking out their own and, as in so much Highland lore, the appeal was not merely to people who still lived in the Highlands but to those who had gone south or overseas.

[1]General D. Stewart, *Manners of the Highlanders*, pp. 140–4.

It is incontrovertible that the Highlanders wore checked fabrics.[1] This can be proved by contemporary documents going back to the sixteenth century, such as rentals and prices fixed for weavers.[2] For practical reasons to weave coloured checks was easier, with the limited equipment of the Highlanders, than to dye a fabric in the piece but, taking a wider view, the complex, stylized designs of the tartan have the same feeling as one finds in Gaelic art—the interlaced patterns, the complex verse forms and the construction of the piobaireachd. The moot point is how far regular clan setts were in use before the '45. The break in continuity due to the proscription of the wearing of Highland dress and of the tartan adds to the difficulty of reaching a conclusion either way that is absolutely incontrovertible.

It is interesting that on the other hand there is definite evidence that the sprig of a plant was used as the badge of many clans, certainly in the seventeenth century, probably earlier. For instance, Lachlan Shaw wrote that every clan had its war-cry and its badge 'whereby they might be known as they had no military habit or livery'.[3] In some cases these badges bear out the traditional theories about the descent of the clans. For instance, all the clans belonging to Clan Donald wear the heather—MacAllisters, MacIains and MacDonnells as well as MacDonalds. All the members of the confederation of Clan Chattan wear the cranberry or some closely allied species of shrublet. For reasons of policy in the sixteenth and seventeenth centuries a common line of descent (almost certainly fictitious) was claimed by the Grants, MacGregors and MacKinnons and they all wear the pine. But, apart from some branches of the MacDonalds, there is not a close correspondence between the tartans of associated clans—those of the Mackintoshes, MacGillivrays, and Farquharsons, very loyal members of Clan Chattan, are quite different. It will be remembered that up till the seventeenth century the principal

---

[1]The word tartan is derived from the French *Tiretaine*, a term for a kind of stuff, not for a colour. See McClintock, *Old Irish and Highland Dress*, p. 5, but it had acquired its present meaning in Lowland Scots by the sixteenth century. The Gaelic word both for tartan and a plaid is *Breacan*, derived from *Breac*—spotted, checked, speckled.

[2]See section on 'Textiles'.

[3]L. Shaw, *History of the Province of Moray*, p. 137. There is other evidence. For a list of some clan badges see J. Logan, *The Scottish Gael* (1831), p. 339.

fighting men wore the mailshirt and they carried a shield on which heraldic devices could be emblazoned. In the older poems and sayings there are no allusions to individual tartans. There is, for instance, no equivalent to the saying that after the Battle of Inverlochy the heather was above the gale.[1]

There is also evidence that district patterns were worn. For instance, Martin wrote: 'Every Isle differs from each other in their fancy of making plaids, as to stripes in breadths and colours. This Humour is as different thro' the Main Land of the Highlands in so far as they who have seen these places are able at first view of a man's plaid to guess the place of his residence.'[2] In the collection of tartans made by Mr. Telfer Dunbar and which he kindly showed me, local differences came out in the wool itself (even nowadays there are local variations in the fleeces of sheep), and in the weave there would naturally be local fashions. For instance, one of the last visitors to St. Kilda told me that all the women had dark blue shawls with overchecks of pink and blue. In much the same way, as a matter of local fashion, J. Logan noticed about 1831 that the men of Badenoch, Strathspey and Strathdearn wore their bonnets cocked.[3] I however much doubt the correctness of a theory that district and clan tartans were influenced by the supply of local dye-plants because most of those in general use are fairly widely distributed.[4]

It is also clear from portraits that the families, at least of the chiefs, tended to wear rather similar patterns of checks, although even in one picture an individual may wear different setts in his coat, plaid, etc. The rather fanciful poem by a Lowlander who was in Dundee's campaign in 1689[5] strongly implies that a chief's immediate following wore rather similar clothes and accoutrements, and in the pictures of the Laird of Grant's piper and champion, painted in 1719, they are wearing checks that are not unlike each other although not identical, and already, in 1703,

[1]The gale or bog myrtle was the badge of the Campbells.
[2]M. Martin, *Western Islands*, p. 247.
[3]J. Logan, *The Scottish Gael*, p. 259.
[4]There was sometimes a local difference in the quality of the dye, I have been told by people in the Islands that crotal gives a better brown there because 'it sees the sea' and in Inverness-shire the same superiority for it was claimed because it was growing inland.
[5]J. Phillip, *The Grameid*, tr. A. D. Murdoch (Scottish History Society).

this chief had ordered all his tenantry to attend him at a great hunt (which was one of their feudal dues) all wearing cloth 'of a red and green tartan set Broad springed or of a red and green dice.' This clearly shows the emergence of the idea, old or new, of a uniform kind of tartan. Other incidents have been cited that can be interpreted as implying that regular clan tartans existed but as many can be shown to prove that they did not.[1] A considerable number of modern clan tartans are copied from eighteenth century portraits. Although one can be sure that such a sett was worn by an individual of the name, it does not prove that it was regularly worn by the whole clan.

Whether regular clan tartans had existed earlier or not, factors came into play in the eighteenth century that greatly stimulated their use if they did not produce them. By that century the Highlanders had found a congenial outlet in service in the armies of Britain, Holland and other countries, and at home many of them served in the Independent Companies formed by the Government to control the Highlands in 1725 and in 1745, and in the Black Watch which had been embodied from the earlier companies. After the collapse of the '45 even the clans who had been 'out' had no hesitation in enlisting in the British Army.[2] The military services of the Highland regiments in the Continental wars of the late eighteenth and early nineteenth centuries form too vast a subject to deal with here. From the formation of the Black Watch till the end of the Napoleonic wars 'the total corps raised in the Highlands amounted to fifty battalions of the Line, three of Reserve, seven of Militia, besides twenty-six battalions of Fencibles and many smaller local Volunteer corps'.[3] It is very significant that these regiments were raised by individual chiefs; an illustration of the survival of their powers. The influence of these regiments in preserving the dress, music, and

[1]For a general statement with many references see J. Telfer Dunbar's article on tartans in H. F. McClintock's *Old Irish and Highland Dress*. For illustrations of actual pictures see that book and also A. E. Haswell Miller, 'The Truth about the Tartans', *Scotland's Magazine*, November 1947, p. 33. See also the Introduction to Sir Thomas Innes of Learney's *Tartans of the Clans*.

[2]In 1745, 400 men of Clan Mackintosh and its septs came out for Charles Edward; by 1754, 500 of them had enlisted in the 42nd Regiment (the Black Watch). Sir E. Mackintosh, *Notes*, p. 15.

[3]J. M. MacKay Scobie, *An Old Highland Fencible Company*, p. 2. See also A. K. Murray, *A History of the Scottish Regiments in the British Army*, pp. 245-8.

the spirit of the Gael through times of severe depression was very great and it can be seen in several of the present-day clan tartans. The Black Watch wore a dark green, blue and black tartan—the Government tartan—and several regiments adopted this with modifications. The Gordon Highlanders wore it with an overcheck of yellow; the regiments raised by MacKenzie of Seaforth and MacKenzie of Cromartie with overchecks of white and red.[1] These are now worn as clan tartans. The Government tartan itself is worn by many Campbells and as a hunting sett by the Grants and Munros and with modifications by the Argyle and Sutherland Highlanders. On the other hand the Cameron's tartan was devised by the mother of Cameron of Errecht who raised the regiment and is said to be the tartan worn by the MacDonnells of Keppoch with a yellow stripe associated with the Camerons added. Like all modern tartans, these regimental tartans are absolutely uniform and the setts are made up of exactly counted numbers of threads of each of the colours.

The equipping of the great number of Highland regiments led to the weaving of tartans by professional weavers, especially those at Tillicoultry, Bannockburn and Killin. Then a demand for their work arose because of the interest in Highland things caused by the great controversy as to whether James Macpherson 'translated' or wrote *Ossian* and the popularity of the writings of Sir Walter Scott. From the order books of one of the most successful of them[2] one can see how designs simply known by numbers or by such names as 'Meg Merrilees' or 'Robin Hood' were replaced by those of a clan. It seems probable that many tartans arose in this way and were produced in response to the growing demand by Lowlanders, especially after George IV's visit, as well as by Highlanders for a tartan to wear.

Since then the making of tartans has gone forward apace. In Logan's Scottish Gael (1831) there is a list of fifty-five tartans; this has now increased to about 400. No one could seriously claim that all these tartans are ancient. Even the most tolerant Gael must regret the uses to which they are sometimes put in creating

[1]Although one of the MacKenzie regiments, the 72 Highlanders between 1823–1881 wore a red tartan.
[2]Mr. Wilson of Bannockburn. Mr. J. Telfer Dunbar most generously deposited some at Am Fasgadh.

souvenirs and in the manner in which one sees them worn by people without any connexion with the north. Yet, whatever views one may hold about the origin of the clan tartans, it is undeniable that to the average Highlander his tartan is to some extent a symbol representing pride of descent and of clanship. In so far as this is not merely a survival but a development it is all the more significant of the tenacity of old habits of thought.

# XV

## SPORTS AND FESTIVALS

THE increased interest in the everyday details of the actual
life lived by the country people has probably largely broken
down older notions of the 'Celtic Gloom' of the Highlanders or
that they lived in an atmosphere steeped in the uncanny and the
violently romantic. When one, however, realizes the extreme
hardness of the old life, one appreciates all the more the resilience
with which they were able to enjoy themselves. The songs and
stories and the nightly meetings at the ceilidhs were so much a
part of their everyday life that I have mentioned them in the
course of trying to give a general picture of it.[1]

The country people also indulged in a good many characteristic
sports and games. The idea pretty generally held, at least in
private by most of the country people, that it is no crime to take
a deer from the hill or a fish from the river goes back a very long
way. There is a wealth of stories and traditions about hunting
the red deer, and the catching of salmon also comes into many of
them. For instance, one of the most usual opening gambits in the
tales about Finn MacCoul and his companions is that they were
on the 'hunting hill' when beautiful maidens or fearsome giants
led them into strange adventures. The climax of the well-known
story of the rivalry of Finn and Diarmid for the lovely Grania is
reached when Diarmid kills the wild boar with poisoned bristles
and is beguiled by Finn into pacing its length and so poisoning
his foot. A proof of the popularity of this tale is that there are
several Ben Gulbains—the place where the boar was said to have
been slain—in Scotland as well as the original in Ireland. Finn
got his supernatural wisdom by sucking his finger which he had
scalded in the bree of the magic salmon that he had caught and

[1]See Chapter VI.

337

was cooking. The ancient kings of Scotland are said to have made the 'Parallel Roads' (a natural feature) in Glen Roy for their hunting and to have kept their hunting dogs on an island in Loch Laggan.

By feudal times there were forestry laws and the Royal Forests were preserved. The murder of the king's forester in Glenartney by some MacGregors in 1589 was the cause (or perhaps the excuse) for the intensification of the bitter persecution of their clan that ended in the proscription of its very name. The Gaelic poets delighted in describing the prowess of the chiefs and heroes in: 'Taking joy of the forest and ascending the rough hills, letting slip the young hounds and inciting the old ones, making the blood flow of the folk of white flank and russet mantle',[1] and in later times, among the finest poems in the language are Duncan Ban Macintyre's *In Praise of Ben Dorain* and *the Misty Corrie (Coire a Cheathaich)* in which the deer are lovingly described. His poetry is full of allusions to hunting. In the *Coire a Cheathaich* he describes the salmon 'in his mail, With back blue-grey, finny, fine speckled, Scaly, red-spotted, white-tailed, slipping',[2] and in the love song to his wife he likens his successful courtship of her to the wiles he employed in catching a beautiful sea-trout with a sheen like moonlight on the sea.[3] Hunting comes into many other poems. Among the best known is *The Owl* by Donald Finlayson.[4]

Among many old tales of hunting is the grim story of how John Ciar, one of the most unpleasant chiefs of the MacLeods, executed a man about 1390 for killing a white stag and of the revenge the family took upon the chief.[5]

Up to the eighteenth century great formal hunts were periodically organized by the Highland nobles and lairds, and one of the dues owed by most Highland tenants was to attend at their superior's hunting. The place to which the game—wolves and foxes as well as deer—were driven was known as the 'Elrick', and this is a common place name in the Highlands. Mary, Queen

[1] J. C. Watson, *Gaelic Songs of Mary MacLeod*, p. 43.
[2] G. Calder, *Songs of Duncan Ban MacIntyre*, pp. 47, 63.
[3] G. Calder, *Songs of Duncan Ban MacIntyre*, p. 400, and N. MacNeill, *The Literature of the Highlands*, p. 398.
[4] Edited by John Mackechnie.
[5] Bannatyne Manuscript, quoted I. F. Grant, *The MacLeods*, p. 64.

of Scots, was nobly entertained by the Earl of Atholl at several of these great hunts but the most historic, at which plans for the Jacobite Rising of the '15 were made, was held by the Earl of Mar. A wandering London poet, J. Taylor, was present at such a hunt in 1618 and has left a vivid account of it.[1] He writes: 'The manner of the hunt is this: five or six-hundred men doe rise early in the morning, and they doe disperse themselves diverse wayes, and seven, eight or ten miles compas they do bring or chase the deer in many herds (two, three or four hundred in a herd) to such and such a place as the nobleman shall appoint them.' He went on to describe how the guests lay on the ground awaiting the coming of the deer but 'as the proverbe says of a bad cooke' the men driving the deer 'doe lick their own fingers' and besides bows and arrows some of them carried 'a harquebusse or musket' and these could be heard from time to time going off. After about three hours 'the deer appear on the hills roundabout us (their heads making a show like a wood)'. They were chased to the appointed valley and 'with dogs, gunnes, arrows, durkes and daggers, all in the space of two hours, fourscore fat deare were slain.'

All the considerable Highland proprietors had deer forests which, like the modern ones, were stretches of hill-ground not necessarily covered with trees. From the seventeenth century several agreements by neighbouring landholders for the preservation of such forests survive. Each one of them undertakes to hand over any of their kinsmen or tenants who killed game there or trespassed without licence. The penalty for killing game for a gentleman tenant was a fine of 100 merks (about £5 7s 9d St.) and in the case of ordinary tenants £40 Scots (3s 6d St.). Both classes of offenders were liable to have their bows or hagbuts forfeited.[2] This would be a severe deprivation, for a gun was the Highlander's darling possession. Like the swords of their ancient heroes, it often had a name. 'The Spaniard' was a common one because many of the earliest guns used in the Highlands had come from Spain, but Duncan Ban Macintyre wrote a poem to his beloved companion, *Cosham's Daughter*.[3] Preserving cannot have

---

[1]Printed in P. Hume Brown, *Early Travellers to Scotland.*
[2]I. F. Grant, *The MacLeods*, p. 275.
[3]G. Calder, *The Songs of Duncan Ban MacIntyre*, p. 243.

been widespread even for red deer. Many are the local tales of adventures that befell lone hunters in the high hills.

We know that in the seventeenth century Highland gentlemen 'diverted' themselves by shooting game because they were specially allowed to carry firearms for the purpose by the Privy Council,[1] but often a servant was employed to shoot game for the pot and, apart from deer, there was no idea of preserving until the nineteenth century. The worthy Bishop Forbes did a little shooting by the way as he travelled to Thurso on an episcopal visitation in 1762. A friend who was with him 'pop'd down one muirfowl'.[2]

Down to the seventeenth century there are stories of wolves being hunted as a public service. With the increase in sheep-farming at the end of the eighteenth century it became usual to employ a fox-hunter. The local farmers combined to pay him a wage or a reward for the foxes he killed and each in turn were liable for feeding him and his dogs when they were working on his farm, but fox-hunting was also a pastime with the country people 'during the Christmas Holy Days' and they arrived 'armed with guns, poles, hooks and spades' and having 'a number of Hounds and Terriers'. When the foxes took to their earths the terriers were put in but the foxes put up a good defence and should one be 'too strong for the Dogs, the pole is put in and the hook being fixed in his body, he is thus dragged out and the tail carried in triumph to the Chief's house, where plenty of good cheer is ready'.[3]

It was not until well on in the first half of the nineteenth century that the shooting of grouse became fashionable and the letting of grouse moors a valuable source of income.[4] In the nineteenth century deer stalking had taken the place of the great deer drives. Landseer's pictures show that the sportsmen were at that time accompanied by deer-hounds for tracking down the wounded stags. At the museum I had the collars used for slipping

[1] *Reg. P.C.S.*, Vol. X, pp. 773–6.
[2] Bishop R. Forbes, *Episcopal Visitations*, 1762, p. 191.
[3] Sir Eneas Mackintosh, *Notes*, p. 131.
[4] For figures showing the dependence of a typical Highland estate upon the letting of its sporting rights see I. F. Grant, *Economic Journal*, 1928, p. 405. See also C. Fraser Mackintosh, *Antiquarian Notes*, Vol. II, p. 360. Anderson's *Guide to the Highlands and Western Islands*, 1850, p. 18.

a brace of these dogs. It was not until after the 1880s, however, that stalking became very fashionable.[1]

The letting of salmon fishings had by that time also become valuable. There is little information about early fishing with rod and line. It is recorded that in 1632 the father of a certain Duncan Campbell became cautioner that his son should not 'put out a wand on the water of Tay'.[2] In 1666 Lord Lovat 'in Highland Cloaths' paid a visit to Glenelg to meet MacLeod of MacLeod, accompanied by one out of every family of the name of Fraser. Their diversions were hunting, hawking, fishing, presumably with rod and line, and archery.[3] At the end of the eighteenth century Sir Eneas Mackintosh of Mackintosh gives a list of the flies used on Loch Moy. People then tied their own flies. But the museum was given some salmon flies about a hundred years old and tied by one of the oldest firms to make flies in Aberdeen. They are heavier but as gaily coloured as the modern varieties. The lines originally were made of white horsehair. To make the line, the horsehairs were threaded through three goose quills, which were rotated between the finger and thumb of the right hand. The twisted line was held in the left hand. Fresh hairs were fed into the quills as needed and they were kept tight in the quills by means of small sticks. Match sticks had been used in the example of line and quills given to the museum. I have never seen the actual process.[4] Old fishing rods would be very simple and I have not seen a survivor but I had old reels made of wood with a hole through which the butt of the rod was pushed.

In spite of preserving most country people continue to get some sport. They are, of course, now legally entitled to shoot ground game—rabbits and hares—on their ground and also marauding stags. Unfortunately, if deer forests are not properly fenced, having to watch for such nightly visitants while the harvest is still out is a great hardship. It would be a churlish and very misguided proprietor who prevented his tenants from fishing the lesser streams for trout. On the quiet many a salmon is lured from the

[1]D. Campbell, *Octogenarian Highlander*, p. 544.

[2]L. A. Barbé, *Sidelights on the History, Industries and Social Life of Scotland*, p. 231.

[3]*Wardlaw Manuscript*, p. 465.

[4]Information given by Mr. Hugh Munro who kindly gave the sample to the museum. Professor Estyn Evans describes the process in *Irish Folk Ways*, p. 248.

pool. Such poaching by local people is, of course, entirely different from the commercial poaching that causes such appalling suffering to the deer and such wanton losses in the salmon pools.[1] I was lucky enough to have been given the rifles of three noted poachers. One, which belonged to a man long since gathered to his fathers, was a flint-lock with an enormously long barrel: one had ingeniously been altered so that the butt unscrewed and the barrel would slip down a man's trouser-leg: the third was an Army rifle of the date of the Crimean War and had been used with great effect up to about thirty years ago.

There were other poaching devices. 'Burning the Water' was practised in the eighteenth century. The fish were attracted to

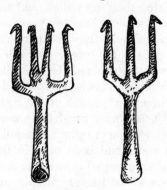

the surface at night by means of a torch or a brazier of glowing peats (of which I had a specimen) and were then speared with a 'leister', a three- or four-pronged iron fork of primitive and of course clandestine manufacture (see Fig. 73). These leisters are so plentiful all over the Highlands that there cannot have been a riverside farm without several. They vary very much in shape according to their maker's fancy. When I was collecting for the museum I was

FIG. 73. Typical leisters. Front and back views.

several times offered a leister, on one occasion by one of my mother's tenants, with the words: 'Here's a queer looking thing. I wonder, would it be a kind of pitchfork?' And politely expressing my own wonder I gratefully accepted the gift. Burning the water generally took place in the autumn when the fish were very 'red' and almost unfit for eating.[2] I have only come across one description of spearing the fish in this way in

[1]The old right of the Highlander to take a stag from the hill has some tacit recognition in the fact that single-handed poaching is excluded from the severe penalties imposed under the Deer (Scotland) Act of 1959 to discourage the barbarities that take place in commercial poaching.

[2]Sir Walter Scott's description in *Guy Mannering* is a classic account.

broad daylight and that was written by Queen Victoria in 1850.[1] In that case the assembled tenants waded in the river, poking under the stones for the fish and watched by their Sovereign, the Prince Consort and the Court. This device has long gone out of use. It is illegal.

Another illegal poaching device was the 'otter'. This was certainly in common use about twenty years ago but seems to have become obsolete, for it was amusing in showing country people round the museum to notice how quickly the older men spotted an otter that was on view, and how innocently the younger ones passed it by. It consisted of a board about 1 × 1½ ft. or a little wider, with a strip of lead nailed along one of the longer sides and four cords fastened through holes in the corners. These were attached to a line and when the otter was put in the water the pull of the line and the weight on one side tilted it in the water and it could be worked against the water much in the same way as a kite can be worked against the wind. A cast of flies or of baited hooks was fastened to it. It was effective on lochs. 'Guddling' trout with the hand as they lie under the bank or slipping a loop of fishing line over the tail of a resting salmon, or spearing him with a gaff on a pole needs no special equipment and are no doubt still carried on. I have seen wickerwork traps that were set in the narrow part of a burn.

Among the other sports indulged in by the Highlanders, one of the most unpleasant was cockfighting. It was, of course, not confined to the Highlands and the terms used were Lowland Scots derived from the Latin. It was almost the invariable custom for the dominie of the parochial school to arrange a cockfight for his pupils every Fastern's Eve (Shrove Thursday). Each boy in the school was entitled to enter a cock (sometimes a couple) and paid 1d sterling (12d Scots) for the privilege. This formed an important part of the schoolmaster's emoluments. He also received the corpses of the cocks that were killed. Those that refused to fight were stoned to death and a charge of a bodle (a half-penny Scots) was made for a throw at them.[2] The owner of the winning cock was hailed with distinction. The museum was

[1]Queen Victoria, *Leaves from the Journal of Our Life in the Highlands*, p. 91.
[2]G. Graham, *Social Life in the Eighteenth Century*, p. 430. See also M. MacLeod Banks, *Calendar Customs, Scotland*, pp. 11, 13.

presented with a tin crown with the imposing legend *Rex Gallorum* painted on the front of it that was worn in the parish of Dyke (see Fig. 74). The sport was not confined to schoolboys.

FIG. 74. The cockfighters crown worn in the parish of Dyke.

In Bernera there was a great contest to which a great many men from Harris used to bring their cocks.[1] This had long fallen into desuetude by the nineteenth century and cockfighting is now illegal. One hopes that it is really obsolete.

In the sixteenth and seventeenth centuries Highland youths, besides being trained to arms, 'Used swimming, archery, football, throwing of the barr, fencing, dancing, wrestling and such manly sprightly exercises and recreations very fit for polishing and refinining youth', and the sons of successive Lords Lovat used to lead their young clansmen in such diversions.[2] Much later, at the end of the eighteenth century, Sir Eneas Mackintosh said that wrestling was popular with boys but that 'it generally ends in earnest fighting'.[3] A *Clach Neart*, a 'stone of strength', which it was a feat of manhood to lift, was to be found in many localities.[4] Such a boulder is still preserved at Moy Hall, the home of Mackintosh of Mackintosh, and there is a tradition about the prodigious strength of one of the MacCrimmons of Skye in lifting a great stone. He put his belt under the boulder and no one else was able to recover this by moving the stone. Long years afterwards the stone was moved by crowbars and there were the remains of the belt beneath it.

From such trials of strength were developed the modern 'Highland Games' as part of the early nineteenth revival of old Highland customs (with a difference). The earliest of these

[1]A. Morrison, *Oiran Chaluim*, p. 17.
[2]*The Wardlaw Manuscript*, pp. 171, 481.
[3]Sir Eneas Mackintosh, *Notes*, p. 32.
[4]J. Logan, *The Scottish Gael*, p. 307.

Highland Games was started by Lord Gwydir at Strathfillan for his tenantry in 1826. By far the best known is the Braemar Gathering. A society of local wrights had been formed early in the nineteenth century and their main activity had been to buy corn to provide against dear years under the Corn Laws. Even before the repeal of these laws in 1846, among other social undertakings, they had begun to organize Highland Games in 1832. In 1849 Queen Victoria was present and the gathering has gone on from strength to strength.[1]

Some of the events in such games are distinctively Highland in character. 'Tossing the caber' has, I think, its origin with the raising of the 'couples' of the traditional Highland houses (Fig. 75E, F). This struck me very forcibly when I saw my own little 'Inverness-shire Cottage' being built at the museum. A tree-trunk—often between 15 and 20 ft. long, about 10 in. at the thickest end and weighing between $1\frac{1}{2}$–2 cwt., is reared on end by two or three men with the thicker end uppermost. The competitor takes hold of it and, resting it against his shoulder works his hands down until he can get them under the lower end, which he cradles in them and then raises the trunk, steps forward a few paces to give him impetus and tosses it. The object is to pitch it so that it will turn a complete somersault. A nice point in judging is that the trunk should reach the absolutely perpendicular as the heavy end hits the ground and the thin end flies over it. When each competitor has had a try a bit is sawn off the trunk and they may each have two more attempts. If there is a breeze it is most exciting to watch the wobbling of the trunk as the competitor prepares to toss it.[2]

Putting the stone has a more ancient pedigree (see Fig. 75A, B, C). One of the ancient folk tales collected by J. F. Campbell tells of a certain Conall Gulban who went out to seek adventure. The 'High Ruler' of the place he came to asked him what feats of skill and strength his people did. He replied casting the stone and hurling the hammer and proceeded to outdo all the company present.[3] It seems to have been a widely practised sport. There

[1]*The Book of the Braemar Gatherings, 1948*, p. 101. Sir Iain Colquhoun of Luss, *Highland Gatherings*, p. 17.

[2]For some of this information see W. McCombie Smith, *Athletes and Athletic Sports of Scotland*, p. 38.

[3]J. F. Campbell, *Tales of the Western Highlands*, Vol. III, p. 256.

Fig. 75. Highland sports. (A), (B) and (C) Putting the stone. (D) Throwing the hammer. (E) and (F) Tossing the caber.

is an Inverness-shire tale that the men of a certain locality were amusing themselves by putting the stone one Sunday morning, and that their new minister, a man renowned for his bodily strength as well as his zeal for the Gospel, pitched the stone an immense distance into the river, after which he herded the men into church. The contest of putting the stone as carried out at modern Highland Games consists of putting (not throwing, the competitor's hand may not be put farther back than his elbow) a stone of 16–23 lb. as far as the competitor can. He may not pass a bound or other mark and may not take a run of more than $7\frac{1}{2}$ ft., and the attitudes he adopts to develop his maximum force are very striking. He stands sideways, with the stone in his right hand and his left arm pointing in the direction of the throw. Then he takes what looks like three rapid hops, bringing his right side forward and hurling the stone.[1] Throwing the hammer is also an old Highland sport but throwing the weight is more modern.[2] Throwing the hammer (see Fig. 75D), seems to have no old stories.

Nowadays some of the other distractions at Highland Games such as bicycle races, are not Highland in character and the purist deplores the prominence given to little girls in male Highland dress and with rows of purchased medals in the dancing competitions. The best of the Highland Games, however, give most valuable encouragement to good piping, including the classical *piobaireachd*. The gold medals competed for at the Highland Games at Inverness and Oban are the highest distinctions that a piper can achieve, but to see piping in a perfect setting one must go to South Uist, to the Games held there upon the machair beside the miles of shimmering silver strand. Before a keen and discriminating audience the local pipers, among the finest in the Highlands, compete against each other in playing the austere and complex music of the Gael. The Highland Games also encourage dancing in the best tradition, but their strongest justification is that they are warmly supported by the country people themselves.

The Highlanders also enjoyed playing football and shinty.

[1] For detailed accounts of how he changes his weight and his feet in the three hops see W. McCombie Smith, *Athletes and Atheltic Sports of Scotland*, p. 31.
[2] W. Mc Combie Op. c. pp. 45, 62.

The former had a character of its own. It was played, especially on New Year's Day, by the men and boys of one parish against those of the next one and the game ranged over the countryside. In Strathdearn a newly married couple was expected to contribute a groat to the schoolboys to keep the ball in order.[1] There is a local tradition that the people of Dalarossie and Moy indulged in this pastime on a Sunday and that in punishment the ghosts of the players are still condemned to play a game upon the anniversary of their misdoings. The place of the ghostly contest has been pointed out to me, but I have never met anyone who saw it.

Modern football is played in the Highlands but a more characteristic game is shinty or *camanachd*. It is played with a bent club or stick and ball and is closely allied to the Irish game of hurley which has a pedigree going back to the Cuchullin saga. As a little boy, that hero went along knocking a hurley ball in front of him as the modern boy will dribble a football, but then, by superhuman prowess he single-handed beat all the sons of the king and nobles in a game. Martin describes an analogous game played at St. Kilda and we have an eighteenth century description of shinty as played in Strathdearn. 'Playing at shiney is thus performed—an equal number of men drawn up on opposite sides, having clubs in their hands; each party has a Goal, and which party drives a Wooden Ball to their adversary's Goal wins the Game, which is rewarded by a share of a cask of Whiskey, on which both parties get drunk. This game is often played upon the Ice, by one Parish against another, when they come to blows if intoxicated. The players' legs being frequently broken may give it the name of Shiney.'[2]

In this district old people have told me of their father's stories of the New Year shinty match. The ball was hit off on the high road at the old boundary between the parishes of Moy and Dalarossie. The game was over walls and fields until darkness fell or, as occasionally happened, the game ended in a free fight in which almost the entire male population joined.[3]

[1]Sir Eneas Mackintosh, *Notes*, p. 35. It was made of a bladder covered with leather.
[2]Sir Eneas Mackintosh, *Notes*, p. 31.
[3]A similar game was played at Rothiemurchus before the ball given to the 'floaters' in the old Strathspey lumbering industry. *Memoirs of a Highland Lady*, p. 218. At Tolsta in Lewis a New Year's shinty match used to be played on the sands.

By the 1870s rules had been evolved and the game had taken its present form. It still flourishes, especially in Badenoch, Lochaber, the Aird, Kintail, Lorn, Oban and Loch Fyneside, and it is organized in Leagues. It derives its name from the *Caman* (from the Gaelic *cam*=crooked) used in playing it. Unlike a hockey stick, its head is almost wedge-shaped so that the ball can be lofted when it is struck. Earlier in the century a ball made of wood was used in Argyll and of tightly twisted hair in Badenoch.[1] Nowadays the ball is covered with leather and is known as 'the leather'. Till quite lately a side consisted of twelve players but nowadays of eleven. As in hockey and association football, the object is to secure the most goals within the time of play. Unlike hockey, there is no rule forbidding a player to lift his caman above his shoulder and the ball flies from end to end of the ground, or a player can balance it on his caman and run with it up the field. To watch shinty at its liveliest one must see a match between the teams from two neighbouring and rival districts. The speed is terrific. The spectators, all local people, are whipped up to vociferous animosity against the opposing side. Casualties are borne off the field (sometimes including spectators hit when the ball flies wide) but they generally soon rise to re-engage in the conflict. After a cup-match the winning team carries the trophy home in triumph and it is filled and refilled with whisky by a public-spirited hotel keeper and carried up and down the village street every passer-by being given a sip out of it. (See Fig: 76.)

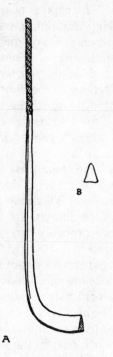

FIG. 76. Head of caman.

Children's games in Lewis were 'Rams' and 'Chickens'; both played with whelks. 'Rams' was a boys' game played like conkers. 'Chickens' was played by the girls who threw up the whelks,

[1]J. Logan, *The Scottish Gael*, p. 309.

trying to keep as many as possible in the air at the same time. The whelks were caught on their palms or on the backs of their hands.[1] In R. C. MacLagan's exhaustive list of games played in Argyllshire most elaborate details are given of this game which required a high degree of skill. Of all the games that he enumerates one of the most popular was said to be a game played in many countries of Europe. In England it is called Hop Scotch, in Argyllshire and elsewhere in the Highlands *Peaver Lal*.[2]

The origins of the typical Highland dances, the reel and the Highland fling are impossible to trace. In the ancient Irish epics dancing is not mentioned among the diversions at feasts and gatherings nor does it come into the poetry and tales of the Highlands of the fourteenth and fifteenth centuries, such as the collections in the *Book of the Dean of Lismore*, nor in the early clan traditions. In the seventeenth century, as already noted, it is alluded to in the account of the training of young Frasers in manly exercises and also as one of the amusements on a hunting expedition,[3] but in the full accounts in the *Wardlaw Manuscript* of entertainments in polite society in the seventeenth century sport, gaming, singing and drinking were the diversions mentioned.[4] This may have been due to the contemporary attitude of the Church. Yet undoubtedly the people danced. In stories that are probably early, the fairies did so, and this was stated in a trial in 1677 at Inveraray to which I have already alluded. The unattractive custom of dancing at a wake is surely old. We have accounts of Irish dances, the 'Rinnce Fada' or the 'Fading' and a sword dance analogous to the English and not to the modern Highland one.[5] In the Lowlands, there were many dances from at least the fifteenth century.[6] But the reel is first mentioned in a witch trial in the Lothians in 1590. How early it was danced in the Highlands one wonders.

[1]'Tolsta bho Thuath', *Stornoway Gazette*, 10.10.51.
[2]R. C. MacLagan, *The Games and Diversions of Argyllshire*, pp. 67, 134.
[3]*Wardlaw MSS.*, pp. 171, 481.
[4]Ibid., pp. 452, 278, 505.
[5]See McClintock, *Old Irish and Highland Dress*, p. 48. G.W. H. Grattan Flood, *Story of the Bagpipe*, p. 90. Bruce Seton, *The Pipes of War*, p. 182, Lily Grove, *Dancing*, pp. 217–18.
[6]Such as the Cockilbie Sow (1450), see *Chryst's Kirk on the Green*, the *Complaint of Scotland* and *Peebles at the Play*. See also Grattan Flood, *The Story of the Bagpipe*, pp. 59–60.

By the seventeenth century the Strathspeys, the tunes in a slower tempo played for the foursome reel were evolving. Tunes of this type called 'ports' are written down in the *Skene* and *Straloch Manuscripts* (1615–25 and 1627–9).[1] They are pre-eminently suited to the fiddle and a school of composers of tunes of this type developed in Strathspey. There is a tradition still told in Badenoch that the earliest of them was a cateran named Macpherson who, in 1700, played a tune of his own composing still known as *Macpherson's Rant* at the foot of the gallows on which he was hanged and smashed his fiddle because no one would accept it. Other traditions say that the first players were a family of Browns in Kincardine (The Speyside Kincardine), The Cummings, hereditary fiddlers to the Laird of Grant, flourished very early and the last of the family is said to have died about the middle of the eighteenth century.[2] If traditions are true the reel of Tulloch, which in swifter tempo generally finishes an ordinary foursome reel, was composed by a proscribed MacGregor. (According to one version he was courting a girl of my own family when he composed it.) Pipers in the old days generally regarded the playing of dance music as below their dignity (how are the mighty fallen!) but a few jigs and 'reels in 6/8 time' were included in the early collections of pipe music of 1760 and 1774[3] to be played for the piper's diversion. The actual dances for these tunes are not known. By the eighteenth century one constantly hears of Highlanders dancing reels and Prince Charles Edward, while on his long flight, danced them to cheer the hearts of his faithful companions, skipping 'so nimbly and knacking his thumbs and clapping his hands' and even singing the tunes for his own dancing.[4] Stoddart, at the end of the century, said that dancing was 'the favourite amusement of the North' and that young boys danced the reel, the 'sheantrews', the hornpipe and the Highland fling with 'a Life and Spirit which few but the native Highlander could attain'.[5] About 1749 the first collection of reels was published by Robert Bremner and contained a large number of our present favourite tunes such as *Gillie Callum* and

---

[1]H. G. Farmer, *History of the Music in Scotland*, p. 233.
[2]J. Logan, *The Scottish Gael*, p. 259.
[3]By Joseph and Patrick MacDonald respectively.
[4]Bishop R. Forbes, *The Lyon in Mourning*, Vol. I, pp. 38, 119, 202. Vol. II, p. 171.
[5]J. Stoddard, *Scenery and Manners in Scotland*, Vol. I, p. 133.

*Tullochgorum*.[1] And it was in the eighteenth century that the 'Scotch Snap' was introduced, defined as 'a short note (on the beat) followed by a long one' occupying the rest of the beat.[2]

Between 1750 and 1830 the playing and composing of reels and strathspeys reached its zenith. Most of the leading composers came from the Central and Eastern Highlands although, so great was southern appreciation, many of them moved to Edinburgh or London. Among the most outstanding were William Marshall (Fochabers) who wrote *The Marquis of Huntly's Farewell*, Neil Gow (Dunkeld) who was better known as a player than as a composer, his son, Nathaniel, the composer of the *Fairy Dance* and Red Rob Mackintosh.[3]

Such was a passing phase of fashion. The country people continued to dance and to take their dancing seriously. In her *Memoirs of a Highland Lady*, Mrs. Smith recalls that all the servants at the Doune took regular dancing lessons, 'all Highlanders considering this art as essential in the education of all classes and never losing an opportunity of acquiring a few more flings and shuffles',[4] and my mother and aunt can remember the regular visits of a dancing master in Strathdearn and Strathspey. He would demonstrate the steps to the class while playing the fiddle and even poking the toes of an awkward dancer with his bow. This carried the old tradition far past the middle of the nineteenth century. My aunt used to be told that the whole of a step ought to be performed on a space as small as a peat. Mr. MacLean tells of itinerant dancing masters in Glen Moriston and on the stress laid on good manners.[5]

There are interesting local dances. Carmichael described a dance in Barra called *Cailleach an Dudain* which is also mentioned by the Fletts and there was a special type of dancing in South Uist and other parts of the Long Island.[6]

[1]A. Mackintosh, *History of Strathspeys and Reels*, p. 282.
[2]A. Scholes, *Oxford Companion of Music*.
[3]A. Mackintosh, *History of Strathspeys and Reels*, p. 284. H. G. Farmer, *History of the Music of Scotland*, p. 344.
[4]*Memoirs of a Highland Lady*, p. 41.
[5]For descriptions of many such dancing masters see J. F. and T. M. Flett, 'Social Dancing in Scotland, 1700–1914', *Scottish Studies*, Vol. II, p. 159. Calum MacLean, *The Highlands*, p. 148.
[6]A. Carmichael, *Carmina Gadelica*, Vol. I, p. 208. J. F. and T. M. Flett, Op. cit., p. 162. G. D. MacLennan, *Highland and Traditional Scottish Dances*, p. 28, gives an

All over the Highlands, whether people dance in the ball-room, the village hall or in their own homes, the foursome reel, generally followed by the reel of Tulloch, is still the principal Highland dance. Less ancient but now a general favourite is the eightsome reel. It was first danced at the Athole Gathering in the early '70s and was evolved from recollections of an earlier 'round reel'.[1] Innovations are the 'Country dances' that were very popular in the Lowlands and enjoyed a considerable vogue about 1800 and spread to the Highlands. They went out of favour in more fashionable society for a time and have now made a come-back. The quadrilles, which came from abroad and have long disappeared from smart ball-rooms, made their way only recently among the country people and are still danced in out of the way places. Later dances, such as the waltz, pas de quatre, scottische, and the more recent ones of Latin American origin, have ap-peared in ball-rooms and worked their way downwards. A very interesting example of the different layers of dances that linger in remoter parts of the Highlands is given by Mrs. Campbell[2] in her description of the dances popular in Glendale, South Uist. They included reels, a country dance (the Petronella), quadrilles, the scottische and the local South Uist dances.

The solo dance as an exhibition of skill and agility is probably very old, but the actual age of those now danced is impossible to fix. They are the *Seann Triubhis*, the sword dance and the High-land fling. The sword dance, danced across two crossed swords is quite different to the north of England sword dances or the ancient sword dance of the Glovers in Perth. The Highland fling consists of a variety of steps, most of which can be danced by men in the foursome and reel of Tulloch. These solo dances are properly men's dances and when, in modern times, women attempt them they wear the men's dress—the kilt. In dancing a reel the showy steps which require the kilt and hose and look very clumsy if danced in trousers are properly danced by men. The women's steps are neat and quiet. Unlike some forms of country

---

especially interesting account of the Hebridean styles of dancing. The Royal Celtic Society gives prizes for such dances.

[1]Such is the tradition told to me. In the 1880s in Inverness-shire it was rather looked down upon as 'an innovation from Perthshire' but it has long been regularly danced and it is great fun to dance it as a sixteenth-some or a thirty-two-some.

[2]M. F. Shaw, *Folk Song and Folk Dance*, p. 16.

dancing, the Scots point their toes and arch their insteps (see Fig. 77). The custom of letting off yells while they dance reels in which some men indulge, is modern. In the old days it was the old men watching the dance who called out occasionally to speed up the tempo of the dancing. My mother as a young girl, was much embarrassed when a gentleman of the old school with rather a resonant voice remarked to her: 'Just you listen to them, yelping like a pack of curs!' One sees the same standard of dancing a reel throughout the Highlands by Highland people of all stations of life. Special heelless brogues are worn for exhibition dancing but a countryman in tackety shoes can do the steps with beautiful neatness and dexterity.

FIG. 77. Position of feet in Highland dancing.

The survival of the custom of dancing varies very much in different districts. The objections by the Established Church have long since died away, but where certain very strict branches of the Presbyterian faith are paramount, dancing and piping are frowned on. The history of religious movements in the Highlands, however, raises too large issues and is too complicated and controversial to deal with in a book of this type.

# XVI

## SEASONS AND GREAT OCCASIONS

THE people's lives were conditioned by the rhythms of their work—the movement of the herds out to pasture in the spring and their return to the stubbles in the autumn, the sowing and reaping of the crops, the movements of the herring shoals—and by the recurrent sequence of events within the life of the family, marriages, child-births and deaths. Worked into the occasions were special observances that have changed in accordance with the changing ideas of the people, and going back through the long years of history to an even remoter past.

The phases of the moon influenced the people's activities. I have always heard that one should not sow when the moon was waning. But Martin recorded that, in Skye, peats were dug at that time because if this were done when she was waxing they would never dry out or burn properly. Earthen dykes were also made during the decrease of the moon, timber felled and rushes cut.[1] To this day, some older people in Skye still believe that peats should not be cut when the moon is waxing or they would not give proper heat. On the other hand, in many parts of the Highlands, it is believed to be lucky to cut one's hair when the moon is waxing and I have heard of a mother taking little snips off her children's hair then for luck. The widespread customs of bowing to the new moon and turning the money in one's pocket are observed in the Highlands and an old relation of my own took that occasion to kiss the woman nearest to him. A Skye superstition that cannot be very ancient is that potatoes are not ready for eating until the autumn Sacrament Sunday. Martin said that in Lewis there had been a custom, even then obsolete, of making

---

[1] M. Martin, *Western Islands*, p. 222.

a fiery circle round the houses, corn and cattle by a man carrying the fire in his right hand and going round sunwise, but he does not say the season when this was done.[1]

The days of the week had their special taboos. I once began to make a list of the things which it was unlucky to do on certain days and found I was supplying myself with excellent pretexts for doing nothing. But the following are a few 'Do's' as well as 'Don'ts'. Monday was good for changing one's dwelling if one were moving from north to south, in spite of a general feeling that it was unlucky to approach one's new abode for the first time from the north. Tuesday was good for reaping and for marriage. If All Saints' Day fell on a Wednesday it portended general bad luck. Thursday, which is specially connected with St. Columba, was the best day in the week to begin things such as the setting up of a warp on a loom or the setting of eggs under a hen. It was also the best day in the week on which to cut one's nails. Friday was not a good day to begin anything; it was unlucky to cut nails or hair, to kill a sheep or to begin to cut the hay, for buying anything or for being buried. (But, *per contra*, Martin said that on Gigha this was the day preferred for funerals.) It was, however, lucky for planting, sowing and for making bargains. On Good Friday it was unlucky to do work that involved putting anything iron into the earth, such as a spade or plough, but sea-ware might be spread or work might be done with a wooden rake. Saturday was lucky for moving one's home if one were moving from south to north. It was unlucky to spin that night and there was a general feeling that it was not a good day to begin anything. Sunday, in Badenoch, was considered the best day to put on clean clothes and it was good to wash in running water.[2] A spring superstition was the catching of the first unfortunate bee to appear and imprisoning it in one's purse to bring about an increase of wealth. Mrs. Campbell mentions this superstition in South Uist. I remember, as a child, hearing the frantic buzzing of the poor bee when my nurse, who came from the Black Isle (Easter Ross), insisted on doing the same thing.[3]

[1] M. Martin, *Western Islands*, p. 177.
[2] A. Goodrich Freer, *The Outer Isles*, p. 238. M. Marten, *The Western Islands*, p. 264. Lachlan Shaw, *History of the Province of Moray*, p. 147. Information kindly given me by Mrs. de Glehn.
[3] M. F. Shaw, *Folk Music and Folk Song*, p. 13.

Something has been said of observances of Beltane that have long since been given up but, all over Scotland, girls still wash their faces in the dew at dawn on the first of May and in Edinburgh crowds go up Arthur's Seat to hail the sunrise. I have also said something about almost forgotten harvest ceremonies. The ancient Samhain, under the more pious title of Hallowe'en, kept some of its pre-christian symbolism, but it has now largely lost its character. As one of the seasonal festivals that are still kept I shall hope to deal with it later on.

The observance of the Festival of St. Bride (1st February) evidently goes back to the worship of a pagan deity, sometimes said to be Brid, the Fire Goddess. I have quoted one description of the making of her bed. Martin says that the custom of doing so on the eve of the Festival was general in his time and Frazer quotes other examples.[1] The essential feature was that it was the women of the household who made up a bed, perhaps with a sheaf of corn dressed as a woman in it, and that Bride was formally invoked and welcomed. This custom seems entirely to have gone out, but the superstition lingers that on St. Bride's Day the sea becomes warmer because she put her hand in it (as a matter of fact it is at its coldest). On that day the fishermen of Barra used to cast lots for their fishing grounds.[2]

Although the celebration of the old festivals of the Church was discouraged it lingered long after the Reformation. Martin mentions that Christmas, Good Friday, Easter and St. Michael's Day were observed in the mainly Protestant islands, as well as in those where the Old Religion retained its hold.[3] Sometimes additional festivals were kept as, for instance, that of St. Barr in Barra,[4] and on this island within living memory, no digging was done on St. Brendan's Day (14th May) although other work, such as sheep shearing was allowed.[5] On Colonsay (Protestant) the birthday of Our Lady was a woman's festival[6].

In the Hebrides there was a special form of keeping St.

---

[1]M. Martin, *Western Islands*, p. 179. Sir J. Frazer, *The Golden Bough*, p. 134.
[2]M. F. Shaw, *Folk Song and Folk Lore*, p. 14. Information kindly given by Mrs. de Glehn.
[3]M. Martin, *Western Islands*, pp. 108, 125, 155, 296, 297, 311.
[4]M. Martin, *Western Islands*, p. 163.
[5]Information kindly given by Mrs. de Glehn.
[6]M. Martin, *Western Islands*, p. 280.

Michael's Day (29th September). Martin has several good descriptions of 'the Cavalcade' that then took place. For instance, on North Uist, it was lawful for anyone to take someone else's horse to ride on that day. Races were ridden by the young men, riding barebacked and without bridles (a feature also mentioned at St. Kilda), and urging their mounts on by pieces of dried tangle. In the actual cavalcade the women were mounted behind the men and in Barra the route was sunwise round the church. In St. Kilda there were not enough horses to go round and so they were ridden by turns.[1] These St. Michael's cavalcades have died out all over the Hebrides. It has been suggested that this was probably due to the increase in the importance of the herring fishery which was generally at its busiest at the end of September.

In the evening of St. Michael's Day special bannocks were baked in many of the Islands. In Barra everyone in the house, including visitors, was expected to eat some of it and it was made of the first grain ground that year.[2] These special bannocks are still baked in Barra but they are now made with ordinary flour with treacle. In South Uist also, the special St. Michael's bannock is still baked. Mrs. Campbell gives the traditional and modern receipts. Some of all the cereals grown on the croft were used in making it and it was coated with beaten egg. The present bannock is made of flour, enriched with currants and carraway seeds and with a coating of treacle, sugar, milk and flour.[3]

In many parts of the Highlands in the old days there was a reluctance to observe Christmas according to the new calendar and it was kept on what is now known as Twelfth Night. Old Balnespick wrote in 1718 of 'our honest old Christmas which we observe as not wishing to be singular in our country'.[4] Mrs. Campbell met an old man in South Uist who still believed in the beautiful idea that the rising sun danced for joy on Easter morning.[5] In some districts, for instance Glen Urquhart and Lewis, people have eggs for breakfast on Easter morning. It is a painful fact that the Church festival most consistently observed in the

[1] M. Martin, *The Western Islands*, pp. 147, 164, 317.
[2] M. Martin, *The Western Islands*, p. 164.
[3] M. F. Shaw, *Folk Song and Folk Life*, p. 58. Father A. MacDonald, *Gaelic Words*.
[4] I. F. Grant, *Old Highland Farm*, p. 235.
[5] M. F. Shaw, *Folk Song and Folk Lore*, p. 14.

Highlands was Shrove Thursday, on which day the cowardly sport of cockfighting was almost universally indulged in.[1]

In the Highlands, like the rest of Scotland, two festivals are widely observed nowadays, Hallowe'en and New Year's Day. Hallowe'en (31st October) is All Souls Day and the eve of All Saints Day and it falls on the old Gaelic season of Samhain, which represented the end of the half year containing the long days of summer and the beginning of the dark and cold second half of the year. Witches and other unchancy beings were said to be specially powerful on that night and it was a specially favourable time for trying to foretell the future. Bonfires were lit. It is, and evidently has long been a light-hearted and festal time. In Lewis the boys and the girls held separate feats and the boys armed themselves with wands and dared other youths to snatch a turnip from them.[2] In Glendale the guests came dressed in disguises.[3] All over the country, in the Lowlands as well as the Highlands, bands of children in fancy dress still come round, sing a song (only too often even in the Highlands some popular hit of the moment) and expect a few pennies or an apple or an orange. Among the older methods of divination were winnowing with an empty wecht and throwing a clue of wool over the kiln (see p. 114) and eating salted herring in the hope that in a dream the future spouse would come and offer a drink. I have seen divination by dropping the white of an egg into a glass of water; if the white spreads the omen is good, if it sinks to the bottom it is bad. But people with the gift would foretell a great deal more and my aunt was present when an old woman foretold a death which actually came to pass: dropping molten lead through the hole at the top of a key: going out into the garden in the dusk and pulling a kail stalk which by its size foretold the stature of the marriage partner. In the Highlands as well as the Lowlands there are the more conventional Hallowe'en ploys of burning two nuts to foretell the love affairs of two people, with a variant of setting two straws upright in the ashes: making a blind-folded person dip his fingers into one of three plates with soot, water, and

[1]For details of other obsolete observances of church festivals see M. MacLeod Banks, *Calendar Customs, Scotland*. She says that the eating of the crowdie on Shrove Thursday was a general Scots custom, p. 10.

[2]'Tolsta bho Thuath', *Stornoway Gazette*, 21.8.51.

[3]M. F. Shaw, *Folk Song and Folk Lore*, p. 14.

nothing in them respectively, and the fun of bobbing for apples in a tub of water. Among the old Highland refreshments was a dish of *fuarag* (oatmeal and cream) into which a button, a thimble and a ring had been put.[1]

Hogmanay, in the Gaelic *a Challuinn*, or *Oidhche nam Bannag*, New Year's Eve, has not got the associations of Hallowe'en, but traces of very ancient rituals seem to survive in its observance in places where old traditions linger. In Lewis the boys formed themselves into bands each with a chosen leader who wore a sheep-skin or hide on his back. Another of the band carried a sack. The bands went from house to house and at the door the leader recited a Gaelic rhyme with responses by the band. It began:

'This is the night of gifts
  Goodwife rise up and bring down the Hogmanay bannock....'
and went on to say that they would be glad of butter, cheese and potatoes, even little ones, but it ended with an invocation of the Trinity. The woman of the house then invited them in and the leader walked clockwise round the fire if it were in the middle of the floor, or round a chair specially placed there in a modern house, while everyone hit the skin with the tongs or sticks. The housewife then gave the band some bannocks and the boys went on to visit other houses till their sack was full and then they feasted on what they had gathered. In South Uist much the same ritual was performed. The leader carried a torch of smouldering sheep-skin smeared with tallow. On reaching a house the boys walked three times round it clockwise and, when they were asked in, the leader passed his smouldering sheep-skin three times round the head of the woman of the house. If it went out during this process the omen was bad. The women then gave the boys three bannocks and received one out of the bag that they carried. She then added other eatables. On leaving, if they had been well treated, the boys called out a blessing on the house but, if they had been given nothing they built a little cairn outside it. Younger boys had to show their fitness to join the band by lifting a weight.[2] Frazer, in *The Golden Bough* gives an account

[1]Father A. MacDonald, *Gaelic Words*. M. F. Shaw, *Folk Song and Folk Lore*, p. 14. E. J. Guthrie, *Old Scottish Customs*, pp. 69–74.

[2]'Tolsta bho Thuath', *Stornoway Gazette*, 21.9.51. M. F. Shaw, *Folk Song and Folk Lore*, pp. 13, 25. She prints two of the songs sung by the boys. They are quite different from the Lewis Song. Father A. MacDonald, *Gaelic Words*.

of similar custom in the Highlands[1] which he said was long obsolete. A man wrapped in a dried cow's hide led the band of youths. A three-fold sunwise turn was made round the house and it was blessed, then each person singed and smelt a bit of the hide and bits were given to the beasts to smell. Frazer considered that the ritual was a relic of the sacrificial killing of a god. In Strathdearn I was once told rather vaguely that in the old days a man dressed in dried hides would come about the houses, which was evidently a dim recollection of this custom.

All over the Highlands and Islands (as in the rest of Scotland) Hogmanay is still an adult festival. At midnight guns are generally fired off. Then the men set out to 'first foot' all the houses where they are friendly. They each carry a bottle of whisky and a bannock of oatcake, and offer everyone in the houses that they visit a dram. The tradition is that this signifies a wish to the house or a blessing and plenty of food for the coming year. Specially thick oatcakes used to be baked for the purpose. Then the owner of the house offers his refreshment to the visitors, generally whisky and port with shortbread and 'scotch bun'.[2] Everyone present must have his or her health drunk separately but it is not necessary to drain the glass each time. It is lucky if the first visitor in the New Year is a dark man, a red-haired one is unlucky and a woman, especially if she is fair-haired, is much worse, but fortunately for such omens, women never go firstfooting alone. If they should go with men the man is always pushed into the house in front.

Events in the family also had their special observances. In the old days there was a mingling of beliefs in the rituals attending the birth and christening of a child. There was a very real fear that the Fairies might steal the baby and substitute a changeling for it. There are many stories about the detection of the changeling and its exposure in order to regain the real child. The precautions taken to protect the mother and baby embodied primitive ideas. Iron was especially valuable and a nail might be knocked into the wood of the mother's bed or a smoothing iron be placed beneath it. Fire also was a protection. Martin writes

[1]Sir J. Frazer. *The Golden Bough*, p. 538. See also Miss E. Hull, *Folk Lore of the British Isles*, p. 235.
[2]An almost solid mass of dried fruit and spice with a thin covering of crust.

that in his days (the end of the sixteenth century) old Skye mid-
wives still carried fire in a circle morning and evening round the
mothers before they were churched and round the unbaptized
babies in order to protect them from abduction.[1] The administration of the Christian rite of baptism, however, made the child
largely immune from this danger. The shadow of this dread has
entirely passed away. The following incident is illuminating: I
was told that two women in Barra, one of whom is still said to be
living, were carrying a child to church to be christened. They took
a short cut over the hills and in a lonely part they heard the fairy
bagpipes and *'they took it to be a good sign'*.

Christening feasts were held among the chiefs and gentry, as
we know from various sixteenth century incidents.[2] The country
people also had their celebrations. James Hall, writing in 1807,
said that they were common in Perthshire, the guests generally
sending a share of the provisions beforehand.[3] Nowadays it is the
Highland custom to bring a small gift or a silver coin when visiting a new baby for the first time.

One reads about the old Highland custom of 'handfasting'[4] and,
according to Scots Law, Marriage by Declaration—the formal
statement by a couple that they were man and wife—constituted
a valid marriage.[5] Nevertheless as a rule weddings in the Highlands were the occasions of some formality and much hospitality.
On the Long Island, where old customs have lingered, there was,
and to some extent there still is, the formal demand for the girl's
hand and the betrothal feast as well as the wedding festivities.
In Lewis, in the old days, the young couple were not supposed to
show much interest in each other until the formal betrothal. But
in such close-knit communities it was a very open secret when the
suitor and his closest friend, who acted as his advocate, called
upon the girl's father to ask for her hand. The same procedure is
followed in Barra and in South Uist, where Mrs. Campbell

[1] M. Martin, *Western Islands*, p. 177.
[2] The tale of the drowning of MacLeod of Raasay on his way home from a christening in Lewis has been told.
[3] J. Hall, *Travels in Scotland*, Vol. II, p. 430.
[4] A couple arranged to live together by private agreement, sometimes by clasping
hands through a hole in a monolith: the agreement was sometimes made for a year
and, if the woman became pregnant, a proper marriage was usual if not obligatory.
[5] This was ended by the 1939 Marriage (Scotland) Act.

describes the thoroughly Highland proceedings. After talk of many things, the friend began to praise the young man and to urge the advantages of the match. The girl would show her concurrence by staying in the room and the father would capitulate, saying 'If she is willing, I am willing, and if this weren't so, this wouldn't be so.' The young couple then drank a dram from the same glass. This interview is nowadays a pleasant formality but there are older traditions of hard bargaining and the interview sometimes took place outside and was attended by a number of male kinsfolk.[1]

The consent of the father was followed by the betrothal feast, *the Reiteach*, so inimitably described by Sir Compton Mackenzie in *Whisky Galore*. It was attended by the nearer relations. In Lewis it was conducted with some formality. The bride's nearest unmarried male relation was the best man. Her bridesmaid was the groom's nearest unmarried female relation. Married relations of the bride presided over the making of the tea and those of the groom handed the whisky to the guests. The issue of the invitations to the wedding also followed a set pattern. Two girls, one for the groom and one for the bride, went round inviting everyone to the feast while the bride and bridegroom invited relations and special friends. If anyone was left out it was regarded as a great slight.

There does not seem to be a tradition of these preliminaries on the mainland. Sir Eneas Mackintosh, writing of Strathdearn in 1774–83, who gives one of the fullest accounts of local wedding customs, said that as soon as the day for the marriage was agreed upon 'a Writting called the contract is signed' (in the presence of the Parish Clerk or the minister) whereby the parties bind themselves to marry and in case of non-performance (without just cause) to pay such a sum as is thought proper.[2] Then 'the night before Marriage, the ceremony of Feet Washing is performed at the Bride and Groom's own Lodgings'.[3] On the

---

[1]M. F. Shaw, *Folk Song and Folk Lore*, p. 14. 'Tolsta bho Thuath', *Stornoway Gazette*, 27.8.51. Information supplied by Mrs. de Glehn. Father Allan MacDonald gives the word *Boigneachas* for the conclusion of the agreement about the dowry as obsolete.

[2]Sir Eneas Mackintosh, *Notes*, p. 33.

[3]I have been told that a coin was put in the water and that there was a general scramble for it, because whoever secured it would be the next to marry.

wedding morning, 'being dressed, the Bridegroom first (preceded by a bagpipe), having a young man on each side of him, next comes the Bride with her two maids, proceed to the Church. When the ceremony is over, and the parties come out, pistols and guns are fired over their heads by their acquaintances who then join, and a cake broken over the bride's head, where a great struggle is made for a piece of it'.[1] 'Upon their return dinner is ready, several Cows and Sheep being frequently killed for that purpose.'[2] Mrs. Murray described wedding feasts in Mull. Breakfast, dinner and supper were provided by the bride's parents. The groom supplied the drinks (whisky and rum). Six sheep might be killed for the feast and long tables were set out in the barn with dishes of meat, potatoes, eggs and outcake down it and a cheese and a lump of butter for every three people.[3] In Strathdearn 'When it is over the Bridegroom goes round the Guests with a plate, when everyone gives according to his Inclination, and if the Bride and Bridegroom are liked, they get as much as will enable them to stock their farm.' Sir Eneas adds that the local laird was often present at the country people's weddings and that he himself had often attended. 'The country people sometimes dance to a pipe but oftener to a Fiddle. At the commencement and finishing of each reel the Swains kiss their Nymphs. The Fiddler receives one penny for each dance. . . . The company continue dancing and drinking till the hour for the young People's going to bed, when the whole company accompany them to the Barn (for they are not allowed to sleep in the house the first night). All the men remain on the outside till the Bride is undressed, then (the Bridegroom being undressed) they kiss the Bride.' He added that the wedding continued for several days.[4]

---

[1]This breaking of the cake, generally shortbread, was done as the bride entered the house. The person who got the largest fragment of cake would be married next. I have talked with people who, as children, remembered scrambling for bits of the cake.

[2]Mrs. Grant, wife of the minister of Laggan, writing of Badenoch about the same time described how the people gloried in being 'splendidly hospitable' and four sheep were killed for their own shepherd's wedding. *Letters from the Mountains*, p. 115.

[3]Mrs. Murray, *Useful Guide*, Vol. II, p. 247.

[4]Sir Eneas MacKintosh, *Notes*, p. 33.

Many accounts of weddings stress the great decorum.[1] but John MacCodrum strikes a more jovial note. The food he says was heaped up like seaweed. 'There was butter and cheese, potatoes and fish being served by women of liberal hand; there were lads and carles fighting and grappling and chewing bones under their back teeth.' After the feast there was dancing. 'Everyone who was at the wedding danced neatly, setting in the double reel and shouting: Hurray, praise the deed as long as the piper and floor last us!'[2]

There were many special observances at the final phases. It was believed that the knots of the bridegroom's clothing must be untied to ensure that the marriage would be fruitful.[3] Another custom was to tie a basket full of stones round the bridegroom's neck and to leave it to the bride's discretion to cut the fastening. A bridegroom might show his activity by making 'the salmon leap' and springing into the bed at a bound from crouching on the ground.

Old people on the mainland have told me of the great wedding feasts of their young days, all the neighbours contributing some of the food, and of the ceremonial dancing of the first reel by the bride, bridegroom, the best man and the bridesmaid, but nowadays, unfortunately, quite often the wedding ceremony as well as the feast after it take place in a hotel in the nearest village or town and, beyond the appearance of a few kilts as garments of ceremony and perhaps the playing of the pipes, there is nothing distinctively Highland about it.

On the Long Island old customs lingered longer. The feast was a communal effort as it largely consisted of fowls contributed by the neighbours. The bridal party walked in procession to and from the church, the pipes were played and guns were fired. The feast took place in the barn and might have to be served in relays. A dance followed to the music of pipes, fiddle, melodeon or mouth music, the opening reel being danced by the bride, groom,

---

[1]Mrs. Grant, *Letters from the Mountains*, p. 115. John Knox, who did so much for Highland fisheries, attended a country wedding in Harris. 'The whole company was decent and orderly. Old and young danced, among the rest Captain MacLeod, who, notwithstanding his years, stepped up to the bride and acquited himself nobly.' He was the proprietor of Harris and over seventy. *Tour*, p. 172.

[2]Translation by Professor W. Matheson, *Songs of John MacCodrum*, p. 117.

[3]Sir James Frazer, *The Golden Bough*, p. 241.

best man and bridesmaid. An old Barra custom was 'the stealing of the bride'. Another girl slipped into her place while she was dancing a reel and while she retired to be undressed by her friends with many pranks. In Barra the two mothers blessed the bridal bed and sprinkled it with holy water. The dancing continued until the next morning. I have mentioned the old custom of the putting on of the curtch by the bride next morning. In Lewis the married couple remained with her parents for a week and then went to their new house. Their appearance at church on the following Sunday was considered the completion of the wedding festivities. There was no honeymoon.[1] Nowadays, even on the Long Island, weddings have not this distinctive character. Friends give money contributions and ordinary food is brought.

The ceremonies connected with death played a most important part in the old social life of the Highland people, and for that matter they do so still. It is tempting to wonder if this attitude of mind goes right back to our remote ancestors who built the megalithic tombs.

There is not space to more than touch upon the mass of superstitions connected with death. The visions of people who had the Second Sight were largely concerned with a future death—the grey mist seen round a person soon to die, the pre-vision of funerals, etc. Objects that would be used at a future funeral were heard to move, lights were seen in the night following the track it would take. Certain families were said to have a tutelary spirit whose weeping foretold the death of a member.[2]

Great importance was attached to the proper observances. The first task of the newly married bride was the making of her winding sheet 'which put her mind of Mortality'.[3] I have seen the remains of a cottage in a remote glen where a lonely old woman in the extremity of death laid herself out lest no one should come to do these last offices for her. The desire among Highland people to be buried with their kin was so strong that one of the curses for breaking the oath imposed under the Proscription of Highland Dress in 1747 was that the taker should be buried far from

[1] M. F. Shaw, *Folk Song and Folk Lore*, p. 15. 'Tolsta bho Thuath', *Stornoway Gazette*, 3.8.51. Information given me by Mrs. de Glehn.
[2] I have spoken with people who have experienced these various manifestations.
[3] I. F. Grant, *Old Highland Farm*, p. 132.

his own kindred. Even nowadays it is usual to bury in the family burial ground even if this involves a long journey. This being so it is curious that old-fashioned Highland graveyards used so often to be uncared for.[1] I have heard of a case where the suggestion that the nettles and dank grass should be cut was opposed as it was thought it would show a lack of respect to the dead. The belief that the spirit of the last person buried had to keep watch until another interment took place seems to have been fairly general and there are tales of how, when two funerals happened to take place on the same day, the two sets of mourners made great efforts, even including a physical struggle, to get their corpse buried first.[2]

In the old days the funeral of a chief was an occasion of great pomp and display. The whole of the clansmen turned out under arms to do him honour and neighbouring chiefs also attended, accompanied by members of their clans. The family piper, with a black flag tied to his pipes, led the procession and the old women cried the coronach. There was, of course, open-handed hospitality to all. The proud remembrance of outstanding funerals still survives in the traditions of some clans.[3]

But I think that of all the descriptions of Highland funerals, the most moving is a much simpler one, 'the Highland Lady's' account of that of an old kinsman. Captain William Grant had lived in great simplicity but, when he died, he lay in state in a room shrouded with white linen (it is still customary to cover mirrors and the glasses of pictures in this way), and the gentle and simple from the whole countryside came to pay their respects. The widow, 'a plain woman in her ordinary, rather shabby attire', had herself made all the preparations, 'streaking the corpse, dressing the chamber, settling her own attire, giving out every bite and every drop that was to be used upstairs and down'. But

---

[1]Nowadays the care of graveyards falls on the Local Authority and it or the Church keep them in decent order.

[2]I. F. Grant, The MacLeods, p. 343.

[3]Master James Fraser, the author of the Wardlaw Manuscript, was a connoisseur in funerals. Among his many accounts is that for a Lord Lovat who died in 1633. He writes: 'This great man's funerals were sumptuous and splendid, nothing was wanting to make it singularly solemn, regular and orderly, the season being very inviting for the neighbouring clans to convene.' Members of eight clans attended, totalling over 5,000 men. Wardlaw Manuscript, p. 252. For a detailed account of a chief's funeral see Sir Eneas Mackintosh, Notes, pp. 19, 34.

now, 'looking an elderly gentlewoman' in her black dress with a white handkerchief pinned on her head, she sat in silence, answering all questions with a sign and although 'the room was full, crowded by comers and goers . . . yet a pin could be heard to drop in it.' Grant of Rothiemurchus, as head of his house, was the chief mourner and a solemn procession consisting of hundreds of mourners, set forth. The extra bearers were close to the coffin. 'Next came the near of kin, then all friends fell in according to their rank without being marshalled.'[1] But it must be admitted that there are also many tales of so much excessive drinking at funerals that the mourners mislaid the coffin, fell to blows or met with other mishaps.

The cost of a funeral of a big chief might amount to £700, a great sum in the eighteenth century.[2] Lesser folk also strained their resources to provide suitable entertainment at the funerals of their relations. Even if they were in debt for the necessaries of life they might spend £1 to £2. For instance, for the funeral of one of old Balnespick's joint-tenants 7s worth of whisky was provided at 1s 6d a Scots pint which would work out at over nine English pints.[3]

Much hospitality was given during the wake. Several writers allude to the ancient custom of dancing led off by the nearest relations.[4] Sir Eneas said that the custom had been given up in Strathdearn by 1740 and that when the relations and friends convened to watch the body—'plenty of whisky and snuff goes round, the young folks play at several country games while the graver sort tell tales of Ghosts and Hobgoblins. . . .'[5] But in Badenoch, very early in the nineteenth century, the husband of the hen-wife at Rothiemurchus 'was waked after the old fashion, shaved and partly dressed, and set up in his bed, all the countryside collecting round him. After abundance of refreshment the company set to dancing when, from the jolting of the floor, out tumbled the corpse into the midst of the reel'.[6]

[1] *Memoirs of a Highland Lady*, p. 249.
[2] Sir Eneas Mackintosh, *Notes*, p. 34.
[3] I. F. Grant, *Old Highland Farm*, p. 133.
[4] Mrs. Murray, *Useful Guide*, Vol. II, p. 248. T. Garnett, *Tour*, Vol. I, p. 119. Lachlan Shaw, *History of the Province of Moray*, p. 155. J. Hall, *Travels in Scotland*, p. 436.
[5] Sir Eneas Mackintosh, *Notes*, p. 34.
[6] *Memoirs of a Highland Lady*, p. 192.

The custom of keening by professional mourning women lasted in the Islands well into the second half of the nineteenth century. Someone who heard it spoke to me of its strangeness and sadness. Carmichael says that there used to be a mid-wife and a mourning woman ( *Bean-tuirim* ) in every township and that the people took it in turn to supply them with summer grass and winter fodder for their beasts. At the funeral the *bean-tuirim* walked behind the coffin intoning a lament and striking it from time to time.[1] There are other old customs as, for instance, that a funeral procession would circle the graveyard *deisal*.

Nowadays wakes of the old kind are never held, but in old-fashioned districts the body lies in the parlour and the closest friends and neighbours, men only, take it in turns to watch it in pairs. They sit in the kitchen, every now and then going to look at the body, and are supplied with food. Everywhere it is an obligatory sign of respect that everyone round about, men and women, should visit the corpse. All over the mainland, even in very sophisticated districts, and in Skye, these visitors always touch the corpse. The reason invariably given is that it prevents unhappy memories of the death. In Barra the corpse is not touched but there a plate of salt is laid on its breast. All over the Highlands and Islands it would be thought a mark of great disrespect to work outside while a neighbour's corpse is still awaiting burial.

Many descriptions of Highland funerals, old and within living memory, mention the orderly way in which mourners took turns in carrying the bier. When roads were few and the traditional desire to be buried with their kinsfolk was strong in Highland people, great distances, sometimes over rough country, had to be covered. There were generally eight bearers and the company walked in two files and at a signal, without interrupting the march, the leading men would slip their shoulders under one of the staves that carried the bier and the relieved bearers would drop behind to the end of the file. At intervals the whole procession would stop to rest and in Skye, Lochaber and the Long Island, each member would add a stone to a little cairn. One can still see whole companies of these 'resting cairns' at places where many funerals had rested on routes often taken to a graveyard as, for instance beside

[1] A. Carmichael, *Carmina Gadelica*, Vol. V. Ed. by A. Matheson, pp. 338–9, 345.

the high road that runs along the shores of Loch Eil.[1] For long there was a prejudice against using any other form of transport, even when it was available, and, even now, when a coffin has to be carried some way to a road it is done in the same orderly fashion. In more sophisticated districts a motor hearse is used for the whole journey to the grave. But in some more out of the way places a lorry may be used for part of the way but when near the graveyard the body is carried.

No invitations are issued for the funeral and it is customary for the men from a very wide area to attend it. In the case of a popular and respected member of the community the concourse is very large. Unless the distance to the graveyard is very great the mourners follow the hearse on foot but it is a mark of respect for the people who have cars or, in the old days, carriages, to arrange for them to follow behind. The utmost solemnity and decorum is observed. Women do not go to funerals. It was my privilege to see a most exceptional and touching tribute when Doctor Kenneth MacKay died at Laggan in 1943, having lost his life as the result of his devoted service in this bleak and hilly district, for numbers of the women came to his funeral service in the church though they did not go on to the grave.

[1]For very full details see 'Tolsta bho Thuath', *Stornoway Gazette*, 3.8.51. Also Osgood MacKenzie, *A Hundred Years in the Highlands*, p. 201. He describes how in the old days before there was a road, a body was carried the 73 miles from Gairloch to Beauly by 150 bearers. They rested two nights on the way.

# INDEX

(Page numbers in italics refer to the illustrations)